숨마 주니어®

119 개 대표 문장으로 끝내는

중학 영문법 MANUAL 119

중학 2학년 영어 교과서 핵심 문법 119개 30일 완성!!

총 2,000여 개 문항 3단계 반복 학습으로 기초 탄탄! 내신 만점!

2

집필진과 검토진 쌤들의 추천 코멘트!!

정지윤 쌤(언남중)

문법이 어렵다는 편견은 이제 그만!
시험에 자주 출제되는 문법 항목별로 개념
설명이 잘 되어 있고, 같은 페이지에 바로
확인 문제들이 있어서 문법 개념을 확실하게
다질 수 있는 좋은 교재입니다. 문법을
어려워하는 학생들도 차근차근 풀어나가다
보면 자신감이 생기고 문법 실력을
쑥쑥 쌓을 수 있는 교재랍니다.

김하경 쌤(당곡중)

학교 시험에서 중요하게 다루는 문법 항목이
일목요연하게 정리되어 있네요.
특히 문법 개념을 익힌 후 학교 시험과
유사한 문제 풀이로 내신을 탄탄하게
대비할 수 있게 되어 있어 좋습니다.
중학 문법! 중학 영문법 매뉴얼 119로
시작해보세요!

홍숙한 쌤
(서울대학교 사범대학 부설여자중)

교과서 분석을 통해 엄선된 핵심 중학 문법
항목을 깔끔하게 정리하여 누구라도 쉽게
이해할 수 있게 했습니다. 또한 내신과
영어 기반 다지기라는 두 마리 토끼를
잡을 수 있도록 구성했습니다. 쉽고 다양한
문제를 내신 적중 실전 문제와
연결하여 단계적인 학습이 가능하게
하였습니다. 이는 학생들의 영어
체력을 확실하게 높여줄 것입니다.

김지영 쌤(상경중)

중학 영문법 매뉴얼 119는
각 학년별로 반드시 알아야 할 영문법을
일목요연하게 정리한 교재입니다.
특히 대표 문장을 제시함으로써,
핵심 문법을 문장 단위로 암기할 수 있도록
하였습니다. 중학 영문법 매뉴얼 119라는
제목처럼 이 교재가 여러분이 급할 때
가장 먼저 찾을 수 있는 교재가
되길 바랍니다.

윤소미 원장(안산 이엘어학원)

각 학년별로 반드시 알아야 할
문법 포인트가 자세히 나누어져 있으며,
하위 카테고리는 어느 것 하나 지나칠 수
없는 알짜 내용으로 구성되어 있습니다.
자칫 지루하게 느껴질 수도 있을 개념 설명에
흥미로운 예문을 곁들였습니다.

윤승희 쌤(필탑학원)

문법 개념 학습 후 베이직 문제,
응용 문제, 마무리 10분 테스트로
이어지는 이 책의 구성은 문법 학습의
첫 시작부터 완벽한 마무리까지
체계적으로 이끌어 줍니다. 책 명칭처럼
이 책은 문법을 어려워하는 학생들에게
119같은 역할이 될 것입니다.

대표 문장 암기표

여러 가지 버전의 mp3 파일을 들으며 완벽하게 외워보자!

LESSON 01 문장의 형태

P 001 1형식 · 2형식 문장	**Spring came and it became warm.**	봄이 와서 날씨가 따뜻해졌다.
P 002 감각동사+형용사	**Her voice sounded shaky on the phone.**	전화상으로 들리는 그녀의 목소리가 떨리는 것 같았다.
P 003 3형식 · 4형식 문장	**He bought a book and gave me the book.**	그는 책을 한 권 사서 내게 그 책을 주었다.
P 004 4형식 문장 → 3형식 문장 전환	**She passed a note *to* me.**	그녀는 나에게 쪽지를 건네주었다.
P 005 5형식 문장의 목적보어 I	**I found the room empty.**	나는 그 방이 비어 있는 것을 발견했다.
P 006 5형식 문장의 목적보어 II (to부정사)	**She encouraged me to follow my dream.**	그녀는 내게 꿈을 좇으라고 격려해 주었다.
P 007 5형식 문장의 목적보어 III (사역동사)	**He makes his children go to bed early.**	그는 아이들을 일찍 자러 가게 한다
P 008 5형식 문장의 목적보어 IV (지각동사)	**She heard the doorbell ring.**	그녀는 초인종이 울리는 소리를 들었다.

LESSON 02 동사의 시제

P 009 현재시제와 현재진행 시제	**She usually complains a lot, but she is not complaining now.**	그녀는 보통 불평을 많이 하지만, 지금은 불평하지 않는다.
P 010 과거시제와 과거진행 시제	**While he was taking a shower, the phone rang.**	그가 샤워를 하고 있는 중에, 전화가 울렸다.
P 011 미래시제	**He will[is going to] be fourteen next year.**	그는 내년에 14살이 된다.
P 012 현재완료의 개념	**I have lived here for five years.**	나는 5년 동안 여기에서 살아왔다.
P 013 현재완료의 용법 (경험)	**I have been to Japan twice.**	나는 일본에 두 번 가 본 적이 있다.
P 014 현재완료의 용법 (완료)	**The bus has *just* left.**	버스가 막 떠났다.
P 015 현재완료의 용법 (계속)	**Mr. Brown has taught science *since* 2011.**	Brown 선생님은 2011년부터 과학을 가르쳐 왔다.
P 016 현재완료의 용법 (결과)	**He has lost his cell phone.**	그는 휴대전화를 잃어버렸다.

LESSON 03 조동사

P 017 can, could	**Can[Could] you do me a favor?**	내 부탁을 들어줄 수 있니[있을까요]?
P 018 may, might	**Your bag may[might] be in the car.**	네 가방은 차 안에 있을지도 모른다.
P 019 will, would	**Will[Would] you help me?**	나 좀 도와줄래요[주시겠어요]?
P 020 must	**You must fasten your seat belt.**	당신은 안전벨트를 매야 한다.
P 021 have to	**I have to finish my homework first.**	나는 먼저 숙제를 끝내야 한다.
P 022 should	**You should help poor people.**	너는 가난한 사람들을 도와야 한다.
P 023 had better	**You had better hurry.**	너는 서두르는 게 좋겠다.
P 024 would like to	**I would like to drink coffee.**	나는 커피를 마시고 싶다.
P 025 used to, would	**I used to exercise every morning.**	나는 매일 아침 운동하곤 했다.
P 026 do	**I do *like* computer games.**	나는 컴퓨터 게임을 정말 좋아한다.

LESSON 04 to부정사

P 027 명사적 용법 (주어, 보어)	**To communicate is to express your ideas to others.**	의사소통하는 것이란 당신의 생각을 다른 사람들에게 표현하는 것이다.
P 028 명사적 용법 (목적어)	**I hope to travel around the world.**	나는 세계를 일주하고 싶다.
P 029 명사적 용법 (의문사+to부정사)	**Do you know how to use this machine?**	너는 이 기계를 어떻게 사용하는지 아니?

P 090 관계대명사 which	I watched a movie which had lots of special effects.	나는 특수효과가 많은 영화를 봤다.
P 091 관계대명사 that	I bought a bag that had many pockets.	나는 주머니가 많은 가방을 샀다.
P 092 관계대명사 that vs. 접속사 that	It's true that I don't know the man that stole your money.	내가 네 돈을 훔친 그 남자를 모른다는 것은 사실이다.
P 093 관계대명사 what	I still remember what you said to me.	나는 아직도 네가 나에게 했던 말을 기억한다.
P 094 관계대명사의 생략 I	This is the first film I've ever made.	이것은 내가 처음으로 만든 영화이다.
P 095 관계대명사의 생략 II	I need a piece of paper I can write on.	나는 쓸 종이가 한 장 필요하다.
P 096 관계대명사의 생략 III	Look at the birds singing in the tree.	나무에서 노래하는 새들을 봐.
P 097 관계부사 when	2002 was the year when the World Cup was held in Korea.	2002년은 한국에서 월드컵이 열린 해였다.
P 098 관계부사 where	Seoul is the city where I live.	서울은 내가 거주하는 도시이다.
P 099 관계부사 why	I don't know the reason why she left me.	나는 그녀가 나를 떠난 이유를 모른다.
P 100 관계부사 how	I remember how you smiled at me.	당신이 나를 향해 미소 짓던 모습을 기억해요.

LESSON 11 가정법

P 101 가정법 과거	If you got more rest, you would feel better.	만약 네가 더 쉰다면 기분이 더 나아질 텐데.
P 102 가정법 과거완료	If I had got up earlier, I could have caught the bus.	만약 내가 더 일찍 일어났다면 버스를 잡을 수 있었을 텐데.
P 103 I wish+가정법 과거	I wish I were taller than now.	내가 지금보다 키가 더 크다면 좋을 텐데.
P 104 I wish+가정법 과거완료	I wish I had followed her advice.	내가 그녀의 충고를 따랐다면 좋았을 텐데.
P 105 as if+가정법 과거	He speaks as if he knew everything.	그는 마치 모든 것을 아는 것처럼 말한다.
P 106 as if+가정법 과거완료	She acted as if she hadn't met me before.	그녀는 마치 전에 나를 만난 적이 없던 것처럼 행동했다.

LESSON 12 접속사

P 107 등위접속사 and, but	I felt sad and happy at the same time.	나는 동시에 슬프고 행복했다.
P 108 등위접속사 or, so	Do you go to school by bus or by bike?	너는 학교에 버스로 가니 아니면 자전거로 가니?
P 109 시간 접속사 when, as, while	When I was 10, my family moved to Canada.	내가 열 살 때, 우리 가족은 캐나다로 이주했다.
P 110 시간 접속사 before, after, until[till]	Please wait until the water boils.	물이 끓을 때까지 기다리세요.
P 111 이유 접속사 because, as, since	I couldn't go to school because I was sick.	나는 아팠기 때문에 학교에 갈 수 없었다.
P 112 결과 접속사 so ~ that	The movie was so boring that I fell asleep.	영화가 너무 지루해서 나는 잠이 들었다.
P 113 조건 접속사 if, unless	If you eat too much pizza, you'll get fat.	피자를 너무 많이 먹는다면, 넌 살이 찔 것이다.
P 114 양보 접속사 though[although]	Although[Though] I studied hard, I failed the test.	나는 공부를 열심히 했음에도 불구하고 시험에 떨어졌다.
P 115 both A and B / not only A but also B	Suji is not only pretty but also kind.	수지는 예쁠 뿐만 아니라 친절하기까지 하다.
P 116 either A or B / neither A nor B	You can drink either coffee or juice.	너는 커피 또는 주스를 마실 수 있다.
P 117 명사절을 이끄는 that	I knew that he was telling the truth.	나는 그가 진실을 말하고 있다는 것을 알고 있었다.
P 118 명사절을 이끄는 if, whether	Do you know whether she will come or not?	너는 그녀가 올지 안 올지 알고 있니?
P 119 명령문+and / 명령문+or	Leave now, and you'll catch the bus.	지금 떠나라, 그러면 너는 버스를 탈 수 있을 것이다.

대표 문장 암기표

여러 가지 버전의 mp3 **파일**을 들으며 완벽하게 외워보자!

P 059 수동태의 시제 (과거시제)	**The telephone was invented by Bell.**	전화는 Bell에 의해 발명되었다.
P 060 수동태의 시제 (미래시제)	**The movie will be released next week.**	그 영화는 다음 주에 개봉될 것이다.
P 061 수동태의 부정문과 의문문	**Was the picnic canceled?**	소풍은 취소되었나요?
P 062 조동사의 수동태	**The paintings should be handled carefully.**	그 그림들은 조심스럽게 다뤄져야 한다.
P 063 4형식 문장의 수동태	**I was given the book by him.**	나는 그에게 그 책을 받았다.
P 064 5형식 문장의 수동태	**He was called *Captain* by his close friends.**	그는 친한 친구들에게 '대장'이라고 불렸다.
P 065 동사구의 수동태	**The meeting was put off by the boss.**	그 회의는 상사에 의해서 연기되었다.
P 066 by 이외의 전치사를 사용하는 수동태	**I am interested in pop songs.**	나는 팝송에 관심이 있다.

LESSON 08 대명사

P 067 부정대명사 one	**I lost my watch, so I have to buy one.**	나는 손목시계를 잃어버려서, 하나 사야 한다.
P 068 부정대명사 another	**Mike ate a hamburger and ordered another.**	Mike는 햄버거 하나를 먹고 또 하나를 주문했다.
P 069 부정대명사 all, both	**Both of them are my friends.**	그들 둘 다 내 친구들이다.
P 070 부정대명사 each, every	**Each of us has our own role.**	우리들 각자에게는 자신만의 역할이 있다.
P 071 부정대명사 some, any	**Some are dying of hunger.**	몇몇 사람들은 굶주림에 죽어가고 있다.
P 072 one ~ the other… / some ~ others…	**Some like spring, and others like fall.**	어떤 사람들은 봄을 좋아하고, 다른 사람들은 가을을 좋아한다.
P 073 each other / one another	**Sora and Minsu like each other.**	소라와 민수는 서로 좋아한다.
P 074 재귀대명사의 재귀 용법	**She looked at herself in the mirror.**	그녀는 거울 속의 자신을 보았다.
P 075 재귀대명사의 강조 용법	**I myself made a pizza.**	내가 직접 피자를 만들었다.
P 076 재귀대명사의 관용적 용법	**The door opened of itself.**	문이 저절로 열렸다.

LESSON 09 비교 구문

P 077 as ~ as 구문	**He is as tall as his brother.**	그는 그의 형만큼 키가 크다.
P 078 비교급, 최상급 만드는 법 (규칙 변화)	**Which is bigger, the sun or the earth?**	태양과 지구 중 어느 것이 더 큰가?
P 079 비교급, 최상급 만드는 법 (불규칙 변화)	**Suji sings better than I do.**	수지는 나보다 노래를 더 잘한다.
P 080 비교급+than	**My sister is taller than me.**	내 여동생은 나보다 키가 더 크다.
P 081 비교 구문을 이용한 표현 I	**Your room is twice as big as mine.**	너의 방은 내 방보다 두 배 더 크다.
P 082 비교 구문을 이용한 표현 II	**The more we have, the more we want.**	우리는 더 많이 가질수록 더 많이 원한다.
P 083 비교 구문을 이용한 표현 III	**The weather is getting colder and colder.**	날씨가 점점 더 추워지고 있다.
P 084 the+최상급	**The Nile is the longest river in the world.**	나일강은 세상에서 가장 긴 강이다.
P 085 최상급을 이용한 표현	**Mt. Halla is one of the high est mountains in Korea.**	한라산은 한국에서 가장 높은 산들 중 하나이다.
P 086 원급, 비교급을 이용한 최상급 표현	**No other teacher is as kind as Ms. Kim.**	다른 어떤 선생님도 김 선생님만큼 친절하지 않다.

LESSON 10 관계사

P 087 주격 관계대명사 who	**I want to be a doctor who can cure cancer.**	나는 암을 낫게 할 수 있는 의사가 되고 싶다.
P 088 소유격 관계대명사 whose	**I have a classmate whose nickname is a walking dictionary.**	내게는 별명이 걸어 다니는 사전인 반 친구가 있다.
P 089 목적격 관계대명사 whom	**Suji is the girl whom I like most.**	수지는 내가 가장 좋아하는 여자아이이다.

P 030 형용사적 용법	It's time to get out of bed.	잠자리에서 일어날 시간이야.
P 031 부사적 용법 (목적)	We got there early to get a good seat.	우리는 좋은 자리를 차지하려고 그곳에 일찍 갔다.
P 032 부사적 용법 (결과)	The boy grew up to be a soldier.	그 소년은 커서 군인이 되었다.
P 033 부사적 용법 (감정의 원인)	I was surprised to hear the news.	나는 그 소식을 듣고 놀랐다.
P 034 부사적 용법 (판단의 근거)	You are brave to challenge me.	나에게 도전하다니 너는 용감하구나.
P 035 부사적 용법 (정도, 조건)	The problem is easy to solve.	그 문제는 풀기 쉽다.
P 036 to부정사의 의미상의 주어	It is hard *for me* to get up on Monday morning.	나는 월요일 아침에 일어나는 것이 어렵다.
P 037 too ~ to부정사	It is too cold to go outside.	너무 추워서 밖에 나갈 수가 없다.
P 038 enough+to부정사	She is tall enough to be a model.	그녀는 모델이 될 수 있을 만큼 충분히 키가 크다.

LESSON 05 동명사

P 039 동명사의 역할 (주어, 보어)	Giving is receiving.	주는 것이 받는 것이다.
P 040 동명사의 역할 (동사의 목적어)	They *enjoy* playing soccer.	그들은 축구하는 것을 즐긴다.
P 041 동명사의 역할 (전치사의 목적어)	He is good *at* dancing.	그는 춤추는 것을 잘한다.
P 042 동명사와 현재분사	Someone is waiting for you in the waiting room.	대기실에서 누군가가 당신을 기다리고 있다.
P 043 동명사와 to부정사 I	She *avoided* talking to strangers.	그녀는 낯선 사람에게 말하는 것을 피했다.
P 044 동명사와 to부정사 II	Do you *like* riding[to ride] a bike?	너는 자전거 타는 것을 좋아하니?
P 045 동명사와 to부정사 III	I *remember* leaving my keys on the desk.	나는 내 열쇠를 책상 위에 놓아둔 것을 기억한다.
P 046 동명사의 관용 표현	He is busy doing his homework.	그는 숙제를 하느라 바쁘다.

LESSON 06 분사

P 047 현재분사	Look at the flying birds.	저 날고 있는 새들을 봐.
P 048 과거분사	The fallen trees blocked the road.	쓰러진 나무들이 길을 막았다.
P 049 분사의 쓰임 (명사 수식)	Who is that pretty girl standing at the door?	저기 문 앞에 서 있는 예쁜 소녀는 누구니?
P 050 분사의 쓰임 (보어 역할)	She stood smiling at me.	그녀는 나를 향해 미소 지으면서 서 있었다.
P 051 감정을 나타내는 분사	A boring French movie made me bored.	한 지루한 프랑스 영화가 나를 지루하게 만들었다.
P 052 분사구문 만드는 법	Seeing the snake, the man ran away.	뱀을 보자, 그 남자는 도망갔다.
P 053 분사구문의 의미 (때)	Walking down the street, I met my old friend.	길을 걷다가, 나는 옛 친구를 만났다.
P 054 분사구문의 의미 (이유)	Having a bad cold, I just stayed home.	심한 감기에 걸려서, 나는 그냥 집에 있었다.
P 055 분사구문의 의미 (조건, 양보)	Being twins, they have very different tastes.	그들은 쌍둥이지만, 취향이 매우 다르다.
P 056 분사구문의 의미 (동시동작, 연속동작)	Eating pizza, I read a comic book.	피자를 먹으면서, 나는 만화책을 읽었다.

LESSON 07 수동태

P 057 수동태의 개념과 기본 형태	Rice is grown in many countries.	쌀은 많은 나라에서 재배된다.
P 058 수동태를 만드는 방법	The character is loved by many children.	그 캐릭터는 많은 아이들에 의해 사랑받는다.

HOW TO STUDY

중학 영문법 매뉴얼 119!

1 대표 문장은 꼭 암기합니다.

Point 상단에 제시된 대표 문장은 해당 문법 항목에서 다루는 내용이 가장 잘 드러나는 문장이므로, 학습 후 암기하는 것이 문법 항목을 이해하는 데 도움이 됩니다. 또한 문장의 실용성이 높아 실생활에서도 활용 가능합니다. 따라서 별도로 제공되는 여러 가지 버전의 mp3 파일을 수시로 들으며 대표 문장을 암기하도록 합니다.

2 틀린 문제는 반드시 확인하고, 부족한 개념은 다시 공부합니다.

틀린 문제를 확인하는 것은 새로운 개념을 공부하는 것보다 더 중요하므로, 문제를 왜 틀렸는지 해설을 통해 반드시 확인합니다. 그리고 내신 적중 실전 문제에는 연계 출제한 문법 point가 표시되어 있으므로, 틀린 문제는 해당 문법 Point를 다시 학습하여 완벽하게 이해하고 넘어가도록 합니다.

3 "마무리 10분 테스트"로 각 Lesson 학습을 마무리 합니다.

마무리 10분 테스트는 해당 Lesson에서 반복 학습할 필요가 있는 중요 문법 문제들로 구성되어 있어 배운 문법을 확실히 정리할 수 있습니다. 무엇보다 중요한 것은 25문항을 10분의 시간을 정해서 푸는 것입니다. 이미 충분히 연습한 개념을 정리하는 것이므로 시간 안에 빠르게 푸는 연습을 하도록 합니다.

4 내신 적중 실전 문제는 중간 • 기말 시험 전에 다시 한 번 학습합니다.

내신 적중 실전 문제는 실제 학교 시험에 출제된 다양한 내신 기출 문제들의 출제 경향, 패턴 및 빈도 등을 분석하여 내신 시험에 출제 가능성이 높은 문제를 수록하였습니다. 따라서 모든 학습을 마친 후 중간·기말 시험 전에 내신 적중 실전 문제만 다시 한 번 풀어보는 것이 학교 내신 시험을 대비하는 데 큰 도움이 될 것입니다.

구성과 특징

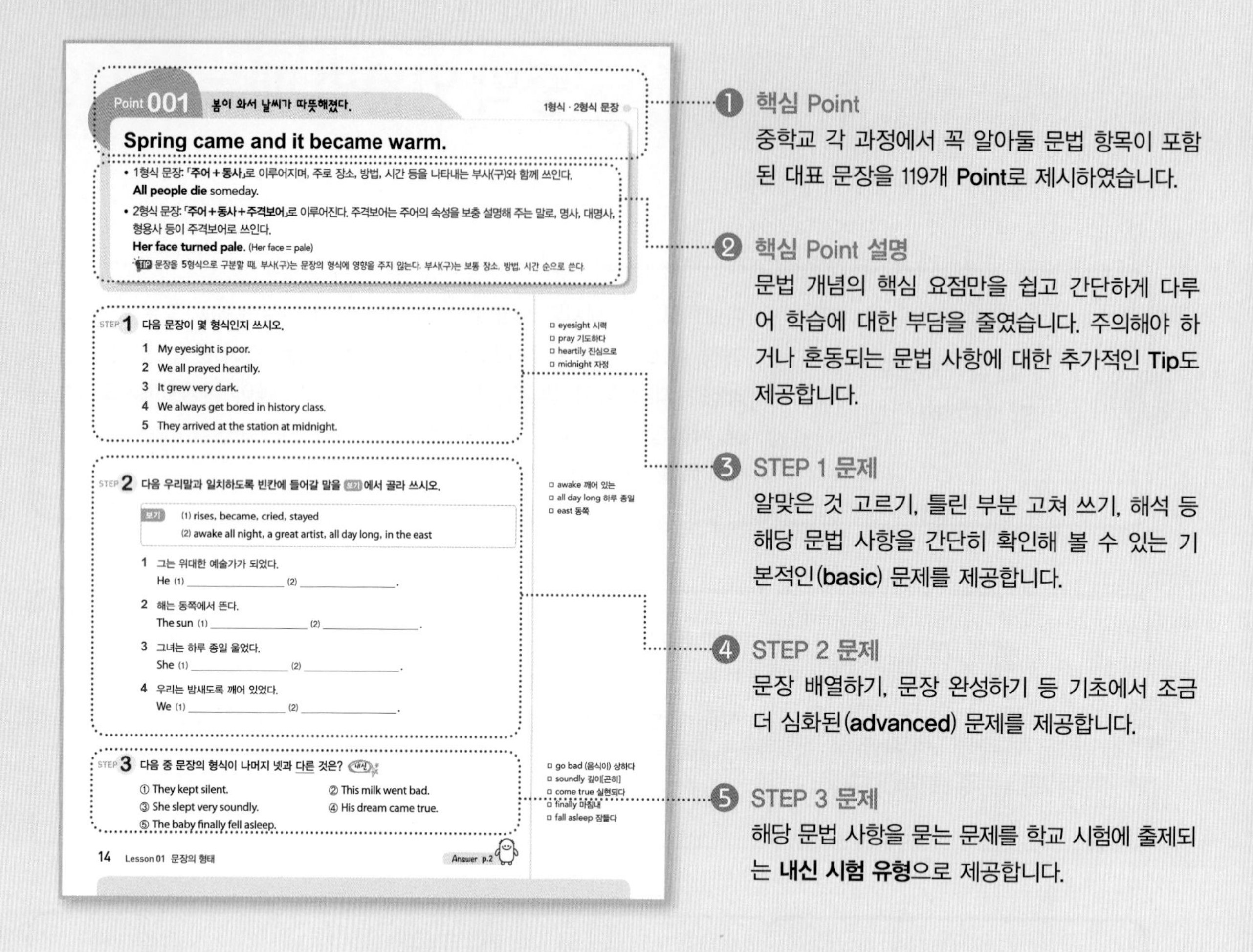

Point 001 봄이 와서 날씨가 따뜻해졌다. 1형식 · 2형식 문장

Spring came and it became warm.

- 1형식 문장: 「주어+동사」로 이루어지며, 주로 장소, 방법, 시간 등을 나타내는 부사(구)와 함께 쓰인다.
  All people die someday.
- 2형식 문장: 「주어+동사+주격보어」로 이루어진다. 주격보어는 주어의 속성을 보충 설명해 주는 말로, 명사, 대명사, 형용사 등이 주격보어로 쓰인다.
  Her face turned pale. (Her face = pale)

TIP 문장을 5형식으로 구분할 때, 부사(구)는 문장의 형식에 영향을 주지 않는다. 부사(구)는 보통 장소, 방법, 시간 순으로 쓴다.

STEP 1 다음 문장이 몇 형식인지 쓰시오.

1 My eyesight is poor.
2 We all prayed heartily.
3 It grew very dark.
4 We always get bored in history class.
5 They arrived at the station at midnight.

□ eyesight 시력
□ pray 기도하다
□ heartily 진심으로
□ midnight 자정

STEP 2 다음 우리말과 일치하도록 빈칸에 들어갈 말을 보기에서 골라 쓰시오.

보기 (1) rises, became, cried, stayed
(2) awake all night, a great artist, all day long, in the east

1 그는 위대한 예술가가 되었다.
He (1) ________ (2) ________.
2 해는 동쪽에서 뜬다.
The sun (1) ________ (2) ________.
3 그녀는 하루 종일 울었다.
She (1) ________ (2) ________.
4 우리는 밤새도록 깨어 있었다.
We (1) ________ (2) ________.

□ awake 깨어 있는
□ all day long 하루 종일
□ east 동쪽

STEP 3 다음 중 문장의 형식이 나머지 넷과 다른 것은? 내신

① They kept silent.
② This milk went bad.
③ She slept very soundly.
④ His dream came true.
⑤ The baby finally fell asleep.

□ go bad (음식이) 상하다
□ soundly 깊이[곤히]
□ come true 실현되다
□ finally 마침내
□ fall asleep 잠들다

14 Lesson 01 문장의 형태 Answer p.2

❶ 핵심 Point
중학교 각 과정에서 꼭 알아둘 문법 항목이 포함된 대표 문장을 119개 **Point**로 제시하였습니다.

❷ 핵심 Point 설명
문법 개념의 핵심 요점만을 쉽고 간단하게 다루어 학습에 대한 부담을 줄였습니다. 주의해야 하거나 혼동되는 문법 사항에 대한 추가적인 **Tip**도 제공합니다.

❸ STEP 1 문제
알맞은 것 고르기, 틀린 부분 고쳐 쓰기, 해석 등 해당 문법 사항을 간단히 확인해 볼 수 있는 기본적인(**basic**) 문제를 제공합니다.

❹ STEP 2 문제
문장 배열하기, 문장 완성하기 등 기초에서 조금 더 심화된(**advanced**) 문제를 제공합니다.

❺ STEP 3 문제
해당 문법 사항을 묻는 문제를 학교 시험에 출제되는 **내신 시험 유형**으로 제공합니다.

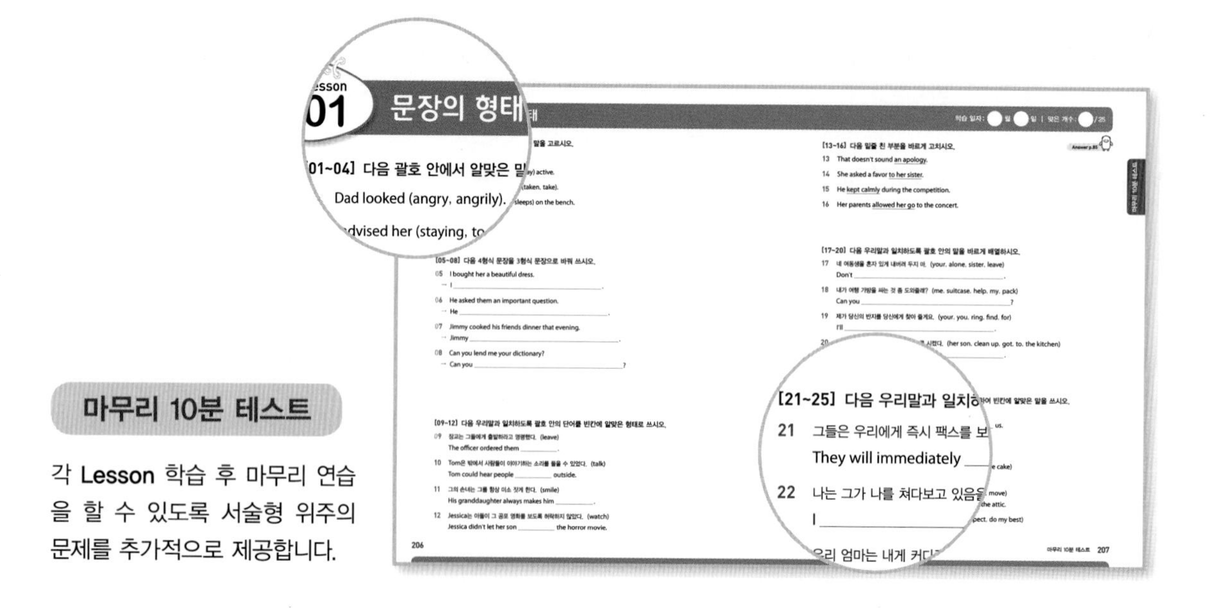

마무리 10분 테스트

각 Lesson 학습 후 마무리 연습을 할 수 있도록 서술형 위주의 문제를 추가적으로 제공합니다.

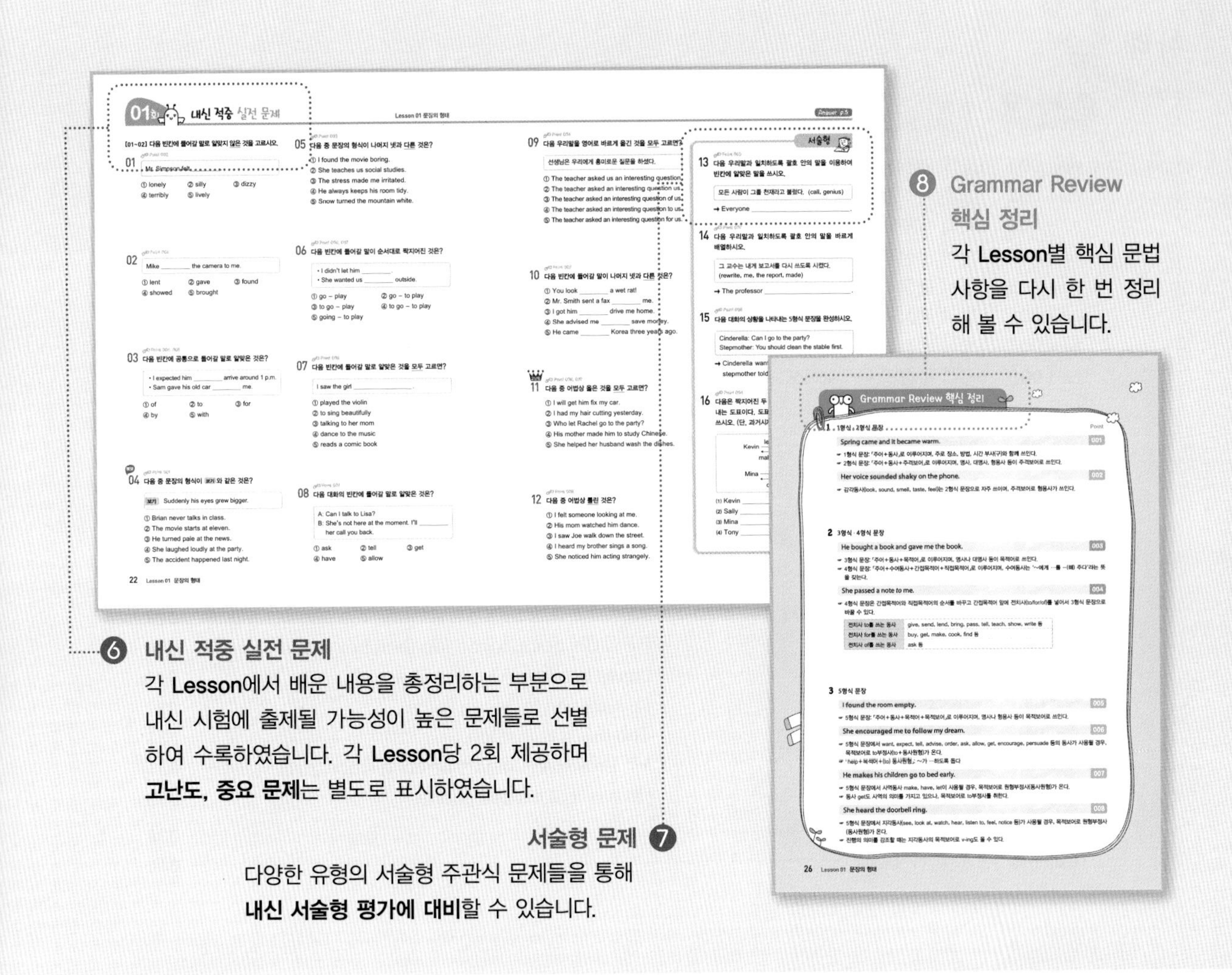

❽ Grammar Review 핵심 정리

각 Lesson별 핵심 문법 사항을 다시 한 번 정리해 볼 수 있습니다.

❻ 내신 적중 실전 문제

각 Lesson에서 배운 내용을 총정리하는 부분으로 내신 시험에 출제될 가능성이 높은 문제들로 선별하여 수록하였습니다. 각 Lesson당 2회 제공하며 **고난도, 중요 문제**는 별도로 표시하였습니다.

서술형 문제 ❼

다양한 유형의 서술형 주관식 문제들을 통해 **내신 서술형 평가에 대비**할 수 있습니다.

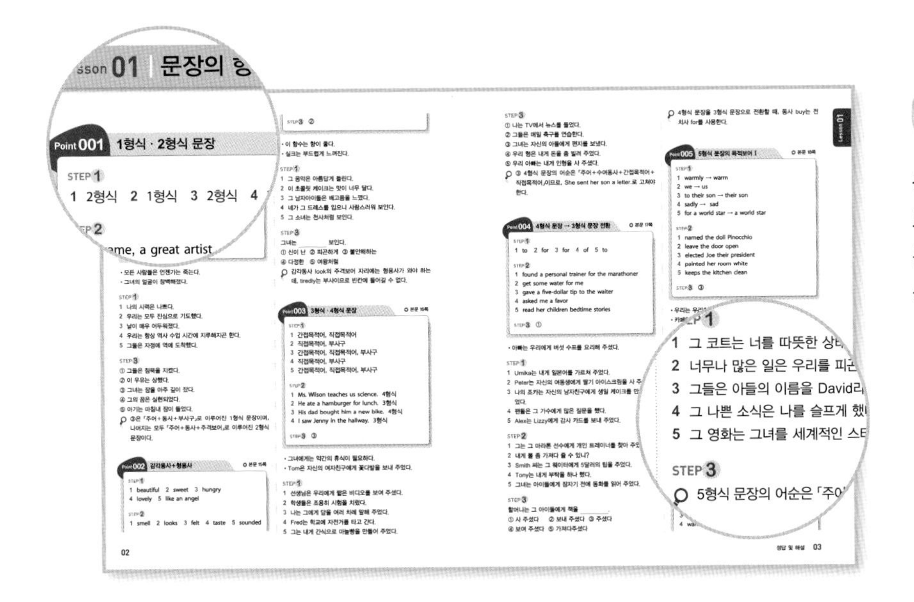

정답 및 해설

문장 해석, 자세한 문제 해설, 중요 어휘를 수록하여 혼자 공부하는 데 어려움이 없도록 구성하였습니다.

차례

CONTENTS

차례

CONTENTS

30일 완성 학습 PROJECT

학습계획표

	학습일	학습 내용	학습 날짜	문법 이해도
LESSON 01	Day 01	문장의 형태 Point 001~008	월 일 월 일	☺😐☹
	Day 02	내신 적중 실전 문제, 핵심 정리, 마무리 10분 테스트	월 일 월 일	☺😐☹
LESSON 02	Day 03	동사의 시제 Point 009~016	월 일 월 일	☺😐☹
	Day 04	내신 적중 실전 문제, 핵심 정리, 마무리 10분 테스트	월 일 월 일	☺😐☹
LESSON 03	Day 05	조동사 Point 017~026	월 일 월 일	☺😐☹
	Day 06	내신 적중 실전 문제, 핵심 정리, 마무리 10분 테스트	월 일 월 일	☺😐☹
LESSON 04	Day 07	to부정사 Point 027~032	월 일 월 일	☺😐☹
	Day 08	to부정사 Point 033~038	월 일 월 일	☺😐☹
	Day 09	내신 적중 실전 문제, 핵심 정리, 마무리 10분 테스트	월 일 월 일	☺😐☹
LESSON 05	Day 10	동명사 Point 039~046	월 일 월 일	☺😐☹
	Day 11	내신 적중 실전 문제, 핵심 정리, 마무리 10분 테스트	월 일 월 일	☺😐☹
LESSON 06	Day 12	분사 Point 047~051	월 일 월 일	☺😐☹
	Day 13	분사 Point 052~056	월 일 월 일	☺😐☹
	Day 14	내신 적중 실전 문제, 핵심 정리, 마무리 10분 테스트	월 일 월 일	☺😐☹
LESSON 07	Day 15	수동태 Point 057~066	월 일 월 일	☺😐☹
	Day 16	내신 적중 실전 문제, 핵심 정리, 마무리 10분 테스트	월 일 월 일	☺😐☹

- 교과서 핵심 문법 Point 119개를 30일 동안 내 것으로 만들어 보자!
- 매일매일 풀 양을 정해놓고 일정 시간 동안 꾸준히 풀어본다.
- 3단계 반복 학습으로 기초 탄탄! 내신 만점!

	학습일	학습 내용	학습 날짜	문법 이해도
LESSON 08	Day 17	대명사 Point 067~071	월 일 월 일	☺😐☹
	Day 18	대명사 Point 072~076	월 일 월 일	☺😐☹
	Day 19	내신 적중 실전 문제, 핵심 정리, 마무리 10분 테스트	월 일 월 일	☺😐☹
LESSON 09	Day 20	비교 구문 Point 077~081	월 일 월 일	☺😐☹
	Day 21	비교 구문 Point 082~086	월 일 월 일	☺😐☹
	Day 22	내신 적중 실전 문제, 핵심 정리, 마무리 10분 테스트	월 일 월 일	☺😐☹
LESSON 10	Day 23	관계사 Point 087~093	월 일 월 일	☺😐☹
	Day 24	관계사 Point 094~100	월 일 월 일	☺😐☹
	Day 25	내신 적중 실전 문제, 핵심 정리, 마무리 10분 테스트	월 일 월 일	☺😐☹
LESSON 11	Day 26	가정법 Point 101~106	월 일 월 일	☺😐☹
	Day 27	내신 적중 실전 문제, 핵심 정리, 마무리 10분 테스트	월 일 월 일	☺😐☹
LESSON 12	Day 28	접속사 Point 107~112	월 일 월 일	☺😐☹
	Day 29	접속사 Point 113~119	월 일 월 일	☺😐☹
	Day 30	내신 적중 실전 문제, 핵심 정리, 마무리 10분 테스트	월 일 월 일	☺😐☹

Note

숨마 주니어® 중학 영문법 매뉴얼 119

LESSON 01

문장의 형태

Point 001 봄이 와서 날씨가 따뜻해졌다.

Spring came and it became warm.

- 1형식 문장: 「**주어+동사**」로 이루어지며, 주로 장소, 방법, 시간 등을 나타내는 부사(구)와 함께 쓰인다.
  All people die someday.
- 2형식 문장: 「**주어+동사+주격보어**」로 이루어진다. 주격보어는 주어의 속성을 보충 설명해 주는 말로, 명사, 대명사, 형용사 등이 주격보어로 쓰인다.
  Her face turned pale. (Her face = pale)

TIP 문장을 5형식으로 구분할 때, 부사(구)는 문장의 형식에 영향을 주지 않는다. 부사(구)는 보통 장소, 방법, 시간 순으로 쓴다.

STEP 1 다음 문장이 몇 형식인지 쓰시오.

1 My eyesight is poor.
2 We all prayed heartily.
3 It grew very dark.
4 We always get bored in history class.
5 They arrived at the station at midnight.

□ eyesight 시력
□ pray 기도하다
□ heartily 진심으로
□ midnight 자정

STEP 2 다음 우리말과 일치하도록 빈칸에 들어갈 말을 보기에서 골라 쓰시오.

보기
(1) rises, became, cried, stayed
(2) awake all night, a great artist, all day long, in the east

1 그는 위대한 예술가가 되었다.
He (1) ________________ (2) ________________.

2 해는 동쪽에서 뜬다.
The sun (1) ________________ (2) ________________.

3 그녀는 하루 종일 울었다.
She (1) ________________ (2) ________________.

4 우리는 밤새도록 깨어 있었다.
We (1) ________________ (2) ________________.

□ awake 깨어 있는
□ all day long 하루 종일
□ east 동쪽

STEP 3 다음 중 문장의 형식이 나머지 넷과 다른 것은? 내신

① They kept silent.
② This milk went bad.
③ She slept very soundly.
④ His dream came true.
⑤ The baby finally fell asleep.

□ go bad (음식이) 상하다
□ soundly 깊이[곤히]
□ come true 실현되다
□ finally 마침내
□ fall asleep 잠들다

Answer p.2

Point 002 전화상으로 들리는 그녀의 목소리가 떨리는 것 같았다.

Her voice sounded shaky on the phone.

- 감각동사(look, sound, smell, taste, feel)는 2형식 문장으로 자주 쓰인다.
  This perfume smells nice.
- 감각동사의 주격보어 자리에는 형용사가 온다.
  Silk feels softly. (×) → **Silk feels soft.**

TIP 감각동사 뒤에 명사(구)가 올 때, 문장을 「**감각동사 + like(~처럼) + 명사(구)**」의 형태로 쓴다.

STEP 1 다음 밑줄 친 부분을 바르게 고치시오. (단, 고칠 필요 없으면 그대로 쓸 것)

1 The music sounds beautifully.
2 This chocolate cake tastes too sweet.
3 The boys felt hungrily.
4 That dress looks lovely on you.
5 The girl looks an angel.

□ angel 천사

STEP 2 다음 우리말과 일치하도록 빈칸에 들어갈 말을 보기 에서 골라 쓰시오.

보기 felt sounded taste smell looks

1 그 쿠키는 냄새가 좋다.
The cookies ____________ good.

2 그 마을은 매우 평화로워 보인다.
The village ____________ very peaceful.

3 나는 수영을 하고 나서 피곤했다.
I ____________ tired after swimming.

4 이 포도는 달고 신맛이 난다.
These grapes ____________ sweet and sour.

5 Karen의 목소리가 전화상에서 슬프게 들렸다.
Karen ____________ sad on the phone.

□ village 마을
□ peaceful 평화로운
□ tired 피곤한
□ sour (맛이) 신

STEP 3 다음 빈칸에 들어갈 말로 알맞지 않은 것은? 내신

She looks ________.

① excited ② tiredly ③ nervous
④ friendly ⑤ like a queen

Answer p.2

Point 003 그는 책을 한 권 사서 내게 그 책을 주었다.

He bought a book and gave me the book.

- 3형식 문장: 「**주어 + 동사 + 목적어**」로 이루어진다. 목적어는 주어가 하는 행위의 대상이 되는 말로, 명사나 대명사 등이 목적어로 쓰인다.
  She needs a little rest.
- 4형식 문장: 「**주어 + 수여동사 + 간접목적어 + 직접목적어**」로 이루어진다.
- 수여동사는 '~에게(간접목적어) …를(직접목적어) –(해) 주다'라는 뜻을 지닌 동사로, give, send, lend, bring, pass, tell, teach, show, write, buy, get, make, cook, find, ask 등이 이에 해당한다.
  Tom sent his girlfriend a bunch of flowers.

STEP 1 다음 밑줄 친 부분의 문장 성분을 보기에서 골라 쓰시오.

□ in silence 조용히
□ several times 여러 차례
□ garlic 마늘
□ snack 간식

보기	간접목적어	직접목적어	부사구

1 The teacher showed us a short video.
2 The students took the exam in silence.
3 I told him the answer several times.
4 Fred rides his bike to school.
5 He made me garlic bread as a snack.

STEP 2 다음 우리말과 일치하도록 괄호 안의 말을 바르게 배열하고, 몇 형식 문장인지 쓰시오.

□ hallway 복도

1 Wilson 선생님은 우리에게 과학을 가르쳐 주신다. (teaches, Ms. Wilson, science, us)
_______________ (   )

2 그는 점심으로 햄버거를 먹었다. (he, a hamburger, for lunch, ate)
_______________ (   )

3 그의 아빠는 그에게 새 자전거를 사 주셨다. (bought, a new bike, his dad, him)
_______________ (   )

4 나는 복도에서 Jenny를 보았다. (saw, I, Jenny, in the hallway)
_______________ (   )

STEP 3 다음 중 어법상 틀린 것은? 내신

□ practice 연습하다
□ lend 빌려주다
□ doll 인형

① I heard the news on TV.
② They practice soccer every day.
③ She sent a letter her son.
④ My brother lent me some money.
⑤ My dad bought a doll for me.

Answer p.2

Point 004 그녀는 나에게 쪽지를 건네주었다. 4형식 문장 → 3형식 문장 전환

She passed a note *to* me.

- 4형식 문장은 간접목적어와 직접목적어의 순서를 바꾸고 간접목적어 앞에 전치사를 넣어서 3형식 문장으로 바꿀 수 있다.
  – 4형식 문장: 「주어 + 동사 + 간접목적어 + 직접목적어」
  – 3형식 문장: **「주어 + 동사 + 직접목적어 + 전치사(to/for/of) + 간접목적어」**

전치사 to를 쓰는 동사	give, send, lend, bring, pass, tell, teach, show, write 등
전치사 for를 쓰는 동사	buy, get, make, cook, find 등
전치사 of를 쓰는 동사	ask 등

Dad cooked us mushroom soup. (4형식) → **Dad cooked mushroom soup *for* us.** (3형식)

STEP **1** 다음 괄호 안에서 알맞은 말을 고르시오.

□ Japanese 일본어
□ niece (여자) 조카

1 Umika taught Japanese (to, for, of) me.
2 Peter bought strawberry ice cream (to, for, of) his sister.
3 My niece made a birthday cake (to, for, of) her boyfriend.
4 The fans asked a lot of questions (to, for, of) the singer.
5 Alex sent a thank-you card (to, for, of) Lizzy.

STEP **2** 다음 4형식 문장은 3형식 문장으로, 3형식 문장은 4형식 문장으로 바꿔 쓰시오.

□ marathoner 마라톤 선수
□ personal 개인의
□ favor 부탁, 호의
□ bedtime story 잠자기 전에 들려주는 동화

1 He found the marathoner a personal trainer.
→ He ______________________________.

2 Can you get me some water?
→ Can you ______________________________?

3 Mr. Smith gave the waiter a five-dollar tip.
→ Mr. Smith ______________________________.

4 Tony asked a favor of me.
→ Tony ______________________________.

5 She read bedtime stories to her children.
→ She ______________________________.

STEP **3** 다음 빈칸에 들어갈 말로 알맞지 <u>않은</u> 것은? 내신

Grandma ________ books to the children.

① bought ② sent ③ gave
④ showed ⑤ brought

Answer p.3

Point 005 나는 그 방이 비어 있는 것을 발견했다.

I found the room empty.

- 5형식 문장: 「**주어+동사+목적어+목적보어**」로 이루어진다. 목적보어는 목적어의 속성을 보충 설명해 주는 말로, 명사나 형용사 등이 목적보어로 쓰인다.
  We called our dog Max. (our dog = Max)
  Caffeine keeps you awake. (you = awake)

STEP 1 다음 문장에서 틀린 부분을 바르게 고치시오.

1 The coat will keep you warmly.
2 Too much work made we tired.
3 They named to their son David.
4 The bad news made me sadly.
5 The movie made her for a world star.

□ keep (~한 상태를) 유지하다
□ name 이름을 지어 주다

STEP 2 다음 우리말과 일치하도록 괄호 안의 말을 이용하여 빈칸에 알맞은 말을 쓰시오.

1 노인은 그 인형의 이름을 피노키오라고 지었다. (name, Pinocchio)
The old man ____________ ____________ ____________ ____________.

2 그 문을 열어 놓은 상태로 두세요. (leave, open)
Please ____________ ____________ ____________ ____________.

3 학생들은 Joe를 자신들의 회장으로 선출했다. (elect, president)
The students ____________ ____________ ____________ ____________.

4 Sophia는 자신의 방을 하얀색으로 칠했다. (paint, white)
Sophia ____________ ____________ ____________ ____________.

5 우리 어머니는 항상 부엌을 깨끗하게 유지하신다. (kitchen, clean)
My mom always ____________ ____________ ____________ ____________.

□ leave (~한 상태로) 두다
□ elect 선출하다
□ president 회장

STEP 3 다음 우리말을 영어로 바르게 옮긴 것은? 내신

엄마는 나를 왕자라고 부르신다.

① My mom calls a prince me.
② My mom calls me to a prince.
③ My mom calls me a prince.
④ My mom calls to a prince me.
⑤ My mom calls to me a prince.

□ prince 왕자

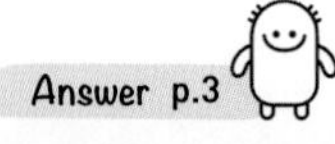

Point 006 그녀는 내게 꿈을 좇으라고 격려해 주었다.

5형식 문장의 목적보어 Ⅱ (to부정사)

She encouraged me to follow my dream.

- 5형식 문장에서 want, expect, tell, advise, order, ask, allow, get, encourage, persuade 등의 동사가 사용될 경우, 목적보어로 to부정사(to + 동사원형)가 온다.

My parents allowed me to go camping.

Harry asked me to marry him.

TIP 「**help** + 목적어 + (**to**) 동사원형」: ~가 …하도록 돕다

STEP 1 다음 밑줄 친 부분을 바르게 고치시오. (단, 고칠 필요 없으면 그대로 쓸 것)

1 His secretary told us wait.
2 Did anyone help you write this report?
3 Ms. Mac advised him selling the house.
4 My parents always encourage me to try new things.
5 The court ordered him paid a $50,000 fine.

□ secretary 비서
□ encourage 격려하다
□ court 법원
□ fine 벌금

STEP 2 다음 우리말과 일치하도록 괄호 안의 말을 바르게 배열하시오.

1 의사는 그에게 금연하도록 권했다. (stop, him, advised, to, smoking)
The doctor ______________________________.

2 너는 내가 널 믿으리라고 기대하니? (believe, to, you, expect, me)
Do you ______________________________?

3 옆집 사람은 그들에게 조용히 해 달라고 요청했다. (to, be, asked, them, quiet)
The neighbor ______________________________.

4 나는 Lily가 나를 이해해 주길 원했다. (me, to, Lily, wanted, understand)
I ______________________________.

5 제 자리를 찾는 것을 도와주시겠어요? (find, me, my seat, help)
Can you ______________________________?

□ expect 기대하다
□ neighbor 옆집 사람, 이웃
□ understand 이해하다
□ seat 자리

STEP 3 다음 빈칸에 들어갈 말로 알맞은 것은? 내신

My mom told me ________ care of my little brother.

① take ② took ③ to taking
④ to take ⑤ to taken

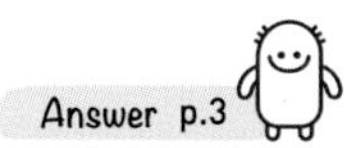

Point 007 그는 아이들을 일찍 자러 가게 한다.

He makes his children go to bed early.

- 5형식 문장에서 사역동사 make, have, let이 사용될 경우, 목적보어로 원형부정사(동사원형)가 온다.
- make: (강제로) ~하게 만들다 / have: ~하게 하다 / let: ~하도록 (허락)해 주다

  Jane had the mechanic check the brakes. / **Tom let me drive** his new car.
- 동사 get도 '~하도록 시키다'라는 사역의 의미를 가지고 있으나, 목적보어로 to부정사를 취한다.

  I got him to clean the table.

TIP 사역동사 **have**의 목적어가 사물인 경우, 목적보어로 **p.p.**가 온다.

STEP 1 다음 괄호 안에서 알맞은 말을 고르시오.

1 I'll have him (help, to help) you.
2 We had to ask him (leave, to leave).
3 Cold water made him (shiver, shivering).
4 How can parents get their children (read, to read) more?
5 Could you have this jacket (wash, washed)?

□ shiver (추위 등으로 몸을) 떨다

STEP 2 다음 빈칸에 들어갈 말을 보기에서 골라 알맞은 형태로 쓰시오.

보기	stop	look	use	take	install

1 She let her students ____________ a dictionary during the test.
2 Did you have the heater ____________?
3 Helen got her son ____________ the medicine.
4 Dylan made his kids ____________ watching TV at night.
5 My aunt wanted me ____________ after her dog for a week.

□ install 설치하다
□ dictionary 사전
□ medicine 약

STEP 3 다음 중 어법상 틀린 것은? 내신

① The sound made the baby cry.
② She got me to wash the dog.
③ I expected him to join my team.
④ She let me to go home early.
⑤ Mom had me turn off the TV.

Answer p.4

Point 008 그녀는 초인종이 울리는 소리를 들었다. 5형식 문장의 목적보어 Ⅳ (지각동사)

She heard the doorbell ring.

- 5형식 문장에서 지각동사(see, look at, watch, hear, listen to, feel, notice 등)가 사용될 경우, 목적보어로 원형부정사(동사원형)가 온다.
- 진행의 의미를 강조할 때는 지각동사의 목적보어로 v-ing도 올 수 있다.
  Mom watched us swim[swimming] in the pool.
  I heard a dog bark[barking] wildly.

STEP 1 다음 밑줄 친 부분을 바르게 고치시오. (단, 고칠 필요 없으면 그대로 쓸 것)

1 I noticed something burning in the kitchen.
2 She felt the ground to shake for about a minute.
3 The professor heard someone knocked on the door.
4 I saw some boys climbed over the fence.
5 We watched her make a tuna sandwich from beginning to end.

□ burn (음식 등이) 타다
□ professor 교수
□ knock 두드리다
□ fence 울타리
□ tuna 참치

STEP 2 다음 우리말과 일치하도록 괄호 안의 말을 바르게 배열하시오.

1 나는 누군가가 내 이름을 부르는 것을 들었다. (heard, my name, I, call, someone)

____

2 아무도 그가 들어오는 것을 보지 못했다. (him, come in, saw, nobody)

____

3 우리는 그 아이들이 모래사장에서 노는 것을 지켜보았다.
(play, watched, we, the kids, in the sand)

____

4 그는 뱀 한 마리가 자신의 어깨를 타고 기어가는 것을 느꼈다.
(felt, crawl, a snake, he, over his shoulder)

____

5 그들은 그가 방에서 나가는 것을 알아차렸다. (leaving, they, him, the room, noticed)

____

□ sand 모래사장
□ crawl 기어가다
□ shoulder 어깨

STEP 3 다음 대화의 빈칸에 들어갈 말로 알맞은 것은? 내신

A: Did I close the window when I went out?
B: Yes, you did. I saw you ________ the window.

① close ② closed ③ to close
④ being closed ⑤ are closing

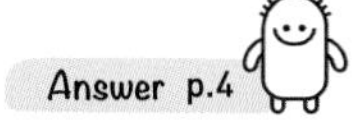

[01~02] 다음 빈칸에 들어갈 말로 알맞지 않은 것을 고르시오.

Point 002

01

Mr. Simpson felt _________.

① lonely ② silly ③ dizzy
④ terribly ⑤ lively

Point 004

02

Mike _________ the camera to me.

① lent ② gave ③ found
④ showed ⑤ brought

Point 004, 006

03 다음 빈칸에 공통으로 들어갈 말로 알맞은 것은?

• I expected him _________ arrive around 1 p.m.
• Sam gave his old car _________ me.

① of ② to ③ for
④ by ⑤ with

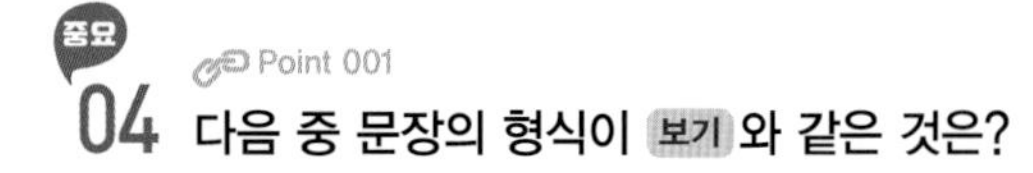

중요

Point 001

04 다음 중 문장의 형식이 보기 와 같은 것은?

보기 Suddenly his eyes grew bigger.

① Brian never talks in class.
② The movie starts at eleven.
③ He turned pale at the news.
④ She laughed loudly at the party.
⑤ The accident happened last night.

Point 003

05 다음 중 문장의 형식이 나머지 넷과 다른 것은?

① I found the movie boring.
② She teaches us social studies.
③ The stress made me irritated.
④ He always keeps his room tidy.
⑤ Snow turned the mountain white.

Point 006, 007

06 다음 빈칸에 들어갈 말이 순서대로 짝지어진 것은?

• I didn't let him _________.
• She wanted us _________ outside.

① go – play ② go – to play
③ to go – play ④ to go – to play
⑤ going – to play

Point 008

07 다음 빈칸에 들어갈 말로 알맞은 것을 모두 고르면?

I saw the girl _______________.

① played the violin
② to sing beautifully
③ talking to her mom
④ dance to the music
⑤ reads a comic book

Point 007

08 다음 대화의 빈칸에 들어갈 말로 알맞은 것은?

A: Can I talk to Lisa?
B: She's not here at the moment. I'll _________ her call you back.

① ask ② tell ③ get
④ have ⑤ allow

Point 004

09 다음 우리말을 영어로 바르게 옮긴 것을 모두 고르면?

선생님은 우리에게 흥미로운 질문을 하셨다.

① The teacher asked us an interesting question.
② The teacher asked an interesting question us.
③ The teacher asked an interesting question of us.
④ The teacher asked an interesting question to us.
⑤ The teacher asked an interesting question for us.

Point 002

10 다음 빈칸에 들어갈 말이 나머지 넷과 다른 것은?

① You look ________ a wet rat!
② Mr. Smith sent a fax ________ me.
③ I got him ________ drive me home.
④ She advised me ________ save money.
⑤ He came ________ Korea three years ago.

고난도 Point 006, 007

11 다음 중 어법상 옳은 것을 모두 고르면?

① I will get him fix my car.
② I had my hair cutting yesterday.
③ Who let Rachel go to the party?
④ His mother made him to study Chinese.
⑤ She helped her husband wash the dishes.

Point 008

12 다음 중 어법상 틀린 것은?

① I felt someone looking at me.
② His mom watched him dance.
③ I saw Joe walk down the street.
④ I heard my brother sings a song.
⑤ She noticed him acting strangely.

서술형

Point 005

13 다음 우리말과 일치하도록 괄호 안의 말을 이용하여 빈칸에 알맞은 말을 쓰시오.

모든 사람이 그를 천재라고 불렀다. (call, genius)

→ Everyone ________________________.

Point 007

14 다음 우리말과 일치하도록 괄호 안의 말을 바르게 배열하시오.

그 교수는 내게 보고서를 다시 쓰도록 시켰다.
(rewrite, me, the report, made)

→ The professor ________________________.

Point 006

15 다음 대화의 상황을 나타내는 5형식 문장을 완성하시오.

Cinderella: Can I go to the party?
Stepmother: You should clean the stable first.

→ Cinderella wanted to go to the party, but her stepmother told her ________________________.

Point 004

16 다음은 짝지어진 두 사람이 서로에게 해 준 일을 나타내는 도표이다. 도표를 참고하여 빈칸에 알맞은 말을 쓰시오. (단, 과거시제로 쓸 것)

Kevin → (lend his camera) → Sally
Kevin ← (make some cookies) ← Sally
Mina → (teach math) → Tony
Mina ← (cook spaghetti) ← Tony

(1) Kevin ________________________ his camera.
(2) Sally ________________________ Kevin.
(3) Mina ________________________ Tony.
(4) Tony ________________________ Mina.

[01~02] 다음 빈칸에 들어갈 말로 알맞지 않은 것을 고르시오.

Point 001

01

She was ________.

① tired ② sadly ③ friendly
④ my cousin ⑤ a writer

중요

Point 006

02

He ________ me read the book.

① let ② saw ③ had
④ made ⑤ allowed

Point 007

03 다음 빈칸에 들어갈 말로 알맞은 것은?

His grandmother made him ________ the housework.

① do ② did ③ does
④ doing ⑤ to do

Point 008

04 다음 두 문장을 한 문장으로 알맞게 바꾼 것은?

I saw the boy. He was dancing on the stage.

① I saw the boy dances on the stage.
② I saw the boy danced on the stage.
③ I saw the boy dancing on the stage.
④ I saw the boy to dance on the stage.
⑤ I saw the boy to dancing on the stage.

Point 003

05 다음 중 문장의 형식이 나머지 넷과 다른 것은?

① He left a great fortune.
② Mom's hands feel warm.
③ You look very nice in blue.
④ She became a hair designer.
⑤ The boy grew bigger and taller.

Point 008

06 다음 밑줄 친 부분 중 어법상 틀린 것은?

All of his family members(①) went to see(②) the soccer game and saw(③) him scored(④) a goal with(⑤) his head.

Point 004

07 다음 빈칸에 들어갈 말이 나머지 넷과 다른 것은?

① Tom told a funny story ________ us.
② Will you find a red cap ________ me?
③ Please get some milk ________ the baby.
④ Can you make potato soup ________ me?
⑤ Mom bought a new pair of shoes ________ me.

Point 002

08 다음 중 문장의 형식이 보기 와 같은 것은?

보기 The fried rice here tastes a bit salty.

① I can't feel Earth move.
② I like the taste of the coffee.
③ Could you show me the way?
④ This cheese smells too strange.
⑤ They looked at the night sky together.

Point 007

09 (A), (B), (C)의 괄호 안에서 알맞은 것끼리 바르게 짝지은 것은?

- The old man let us (A) [feed / to feed] the sheep.
- Jordan got me (B) [join / to join] his club.
- I had my daughter (C) [set / to set] the table.

	(A)	(B)	(C)
①	feed	join	set
②	feed	to join	set
③	to feed	join	set
④	feed	to join	to set
⑤	to feed	to join	set

Point 006, 007

10 다음 중 어법상 옳은 문장의 개수는?

- She ordered me follow her.
- I made him clean the house.
- I wanted them to being careful.
- He asked me to be his partner.
- She allowed him uses the computer.

① 1개 ② 2개 ③ 3개 ④ 4개 ⑤ 5개

Point 005

11 다음 중 어법상 옳은 것은?

① They named their baby Joseph.
② My uncle bought for me a pizza.
③ Refrigerators keep vegetables freshly.
④ Bob found that the chair very comfortable.
⑤ The teacher gives students with too much homework.

Point 004

12 다음 중 어법상 틀린 것은?

① Can I ask a favor of you?
② I will show his pictures to you.
③ Dave teaches English to children.
④ He wrote an apology letter for me.
⑤ Did you get the newspaper for him?

서술형

Point 008

13 다음 우리말과 일치하도록 괄호 안의 말을 바르게 배열하시오.

나는 빗방울이 머리 위로 떨어지는 것을 느꼈다.
(drops of rain, my head, falling, felt, on)

→ I ____________________.

Point 006

14 다음 우리말과 일치하도록 괄호 안의 말을 이용하여 빈칸에 알맞은 말을 쓰시오.

나는 네가 내 제안을 맘에 들어 할 거라고 예상하지 못했어. (expect, like)

→ I didn't ____________ my suggestion.

Point 004

15 다음 4형식 문장은 3형식 문장으로, 3형식 문장은 4형식 문장으로 바꿔 쓰시오.

(1) He bought his girlfriend a necklace.
→ ____________________

(2) Becky sent a text message to her brother.
→ ____________________

고난도

Point 006, 007

16 다음 대화문을 다음과 같이 요약할 때, 괄호 안의 말을 이용하여 빈칸에 알맞은 말을 쓰시오.

Semin: Mom, can I play video games?
Mom: Sorry, you can't. You have to help me clean the floor.

→ Semin's mom doesn't (1) ____________ ____________. (let) She (2) ____________ ____________. (want)

Grammar Review 핵심 정리

1 1형식 · 2형식 문장

Point

Spring came and it became warm. 001

☞ 1형식 문장: 「주어+동사」로 이루어지며, 주로 장소, 방법, 시간 부사(구)와 함께 쓰인다.
☞ 2형식 문장: 「주어+동사+주격보어」로 이루어지며, 명사, 대명사, 형용사 등이 주격보어로 쓰인다.

Her voice **sounded shaky** on the phone. 002

☞ 감각동사(look, sound, smell, taste, feel)는 2형식 문장으로 자주 쓰이며, 주격보어로 형용사가 쓰인다.

2 3형식 · 4형식 문장

He bought a book and gave me the book. 003

☞ 3형식 문장: 「주어+동사+목적어」로 이루어지며, 명사나 대명사 등이 목적어로 쓰인다.
☞ 4형식 문장: 「주어+수여동사+간접목적어+직접목적어」로 이루어지며, 수여동사는 '~에게 …를 -(해) 주다'라는 뜻을 갖는다.

She passed a note *to* me. 004

☞ 4형식 문장은 간접목적어와 직접목적어의 순서를 바꾸고 간접목적어 앞에 전치사(to/for/of)를 넣어서 3형식 문장으로 바꿀 수 있다.

전치사 to를 쓰는 동사	give, send, lend, bring, pass, tell, teach, show, write 등
전치사 for를 쓰는 동사	buy, get, make, cook, find 등
전치사 of를 쓰는 동사	ask 등

3 5형식 문장

I **found** the room **empty**. 005

☞ 5형식 문장: 「주어+동사+목적어+목적보어」로 이루어지며, 명사나 형용사 등이 목적보어로 쓰인다.

She **encouraged** me **to follow** my dream. 006

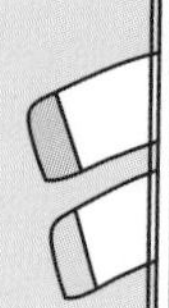

☞ 5형식 문장에서 want, expect, tell, advise, order, ask, allow, get, encourage, persuade 등의 동사가 사용될 경우, 목적보어로 to부정사(to+동사원형)가 온다.
☞ 「help+목적어+(to) 동사원형」: ~가 …하도록 돕다

He **makes** his children **go** to bed early. 007

☞ 5형식 문장에서 사역동사 make, have, let이 사용될 경우, 목적보어로 원형부정사(동사원형)가 온다.
☞ 동사 get도 사역의 의미를 가지고 있으나, 목적보어로 to부정사를 취한다.

She **heard** the doorbell **ring**. 008

☞ 5형식 문장에서 지각동사(see, look at, watch, hear, listen to, feel, notice 등)가 사용될 경우, 목적보어로 원형부정사(동사원형)가 온다.
☞ 진행의 의미를 강조할 때는 지각동사의 목적보어로 v-ing도 올 수 있다.

LESSON 02

동사의 시제

Point 009 그녀는 보통 불평을 많이 하지만, 지금은 불평하지 않는다.

She usually complains a lot, but she is not complaining now.

- 현재시제는 현재의 동작이나 상태, 습관, 반복적인 일 또는 일반적인 사실이나 진리를 나타낸다.
  He **is** in a good mood now. (현재의 상태)
  Light **travels** faster than sound. (일반적인 사실 · 진리)
- 현재진행 시제는 현재 진행 중인 일이나, 현재를 포함하여 일정 기간 일시적으로 진행되는 일을 나타낸다.
  The boy **is dancing** now. (말하는 시점에 진행)
  Julia **is studying** hard this semester. (일시적으로 진행되는 일)

TIP always, usually, often, sometimes, rarely[seldom], never는 현재시제에 자주 쓰이는 빈도부사로 보통 일반동사 앞이나 be동사, 조동사 뒤에 온다.

STEP 1 다음 괄호 안에서 알맞은 말을 고르시오.

1 Joe (has, is having) lunch at noon every day.
2 I can't use the computer now. My brother (uses, is using) it.
3 The Olympic games (take, are taking) place every four years.
4 The sun (rises, is rising) in the east every morning.
5 She (is always, always is) on time for her appointment.

□ take place 개최되다
□ appointment 약속

STEP 2 다음 우리말과 일치하도록 괄호 안의 말을 이용하여 빈칸에 알맞은 말을 쓰시오.

1 Philip은 여가 시간에 우표를 수집해. 그것은 그의 취미야. (collect)
Philip ____________ stamps in his spare time. It's his hobby.

2 너는 TV를 보고 있니, 아니면 그것을 꺼도 되니? (watch)
____________ ____________ ____________ TV, or can I turn it off?

3 Sarah는 이번 주에 일하지 않고 있다. 그녀는 휴가 중이다. (work)
Sarah ____________ ____________ ____________ this week. She's on vacation.

4 지구는 태양 주변을 돈다. (go)
The earth ____________ around the sun.

□ collect 수집하다
□ spare time 여가 시간
□ turn off 끄다
□ vacation 휴가

STEP 3 다음 빈칸에 들어갈 말로 알맞은 것은? 내신

The water ____________ out of the bathtub. Turn off the water tap right now!

① run ② runs ③ ran
④ is running ⑤ was running

□ bathtub 욕조
□ tap (수도 등의) 꼭지

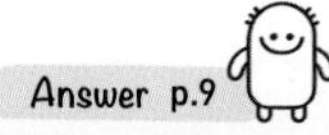

Point 010 그가 샤워를 하고 있는 중에, 전화가 울렸다. 과거시제와 과거진행 시제

While he was taking a shower, the phone rang.

- 과거시제는 과거에 이미 끝난 동작이나 상태, 과거에 있었던 역사적 사실을 나타낸다.
  We **went** hiking last weekend. (과거의 동작)
  World War Ⅱ **ended** in 1945. (역사적 사실)
- 과거진행 시제는 과거 한 시점에서 진행 중이었던 일을 나타내고 '~하는 중이었다'라고 해석한다.
  I **was playing** computer games at 10 last night. (과거에 진행 중이었던 일)

TIP 과거에 어떤 일이 진행 중인 도중에 다른 일이 일어나면, 진행 중이었던 일은 과거진행 시제를 사용하고 도중에 일어난 일은 과거 시제를 사용한다. While he **was peeling** an apple, he **cut** his finger.

STEP 1 다음 문장을 밑줄 친 부분에 유의하여 우리말로 해석하시오.

□ hurt 다치게 하다
□ knee 무릎

1 David was riding a bike at 10 yesterday morning.
2 Cathy went shopping last Saturday.
3 The brothers were watching the baseball game 30 minutes ago.
4 While Henry was playing soccer, he hurt his knee.
5 When I got home, Mom was washing the dishes.

STEP 2 다음 우리말과 일치하도록 빈칸에 알맞은 말을 쓰시오.

□ accident 사고
□ arrive 도착하다

1 그녀는 지난주에 열 권의 책을 읽었다.
She ____________ ten books last week.

2 너는 어제 이맘때 쯤 무엇을 하고 있었니?
What ____________ ____________ ____________ at this time yesterday?

3 그 사고가 일어났을 때 그 차는 얼마나 빨리 달리고 있었니?
How fast ____________ the car going at the time of the accident?

4 내가 도착했을 때, Ryan이 나를 기다리고 있었다.
Ryan ____________ ____________ for me when I ____________.

STEP 3 다음 우리말과 일치하도록 할 때, 빈칸에 들어갈 말이 순서대로 짝지어진 것은? 내신

□ fall asleep 잠들다

Andy는 TV를 보던 중에 잠이 들었다.
→ Andy ________ asleep while he ________ TV.

① falls – watches
② is falling – watches
③ fell – watched
④ was falling – watched
⑤ fell – was watching

Answer p.9

Point 011 그는 내년에 14살이 된다.

He will[is going to] be fourteen next year.

- 「will + 동사원형」은 미래에 일어날 일을 예측하거나 말하는 사람의 의지 또는 순간적인 결정을 나타낼 때 사용하고 '~할 것이다', '~하겠다'로 해석한다. 의문형은 「**Will + 주어 + 동사원형 ~?**」, 부정형은 「**will not[won't]**」이다.
  I **will** keep my words. (말하는 사람의 의지)
- 「be going to + 동사원형」은 이미 계획한 일이나 가까운 미래를 나타낼 때 사용하고 '~할 예정이다', '~할 것이다'로 해석한다. 의문형은 「**Be동사 + 주어 + going to + 동사원형 ~?**」, 부정형은 「**be not going to + 동사원형**」이다.
  I'**m going to** give her a special gift. (이미 계획한 일)

STEP 1 다음 밑줄 친 부분을 바르게 고치시오.

1 Nancy will gets there tomorrow.
2 I'm going to playing soccer this Saturday.
3 Are you going stay here tomorrow?
4 He not is gong to make a cake for her.
5 Will you is at home tonight?

STEP 2 다음 우리말과 일치하도록 괄호 안의 말을 바르게 배열하시오.

□ problem 문제
□ huge 엄청난
□ cook 요리하다

1 공기 오염은 미래에 엄청난 문제가 될 것이다.
(air, pollution, will, problem, be, a, huge, future, in, the)
____

2 영어 시험은 쉽지 않을 것이다. (easy, the, will, be, English, test, not)
____

3 영화가 곧 시작될 것이다. (soon, the, movie, is, start, to, going)
____

4 저녁 식사로 불고기와 비빔밥을 요리하실 거예요?
(going, are, you, dinner, to, cook, for, bulgogi, bibimbap, and)
____

STEP 3 다음 대화의 빈칸에 들어갈 말로 알맞은 것은? 내신

□ weekend 주말

A: What are you going to do this weekend?
B: ______________________

① I played soccer.
② I watched a movie.
③ I was talking to mom.
④ I was doing my homework.
⑤ I'm going to ride a bike.

Answer p.9

Point 012 나는 5년 동안 여기에서 살아왔다.

I have lived here for five years.

• 현재완료는 「**have[has] + p.p.**」의 형태로, 과거에 일어난 일이 현재까지 영향을 미치고 있음을 나타낸다.

	의미	예문
경험	과거부터 현재까지의 경험	I **have been** to Canada twice.
완료	과거의 동작이 현재에 막 완료됨	I **have** just **finished** lunch.
계속	과거부터 현재까지 어떤 일이 계속 됨	I **have stayed** at home all day long.
결과	과거의 일로 인해 생긴 결과가 현재에도 영향을 미침	I **have spilt** juice on my shirt.

• 부정형은 「**have[has] + not + p.p.**」이고 의문형은 「**Have[Has] + 주어 + p.p. ~?**」이다.
Jane **hasn't seen** Chris since this morning.
Have you ever **traveled** by ship?

TIP 현재완료는 yesterday, last week, two years ago 등과 같이 명백한 과거 시점을 나타내는 부사(구)와 함께 쓸 수 없다.

STEP 1 다음 괄호 안에서 알맞은 말을 고르시오.

□ traffic 교통
□ all one's life 평생, 일생 내내

1 The traffic accident (happened, has happened) last Friday.
2 Tylor (took, has taken) violin lessons for three years.
3 Jenny lives in Los Angeles. She (lived, has lived) there all her life.
4 My uncle (worked, has worked) at the bank in 2016.
5 I (am, have been) in the cafe for an hour.

STEP 2 다음 우리말과 일치하도록 괄호 안의 말을 빈칸에 알맞은 형태로 쓰시오.

□ each other 서로
□ since ~이후로
□ go skiing 스키 타러 가다
□ recently 최근에

1 우리는 서로 알고 지낸지 5년이 되었다. (know)
We ______________________ each other for five years.

2 그녀는 그 병원에서 2015년부터 일해 왔다. (work)
She ______________________ in the hospital since 2015.

3 우리는 지난 겨울에는 스키를 타러 가지 않았다. (go skiing)
We ______________________ last winter.

4 너는 최근에 David를 본 적 있니? (see)
______________________ David recently?

STEP 3 다음 빈칸에 들어갈 말로 알맞은 것은? 내신

□ last year 작년

Jim ________ tennis lessons since last year.

① takes ② took ③ taken ④ has took ⑤ has taken

Answer p.10

Point 013 나는 일본에 두 번 가 본 적이 있다.

현재완료의 용법 (경험)

I have been to Japan twice.

- 현재완료 용법의 경험은 과거부터 현재까지 경험한 일을 나타내며 '~한 적이 있다'로 해석한다. 정확하게 일어난 때를 알 수 없거나 밝힐 필요 없을 때 사용하며, 주로 ever, never, once, before 등과 함께 쓴다.
  I **have seen** the movie *before*.
  I **have** *never* **eaten** snails.
  Have you *ever* **been** to Ireland?

TIP 「**have[has]** + **never** + **p.p.**」는 '(결코) ~한 적이 없다'의 의미로 자주 쓰이는 표현이니 알아두면 좋다.

STEP 1 다음 밑줄 친 부분을 바르게 고치시오.

1 Has she ever try bungee jumping?
2 He have been to London once.
3 I have meet Tom four times.
4 The girl has eaten never lobster before.
5 Were you ever seen the movie *Gone with the Wind*?

□ bungee jumping 번지 점프
□ lobster 바닷가재

STEP 2 다음 우리말과 일치하도록 괄호 안의 말을 바르게 배열하시오.

1 Henry는 그 박물관을 여러 번 방문한 적이 있다.
(the, museum, visited, several, times, Henry, has)

2 너는 그를 만난 적이 있니? (you, ever, have, him, met)

3 그녀는 스페인에 가본 적이 없다. (never, has, Spain, she, to, been)

4 그는 이제까지 마라톤을 해 본 적이 있나요? (he, ever, a, marathon, run, has)

□ marathon 마라톤

STEP 3 다음 중 어법상 틀린 것은? 내신

① I have met Rachel twice.
② Has he ever visited Italy?
③ I have see the actor before.
④ Have you ever tried Greek food?
⑤ He has been to the Orsay Museum.

□ Greek food 그리스 음식

Answer p.10

Point 014 버스가 막 떠났다.

The bus has *just* left.

- 현재완료 용법의 완료는 '벌써[이미,막] ~했다'라는 뜻으로 과거에 시작한 어떤 동작이 현재에 막 완료되었음을 나타내며, 주로 just, already, yet 등과 함께 쓴다.
  I **haven't finished** my homework *yet*.

TIP just, already는 have[has]와 p.p.사이에 위치하고, yet는 부정문이나 의문문에 주로 쓰이며 문장 끝에 온다.

STEP 1 다음 밑줄 친 부분에 유의하여 우리말로 해석하시오.

□ solution 해결책

1 We have just arrived home.
2 He has already moved to a new house.
3 I have just finished my science report.
4 They haven't found a solution yet.
5 I have already had dinner with my family.

STEP 2 다음 괄호 안의 말과 현재완료를 사용하여 대화를 완성하시오.

1 A: Are you hungry? (just, have)
B: No, I ______________________ lunch.

2 A: What do your parents think about your plans? (not, tell, yet)
B: Actually, I ______________________.

3 A: Did Tony call you? (just, get)
B: Yes, I ______________________ a call from him.

4 A: Don't forget to turn off the gas. (already, do)
B: Don't worry. I ______________________ it.

STEP 3 다음 중 어법상 틀린 것은? 내신

□ receive 받다

① The rain hasn't stopped yet.
② I have sent you an e-mail just.
③ I haven't received a letter from him yet.
④ I have never seen such a beautiful dress.
⑤ The bus hasn't arrived at the bus stop yet.

Answer p.10

Point 015 Brown 선생님은 2011년부터 과학을 가르쳐 왔다.

Mr. Brown has taught science *since* 2011.

- 현재완료 용법의 계속은 과거부터 현재까지 지속되고 있는 동작이나 상태를 나타내며 '계속 ~해 왔다'로 해석한다. 주로 for, since, lately, recently, how long 등과 함께 쓴다.
  I **have used** this cell phone *for* 2 years.
  How long **have** you **had** the pain?
  TIP 「**for** + 기간」은 '~동안'의 의미이고, 「**since** + 과거 시점」은 '~이래로'의 의미이다.

STEP 1 다음 괄호 안에서 알맞은 말을 고르시오.

□ tough 힘든, 어려운

1 Mr. Smith has taught English (for, since) 3 years.
2 We haven't heard from him (for, since) last month.
3 Kevin (had / has had) a dog since he was 5 years old.
4 How long (have you know / have you known) each other?
5 Life has been tough (last year, lately).

STEP 2 다음 두 문장을 for 또는 since를 사용하여 보기 와 같이 한 문장으로 바꿔 쓰시오.

□ still 여전히
□ then 그 때
□ pilot 조종사, 비행사

보기 I started to play the piano seven years ago. I still play the piano.
→ I have played the piano for seven years.

1 Amy became sick on Sunday. She is still sick.
→ Amy ______________________ Sunday.

2 He started to love music then. He still loves it.
→ He ______________________ then.

3 Kevin and Jenny became friends ten years ago. They are still friends.
→ Kevin and Jenny ______________________ ten years.

4 Peter wanted to be a pilot when he was young. He still wants to be a pilot.
→ Peter ______________________ he was young.

STEP 3 다음 빈칸에 들어갈 말이 순서대로 짝지어진 것은? 내신

□ as (자격이) …로(서)
□ nurse 간호사

• Sarah has worked as a nurse ________ last year.
• Ms. Green has taught English ________ two years.

① for – for ② for – since ③ since – for
④ since – since ⑤ in – since

Answer p.11

Point 016 그는 휴대전화를 잃어버렸다.

He has lost his cell phone.

- 현재완료 용법의 결과는 과거에 행한 동작이 현재 어떠한 결과로 나타났을 때 사용한다. 해석은 '~했다'로 과거와 같지만 '그래서 현재는 ~하다'라는 결과의 의미를 내포하고 있다.
  He **has gone** out. (= He went out, so he is not here now.)

TIP 「**have[has] been to**」 '~에 가 본 적이 있다'의 의미로 모든 인칭에 사용 가능하지만, 「**has gone to**」는 '~에 가고 없다'의 의미로 3인칭에만 사용 가능하다.

STEP 1 다음 괄호 안에서 알맞은 말을 고르시오.

1 I have lost my car keys. I (can, can't) get in the car.
2 He has cleaned his room. Now his room is (tidy, messy).
3 She has left Africa, so she (is, isn't) here.
4 I (have been to, have gone to) my father's office.
5 Michael has broken his leg. So he (can't, couldn't) walk now.

□ tidy 깔끔한, 잘 정돈된
□ messy 지저분한
□ break one's leg ~의 다리가 부러지다

STEP 2 다음 두 문장을 현재완료를 사용하여 보기 와 같이 한 문장으로 바꿔 쓰시오.

보기 He fell into a deep hole. He's still there.
→ He has fallen into a deep hole.

1 My sunglasses disappeared. They are not here now.
→ ____________________

2 Katie lost her ring. So she doesn't have it now.
→ ____________________

3 I left my math homework at home. So I don't have it now.
→ ____________________

4 Cathy went to the library. So she's not here now.
→ ____________________

□ deep 깊은
□ disappear 사라지다

STEP 3 다음 빈칸에 들어갈 말로 알맞은 것은? 내신

Somebody has ________ my coffee. The cup is empty.

① drink ② drank ③ drunk ④ drinking ⑤ to drink

Answer p.11

01회 내신 적중 실전 문제

[01~02] 다음 빈칸에 들어갈 말로 알맞은 것을 고르시오.

Point 010

01

When he came home, his brother _________ TV.

① watch ② was watch
③ watching ④ is watching
⑤ was watching

Point 015

02

Peter has studied Spanish ___________.

① in 2015 ② tomorrow
③ last year ④ since last month
⑤ three years ago

[03~05] 다음 대화의 빈칸에 들어갈 말로 알맞은 것을 고르시오.

Point 011

03

A: Erica is in the hospital.
B: I know. _________ her tomorrow.

① I visit ② I visited
③ I didn't visit ④ I was visiting
⑤ I'm going to visit

Point 016

04

A: Where is Judy?
B: She has already _________ to New York on business. She left a week ago.

① go ② going ③ gone
④ went ⑤ to go

Point 015

05

A: How long have you stayed here?
B: I've _________ here for two weeks.

① be ② is ③ are
④ were ⑤ been

Point 016

06 다음 두 문장을 한 문장으로 바꿀 때 빈칸에 들어갈 말로 알맞은 것은?

He lost his watch. He still can't find it.
➜ He _________ his watch.

① loses ② is losing ③ has lost
④ had lost ⑤ was losing

[07~08] 다음 빈칸에 들어갈 말이 순서대로 짝지어진 것을 고르시오.

Point 015

07

• He hasn't eaten anything _________ three days.
• She hasn't attended class _________ last Tuesday.

① for – since ② for – before
③ since – for ④ since – before
⑤ before – for

Point 009

08

• Hurry up! Everybody _________ for you.
• Time _________ for no man.

① waited – waits
② is waiting – waits
③ waits – is waiting
④ was waiting – waited
⑤ is waiting – was waiting

Answer p.12

Point 015

09 다음 우리말을 영어로 바르게 옮긴 것은?

그들은 이틀째 과학 캠프에 참가하고 있다.

① They are at the science camp for two days.
② They were at the science camp two days ago.
③ They have been at the science camp two days ago.
④ They have been at the science camp for two days.
⑤ They have been at the science camp since two days.

[10~11] 다음 중 어법상 틀린 것을 고르시오.

Point 016

10

① Tony has lost his bike.
② I has gone to England.
③ I have been to Japan twice.
④ I've watched the movie before.
⑤ He's already arrived at the airport.

Point 014

11

① I have met him once.
② He has never been to Italy.
③ It has rained a lot a year ago.
④ Mom has just made cookies.
⑤ Someone has eaten my soup.

고난도 Point 015

12 다음 보기 의 두 문장을 한 문장으로 바르게 나타낸 것은?

보기 Jason moved to Chicago three years ago. He still lives there.

① Jason lived in Chicago for three years.
② Jason has lived in Chicago for three years.
③ Jason has moved to Chicago for three years.
④ Jason has lived in Chicago three years ago.
⑤ Jason has been to Chicago three years ago.

서술형

Point 010

13 다음 우리말과 일치하도록 괄호 안의 말을 이용하여 영작하시오.

그 소녀들은 인형 놀이를 하고 있는 중이었다.
(play with dolls)

→ ______________________

Point 014

14 다음 대화의 흐름에 맞도록 괄호 안의 말을 바르게 배열하시오.

A: Let's have lunch. I'm hungry.
B: Sorry, but I ______________________.
(already, lunch, have, eaten)

[15~16] 다음 두 문장을 한 문장으로 바꿀 때, 빈칸에 알맞은 말을 쓰시오.

Point 013

15

Diana started to work at the bank in 2012. She still works there.

→ Diana ________ ________ at the bank ________ 2012.

Point 016

16

I forgot my online banking password. I can't access my account.

→ I ________ ________ my online banking password.

02회 내신 적중 실전 문제

[01~02] 다음 빈칸에 들어갈 말이 순서대로 짝지어진 것을 고르시오.

Point 009

01

Kelly usually _________ her homework from 8:00 to 9:00 in the evening. It's 8:20. She's _________ her homework now.

① do – do ② does – do
③ does – does ④ does – doing
⑤ doing – doing

Point 010, 015

02

• Jessica sent the letter _________.
• I haven't heard from him _________.

① for 3 hours – last week
② last Friday – 2 years ago
③ yesterday – since last year
④ since this morning – lately
⑤ since 4 o'clock – for days

Point 010

03 다음 대화의 빈칸에 들어갈 말이 순서대로 짝지어진 것은?

A: _________ Tony studying when you came back?
B: No, he _________ computer games at that time.

① Is – is playing ② Was – is playing
③ Was – was playing ④ Did – played
⑤ Did – was playing

Point 013

04 다음 대화의 빈칸에 공통으로 들어갈 말로 알맞은 것은?

A: Have you ever _________ to Hawaii?
B: Yes, I've _________ there twice.

① gone ② gotten ③ done
④ been ⑤ went

[05~06] 다음 빈칸에 들어갈 말로 알맞은 것을 고르시오.

Point 016

05

She _________ the boy a year ago.

① like ② likes ③ liked
④ has liked ⑤ have liked

Point 015

06

I have studied Japanese _________.

① in 2015 ② last month
③ three years ago ④ since 2012
⑤ when I was young

Point 009

07 다음 문장에서 usually가 들어가기에 알맞은 곳은?

I (①) have (②) cereal (③) for (④) breakfast (⑤).

Point 015

08 다음 우리말을 영어로 바르게 옮긴 것은?

Gini는 일주일째 아프다.

① Gini is sick since a week.
② Gini was sick for a week.
③ Gini has been sick for a week.
④ Gini has been sick since a week.
⑤ Gini has already been sick since a week.

중요

Point 015

09 다음 우리말과 일치하도록 할 때, 빈칸에 들어갈 말로 알맞은 것은?

> 나의 형은 작년부터 캐나다에 머무르고 있다.
> → My brother ________ in Canada since last year.

① stay ② stays ③ stayed
④ to stay ⑤ has stayed

Point 013

10 다음 중 밑줄 친 부분의 용법이 보기 와 같은 것은?

> 보기 I have seen the movie before.

① She has gone to Paris.
② He has just opened the box.
③ Have you ever caught a big fish?
④ How long have you used this computer?
⑤ I have lost my book. So I can't read it.

Point 013

11 다음 중 어법상 틀린 것은?

① I have never drove a car.
② She hasn't drunk coffee for years.
③ How long have you had your pet?
④ You have grown since the last time I saw you.
⑤ He has liked soccer since he was a little child.

고난도

Point 013

12 다음 중 어법상 옳은 것은?

① Do you have ridden a horse before?
② Henry have been very busy for a week.
③ I have been to New York two years ago.
④ We have kept this rule for over ten years.
⑤ She didn't have anything since this morning.

서술형

Point 012

13 다음 주어진 문장을 지시에 맞게 바꿔 쓰시오.

(1) I have met her before. (부정문)
→ ________________________

(2) He has finished his report. (의문문)
→ ________________________

[14~15] 다음 두 문장을 한 문장으로 바꿔 쓰시오.

Point 015

14

> He started to use the computer 5 years ago. He still uses the computer.

→ ________________________

Point 016

15

> I left my umbrella on the bus. I don't have it with me.

→ ________________________

Point 016

16 다음은 미나의 과제 수행 상태를 나타낸 표이다. 표의 정보를 이용하여 대화를 완성하시오.

Homework	Done
science homework	○
math homework	×

> 조건 1 현재완료와 괄호 안의 말을 사용할 것
> 조건 2 각각 총 4단어로 쓸 것

A: Have you finished your science homework?
B: Yes, I (1) ____________. (already, do)
A: How about your math homework? Have you finished it?
B: No, I (2) ____________. (finish, yet)

Grammar Review 핵심 정리

1 현재시제와 현재진행 시제

Point

She usually **complains** a lot, but she **is** not **complaining** now. **009**

☞ 현재시제는 현재의 동작이나 상태, 습관, 반복적인 일 또는 일반적인 사실이나 진리를 나타낸다.
☞ 현재진행 시제는 현재 진행 중인 일이나, 현재를 포함하여 일정 기간 일시적으로 진행되는 일을 나타낸다.

2 과거시제와 과거진행 시제

While he **was taking** a shower, the phone **rang**. **010**

☞ 과거시제는 과거에 이미 끝난 동작이나 상태, 또는 과거에 있었던 역사적인 사실을 나타낸다.
☞ 과거진행 시제는 과거 한 시점에서 진행 중이었던 일을 나타내고 '~하는 중이었다'라고 해석한다.

3 미래시제

He **will[is going to]** be fourteen next year. **011**

☞ 「will+동사원형」은 미래에 일어날 일을 예측하거나 말하는 사람의 의지 또는 순간적인 결정을 나타낼 때 사용하고 '~할 것이다'로 해석한다.
☞ 「be going to+동사원형」은 이미 계획한 일이나 가까운 미래를 나타낼 때 사용하고 '~할 예정이다'로 해석한다.

4 현재완료의 개념

I **have lived** here for five years. **012**

☞ 현재완료는 「have[has]+p.p.」의 형태로, 과거에 일어난 일이 현재까지 영향을 미치고 있음을 나타낸다.

5 현재완료의 용법

I **have been** to Japan twice. **013**

☞ 경험: 과거부터 현재까지 경험한 일을 나타내며 '~한 적이 있다'로 해석 하고 주로 ever, never, once, before 등과 함께 쓴다.

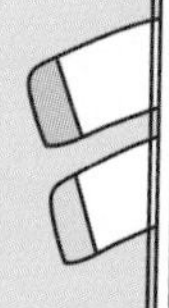

The bus **has** *just* **left**. **014**

☞ 완료: '벌써[이미, 막] ~했다'라는 뜻으로 과거에 시작된 동작이 현재에 막 완료되었음을 나타내고 just, already, yet 등과 함께 쓴다.

Mr. Brown **has taught** science *since* 2011. **015**

☞ 계속: '계속 ~해 왔다'의 뜻으로 과거부터 현재까지 지속되고 있는 상태를 나타내고 for, since, lately, recently, how long 등과 자주 쓴다.
☞ 「for+기간」 ~동안 / 「since+과거 시점」 ~이래로

He **has lost** his cell phone. **016**

☞ 결과: 과거에 행한 동작이 어떠한 결과로 나타났을 때 쓴다. 해석은 '~했다'로 과거와 같지만 '그래서 현재는 ~하다'라는 결과의 의미를 내포하고 있다.

조동사

Point 017 내 부탁을 들어줄 수 있니[있을까요]?

Can[Could] you do me a favor?

- 능력: '~할 수 있다'의 의미로 능력 · 가능한 일을 나타내며, 이때 과거는 could 또는 was[were] able to, 미래는 will be able to로 쓴다.
  My child **can**[is able to] swim well.
- 허가 · 허락: '~해도 된다[좋다]'의 의미로 허가 · 허락을 나타낸다.
  You **can** leave now.
- 요청 · 부탁: '~해 주시겠어요?'의 의미로 요청 · 부탁을 나타내고, could는 보다 정중한 부탁의 표현으로 사용할 수 있다.
  Can[Could] you give me a ride to the station?

STEP 1 다음 문장의 밑줄 친 부분의 의미를 고르시오.

□ concentrate 집중하다
□ borrow 빌리다
□ language 언어

1 Could you please open the door? (능력, 부탁)
2 I was very sleepy, so I couldn't concentrate. (능력, 허가)
3 You can borrow my pen if you like. (허가, 부탁)
4 My grandfather could speak three languages. (능력, 부탁)
5 Can I see your picture? (능력, 허가)

STEP 2 다음 우리말과 일치하도록 can 또는 could와 괄호 안의 말을 이용하여 빈칸에 알맞은 말을 쓰시오. (can과 could가 둘 다 가능한 것도 있음)

□ pass 건네주다

1 너는 바이올린을 연주할 수 있니? (play)
  ____________ you ____________ the violin?
2 나에게 소금 좀 전해줄래? (pass)
  ____________ you ____________ me the salt, please?
3 저희가 여기서 머물러도 되나요? (stay)
  ____________ we ____________ here?
4 나는 토마토 스프를 만들 수 있다. (make)
  I ____________ ____________ tomato soup.

STEP 3 다음 대화의 빈칸에 들어갈 말로 알맞은 것은? 내신

A: You look tired.
B: Yes, I __________ sleep well last night.

① can ② can't ③ could ④ couldn't ⑤ was able to

Answer p.15

Point 018 네 가방은 차 안에 있을지도 모른다.

Your bag may[might] be in the car.

- 허가: '~해도 좋다[된다]'의 의미로 허가를 나타낸다. 이때 can으로 바꿔 쓸 수 있는데, can은 may보다 격식을 차리지 않는 관계에서 주로 사용한다.
  May I come in?
- 불확실한 추측: '~일지도 모른다'의 의미로 불확실한 추측을 나타내고 might는 may보다 약한 추측을 나타낸다. 부정형은 「**may[might] not+동사원형**」이다.
  She **may[might]** be at school.
  It **may[might] not** be true.

STEP 1 다음 문장의 밑줄 친 부분의 의미를 고르시오.

1 May I go to the bathroom? (허가, 추측)
2 It may rain this afternoon. (허가, 추측)
3 He might be taking a shower now. (허가, 추측)
4 I may be a little late for the meeting. (허가, 추측)
5 You may look around, but don't break anything. (허가, 추측)

□ take a shower 샤워를 하다
□ be late for ~에 늦다
□ look around 구경하다
□ break 깨다, 부수다

STEP 2 다음 우리말과 일치하도록 may 또는 might와 괄호 안의 말을 이용하여 빈칸에 알맞은 말을 쓰시오. (may와 might가 둘 다 가능한 것도 있음)

1 제가 창문을 닫아도 될까요? (close)
_______ _______ _______ the window?

2 너는 기차를 놓칠지도 몰라. (miss)
_______ _______ _______ the train.

3 내 카메라를 빌려도 좋은데, 그것을 조심히 다루렴. (borrow)
You _______ _______ my camera, but be careful with it.

4 그것은 좋아 보이지만, 매우 비쌀지도 모른다. (be)
It looks nice, but it _______ _______ very expensive.

□ miss 놓치다
□ borrow 빌리다
□ be careful with ~에 조심하다

STEP 3 다음 밑줄 친 부분의 의미가 나머지 넷과 다른 것은? 내신

① She may be hungry.
② You might need this.
③ He might be in the attic.
④ You may go home early today.
⑤ They may not believe your story.

□ attic 다락방

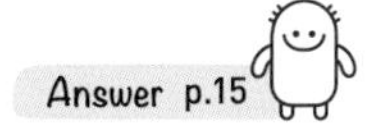
Answer p.15

Point 019 나 좀 도와줄래요[주시겠어요]?

Will[Would] you help me?

- will
  a. 예정 · 의지: '~할 것이다'의 의미로 미래의 일이나 의지를 나타낸다. 부정형은 will not[won't]이다.
  They **will** have a pajama party this weekend.
  b. 요청: '~할래'의 의미로 요청이나 제안을 나타낸다. A: **Will** you be my partner? B: No, I **won't**.
- would
  a. will의 과거형 She said she **would** support us.
  b. 정중한 부탁: '~해 주실래요?'의 의미로 will보다 정중한 표현이다. **Would** you speak more slowly?
  c. 과거의 불규칙적 습관: '~하곤 했다'의 의미로 과거의 반복적인 행동이나 습관을 나타낸다.
  Whenever Peter got angry, he **would** take a walk.

STEP 1 다음 괄호 안에서 알맞은 말을 고르시오.

1 I (will, would) go to the dance tomorrow.
2 I knew she (won't, wouldn't) show up on time.
3 It is raining. I (not will, won't) go outside.
4 I'm in the library now. I (will, would) call you later.
5 When I was in the army, I (will, would) get up at 5:30 a.m.

□ show up 나타나다
□ on time 제 시간에
□ army 군대
□ get up 일어나다

STEP 2 다음 빈칸에 들어갈 말을 will 또는 would와 함께 보기 에서 골라 쓰시오. (will 또는 would가 둘 다 가능한 것도 있음)

보기 study be visit carry

1 My sister ____________ ____________ 10 years old next year.
2 I have a test tomorrow. I ____________ ____________ late tonight.
3 ____________ you ____________ this bag for me, please?
4 I ____________ ____________ my grandparents on weekends when I was young.

□ carry 나르다
□ grandparents 조부모

STEP 3 다음 빈칸에 공통으로 들어갈 말로 알맞은 것은? 내신

- ________ you have dinner with me on Friday?
- I thought she ________ wait for me.
- When I was young, I ________ spend my vacations at my grandmother's.

① Can[can] ② Will[will] ③ Would[would]
④ May[may] ⑤ Might[might]

□ vacation 방학

Answer p.15

Point 020 당신은 안전벨트를 매야 한다.

You must fasten your seat belt.

- 의무: '~해야 한다'의 의미로 필요 · 의무를 나타내고, must not[mustn't]은 '~해서는 안 된다'의 뜻으로 금지를 나타낸다.
  You **must** come back before 12 o'clock.
  You **must not** be late.
- 강한 추측: '~임이 틀림없다'의 의미로 확실한 추측을 나타낸다.
  You **must** be hungry after all that walking.

TIP cannot be[can't be]는 '~일 리가 없다'의 뜻으로 강한 부정의 추측을 나타낸다.

STEP 1 다음 괄호 안에서 알맞은 말을 고르시오.

1 You (must, must not) ride a bike in the rain. It's dangerous.
2 Ted already left the classroom. He (must, can't) be at school.
3 You (must, can not) be quiet in the library.
4 You (must, cannot) be Julie's sister. You look just like her.
5 Sarah is absent today. She (must, cannot) be sick.

□ dangerous 위험한
□ already 이미
□ absent 결석한, 결근한

STEP 2 다음 우리말과 일치하도록 빈칸에 알맞은 말을 쓰시오.

1 너는 수업 중에 휴대전화를 사용해서는 안 된다.
You ________ ________ ________ your cell phone in class.

2 너는 그것을 비밀로 해야 한다.
You ________ ________ it a secret.

3 그는 의사인 것이 틀림없다.
He ________ ________ a doctor.

4 그 소문은 사실일 리가 없다.
The rumor ________ ________ true.

5 그는 내가 그를 좋아한다는 것을 아는 것이 틀림없다.
He ________ ________ that I like him.

□ in class 수업 중에
□ keep ~ a secret ~을 비밀로 하다
□ rumor 소문

STEP 3 다음 빈칸에 들어갈 말로 알맞은 것은? 내신

Lisa is crying. She ________ be sad.

① won't ② can't ③ must ④ must not ⑤ may not

Answer p.16

Point 021 나는 먼저 숙제를 끝내야 한다.

I have to finish my homework first.

- 「**have[has] to + 동사원형**」은 '~해야 한다'는 뜻으로 필요 · 의무를 나타내며, must와 바꿔 쓸 수 있다.
  I **have to**[must] work late tonight.
- have to는 일반동사와 같은 방법으로 do/does/did를 이용하여 부정문과 의문문을 만든다. 부정문은 「**don't have to + 동사원형**」으로 '~할 필요가 없다'로 해석하고, 의문문은 「**Do + 주어 + have to + 동사원형 ~?**」으로 '~해야 하나요?'로 해석한다.
  You **don't have to** hurry. **Do I have to** go to the hospital?
- 과거형은 「**had to + 동사원형**」으로 '~해야 했다'라고 해석한다.
  He **had to** cook dinner all by himself.

TIP have to와 must는 둘 다 필요 · 의무의 뜻이지만, don't have to는 불필요를 나타내고, must not은 금지를 나타낸다.

STEP 1 다음 문장을 밑줄 친 부분에 유의하여 우리말로 해석하시오.

□ suit 정장

1 We don't have to wait in the long line.
2 Does he have to work tomorrow?
3 Do I have to wear a suit to work?
4 She doesn't have to clean the bathroom.
5 They had to go back to school.

STEP 2 다음 우리말과 일치하도록 빈칸에 알맞은 말을 쓰시오.

□ report 보고서

1 우리가 그를 도와야 한다.
We ____________ ____________ help him.

2 너는 파티를 위해 아무 것도 가지고 올 필요가 없다.
You ____________ ____________ ____________ bring anything for the party.

3 그녀는 시험을 위해 공부를 해야 했다.
She ____________ ____________ study for the exam.

4 제가 보고서를 영어로 써야 합니까?
____________ I ____________ ____________ write the report in English?

STEP 3 다음 우리말과 일치하도록 할 때, 빈칸에 들어갈 말로 알맞은 것은? 내신

□ get up early 일찍 일어나다

> 나는 내일 일을 하지 않아서, 나는 일찍 일어날 필요가 없다.
> → I'm not working tomorrow, so I ________ get up early.

① cannot ② may not ③ must not ④ would not ⑤ don't have to

Answer p.16

Point 022 너는 가난한 사람들을 도와야 한다.

You should help poor people.

- should는 '~하는 것이 좋겠다', '~해야 한다'라는 뜻으로 의무 · 당연 · 충고를 나타낸다.
  You **should** get some rest.
- 부정문은 「**should not[shouldn't] + 동사원형**」, 의문문은 「**Should + 주어 + 동사원형~?**」으로 나타낸다.
  You **should not** go to bed so late.
  Should I apologize to her?

TIP must는 강제성이 있는 의무인 반면, should는 도덕적으로 옳거나 그렇게 하는 것이 좋을 때 주로 쓰인다.

STEP 1 다음 괄호 안에서 알맞은 말을 고르시오.

1 You (should, shouldn't) eat too much. You're on a diet.
2 You (should, shouldn't) go to London. It's a great city.
3 You've hurt her feelings. I think you (should, shouldn't) apologize to her.
4 You (should, shouldn't) cross the street on a red crosswalk light.
5 You look tired. You (should, shouldn't) take a few days off.

□ be on a diet 다이어트 중이다
□ hurt 다치게 하다
□ feeling 감정
□ apologize 사과하다

STEP 2 다음 우리말과 일치하도록 괄호 안의 말을 바르게 배열하시오.

1 우리는 환경을 보호해야 한다. (should, environment, protect, we, the)
____

2 파티에 뭔가를 가져가야 하나요? (I, bring, should, party, to, something, the)
____

3 너는 약속을 어기면 안 된다. (promise, you, break, should, not, the)
____

4 실내에서 자외선 차단제를 발라야 하나요? (wear, I, should, sunscreen, indoors)
____

5 그는 그의 부모님의 말씀을 들어야 한다. (he, his, to, listen, should, parents)
____

□ protect 보호하다
□ environment 환경
□ promise 약속
□ sunscreen 자외선 차단제

STEP 3 다음 빈칸에 들어갈 말로 알맞은 것은? 내신

Be quiet! You __________ make a noise in the library!

① must ② should ③ shouldn't ④ had to ⑤ don't have to

□ make a noise 시끄럽게 하다

Answer p.16

Point 023 너는 서두르는 게 좋겠다. had better

You had better hurry.

- 「had better + 동사원형」은 '~하는 것이 좋겠다'라는 뜻으로 경고성의 충고나 조언을 나타내고, 「주어'd better」으로 축약하기도 한다. 부정문은 「had better not + 동사원형」으로 '~하지 않는 편이 낫다'로 해석한다.
  You **had better** leave soon, or you'll miss the train.
  You **had better not** go out in this bad weather.

TIP had better는 그렇게 하지 않으면 불이익이 따르는 특정한 상황에서 경고성이 있는 조언이나 충고를 할 때 사용한다.

STEP 1 다음 괄호 안에서 알맞은 말을 고르시오.

1 They don't take checks. We (have better, had better) get some cash.
2 You (had better, had better to) tidy up your room, or your mom will be angry.
3 It looks dangerous. You (had not better, had better not) try.
4 You (had better be not, had better not be) late again, or you'll lose your job.
5 He (has better, had better) stay at home. It is raining hard.

□ check 수표
□ cash 현금
□ tidy up 정리하다
□ lose one's job 실직하다

STEP 2 다음 빈칸에 들어갈 말을 had better 또는 had better not과 괄호 안의 말을 이용하여 쓰시오.

1 I ______________ that away. It might come in useful. (throw)
2 I ______________ now before the traffic gets too bad. (go)
3 You ______________ too much if you don't want to take it out at the airport. (pack)
4 We ______________ the tickets now. There won't be any left tomorrow. (book)
5 You ______________ between meals if you want to lose weight. (eat)

□ throw away ~을 버리다
□ come in useful 쓸모 있다
□ book 예약하다
□ eat between meals 간식을 먹다

STEP 3 다음 대화의 빈칸에 들어갈 말로 알맞은 것은? 내신

A: Oh, it's raining!
B: I don't want to get my dress wet. I ________ an umbrella.

① had better bring
② had better not bring
③ had better to bring
④ had better not to bring
⑤ had not better to bring

□ wet 젖은

Answer p.17

Point 024 나는 커피를 마시고 싶다.

I would like to drink coffee.

- 「**would like to＋동사원형**」은 '~하고 싶다'라는 뜻으로 자신의 의사를 공손하게 표현하거나, 상대방의 의향을 정중히 물을 때 사용한다. 「**주어'd like**」로 축약하기도 한다.
  I **would like to** ask you a question.
  What **would** you **like to** eat?
- 「**would like＋명사**」의 형태도 '~를 원하다'의 뜻이다.
  A: **Would** you **like** a cup of tea?　B: **I'd like** some coffee, please.

STEP 1 다음 문장을 밑줄 친 부분에 유의하여 우리말로 해석하시오.

1 I would like to eat a hamburger with Coke.
2 I would like to show you my new shoes.
3 What would you like to do this weekend?
4 Would you like first class or economy class?
5 What would you like to know about her?

□ first class 일등석
□ economy class 일반석

STEP 2 다음 우리말과 일치하도록 괄호 안의 말과 would like to를 이용하여 빈칸에 알맞은 말을 쓰시오.

1 저는 저 영화를 보고 싶어요. (watch)
______________________________ that movie.

2 저와 데이트할래요? (go out with)
______________________________ me?

3 당신은 오늘 밤에 무엇을 하고 싶나요? (do)
______________________________ tonight?

4 저는 터키로 여행을 가고 싶어요. (travel)
______________________________ to Turkey.

□ go out with ~와 데이트하다

STEP 3 다음 빈칸에 들어갈 말로 알맞은 것은? 내신

Would you like ________ with me?

① come　② came　③ coming
④ to come　⑤ to coming

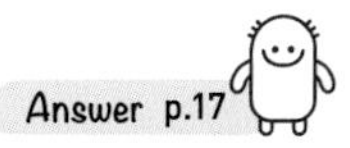

Point 025 나는 매일 아침 운동하곤 했다.

I used to exercise every morning.

- 「**used to + 동사원형**」은 현재에는 더 이상 지속되지 않는 과거의 상태 또는 과거의 규칙적, 계속적인 습관을 나타낸다. 부정형은 「**didn't used to**」 또는 「**used not to**」로 쓴다.
  a. 과거의 상태: '(전에는) ~이었다' There **used to be** a park here.
  b. 과거의 습관: '~하곤 했다' Bob **used to play** soccer after school.
- 「**would + 동사원형**」은 '~하곤 했다'라는 뜻으로 과거의 불규칙하게 반복되는 동작을 나타낸다.
  We **would go** swimming every Saturday.
  TIP 과거의 상태를 나타낼 때는 「**used to** + 동사원형」만 쓸 수 있다.

STEP 1 다음 괄호 안에서 알맞은 말을 모두 고르시오.

□ pond 연못
□ teenager 십 대

1 We (used to, would) go to the park and play baseball.
2 There (used to, would) be a big pond around here.
3 I (used to, would) have a short hair when I was a teenager.
4 He (used to, would) walk along the beach before bed.
5 My hometown (used to, would) be very peaceful.

STEP 2 다음 우리말과 일치하도록 괄호 안의 말을 바르게 배열하시오.

1 우리는 매주 토요일마다 자전거 주행을 하곤 했다.
(a, go, on, bike, used, every, Saturday, we, to, ride)
____

2 우리 가족은 내가 아이였을 때 Los Angeles에서 살았었다.
(my, family, Los Angeles, when, a, kid, used, to, live, in, I, was)
____

3 나는 학교에 가기 위해 6시에 일어나곤 했다.
(go, to, I, at, to, would, get, school, 6, up)
____

4 나의 할아버지는 그의 직업에 대해 이야기하곤 했다.
(grandfather, tell, stories, my, would, about, job, his)
____

STEP 3 다음 두 문장이 같은 뜻이 되도록 할 때, 빈칸에 들어갈 말로 알맞은 것은? 내신

□ post office 우체국

There was a post office on this street, but it's not there now.
= There ________ a post office on this street.

① use ② using ③ used
④ is using ⑤ used to be

Answer p.17

Point 026 나는 컴퓨터 게임을 정말 좋아한다.

I do *like* computer games.

- do는 일반동사 앞에서 부정문과 의문문을 만든다. **Do** you know the answer?
- 대동사 do: 앞 문장이나 절에 나온 동사(구)의 반복을 피하기 위해 do/does/did를 사용한다.
  He writes better than I **do**.
- 강조의 do: 동사의 의미를 강조하기 위해 do/dose/did가 쓰인다. 이어서 나오는 동사의 형태는 동사원형이 되어야 한다. Mike **does** *work* hard.

TIP do가 일반동사로 쓰일 때는 '하다', '적절하다, 충분하다'의 의미 등으로 쓰인다.

STEP 1 다음 괄호 안에서 알맞은 말을 고르시오.

□ pay 지불하다

1 A: (Do, Does) cats like dogs? B: No, they (don't, doesn't).

2 A: I think you should pay him. B: I already (do, did).

3 A: Oh, no. Mike is singing that song again.
B: He (do, does) love that song. I've heard that song ten times today.

4 A: Who runs faster, you or your brother?
B: I run faster than my brother (do, does).

5 A: Why didn't you call me last night?
B: I (do, did) call you last night! But you didn't answer.

STEP 2 다음 밑줄 친 동사를 강조하여 문장을 다시 쓰시오.

□ understand 이해하다

1 We want to help you. → ______________________

2 He looks tired. → ______________________

3 I enjoyed the party last night. → ______________________

4 I knew the answer. → ______________________

5 I understand how you feel. → ______________________

STEP 3 다음 밑줄 친 부분의 쓰임이 보기 와 같은 것은? 내신

□ make money 돈을 벌다
□ truth 진실

보기	I make more money than he does.

① Does she like shopping?
② She does look great in that dress.
③ The box will do fine as a table.
④ He does not know the truth.
⑤ You play better than you did a year ago.

Answer p.18

[01~02] 다음 빈칸에 공통으로 들어갈 말로 알맞은 것을 고르시오.

Point 017

01

- _________ I borrow your camera, please?
- She _________ not sleep last night.

① Can[can] ② Must[must]
③ Would[would] ④ Might[might]
⑤ Could[could]

Point 021

02

- Yesterday, I _________ study all day for the mid-term.
- I _________ buy new clothes because I gained a lot of weight.

① can ② must ③ had to
④ had better ⑤ should

Point 025

03 다음 우리말과 일치하도록 할 때, 빈칸에 들어갈 말로 알맞은 것은?

그 당시는 사람들이 마을 우물에서 물을 기르곤 했다.
→ In those days, people _________ draw water from the village well.

① will ② would ③ must
④ may ⑤ might

Point 017

04 다음 보기 의 밑줄 친 부분과 의미상 바꿔 쓸 수 있는 것은?

보기 May I use your phone, please?

① Do ② Will ③ Must
④ Could ⑤ Should

Point 023

05 다음 우리말을 영어로 바르게 옮긴 것은?

너는 짠 음식을 먹지 않는 게 좋겠다.

① You'd not better to eat salty food.
② You had better not eat salty food.
③ You have better not eat salty food.
④ You had better not eating salty food.
⑤ You had better not to eat salty food.

[06~07] 다음 대화의 빈칸에 들어갈 말로 알맞은 것을 고르시오.

Point 020

06

A: Someone is at the door.
B: It _________ be Andy. He is still at work now.

① must not ② may not ③ do not
④ would not ⑤ doesn't have to

Point 025

07

A: _________ you like to have more dessert?
B: No, thanks. I'm full.

① May ② Can ③ Will
④ Could ⑤ Would

Point 021

08 다음 빈칸에 들어갈 말이 순서대로 짝지어진 것은?

- Don't make so much noise. We _________ wake the baby.
- There's an elevator in the building, so we _________ climb the stairs.

① must not – must
② have to – must not
③ should – must not
④ have to – don't have to
⑤ must not – don't have to

[09~10] 다음 밑줄 친 부분 중 쓰임이 나머지 넷과 다른 것을 고르시오.

Point 018

09 ① This map may be helpful.
② She may not like your answer.
③ He may remember your name.
④ May I use a calculator on the test?
⑤ He may be our new English teacher.

Point 025

10 ① My father would smoke a lot.
② Would you introduce yourself?
③ He would walk his dog every morning.
④ I would follow my older sister everywhere.
⑤ My father and I would go fishing when I was little.

고난도

Point 026

11 다음 중 어법상 틀린 것을 모두 고른 것은?

① I do believe him.
② He did come again.
③ She does like it a lot.
④ He do look happy today.
⑤ I did saw her in the hallways.

중요

Point 022

12 다음 중 어법상 옳은 것은?

① You must not telling a lie.
② She don't have to buy the book.
③ She may be not at school now.
④ She should take care of her brother.
⑤ I have to get home before my dad arrived.

서술형

[13~14] 다음 대화의 흐름에 맞도록 괄호 안의 말을 바르게 배열하시오.

Point 024

13
A: May I take your order?
B: Yes, ______________________________ a shrimp burger. (have, like, I, to, would)

Point 026

14
A: You failed the math test again. Did you study?
B: ______________________________. (did, I, hard, study) But the math test was too difficult.

Point 025

15 다음 두 문장이 같은 뜻이 되도록 할 때, 빈칸에 알맞은 말을 쓰시오.

The river was clean, but now it is dirty.
= The river __________ __________ __________ clean.

Point 020

16 다음은 지하철에서 지켜야 할 에티켓이다. must 또는 must not을 이용하여 빈칸에 알맞은 말을 쓰시오.

On the subway...
(1) You ______________ talk loudly.
(2) You ______________ eat or drink.
(3) You ______________ keep your pet in a carrier.

02회 내신 적중 실전 문제

[01~03] 다음 빈칸에 들어갈 말로 알맞은 것을 고르시오.

Point 018

01

You broke his new smart phone. He _________ be angry.

① may ② cannot
③ have to ④ doesn't have to
⑤ do

Point 020

02

The boys _________ be twins. They look the same.

① must ② cannot ③ do
④ have to ⑤ had better

Point 025

03

We _________ live in the country when we were young. But we live in the city now.

① must ② can ③ do
④ used to ⑤ had better

[04~05] 다음 밑줄 친 부분 중 쓰임이 나머지 넷과 다른 것을 고르시오.

Point 017

04
① Most birds can fly.
② I can swim without a tube.
③ Can you run faster than Jake?
④ Can I bring a friend to the party?
⑤ Can you remember the number?

중요 Point 025

05
① I do like my job.
② She does look tired.
③ Do you take credit cards?
④ I do believe she is right.
⑤ We did have a great time at the party.

Point 026

06 다음 대화의 빈칸에 들어갈 말로 알맞은 것은?

A: Did he apologize to her yesterday?
B: Yes, he _________ to her.

① do apologize ② does apologize
③ did apologize ④ didn't apologized
⑤ did apologized

Point 019

07 다음 빈칸에 공통으로 들어갈 말로 알맞은 것은?

• His dad _________ always read to him before bed when he was young.
• He said that he _________ pay back the money within a week.

① can ② must ③ may
④ will ⑤ would

Point 017

08 다음 빈칸에 들어갈 말로 알맞지 않은 것은?

_________ you help me with my report?

① Can ② Could ③ Will
④ Should ⑤ Would

Point 025

09 다음 보기 의 밑줄 친 부분과 의미상 바꿔 쓸 수 있는 것은?

보기	We <u>used to</u> play computer games for hours after school.

① might ② should ③ would
④ had to ⑤ had better

Point 025

10 다음 문장에서 알 수 있는 것을 <u>모두</u> 고른 것은?

They used to be friends.

① They are friends now.
② They were friends in the past.
③ They are not friends any more.
④ They were not friends in the past.
⑤ They have been friends for a long time.

고난도

Point 023

11 다음 우리말과 일치하도록 할 때, 빈칸에 들어갈 말이 순서대로 짝지어진 것은?

너는 지금 그에게 말을 걸지 않는 것이 좋겠다. 그는 너에게 화가 나있을지도 모른다.
➜ You ________ talk to him now. He ________ be angry with you.

① must not – can't
② should not – won't
③ would like to – has to
④ don't have to – must
⑤ had better not – may

Point 024

12 다음 중 어법상 <u>틀린</u> 것은?

① I would like to join the club.
② Would you like to some tea?
③ What would you like to drink?
④ I would like to get some help.
⑤ Would you like to play board games?

서술형

Point 020

13 다음 두 문장이 같은 뜻이 되도록 할 때, 빈칸에 알맞은 말을 쓰시오.

(1) I'm sure that he is a spy.
= He ________ be a spy.
(2) She could sing well.
= She ________ ________ ________ sing well.

[14~15] 다음 대화의 흐름에 맞도록 괄호 안의 말을 바르게 배열하시오.

Point 023

14

A: I'm allergic to nuts.
B: Oh, ________________________ any of this walnut pie. (you, better, had, not, eat)

Point 021

15

A: How's the weather outside?
B: It's warm. ________________________ a coat. (wear, have, you, to, don't)

Point 022

16 다음 대화의 흐름에 맞도록 should 또는 shouldn't와 보기 의 단어를 이용하여 빈칸에 알맞은 말을 쓰시오.

보기	do	eat	lose

A: Mom, I gained some weight these days. I think I (1) ________________ weight.
B: You (2) ________________ snacks at night. And you (3) ________________ some exercises.

Grammar Review 핵심 정리

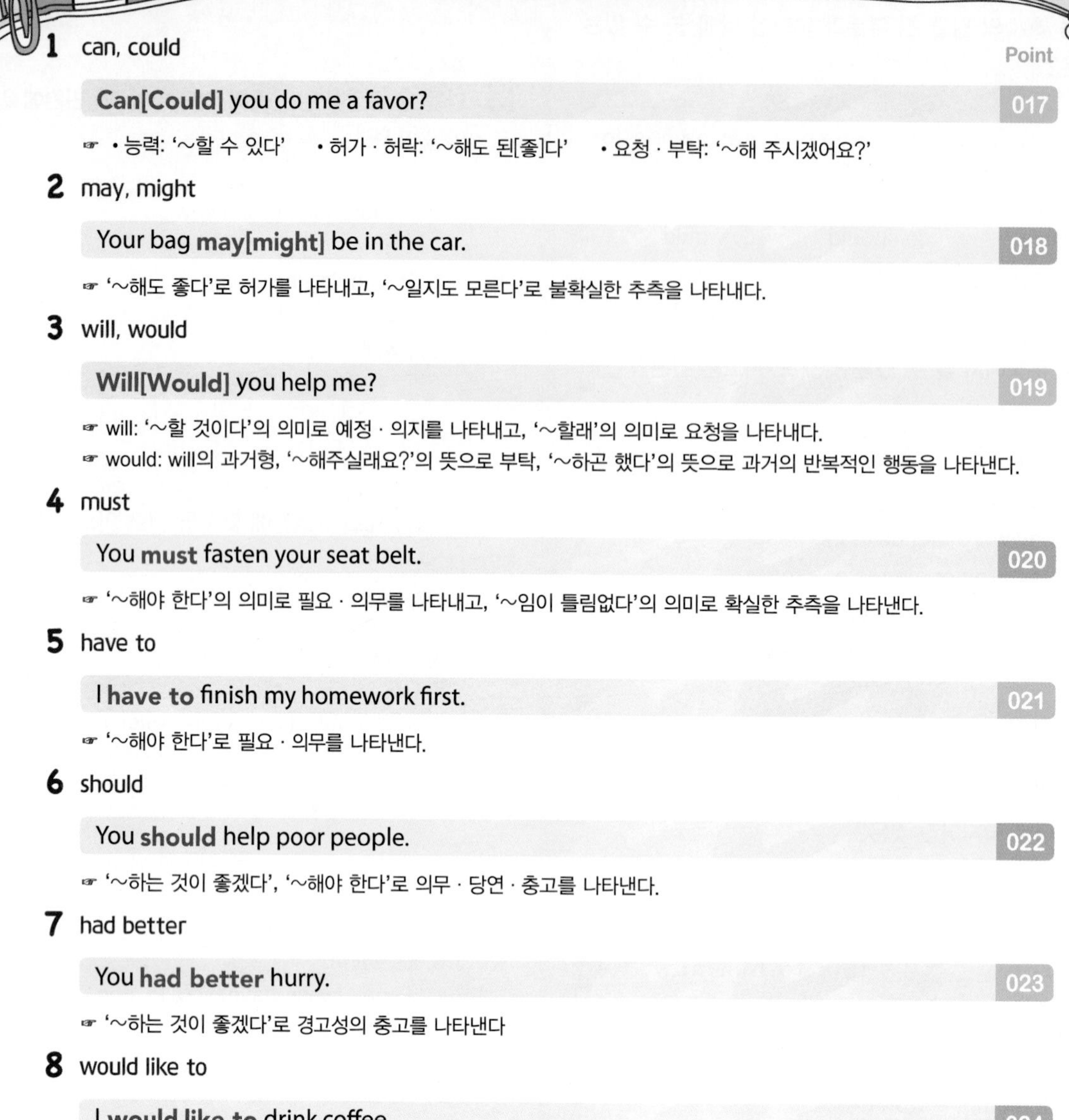

Point

1 can, could

Can[Could] you do me a favor? 017

☞ • 능력: '~할 수 있다' • 허가 · 허락: '~해도 된[좋]다' • 요청 · 부탁: '~해 주시겠어요?'

2 may, might

Your bag **may[might]** be in the car. 018

☞ '~해도 좋다'로 허가를 나타내고, '~일지도 모른다'로 불확실한 추측을 나타내다.

3 will, would

Will[Would] you help me? 019

☞ will: '~할 것이다'의 의미로 예정 · 의지를 나타내고, '~할래'의 의미로 요청을 나타내다.
☞ would: will의 과거형, '~해주실래요?'의 뜻으로 부탁, '~하곤 했다'의 뜻으로 과거의 반복적인 행동을 나타낸다.

4 must

You **must** fasten your seat belt. 020

☞ '~해야 한다'의 의미로 필요 · 의무를 나타내고, '~임이 틀림없다'의 의미로 확실한 추측을 나타낸다.

5 have to

I **have to** finish my homework first. 021

☞ '~해야 한다'로 필요 · 의무를 나타낸다.

6 should

You **should** help poor people. 022

☞ '~하는 것이 좋겠다', '~해야 한다'로 의무 · 당연 · 충고를 나타낸다.

7 had better

You **had better** hurry. 023

☞ '~하는 것이 좋겠다'로 경고성의 충고를 나타낸다

8 would like to

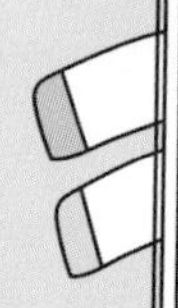

I **would like to** drink coffee. 024

☞ 「would like to+동사원형」: '하고 싶다' ☞ 「would like+명사」: '~을 원하다'

9 used to, would

I **used to** exercise every morning. 025

☞ 「used to+동사원형」: '(전에는) ~이었다'의 의미로 과거의 상태와 '~하곤 했다'의 의미로 과거의 습관을 나타낸다.
☞ 「would+동사원형」: '~하곤 했다'의 의미로 과거의 불규칙하게 반복되는 행동을 나타낸다.

10 do

I **do** *like* computer games. 026

☞ 부정문과 의문문을 만든다. • 대동사 do: 동사(구)의 반복을 피하기 위해 사용한다.
☞ 강조의 do: 동사를 강조하기 위해 do/does/did가 쓰인다.

LESSON

04

to부정사

Point 027 의사소통하는 것이란 당신의 생각을 다른 사람들에게 표현하는 것이다.

To communicate is to express your ideas to others.

- to부정사는 「**to + 동사원형**」의 형태로, 명사 역할을 하여 주어, 보어, 목적어로 쓰일 수 있다.
- to부정사가 주어로 쓰일 때 '~하는 것은[이]'로 해석한다. to부정사(구)는 문장의 맨 앞에 올 수도 있지만, 흔히 가주어 it을 주어 자리에 쓰고 진주어인 to부정사(구)를 문장 뒤로 옮긴다.
  To play computer games is fun. = **It** is fun **to play computer games**.
- to부정사가 보어로 쓰일 때 '~하는 것(이다)'로 해석하며, 이때 to부정사는 동사 뒤에서 주어를 보충 설명한다.
  His goal is **to get** into the World Cup finals.

STEP 1 다음 괄호 안에서 알맞은 말을 고르시오.

1 (Learn, To learn) our history is important.
2 Her mission is (get, to get) rid of the bomb.
3 (It, That) is wrong to cheat on exams.
4 She seemed (to have, have) many friends in town.
5 Mr. Smith appeared to (be, being) in his late thirties.

□ mission 임무
□ get rid of ~을 제거하다
□ bomb 폭탄
□ cheat (시험 등에서) 부정 행위를 하다

STEP 2 다음 우리말과 일치하도록 괄호 안의 말을 바르게 배열하시오.

1 다른 사람들을 탓하는 것은 쉬운 일이다. (blame, easy, it, to, is, other people)

____

2 내 꿈은 과학 교사가 되는 것이다. (be, to, is, my dream, a science teacher)

____

3 사용 설명서를 읽는 것은 중요하다. (read, it, to, important, is, the instructions)

____

4 그의 계획은 시골에 집을 짓는 것이다. (build, is, his plan, a house, to, in the country)

____

5 좋은 부모가 되는 것은 좋은 경청자가 되는 것이다.
(be, a good listener, a good parent, to, is, to, be)

____

□ blame ~을 탓하다
□ instructions 사용 설명서
□ build 짓다
□ country 시골

STEP 3 다음 밑줄 친 부분 중 쓰임이 나머지 넷과 다른 것은? 내신

① It is safe to walk on the sidewalk.
② To ride a bike in the rain is dangerous.
③ The dog's duty is to keep the owner's house.
④ Her voice sounded like music to me.
⑤ It's impossible to please everyone.

□ sidewalk 인도
□ duty 의무
□ owner 주인
□ please 기쁘게 하다

Answer p.22
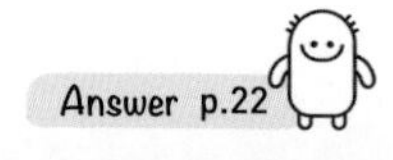

Point 028 나는 세계를 일주하고 싶다.

I hope to travel around the world.

- to부정사가 목적어로 쓰일 때 '~하기를', '~하는 것을'로 해석한다.
- to부정사를 목적어로 취하는 동사: need, want, wish, hope, choose, decide, plan, promise, learn, expect, agree, fail 등

  He decided **to join** the club.

  They planned **to open** their restaurant.

STEP 1 다음 문장을 밑줄 친 부분에 유의하여 우리말로 해석하시오.

1. Do you want to talk about your problems?
2. You need to explain this to us.
3. I didn't expect to see you here.
4. He hopes to get into medical school.
5. Tom failed to keep his promise.

- □ explain 설명하다
- □ expect 예상하다
- □ medical school 의과대학
- □ promise 약속

STEP 2 다음 우리말과 일치하도록 괄호 안의 말을 이용하여 빈칸에 알맞은 말을 쓰시오.

1. 나는 며칠간 더 머무르기를 바란다. (hope, stay)
   I ______________________ for a few more days.
2. 그들은 함께 새로운 사업을 시작하기로 결정했다. (decide, start)
   They ______________________ a new business together.
3. 당신은 나를 영원히 사랑할 것을 약속하나요? (promise, love)
   Do you ______________________ me forever?
4. 그녀는 런던으로 돌아가기로 계획했다. (plan, go back)
   She ______________________ to London.
5. 그가 그들의 제의를 받아들이기로 선택했나요? (choose, accept)
   Did he ______________________ their offer?

- □ decide 결정하다
- □ plan 계획하다
- □ accept 받아들이다
- □ offer 제의, 제안

STEP 3 다음 밑줄 친 부분의 쓰임이 보기와 같은 것은? 내신

보기 I learned to knit a sweater.

① To give advice is easy.
② His job is to train horses.
③ She wishes to study abroad.
④ It's necessary to have a passport.
⑤ His goal was to become a well-known writer.

- □ knit 뜨다[짜다]
- □ advice 충고
- □ necessary 필요한
- □ passport 여권

Answer p.22

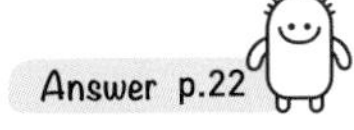

Point 029 너는 이 기계를 어떻게 사용하는지 아니?

Do you know how to use this machine?

- 「의문사 + to부정사」는 문장 안에서 명사적 용법으로 쓰이며, 주로 목적어 역할을 한다.

who(m) to부정사: 누가[누구를] ~할지	when to부정사: 언제 ~할지
where to부정사: 어디서 ~할지	what to부정사: 무엇을 ~할지
how to부정사: 어떻게 ~할지, ~하는 방법	why는 to부정사와 함께 쓸 수 없음

Please tell me **when to stop**. = Please tell me **when I should stop**.
He didn't explain **why to do** it. (×)

STEP 1 다음 문장을 밑줄 친 부분에 유의하여 우리말로 해석하시오.

1 I don't know what to wear tomorrow.
2 Do you know how to bake a cake?
3 They talked about where to live.
4 We have to decide whom to choose for our team.
5 Can you teach me when to use italics?

□ bake 굽다
□ italics 이탤릭체

STEP 2 다음 주어진 문장을 보기 와 같이 바꿔 쓰시오.

보기 Please tell me what I should do. → Please tell me what to do.

1 I'm not sure where I should start.
→ ______________________________

2 Did you carefully pick whom you should follow?
→ ______________________________

3 Please let me know when I should book the hotel.
→ ______________________________

4 I asked him how I should use the camera.
→ ______________________________

□ pick 선택하다
□ follow 따르다, 뒤쫓다
□ book 예약하다
□ use 사용하다

STEP 3 다음 빈칸에 들어갈 말이 순서대로 짝지어진 것은? 내신

- We're going on a trip tomorrow. But we haven't decided ________ to stay.
- I'm sorry. I don't know ________ to say.

① what – how
② where – what
③ what – why
④ where – why
⑤ what – when

Answer p.22

Point 030 잠자리에서 일어날 시간이야.

It's time to get out of bed.

- to부정사가 형용사 역할을 할 때 '~하는', '~할'로 해석하며, 이때 to부정사는 앞에 있는 명사(구)를 수식한다.
- to부정사의 수식을 받는 명사(구)가 전치사의 목적어일 경우, 반드시 to부정사 뒤에 전치사를 써야 한다.
  I need **a chair to sit on.** (← sit on a chair)

TIP 「-thing으로 끝나는 명사 + 형용사 + to부정사」
I want **something tasty to eat**.

STEP 1 다음 밑줄 친 부분을 바르게 고치시오.

1 What is the best way learning English?
2 I want to buy a new dress wear at the party.
3 He has no friends to hang out.
4 I can't find good anything to read.
5 You should bring some paper to write.

□ way 방법
□ hang out 어울려 다니다

STEP 2 다음 우리말과 일치하도록 괄호 안의 말을 바르게 배열하시오.

□ bring 가져오다

1 선생님은 우리에게 풀어야 할 문제 몇 개를 내 주셨다.
(some, gave, solve, us, to, problems)
The teacher ______________________________.

2 나는 비행기에서 읽을 책을 가져왔다. (read, a book, to, brought, on the plane)
I ______________________________.

3 그들에게는 쓸 돈이 전혀 없다. (have, to, any, spend, money)
They don't ______________________________.

4 차가운 마실 거리 좀 드시겠어요? (cold, to, like, anything, drink)
Would you ______________________________?

5 우리는 살 집이 필요하다. (need, to, in, a house, live)
We ______________________________.

STEP 3 다음 대화의 빈칸에 들어갈 말로 알맞은 것은? 내신

A: Can you give me ______________?
B: Sure. Here is a pen.

① something to write
② something write with
③ something for write on
④ something to write with
⑤ something to write on

Answer p.23

Point 031 우리는 좋은 자리를 차지하려고 그곳에 일찍 갔다.

부사적 용법 (목적)

We got there early to get a good seat.

- to부정사는 동사, 형용사, 부사를 수식하는 부사 역할을 할 수 있다. 이때 문맥에 따라 목적, 결과, 감정의 원인, 판단의 근거, 정도, 조건 등의 다양한 의미를 나타낸다.
- 목적을 나타내는 to부정사는 '~하기 위해'로 해석하며, 「**in order to + 동사원형**」, 「**so as to + 동사원형**」, 「**so that + 주어 + can/could + 동사원형**」으로 바꿔 쓸 수 있다.

  He went out **to get** some fresh air.

  = He went out **in order[so as] to get** some fresh air.

  = He went out **so that he could get** some fresh air.

STEP 1 다음 문장을 밑줄 친 부분에 유의하여 우리말로 해석하시오.

1 Mom bought some flour to bake cookies.

2 I planned to stay at home all day tomorrow.

3 She jumped rope every day to lose weight.

4 We gave him a chance to run away.

5 They went to the stadium to watch the baseball game.

□ flour 밀가루
□ jump rope 줄넘기를 하다
□ lose weight 살을 빼다
□ stadium 경기장

STEP 2 다음 빈칸에 들어갈 말을 보기에서 골라 알맞은 형태로 쓰시오.

보기	look	get	avoid	ask

1 우리는 교통 체증을 피하기 위해 일찍 출발했다.
We set off early ____________ the heavy traffic.

2 그녀는 숙제를 도와 달라고 부탁하기 위해 친구에게 전화했다.
She called her friend ____________ for help with her homework.

3 그는 용돈을 추가로 받기 위해 일요일마다 아빠의 차를 세차한다.
He washes his father's car every Sunday ____________ extra allowance.

4 나는 단어를 찾기 위해 그의 사전을 빌렸다.
I borrowed his dictionary ____________ up a word.

□ set off 출발하다
□ extra 추가의
□ allowance 용돈
□ dictionary 사전

STEP 3 다음 중 문장의 의미가 나머지 넷과 다른 것은? 내신

① I woke up early, so I caught the first train.
② I woke up early in order to catch the first train.
③ I woke up early so that I could catch the first train.
④ To catch the first train, I woke up early.
⑤ I woke up early so as to catch the first train.

□ catch 타다, 잡다

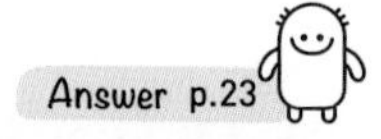

Point 032 그 소년은 커서 군인이 되었다.

The boy grew up **to be** a soldier.

- 결과를 나타내는 to부정사는 live, grow, wake 등과 같은 동사 뒤에 오며, '그래서 (결국) ~하다[되다]'로 해석한다.

TIP to부정사가 only와 함께 쓰이면 but의 의미를 포함하여 '하지만 (결국) ~하다[되다]'의 뜻이 된다.
He worked hard, **only to fail**. = He worked hard, **but** he **failed**.

STEP 1 자연스러운 문장이 되도록 다음을 연결하시오.

1 Diana got home •
2 He grew up •
3 My grandma lived •
4 I tried to save his eyesight, •
5 I hurried to the bank, •

• ⓐ to be 100 years old.
• ⓑ to find her cat dead.
• ⓒ only to find it closed.
• ⓓ to be a famous actor.
• ⓔ only to fail.

□ save (손상 · 손실 등에서) 구하다
□ eyesight 시력
□ hurry 서둘러 가다

STEP 2 다음 주어진 문장을 to부정사를 이용하여 바꿔 쓰시오.

1 He got home and found his wallet on the desk.
→ He got home ______________________.

2 I tried to forget her, but I failed.
→ I tried to forget her, ______________________.

3 He woke up and found himself late for the meeting.
→ He woke up ______________________.

4 She did her best to stay awake, but she fell asleep.
→ She did her best to stay awake, ______________________.

5 We ran to the station, but we missed the last train.
→ We ran to the station, ______________________.

□ wallet 지갑
□ forget 잊다
□ stay awake 자지 않고 깨어 있다
□ fall asleep 잠들다

STEP 3 다음 밑줄 친 부분 중 쓰임이 나머지 넷과 다른 것은? 내신

① She woke up to notice a light on.
② They promised to live together forever, only to get divorced.
③ I used sponges and soft cloths to clean the windows.
④ The curious boy grew up to invent a light bulb.
⑤ We tried to reach the summit, only to give up halfway.

□ get divorced 이혼하다
□ light bulb 전구
□ summit 정상
□ halfway 중간에

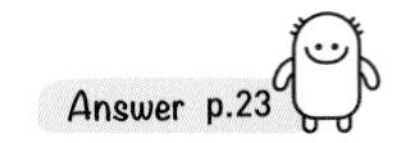
Answer p.23

Point 033 나는 그 소식을 듣고 놀랐다.

부사적 용법 (감정의 원인)

I was surprised to hear the news.

- 감정의 원인을 나타내는 to부정사는 glad, pleased, sorry, surprised, disappointed 등의 감정을 나타내는 형용사 뒤에 오며 '~해서', '~하니'로 해석한다.
  I'm **glad to see** you again.

STEP 1 다음 문장을 밑줄 친 부분에 유의하여 우리말로 해석하시오.

1 He was touched to read their story.
2 She was really pleased to meet her old friends.
3 He was upset to receive a red card.
4 I was happy to get many birthday gifts.
5 He was disappointed to miss the chance.

□ touched 감동한
□ receive 받다
□ disappointed 실망한

STEP 2 다음 우리말과 일치하도록 괄호 안의 말을 이용하여 빈칸에 알맞은 말을 쓰시오.

1 우리는 긴 여행을 마치게 되어서 기뻤다. (glad, finish our long journey)

____

2 그는 그 영화배우의 죽음에 대한 소식을 듣고 충격을 받았다.
(shocked, hear of the movie star's death)

____

3 그들은 경기에서 이겨서 흥분했다. (excited, win the game)

____

4 그녀는 그가 떠나는 것을 보고 슬퍼했다. (sad, see him go away)

____

5 나는 문이 잠겨 있는 것을 발견하고 화가 났다. (angry, find the door locked)

____

□ journey 여행
□ shocked 충격을 받은
□ locked (자물쇠 등으로) 잠긴

STEP 3 다음 밑줄 친 부분의 쓰임이 보기 와 같은 것은? 내신

보기 I am sorry to bother you at this hour.

① I came home to babysit my cousin.
② I was surprised to see the results.
③ She woke up to find herself famous overnight.
④ I went to the post office to buy some stamps.
⑤ All her children grew up to be teachers.

□ bother 귀찮게 하다
□ babysit (아이를) 봐주다
□ result 결과
□ overnight 밤사이에, 하룻밤 동안

Answer p.24
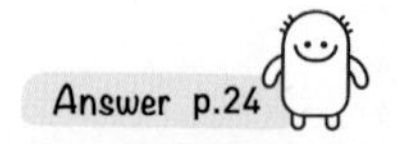

Point 034 나에게 도전하다니 너는 용감하구나.

You are brave to challenge me.

- 판단의 근거를 나타내는 to부정사는 '~하다니', '~하는 것을 보니'로 해석한다.
  He was foolish **to waste** so much money.
  She must be wise **to say** so.

STEP 1 자연스러운 문장이 되도록 다음을 연결하시오.

1 The boy is naughty •
2 John must be tired •
3 She must be kind •
4 She was very smart •
5 He must be a fool •

• ⓐ to go to bed so early.
• ⓑ to get into law school.
• ⓒ to make such a mess.
• ⓓ to believe such a lie.
• ⓔ to help the homeless.

□ naughty 말을 안 듣는, 버릇없는
□ law school 법대
□ make a mess 엉망을 만들다
□ the homeless 노숙자들

STEP 2 다음 우리말과 일치하도록 괄호 안의 말을 바르게 배열하시오.

1 모든 질문에 답하는 것을 보니 그는 똑똑한 것이 틀림없다.
(be, answer, must, clever, he, to, all the questions)

____

2 아무 말도 안 하는 것을 보니 그녀는 화난 것이 틀림없다.
(angry, not a word, she, to, be, say, must)

____

3 나에게 두 번째 기회를 주다니 그는 너그러웠다.
(me, was, give, to, generous, he, a second chance)

____

4 엄마가 가장 좋아하시는 컵을 깨뜨리다니 내 남동생은 부주의했다.
(my mom's, break, was, my brother, to, careless, favorite cup)

____

5 그 남자에게 자신의 비밀번호를 알려 주다니 그녀는 어리석었다.
(to, silly, her password, the man, was, she, tell)

____

□ clever 똑똑한
□ generous 너그러운
□ careless 부주의한
□ silly 어리석은

STEP 3 다음 두 문장이 같은 뜻이 되도록 할 때, 빈칸에 들어갈 말로 알맞은 것은? 내신

He sends her flowers every day. He must like her.
= He must like her ________ her flowers every day.

① send ② sent ③ to send
④ sending ⑤ to sending

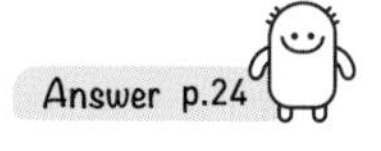

Point 035 그 문제는 풀기 쉽다.

The problem is easy to solve.

- 정도를 나타내는 to부정사는 easy, hard, difficult, safe, convenient 등의 형용사 뒤에 와서 형용사를 수식하며 '~하기에'로 해석한다.
  The theory is **difficult to understand**.
- 조건을 나타내는 to부정사는 주로 조동사 would, could 등과 함께 쓰이며 '만약 ~한다면'으로 해석한다.
  We **would** be very happy **to work** with you.
  = We **would** be very happy **if** we **worked** with you.

STEP 1 다음 문장을 밑줄 친 부분에 유의하여 우리말로 해석하시오.

1 The motorcycle is unsafe to ride.
2 His questions were difficult to answer.
3 This blender is convenient to use.
4 To see him play basketball, you would consider him a pro.
5 To hear her talk, you would take her for a liar.

□ motorcycle 오토바이
□ blender 믹서기
□ convenient 편리한
□ take A for B A를 B로 여기다

STEP 2 다음 두 문장이 같은 뜻이 되도록 할 때, 빈칸에 알맞은 말을 쓰시오.

1 It is safe to drink this water.
= This water is ________ ________ ________.

2 It is not easy to persuade her.
= She is not ________ ________ ________.

3 If you heard her play the piano, you would be amazed at her skills.
= ________ ________ ________ the piano, you would be amazed at her skills.

4 If you saw her dance, you would think she was a ballerina.
= ________ ________ ________ ________, you would think she was a ballerina.

□ persuade 설득하다
□ amazed 놀란

STEP 3 다음 우리말을 영어로 바르게 옮긴 것을 모두 고르면? 내신

그 창문은 열기가 쉽지 않았다.

① It was not easy to open the window.
② This was not easy to open the window.
③ That was not easy to open the window.
④ The window was not easy to open.
⑤ The window was not easy to open it.

Answer p.24

Point 036 나는 월요일 아침에 일어나는 것이 어렵다.

It is hard *for me* to get up on Monday morning.

- to부정사의 행위나 상태의 주체를 의미상의 주어라고 하고 「**for + 목적격**」으로 나타낸다.
  It is natural *for you* **to get** angry. (to get angry하는 사람은 you)
- 사람의 성격 · 태도를 나타내는 형용사(kind, nice, careful, careless, polite, rude, smart, wise, foolish, stupid, silly 등) 다음에 나오는 to부정사의 의미상의 주어는 「**of + 목적격**」으로 나타낸다.
  It was careless *of her* **to take** the wrong bus.

STEP 1 다음 괄호 안에서 알맞은 말을 고르시오.

1 It was foolish (of, for) me to trust him.
2 It is kind (of, for) you to take care of my dog.
3 It is necessary (of, for) him to stop smoking.
4 It was rude (of, for) him to talk back to his teacher.
5 It is impossible (of, for) her to reach the top of the mountain.

□ trust 믿다
□ take care of ~을 돌보다
□ rude 무례한
□ talk back to ~에게 말대답하다

STEP 2 다음 우리말과 일치하도록 괄호 안의 말을 바르게 배열하시오.

1 아이를 구하다니 그는 용감했다. (save, to, it, was, of, him, the child, brave)

____

2 우리가 그 프로젝트를 24시간 안에 끝내는 것은 어렵다.
(to, us, is, difficult, it, for, finish, the project)
______________________________ in 24 hours.

3 그들에게는 새로운 게임을 하는 것이 신나는 일이다.
(play, is, a new game, to, exciting, for, it, them)

____

4 노인에게 자리를 양보하다니 그녀는 매우 공손했다.
(to, give up, polite, was, it, very, of, her, her seat)
______________________________ to the old man.

5 아이들이 실외에서 노는 것은 중요하다. (to, children, play, is, for, it, important)
______________________________ outdoors.

□ brave 용감한
□ exciting 신나는
□ outdoors 실외에서

STEP 3 다음 빈칸에 들어갈 말이 순서대로 짝지어진 것은? 내신

- It is not easy ________ her to lose weight.
- It was stupid ________ him to press the emergency button.

① for – for ② for – of ③ of – for
④ for – by ⑤ by – of

□ emergency 비상 (사태)

Answer p.25

Point 037 너무 추워서 밖에 나갈 수가 없다. too ~ to부정사

It is too cold to go outside.

- 「**too + 형용사/부사 + to부정사**」는 '너무 ~하여 …할 수 없다'로 해석하며, 「**so + 형용사/부사 + that + 주어 + can't/couldn't + 동사원형**」으로 바꿔 쓸 수 있다.
  I am **too tired to go** shopping. = I am **so tired that I can't go** shopping.
  The box was **too heavy for me to carry**. = The box was **so heavy that I couldn't carry** it.

STEP 1 다음 문장을 밑줄 친 부분에 유의하여 우리말로 해석하시오.

1 The pie is so hot that I can't eat it.
2 He was too sick to leave the hospital.
3 She was too busy to take a break.
4 She has become so fat that she can't wear her jeans.
5 The ring was too expensive for me to buy.

□ leave the hospital 퇴원하다
□ take a break 휴식을 취하다
□ jeans 청바지

STEP 2 다음 두 문장이 같은 뜻이 되도록 할 때, 빈칸에 알맞은 말을 쓰시오.

1 I'm so sleepy that I can't drive.
= I'm too ________ ________ ________.

2 He was so scared that he couldn't move.
= He was ________ ________ to ________.

3 I woke up too late to catch the bus.
= I woke up so ________ ________ I ________ ________ the bus.

4 The test was too difficult for her to pass.
= The test was ________ ________ that ________ ________ ________ it.

□ scared 겁이 난
□ pass 통과하다

STEP 3 다음 중 보기와 의미가 같은 것은? 내신

보기 She is too slow to catch up with him.

① She is slow not to catch up with him.
② She is slow enough to catch up with him.
③ She is not slow enough to catch up with him.
④ She is so slow that she can catch up with him.
⑤ She is so slow that she can't catch up with him.

□ catch up with ~을 따라잡다

Answer p.25

Point 038 그녀는 모델이 될 수 있을 만큼 충분히 키가 크다.

She is tall enough to be a model.

- 「**형용사/부사 + enough + to부정사**」는 '~할 수 있을 만큼 충분히 …한[하게]'로 해석하며, 「**so + 형용사/부사 + that + 주어 + can/could + 동사원형**」으로 바꿔 쓸 수 있다.

  He is **fast enough to win** the race. = He is **so fast that he can win** the race.

  She was **rich enough to buy** a yacht. = She was **so rich that she could buy** a yacht.

STEP 1 자연스러운 문장이 되도록 다음을 연결하시오.

1 Your shirt is so small •
2 I'm tall enough •
3 He is too young •
4 The driving test was so easy •
5 The pizza was big enough •

• ⓐ to watch this program.
• ⓑ that I can't wear it.
• ⓒ for everyone to share.
• ⓓ that she was able to pass it.
• ⓔ to reach the top shelf.

□ share 나눠 먹다[갖다]
□ shelf 선반

STEP 2 다음 두 문장을 한 문장으로 바꿀 때 빈칸에 알맞은 말을 쓰시오. (단, too ~ to 또는 enough to를 이용할 것)

1 I'm very strong. I can lift the rock.
→ I'm ________ ________ ________ ________ the rock.

2 The girls were very shy. They couldn't perform well in the play.
→ The girls were ________ ________ ________ ________ well in the play.

3 It was very late. We couldn't change our plan.
→ It was ________ ________ for us ________ ________ our plan.

4 My suitcase is very large. It can hold all these clothes.
→ My suitcase is ________ ________ ________ ________ all these clothes.

5 The door is very narrow. The piano can't go in.
→ The door is ________ ________ for the piano ________ ________ in.

□ perform 연기하다, 공연하다
□ suitcase 여행 가방
□ hold 담다
□ narrow 좁은

STEP 3 다음 문장에서 enough가 들어가기에 알맞은 곳은? 내신

The water (①) is (②) clean (③) to (④) drink (⑤) without worry.

Answer p.26

Point 027

01 다음 밑줄 친 부분 중 쓰임이 나머지 넷과 다른 것은?

① I was sad to move to another city.
② Her goal is to be a top student in her class.
③ Do you want to learn about Korean culture?
④ He told a funny story to the children in the hospital.
⑤ My son is smart enough to speak three languages.

[02~03] 다음 밑줄 친 부분의 용법이 보기 와 같은 것을 고르시오.

Point 035

02

보기 The song was easy to sing along to.

① I need someone to assist me.
② Old habits are hard to break.
③ He decided to climb Mt. Everest.
④ I bought some toothbrushes to use.
⑤ Our plan is to hold a surprise party for her.

Point 027, 028

03

보기 I agreed to join the charity campaign.

① Can I have something to eat?
② She was surprised to hear that.
③ It is dangerous to climb a tall tree.
④ I was disappointed to lose the game.
⑤ Who was the first person to land on the moon?

[04~05] 다음 두 문장이 같은 뜻이 되도록 할 때, 빈칸에 들어갈 말로 알맞은 것을 고르시오.

Point 029

04

The old man told me where I should go.
= The old man told me where ________.

① go ② went ③ to go
④ going ⑤ to going

Point 032

05

He worked very hard but lost his job again.
= He worked very hard, ________ lose his job again.

① only to ② so only ③ to only
④ that only ⑤ only that

Point 037

06 다음 중 보기 와 의미가 같은 것은?

보기 She was too tired to do her homework.

① She was so tired that she can do her homework.
② She was so tired that she could do her homework.
③ She was not tired that she can't do her homework.
④ She was so tired that she couldn't do her homework.
⑤ She was not tired that she couldn't do her homework.

Point 033, 034

07 다음 밑줄 친 부분의 쓰임이 보기 와 다른 것은?

보기 I was satisfied to finish first in the race.

① We were excited to watch the parade.
② He must be smart to invent this machine.
③ She was surprised to see such a big dog.
④ The lady was pleased to get a free ticket.
⑤ The boy was scared to be alone in the dark.

Point 036

08 다음 빈칸에 들어갈 말이 순서대로 짝지어진 것은?

• It is impossible ________ him to do this project.
• It was stupid ________ you to do such a thing.

① with – for ② for – of ③ of – with
④ for – with ⑤ of – for

Answer p.26

Point 038

09 다음 우리말을 영어로 바르게 옮긴 것은?

그의 말은 경주에서 이길 수 있을 정도로 충분히 빠르다.

① His horse is too fast to win the race.
② His horse is to fast too win the race.
③ His horse is fast enough to win the race.
④ His horse is enough fast to win the race.
⑤ His horse is fast to enough win the race.

Point 034

10 다음 밑줄 친 부분의 쓰임이 보기 와 같은 것은?

보기 He must be rich to buy a sports car.

① She was glad to receive his letter.
② The twins were hard to take care of.
③ You are lucky to have a friend like him.
④ I returned home to find my sister crying.
⑤ He went to the store to buy some clothes.

고난도

Point 030

11 다음 중 어법상 틀린 것은?

① I really need a friend to talk.
② He gave me a form to fill out.
③ There is nobody to help you here.
④ We want someone to fix this problem.
⑤ Are you looking for a roommate to live with?

Point 031

12 다음 중 문장의 의미가 나머지 넷과 다른 것은?

① I worked out a lot to keep in shape.
② I worked out a lot so as to keep in shape.
③ I worked out a lot, so I could keep in shape.
④ I worked out a lot in order to keep in shape.
⑤ I worked out a lot so that I could keep in shape.

서술형

Point 028

13 다음 대화의 흐름에 맞도록 괄호 안의 말을 이용하여 빈칸에 알맞은 말을 쓰시오.

A: What is your dream?
B: ______________________
(want, reporter)

Point 029

14 다음 대화의 흐름에 맞도록 괄호 안의 말을 바르게 배열하시오.

A: Did you decide ______________________?
(to, the, have, party, where)
B: Yes, we will hold the party at Julie's house.

Point 038

15 다음 두 문장이 같은 뜻이 되도록 할 때, 빈칸에 알맞은 말을 쓰시오.

The phone is so small that it can fit into my pocket.
= The phone is ________ ________ ________ ________ into my pocket.

Point 030

16 민수는 캠핑을 가기 위해 짐을 챙기고 있다. 괄호 안의 말을 바르게 배열하여, 챙겨 가야 할 물건에 관해 말하는 문장을 완성하시오.

(1) I need ______________________.
(to, my eyes, sunglasses, protect)
(2) I need some ______________________.
(eat, the hike, during, snacks, to)
(3) I need ______________________.
(with, take, to, a camera, pictures)

Point 027, 035

01 다음 빈칸에 들어갈 말이 순서대로 짝지어진 것은?

- ________ is fun to learn new things.
- ________ him speak English, you would consider him a native speaker.

① It – Hear ② It – If hear
③ It – To hear ④ That – Hear
⑤ That – To hear

Point 031

02 다음 대화의 빈칸에 들어갈 말로 알맞은 것은?

A: Why did he go to Daegu?
B: He went there ________ his uncle.

① visit ② visited ③ visiting
④ to visit ⑤ to visiting

중요

Point 036

03 다음 빈칸에 들어갈 말이 나머지 넷과 <u>다른</u> 것은?

① It is difficult ________ me to write a letter.
② It was brave ________ him to save the child.
③ It is important ________ you to try your best.
④ It was impossible ________ her to climb the wall.
⑤ It is dangerous ________ you to swim in this river.

Point 037

04 다음 중 문장의 의미가 나머지 넷과 <u>다른</u> 것은?

① He is too young to drive a car.
② He is so young, but he can drive a car.
③ He is so young that he can't drive a car.
④ He is very young, so he can't drive a car.
⑤ He can't drive a car because he is very young.

Point 030

05 다음 우리말과 일치하도록 할 때, 빈칸에 들어갈 말로 알맞은 것은?

나에게는 같이 일할 파트너가 있다.
I have ________________.

① with a partner to work
② a partner with to work
③ to work a partner with
④ a partner to work with
⑤ with work a partner to

Point 032

06 다음 중 보기 와 의미가 같은 것은?

보기 He ran so fast after the bus, only to miss it.

① He ran so fast after the bus, but he missed it.
② He ran so fast after the bus that he didn't miss it.
③ He didn't run so fast after the bus, so he missed it.
④ He ran so fast after the bus that he couldn't miss it.
⑤ He didn't run so fast after the bus, but he didn't miss it.

Point 033

07 다음 빈칸에 들어갈 말로 알맞지 <u>않은</u> 것은?

I was ________ to hear the news.

① sad ② glad ③ possible
④ happy ⑤ sorry

Point 030

08 다음 밑줄 친 부분 중 용법이 나머지 넷과 <u>다른</u> 것은?

① He watches TV <u>to relax</u> after work.
② I came here <u>to get</u> a good education.
③ We need someone <u>to teach</u> us Chinese.
④ She went to the market <u>to buy</u> some fruits.
⑤ They left for the island <u>to find</u> the treasure.

Answer p.28

Point 027

09 다음 밑줄 친 부분의 용법이 보기 와 같은 것은?

보기 It is not easy to get up early.

① He grew up to be a professor.
② I was pleased to see them again.
③ I need something to eat on the train.
④ To win first prize, I would be happy.
⑤ To follow his advice seemed impossible.

고난도 Point 034

10 다음 중 어법상 옳은 것은?

① This water is safe to drink it.
② I have important something to do.
③ She doesn't have any friends to play.
④ She needed somebody for repair her car.
⑤ He cannot be a fool to solve the problem.

Point 028

11 다음 중 어법상 틀린 것은?

① Ted wanted to eat Italian food.
② He chose to run for the election.
③ Dad promised to buy me the bike.
④ She planned traveling with her aunt.
⑤ He decided to go back to his country.

Point 029, 036

12 다음 중 어법상 틀린 것을 모두 고르면?

① It is kind of you to help the child.
② The teacher taught me why to live.
③ Tell me when to turn off the oven.
④ They bought a leather sofa to sit on.
⑤ It was difficult for he to understand it.

서술형

Point 030

13 다음 글의 흐름에 맞도록 괄호 안의 말을 바르게 배열하시오.

I'm thirsty. Can you ______________________?
(drink, give, to, something, me)

[14~15] 다음 주어진 문장을 too ~ to 또는 enough to를 이용한 문장으로 바꿔 쓰시오.

Point 038

14 The dog is so smart that it can understand its master's orders.

→ The dog is ______________________.

Point 037

15 We were so late that we couldn't get good seats.

→ We were ______________________.

Point 034

16 다음 두 문장을 to부정사를 이용하여 한 문장으로 바꿔 쓰시오.

He complained to his boss. He was so stupid.

→ He was so stupid ______________________.

Grammar Review 핵심 정리

1 to부정사의 명사적 용법

Point

To communicate is **to express** your ideas to others. 027

☞ to부정사는 「to+동사원형」의 형태로, 명사 역할을 할 때 '~하는 것'으로 해석하며 주어, 보어, 목적어로 쓰일 수 있다.

I hope **to travel** around the world. 028

☞ to부정사를 목적어로 취하는 동사: need, want, wish, hope, choose, decide, plan, promise, expect, agree 등

Do you know **how to use** this machine? 029

☞ who(m) to부정사: 누가[누구를] ~할지 / when to부정사: 언제 ~할지 / where to부정사: 어디서 ~할지
what to부정사: 무엇을 ~할지 / how to부정사: 어떻게 ~할지, ~하는 방법 / why to부정사 (×)

2 to부정사의 형용사적 용법

It's time **to get** out of bed. 030

☞ to부정사가 형용사 역할을 할 때 '~하는', '~할'로 해석하며, to부정사의 수식을 받는 명사(구)가 전치사의 목적어일 때 반드시 to부정사 뒤에 전치사를 써야 한다.

3 to부정사의 부사적 용법

We got there early **to get** a good seat. 031

☞ to부정사가 부사 역할을 할 때 목적, 결과, 감정의 원인, 판단의 근거, 정도, 조건 등의 다양한 의미로 해석한다.
☞ 목적을 나타내는 to부정사는 '~하기 위해'로 해석한다.

The boy grew up **to be** a soldier. 032

☞ 결과를 나타내는 to부정사는 '그래서 (결국) ~하다[되다]'로 해석한다.

I was surprised **to hear** the news. 033

☞ 감정의 원인을 나타내는 to부정사는 감정을 나타내는 형용사 뒤에 오며 '~해서', '~하니'로 해석한다.

You are brave **to challenge** me. 034

☞ 판단의 근거를 나타내는 to부정사는 '~하다니', '~하는 것을 보니'로 해석한다.

The problem is easy **to solve**. 035

☞ 정도를 나타내는 to부정사는 easy, hard, difficult 등의 형용사 뒤에서 형용사를 수식하며 '~하기에'로 해석한다.
☞ 조건을 나타내는 to부정사는 주로 조동사 would, could 등과 함께 쓰이며 '만약 ~한다면'으로 해석한다.

4 to부정사의 의미상의 주어

It is hard *for me* **to get** up on Monday morning. 036

☞ to부정사의 의미상의 주어는 보통 「for+목적격」으로 나타낸다.
☞ 사람의 성격 · 태도를 나타내는 형용사 다음에 나오는 to부정사의 의미상의 주어는 「of+목적격」으로 나타낸다.

5 too ~ to부정사 / enough + to부정사

It is **too cold to go** outside. 037

☞ 「too+형용사/부사+to부정사」는 '너무 ~하여 …할 수 없다'로 해석한다.

She is **tall enough to be** a model. 038

☞ 「형용사/부사+enough+to부정사」는 '~할 수 있을 만큼 충분히 …한[하게]'로 해석한다.

LESSON

05

동명사

Point 039 주는 것이 받는 것이다.

Giving is receiving.

- 동명사는 「**동사원형 + -ing**」의 형태로 문장에서 명사처럼 쓰여 주어, 목적어, 보어 역할을 한다.
- 주어 역할: '~하는 것은[이]'으로 해석한다. 동명사가 주어로 쓰일 경우, 동사는 단수 취급한다.
  Exercising regularly **is** important for your health.
  동명사 주어 단수 동사
- 보어 역할: '~하는 것(이다), ~하기(이다)'로 해석한다.
  Her plan is **planting** roses in the garden.

STEP 1 다음 괄호 안에서 알맞은 말을 고르시오.

1 (Get, Getting) a good job is not easy.
2 Using computers (save, saves) your time.
3 One of his duties is (attends, attending) meetings.
4 Crossing the ocean in a few days (is, are) impossible.
5 My uncle's habit is (to singing, singing) in the shower.

□ save 절약하다
□ duty 의무
□ attend 참석하다
□ cross 건너다

STEP 2 다음 우리말과 일치하도록 괄호 안의 말을 바르게 배열하시오.

1 호랑이를 사냥하는 것은 위험하다. (is, tigers, hunting, dangerous)

____

2 그녀의 취미는 오래된 우표를 모으는 것이다. (old stamps, is, her hobby, collecting)

____

3 그의 직업은 학교 버스를 운전하는 것이다. (driving, is, his job, a school bus)

____

4 외국어를 배우는 것은 많은 시간을 필요로 한다.
(a lot of time, a foreign language, learning, requires)

____

□ collect 수집하다
□ foreign language 외국어
□ require 필요로 하다

STEP 3 다음 우리말을 영어로 바르게 옮긴 것은? 내신

다른 사람들 앞에서 말하는 것은 나를 긴장시킨다.

① Speak in front of others make me nervous.
② Speak in front of others makes me nervous.
③ To Speak in front of others make me nervous.
④ Speaking in front of others make me nervous.
⑤ Speaking in front of others makes me nervous.

□ in front of ~앞에
□ nervous 긴장한

Point 040 그들은 축구하는 것을 즐긴다.

They *enjoy* playing soccer.

- 목적어 역할: 동명사가 문장에서 동사의 목적어로 쓰이는 경우, '~하는 것을, ~하기를'로 해석한다.
  He *avoided* **answering** my question.

STEP 1 다음 문장을 밑줄 친 부분에 유의하여 우리말로 해석하시오.

1 Susan likes reading fantasy novels.
2 Can you imagine living without water?
3 Living in a big city is convenient.
4 John admitted cheating on the test.
5 My favorite activity is listening to music.

□ novel 소설
□ without ~없이
□ admit 인정하다
□ cheat (시험 등에서) 부정행위를 하다

STEP 2 다음 빈칸에 들어갈 말을 보기 에서 골라 알맞은 형태로 쓰시오.

보기 tell paint buy clean write

1 당신은 욕실 청소하는 것을 싫어하나요?
Do you hate __________ the bathroom?

2 나는 사람들에게 내 나이를 말하는 것을 개의치 않는다.
I don't mind __________ people my age.

3 내 여동생은 알파벳 쓰는 것을 연습하고 있다.
My little sister is practicing __________ the alphabet.

4 아빠는 아직 울타리를 페인트칠하는 것을 끝내지 못했다.
Dad hasn't finished __________ the fence yet.

5 그는 새 차를 한 대 사는 것을 생각 중이다.
He is considering __________ a new car.

□ mind 언짢아하다, 상관하다
□ practice 연습하다
□ paint 페인트칠하다
□ fence 울타리

STEP 3 다음 중 어법상 틀린 것은? 내신

① Taking a bath is relaxing.
② The baby began cry loudly.
③ Walking helps you feel better.
④ They continued shouting slogans.
⑤ His job is answering calls from customers.

□ take a bath 목욕을 하다
□ loudly 크게
□ customer 고객

Answer p.30

Point 041 그는 춤추는 것을 잘한다.

He is good *at* dancing.

- 목적어 역할: 동명사가 문장에서 전치사의 목적어로 쓰이는 경우, '~하는 것'으로 해석한다.
  We were excited *about* **making** our own film.

  TIP 동명사의 부정은 동명사 바로 앞에 not을 쓴다.
  I felt sorry ***for*** **not being** on time.

STEP 1 다음 문장에서 밑줄 친 부분의 역할을 보기 에서 골라 쓰시오.

보기 주어 보어 동사의 목적어 전치사의 목적어

1 Peter gave up memorizing the poem. (　　　　　)
2 Making wooden toys is my favorite pastime. (　　　　　)
3 I'm tired of waiting for the bus. (　　　　　)
4 The important thing is eating a balanced diet. (　　　　　)
5 They are talking about buying a new house. (　　　　　)

□ memorize 암기하다
□ pastime 취미
□ be tired of ~에 지치다
□ diet 식사

STEP 2 다음 우리말과 일치하도록 괄호 안의 말을 바르게 배열하시오.

1 Jenny는 작은 섬에 사는 것을 꿈꾼다. (of, living, dreams)
Jenny ______________________ on a small island.

2 Scot은 늦은 것에 대해 사과했다. (for, late, apologized, being)
Scot ______________________.

3 날 잊지 않아줘서 고마워. (not, for, me, forgetting)
Thank you ______________________.

4 Andrew는 친구를 사귀는 것에 대해 절대 걱정하지 않는다.
(friends, worries, making, about)
Andrew never ______________________.

5 그는 한국 문화에 대해 배우는 데 관심이 있다. (in, interested, learning, is)
He ______________________ about Korean culture.

□ island 섬
□ apologize 사과하다
□ forget 잊다
□ worry 걱정하다

STEP 3 다음 빈칸에 들어갈 말로 알맞은 것은? 내신

He left without ________ goodbye.

① say ② says ③ saying ④ said ⑤ to say

□ leave 떠나다(-left-left)

Answer p.30

Point 042 대기실에서 누군가가 당신을 기다리고 있다.

Someone is **waiting** for you in the **waiting** room.

- 동명사와 현재분사는 둘 다 「**동사원형 + -ing**」의 형태이지만 동명사는 명사의 역할을, 현재분사는 형용사의 역할을 한다.

동명사	현재분사
(1) 쓰임: 문장에서 주어, 목적어, 보어의 명사 역할 의미: ~하는 것 My plan is **driving** along the beach.	(1) 쓰임: be동사와 함께 쓰여 진행의 의미를 나타냄. 의미: ~하는 중인 He **is driving** a truck.
(2) 쓰임: 뒤에 오는 명사의 목적이나 용도를 나타냄. 의미: ~를 위한, ~로 사용되는 a **sleeping** bag 침낭 (= a bag for sleeping)	(2) 쓰임: 뒤에 오는 명사를 수식하며, 명사의 동작이나 상태를 나타내는 형용사 역할 의미: ~을 하고 있는 a **sleeping** baby 자고 있는 아기 (= a baby who is sleeping)

STEP 1 다음 밑줄 친 부분이 동명사인지 현재분사인지 구별하여 쓰시오.

1 His habit is biting his nails. (　　　　　　)
2 She is blowing a balloon. (　　　　　　)
3 They called him a "walking dictionary." (　　　　　　)
4 She bought a new washing machine. (　　　　　　)
5 The best part of my job is making people laugh. (　　　　　　)

□ bite 깨물다
□ nail 손톱
□ blow 불다
□ washing machine 세탁기

STEP 2 다음 문장을 밑줄 친 부분에 유의하여 우리말로 해석하시오.

1 (a) Look at the dancing girls.
(b) The girls were wearing dancing shoes.

2 (a) His favorite pastime is taking pictures.
(b) The man is taking pictures.

3 (a) The boy is wearing a swimming suit.
(b) The swimming boy is my brother.

4 (a) Jason is fixing his bicycle.
(b) My grandpa likes fixing things.

□ take a picture 사진을 찍다
□ swimming suit 수영복

STEP 3 다음 밑줄 친 부분 중 쓰임이 나머지 넷과 다른 것은? 내신

① a smoking room
② a walking stick
③ a shopping mall
④ a burning house
⑤ a swimming pool

□ walking stick 지팡이

Point 043 그녀는 낯선 사람에게 말하는 것을 피했다.

She *avoided* talking to strangers.

• 동사의 종류에 따라 동명사만을 목적어로 취하는 동사와 to부정사만을 목적어로 취하는 동사가 있다.

동명사	to부정사
enjoy, finish, mind, give up, stop, quit, avoid, practice, consider, suggest 등	want, hope, plan, wish, promise, decide, agree, refuse 등

TIP 동명사에는 과거의 의미가 담겨 있어서 '이전에 한 일을 ~하다' 또는 '이미 하고 있는 일을 ~하다'라는 뜻의 동사와 주로 함께 쓴다. 반면 to부정사는 미래지향적인 의미를 가져서 소망, 계획, 의도 등을 나타내는 동사와 주로 함께 쓴다.

STEP 1 다음 괄호 안에서 알맞은 말을 고르시오.

1 I don't want (to move, moving) to another city.
2 Peter quit (to complain, complaining) about his job.
3 Do you practice (to play, playing) the violin every day?
4 John decided (to study, studying) economics in London.
5 Would you mind (to watch, watching) my bag for a moment?

□ move 이사하다
□ economics 경제학
□ watch (잠깐 동안) 봐 주다

STEP 2 다음 우리말과 일치하도록 괄호 안의 단어를 빈칸에 알맞은 형태로 쓰시오.

1 그는 공상 과학소설을 읽는 것을 즐긴다. (read)
He enjoys ____________ science fiction.

2 우리는 마을의 어린이들을 위해 학교를 지을 계획이다. (build)
We plan ____________ a school for the village children.

3 옳은 일을 하는 것을 절대 포기하지 마라. (do)
Never give up ____________ the right thing.

4 나는 방금 짐을 다 쌌다. (pack)
I've just finished ____________ my suitcase.

5 나는 좋은 성적을 받을 거라고 예상하지 못했다. (get)
I didn't expect ____________ a good grade.

□ fiction 소설
□ pack (짐을) 싸다
□ expect 예상하다
□ grade 성적

STEP 3 다음 빈칸에 들어갈 말이 순서대로 짝지어진 것은? 내신

• She hoped __________ the gold medal.
• They are considering __________ to Hawaii for a week.

① win – go
② to win – going
③ to win – to go
④ winning – going
⑤ winning – to go

□ gold medal 금메달
□ consider 고려하다, 숙고하다

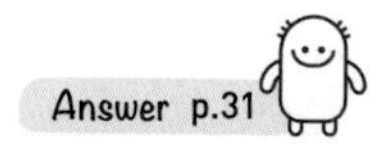

Point 044 너는 자전거 타는 것을 좋아하니?

Do you *like* riding[to ride] a bike?

- 다음 동사들은 동명사와 to부정사를 모두 목적어로 취할 수 있으며 그 뜻의 차이가 거의 없다.

like love hate start begin continue 등

They *began* **to clean** the house.
= They *began* **cleaning** the house.

STEP 1 다음 괄호 안에서 알맞은 말을 모두 고르시오.

1 The water in the pot started (to boil, boiling).
2 Thomas is considering (to get, getting) a new job.
3 The boy hates (to eat, eating) carrots.
4 Dad promised (to take, taking) us to the beach.
5 She doesn't like (to watch, watching) horror movies.

□ pot 냄비
□ boil 끓다
□ horror movie 공포영화

STEP 2 다음 두 문장이 같은 뜻이 되도록 할 때, 빈칸에 알맞은 말을 쓰시오.

1 He likes to sing when he is alone at home.
= He likes ____________ when he is alone at home.

2 Mr. Porter began teaching English two years ago.
= Mr. Porter began ____________ English two years ago.

3 People love talking about themselves.
= People love ____________ about themselves.

4 She continued to swim with all her strength.
= She continued ____________ with all her strength.

5 The president started to give a speech.
= The president started ____________ a speech.

□ alone 혼자, 다른 사람 없이
□ strength 힘
□ president 대통령
□ give a speech 연설하다

STEP 3 다음 빈칸에 공통으로 들어갈 말로 알맞은 것은? 내신

- Cindy __________ to spend money on clothes.
- Eddie __________ playing basketball on weekends.

① plans ② likes ③ wants ④ hopes ⑤ enjoys

□ spend money on ~ 에 돈을 쓰다
□ on weekends 주말에

Answer p.31

Point 045 나는 내 열쇠를 책상 위에 놓아둔 것을 기억한다.

I *remember* leaving my keys on the desk.

- 다음 동사들은 동명사와 to부정사를 모두 목적어로 취하지만 의미가 달라진다.

remember + v-ing: (과거에) ~했던 것을 기억하다 remember + to-v: (앞으로) ~할 것을 기억하다	forget + v-ing: (과거에) ~했던 것을 잊다 forget + to-v: (앞으로) ~할 것을 잊다
try + v-ing: 시험 삼아 ~해보다 try + to-v: ~하려고 노력하다	regret + v-ing: (과거에) ~했던 것을 후회하다 regret + to-v: (앞으로) ~하게 되어 유감이다

TIP **stop + v-ing**: ~하던 것을 멈추다
stop + to-v: ~하기 위해 멈추다(이때 to부정사는 stop의 목적어가 아니라 목적을 나타내는 to부정사의 부사적 용법으로 쓰임)

STEP 1 다음 문장을 밑줄 친 부분에 유의하여 우리말로 해석하시오.

1 Did you forget to call your grandma?
2 I remember visiting the museum when I was a kid.
3 She regrets leaving school when she was sixteen.
4 I stopped to have a rest because I was so sleepy.
5 He tried to get a job, but he couldn't.

STEP 2 다음 우리말과 일치하도록 괄호 안의 단어를 빈칸에 알맞은 형태로 쓰시오.

1 집에 올 때 빵을 사오는 것을 기억하세요. (buy)
Please remember ____________ bread when you come home.

2 나는 Grand Canyon 위로 비행했던 것을 절대 잊을 수 없을 것이다. (fly)
I'll never forget ____________ over the Grand Canyon.

3 나는 잠이 오지 않아서 시험 삼아 따뜻한 우유를 조금 마셔 보았다. (drink)
I couldn't sleep, so I tried ____________ some hot milk.

4 우리 할머니는 85세 때 운전하는 것을 그만두셨다. (drive)
My grandmother stopped ____________ when she was 85.

STEP 3 다음 빈칸에 들어갈 말이 순서대로 짝지어진 것은? 내신

- Max regrets __________ to the meeting. It was a waste of time.
- Don't forget __________ your swimsuits! There's a lovely pool at the hotel.

① go – pack ② going – packing ③ to go – to pack
④ going – to pack ⑤ to go – packing

□ waste 낭비
□ lovely 훌륭한, 멋진
□ pool 수영장

Answer p.32

Point 046 그는 숙제를 하느라 바쁘다.

He is busy doing his homework.

- go v-ing	~하러 가다	- It is no use v-ing	~해도 소용없다
- be busy v-ing	~하느라 바쁘다	- look forward to v-ing	~하기를 기대하다
- feel like v-ing	~하고 싶다	- be worth v-ing	~할 만한 가치가 있다
- keep (on) v-ing	계속해서 ~하다	- have trouble v-ing	~하는 데 어려움을 겪다
- on v-ing (= as soon as+주어+동사)	~하자마자	- cannot help v-ing (= cannot (help) but+동사원형)	~하지 않을 수 없다

STEP 1 다음 문장을 밑줄 친 부분에 유의하여 우리말로 해석하시오.

1 On seeing me, he ran away.

2 It is no use crying over spilt milk.

3 We look forward to seeing you soon.

4 I can't help falling in love with you.

5 He had trouble making friends.

□ run away 도망가다
□ spill 엎지르다(-spilt-spilt)
□ fall in love with ~와 사랑에 빠지다

STEP 2 다음 우리말과 일치하도록 괄호 안의 말을 이용하여 빈칸에 알맞은 말을 쓰시오.

1 나는 계속해서 뛸 기력이 없다. (keep, run)
I have no energy to ____________ ____________ ____________.

2 나는 빗속에서 걷고 싶다. (feel, walk)
I ____________ ____________ ____________ in the rain.

3 그녀는 전화를 받느라고 바빴다. (busy, answer)
She ____________ ____________ ____________ the phones.

4 그것은 시도해볼 만한 가치가 있다. (worth, try)
It ____________ ____________ ____________.

5 Kevin은 아빠와 낚시하러 가는 것을 좋아한다. (go)
Kevin loves to ____________ ____________ with his father.

□ try 시도하다

STEP 3 다음 빈칸에 들어갈 말로 알맞은 것은? 내신

I'm hungry. I feel like ________ a snack.

① had ② have ③ having
④ to have ⑤ to having

□ snack 간식

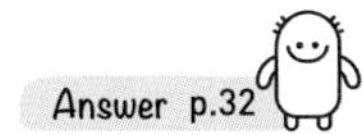
Answer p.32

01회 내신 적중 실전 문제

[01~02] 다음 빈칸에 들어갈 말로 알맞은 것을 고르시오.

Point 039

01

_________ friendship is not an easy thing.

① Keep ② Kept ③ Keeps
④ Keeping ⑤ Being kept

Point 040

02

I'll finish _________ the essay by the end of the month.

① write ② wrote ③ writing
④ to write ⑤ being written

중요

Point 041

03 다음 문장에서 not이 들어가기에 알맞은 곳은?

Larry (①) started (②) to (③) regret (④) going (⑤) to university.

Point 043

04 다음 빈칸에 들어갈 말로 알맞지 않은 것은?

Cathy _________ watching a horror movie.

① wants ② enjoys ③ loves
④ likes ⑤ hates

Point 039

05 다음 밑줄 친 부분 중 어법상 틀린 것은?

Respect(①) each other(②) is(③) the key to(④) every successful relationship(⑤).

Point 045

06 다음 두 문장이 같은 뜻이 되도록 할 때, 빈칸에 들어갈 말로 알맞은 것은?

I'm sure I locked the door.
= I remember _________ the door.

① lock ② to lock ③ locking
④ locked ⑤ to locking

[07~08] 다음 빈칸에 들어갈 말이 순서대로 짝지어진 것을 고르시오.

Point 043

07

- He avoids _________ new people.
- The couple agreed _________ as soon as possible.

① meet – to marry ② to meet – to marry
③ meeting – marrying ④ to meet – marrying
⑤ meeting – to marry

Point 043, 046

08

- This book is worth _________ twice.
- Do you mind _________ me your name?

① to read – tell ② to read – telling
③ to read – to tell ④ reading – telling
⑤ reading – to tell

Answer p.32

Point 045

09 다음 괄호 안의 단어를 알맞은 형태로 고친 것은?

Stop (talk) and be quiet. You're in the library.

① talks ② talking ③ talked
④ to talk ⑤ to talking

Point 042

10 다음 밑줄 친 부분 중 쓰임이 나머지 넷과 다른 것은?

① The baby likes playing with a ball.
② Can you see the falling snowflakes?
③ Being a movie director is my dream.
④ We finally arrived at the wedding hall.
⑤ His favorite free-time activity is playing tennis.

Point 046

11 다음 우리말을 영어로 바르게 옮긴 것은?

나는 뭔가 단 것이 먹고 싶다.

① I feel like eat something sweet.
② I feel like to eat something sweet.
③ I feel like eating something sweet.
④ I feel like to eating something sweet.
⑤ I feel like for eating something sweet.

고난도

Point 043

12 다음 중 어법상 틀린 것은?

① She loves to play with her pet.
② Did you practice playing the flute?
③ We're considering to travel to Egypt.
④ I will stop buying unnecessary things.
⑤ The kids kept on making a snowman.

서술형

[13~14] 다음 괄호 안의 단어를 빈칸에 알맞은 형태로 쓰시오.

Point 043

13

Don't give up ____________ your true love. (find)

Point 045

14

It is a very busy restaurant. Don't forget ____________ a table. (book)

Point 044

15 다음 두 문장이 같은 뜻이 되도록 할 때, 빈칸에 알맞은 말을 쓰시오

I hate to work late at night.
= I hate ____________ late at night.

고난도

Point 043, 045

16 다음 우리말과 일치하도록 (A)와 (B)에서 알맞은 단어를 각각 하나씩 골라 문장을 완성하시오. (단, 필요하면 형태를 바꿀 것)

(A)	(B)
finish	do
try	keep
decide	paint

(1) 너는 최선을 다하려고 노력해야 된다.
You should ______________ your best.

(2) Lisa는 일기를 쓰기로 결심했다.
Lisa ______________ a journal.

(3) Robin은 그의 집을 페인트칠하는 것을 끝냈다.
Robin ______________ his house.

02회 내신 적중 실전 문제

[01~02] 다음 빈칸에 들어갈 말로 알맞은 것을 고르시오.

Point 041

01

Are you interested in _________ plants?

① grow ② grew ③ grown
④ growing ⑤ to grow

Point 045

02

Remember _________ your grandmother tomorrow. It's her birthday.

① call ② called ③ calling
④ to call ⑤ to calling

[03~04] 다음 빈칸에 들어갈 말로 알맞은 것을 모두 고르시오.

Point 044

03

He began _________ his homework after dinner.

① do ② doing ③ to do
④ have done ⑤ to doing

Point 043

04

My brother _________ making model airplanes.

① wanted ② enjoyed ③ hoped
④ planned ⑤ gave up

Point 041

05 다음 대화의 빈칸에 들어갈 말로 알맞은 것은?

A: How about _________ an action movie?
B: That sounds great! I love action movies.

① watch ② to watch ③ watching
④ watched ⑤ to watching

Point 045

06 다음 두 문장이 같은 뜻이 되도록 할 때, 빈칸에 들어갈 말로 알맞은 것은?

I am sorry that I spent so much money last month.
= I regret _________ so much money last month.

① spent ② to spend ③ spending
④ spend ⑤ to spending

[07~08] 다음 우리말을 영어로 바르게 옮긴 것을 고르시오.

Point 046

07

나는 당신과 함께 일하는 것이 기대됩니다.

① I'm looking forward work with you.
② I'm looking forward to work with you.
③ I'm looking forward working with you.
④ I'm looking forward to worked with you.
⑤ I'm looking forward to working with you.

중요

Point 039

08

채소를 먹는 것은 건강에 좋다.

① Eat vegetables are good for your health.
② Eating vegetables is good for your health.
③ Eating vegetables are good for your health.
④ To eating vegetables is good for your health.
⑤ To eating vegetables are good for your health.

Answer p.33

Point 043, 046

09 다음 빈칸에 들어갈 말이 순서대로 짝지어진 것은?

• My mom quit ________ coffee.
• I want ________ this singing contest.
• On ________ home, she ran to her room.

① to drink – win – to return
② drinking – to win – returning
③ drinking – winning – returning
④ drinking – to win – to return
⑤ to drink – winning – to return

Point 042

10 다음 밑줄 친 부분의 쓰임이 보기 와 같은 것을 모두 고르면?

보기 Imagine lying on the beach.

① Look at the flying birds.
② He is playing the guitar.
③ His job is teaching English.
④ They are helping the children.
⑤ I bought a new pair of running shoes.

[11~12] 다음 중 어법상 틀린 것을 고르시오.

Point 041

11 ① Mike is planning to sell his house.
② She continued to clean the bathroom.
③ I'll never forget seeing her for the first time.
④ I regret to say that it's time to say good-bye.
⑤ Please forgive me for answering not your letter.

고난도

Point 043

12 ① I promise to take you home.
② Jessica doesn't mind to eat alone.
③ Jennifer avoided meeting me at school.
④ I tried eating the soup, but I didn't like it.
⑤ Please consider giving me a second chance.

서술형

[13~14] 다음 우리말과 일치하도록 괄호 안의 말을 이용하여 빈칸에 알맞은 말을 쓰시오.

Point 046

13 그것에 관해 불평해봤자 소용없다. (use, complain)

→ It is ________ ________ ________ about it.

Point 046

14 나는 그의 농담에 웃지 않을 수 없었다. (help, laugh)

→ I ________ ________ ________ at his joke.

Point 041

15 다음 우리말과 일치하도록 괄호 안의 말을 바르게 배열하시오.

그는 그의 권력을 잃을까 봐 두려워하고 있다.
(his power, afraid, is, he, losing, of)

→ ________________________

Point 045

16 다음 글에서 어법상 틀린 부분을 찾아 바르게 고쳐 쓰시오.

At the beginning of this year, I decided to lose weight. So, I started jogging every morning. I also stopped to eat fast food.

________ → ________

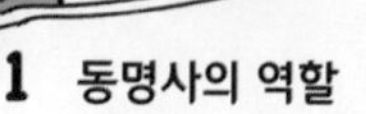

Grammar Review 핵심 정리

1 동명사의 역할

문장에서 명사처럼 쓰여 주어, 보어, 목적어의 역할을 한다.

Point

Giving is **receiving.** 039

☞ 주어 역할: '~하는 것은[이]'으로 해석한다.
☞ 보어 역할: '~하는 것(이다), ~하기(이다)'로 해석한다.

They *enjoy* **playing** soccer. 040

☞ 목적어 역할: 동사의 목적어로 쓰이는 경우, '~하는 것을, ~하기를'로 해석한다.

He is good *at* **dancing.** 041

☞ 목적어 역할: 전치사의 목적어로 쓰이는 경우, '~하는 것'으로 해석한다.

2 동명사 vs. 현재분사

Someone is **waiting** for you in the **waiting** room. 042

☞ 동명사는 명사의 역할을, 현재분사는 형용사의 역할을 한다.
☞ 동명사는 명사 앞에서 명사의 목적이나 용도를 나타내고, 현재분사는 명사를 수식한다.

3 동명사와 to부정사

She *avoided* **talking** to strangers. 043

☞ 동명사만을 목적어로 취하는 동사: enjoy, finish, mind, give up, stop, quit, avoid 등
☞ to부정사만을 목적어로 취하는 동사: want, hope, plan, wish, promise, decide, agree 등

Do you *like* **riding[to ride]** a bike? 044

☞ 동명사와 to부정사를 모두 목적어로 취하는 동사: like, love, hate, start, begin, continue 등

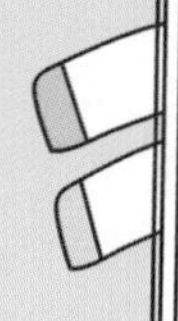

I *remember* **leaving** my keys on the desk. 045

☞ 동명사와 to부정사를 모두 목적어로 취하지만 의미가 달라지는 동사: forget, remember, try, regret 등

4 동명사의 관용 표현

He **is busy doing** his homework. 046

☞ go v-ing (~하러 가다) / be busy v-ing (~하느라 바쁘다) / feel like v-ing (~하고 싶다) / have trouble v-ing (~하는 데 어려움을 겪다) / keep (on) v-ing (계속해서 ~하다) / It is no use v-ing (~해도 소용없다) / on v-ing (~하자마자) / look forward to v-ing (~하기를 기대하다) / be worth v-ing (~할 만한 가치가 있다) / cannot help v-ing (~하지 않을 수 없다) 등이 있다.

분사

Point 047 저 날고 있는 새들을 봐.

Look at the flying birds.

- 분사는 동사원형에 -ing나 -ed를 붙여 동사를 형용사처럼 쓸 수 있게 변형한 것으로 분사에는 현재분사와 과거분사가 있다.
- 현재분사: 「**동사원형 + -ing**」의 형태로 '능동(~하는), 진행(~하고 있는)'의 의미를 갖는다.
  It was an **exciting** game. (능동)
  I saw the **rising** sun from the mountain top. (진행)
  TIP 현재분사는 be동사와 결합하여 진행형을 만든다.
  She **is listening** to music.

STEP 1 다음 문장을 밑줄 친 부분에 유의하여 우리말로 해석하시오.

1 He ran out of the burning house.
2 Several ducks were swimming in the pond.
3 Did you see a man smoking in the room?
4 Mom is making egg sandwiches for lunch.
5 There's a train leaving for Paris at twelve.

□ burn 타다
□ several (몇)몇의
□ pond 연못

STEP 2 다음 우리말과 일치하도록 괄호 안의 단어를 빈칸에 알맞은 형태로 쓰시오.

1 모두가 춤추고 있는 소녀들을 위해 박수를 쳐주었다. (dance)
Everybody clapped for the ____________ girls.

2 그 개는 낯선 사람을 향해 짖고 있었다. (bark)
The dog was ____________ at a stranger.

3 그는 하늘의 반짝이는 별들을 쳐다보았다. (shine)
He looked at the ____________ stars in the sky.

4 그 남자는 땅에 구멍을 파고 있다. (dig)
The man is ____________ a hole in the ground.

□ clap 박수를 치다
□ bark (개 · 여우 등이) 짖다
□ shine 반짝이다
□ dig (구멍 등을) 파다

STEP 3 다음 빈칸에 공통으로 들어갈 말로 알맞은 것은? 내신

- Eric is _________ on the bed.
- She gently put down the _________ baby.

① sleep ② sleeps ③ slept
④ sleeping ⑤ to be slept

□ gently 부드럽게
□ put down 내려놓다

Answer p.35

Point 048 쓰러진 나무들이 길을 막았다.

The fallen trees blocked the road.

- 과거분사: 「**동사원형+-ed**」의 형태로 '수동(~된, ~당한), 완료(~되어 있는)'의 의미를 갖는다.
  There was a **broken** bike in the garage. (수동)
  Can I eat these **boiled** eggs? (완료)
  TIP 과거분사는 have동사와 결합하여 완료형을 만들거나 be동사와 결합하여 수동태를 만든다.

STEP 1 다음 문장을 밑줄 친 부분에 유의하여 우리말로 해석하시오.

1 She swept away the fallen leaves.
2 The plane has just arrived at the airport.
3 The menu at this restaurant is changed regularly.
4 She showed her newly painted house to us.
5 All the doors and windows were closed tightly.

□ sweep away ~을 쓸어 내다
□ regularly 정기적으로
□ newly 새롭게
□ tightly 단단히, 꽉

STEP 2 다음 우리말과 일치하도록 괄호 안의 단어를 빈칸에 알맞은 형태로 쓰시오.

1 너는 저 충격 받은 사람들이 보이지 않니? (shock)
Can't you see those ____________ people?

2 우리는 동굴에서 그 보물을 발견했다. (find)
We have ____________ the treasure in the cave.

3 나는 Jenny의 생일 파티에 초대받았다. (invite)
I was ____________ to Jenny's birthday party.

4 부상을 당한 여자는 병원으로 이송되었다. (injure)
The ____________ woman was carried to the hospital.

5 대학에서 그는 Jake라고 불리는 친구를 만났다. (name)
At college, he met a friend ____________ Jack.

□ treasure 보물
□ cave 동굴
□ injure 부상을 입히다
□ college 대학
□ name 이름을 붙이다[짓다]

STEP 3 다음 빈칸에 들어갈 말로 알맞은 것은? 내신

I saw a ____________ letter in the trash can.

① tear ② tore ③ torn
④ tearing ⑤ to tear

□ tear 찢다(-tore-torn)
□ trash can 쓰레기통

Answer p.35

Point 049 저기 문 앞에 서 있는 예쁜 소녀는 누구니?

Who is that pretty girl standing at the door?

• 분사가 단독으로 명사를 수식할 때는 명사 앞에, 구를 이루어 명사를 수식할 때는 명사 뒤에 온다.

The police found the **stolen** wallet. (명사 앞에서 수식)

The boy **wearing** a blue cap is my brother. (명사 뒤에서 수식)

STEP 1 다음 괄호 안에서 알맞은 말을 고르시오.

1 She gave me a dress (designing, designed) by Valentino.
2 I heard the (beeping, beeped) sound of the alarm clock.
3 The tall girl (dancing, danced) in the parade is my sister.
4 I found the (losing, lost) ring under the bed.
5 Most of the people (inviting, invited) to the party didn't turn up.

□ beep (전자기기가) 삐 소리를 내다
□ parade 퍼레이드, 행진
□ turn up 나타나다

STEP 2 다음 보기 와 같이 분사를 이용하여 두 문장을 한 문장으로 바꿔 쓰시오.

보기 Look at the birds. + They are building a nest.
→ Look at the birds building a nest.

1 Do you know that lady? She is talking to Ms. Wilson.
→ ______________________________

2 My dad bought my mom a bag. It was made in Italy.
→ ______________________________

3 The picture was taken ten years ago. It is hanging on the wall.
→ ______________________________

4 The boy is in the hospital now. He was bitten by a snake.
→ ______________________________

5 Have you read any books? The books were written by Tolstoy.
→ ______________________________

□ nest (새의) 둥지
□ bite 물다(-bit-bitten)

STEP 3 다음 우리말과 일치하도록 할 때, covered가 들어가기에 알맞은 곳은? 내신

그는 서류로 덮여 있는 탁자에 앉아 있었다.
→ He (①) was (②) sitting (③) at the (④) table (⑤) with papers.

□ cover 덮다
□ papers 서류

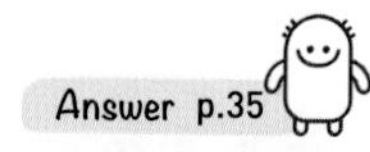

Point 050 그녀는 나를 향해 미소 지으면서 서 있었다.

She stood smiling at me.

- 주격 보어: 주어의 상태나 행동을 보충 설명하는 역할을 한다.
  He sat **watching** TV. (능동)
  The actor stood **surrounded** by his fans. (수동)
- 목적격 보어: 목적어의 상태나 행동을 보충 설명하는 역할을 한다.
  She kept him **waiting** for too long. (능동)
  Jack found his room **cleaned**. (수동)

TIP 분사가 주격 보어이거나 목적격 보어일 경우, 주어와 보어 또는 목적어와 보어의 관계가 능동이면 현재분사, 수동이면 과거분사를 쓴다.

STEP 1 다음 괄호 안에서 알맞은 말을 고르시오.

1 Alice was lying (listened, listening) to music.
2 She left her food (untouching, untouched).
3 Peter saw her (walked, walking) down the stairs.
4 I wanted the problem (solving, solved) immediately.
5 He looked a little (disappointing, disappointed) at the news.

□ lie 누워 있다
□ stairs 계단
□ solve 해결하다
□ disappoint 실망시키다

STEP 2 다음 우리말과 일치하도록 괄호 안의 말을 바르게 배열하시오.

1 그는 그의 차가 일주일 내에 수리되도록 했다. (repaired, he, his car, had)
______________________ within a week.

2 그의 남동생은 크게 울며 그에게 왔다. (crying, came, loudly, his younger brother)
______________________ to him.

3 그 역은 30년 넘게 사용되지 않은 채로 있었다. (unused, the station, remained)
______________________ for over thirty years.

4 그녀가 돌아왔을 때, 나는 그녀의 태도가 바뀐 것을 알아차렸다.
(her attitude, noticed, I, changed)
When she returned, ______________________.

5 제가 당신을 오래 기다리게 했나요? (you, I, waiting, keep)
Did ______________________ for a long time?

□ repair 수리하다
□ station 역
□ unused 사용되지 않는
□ attitude 태도

STEP 3 다음 빈칸에 들어갈 말로 알맞은 것은? 내신

We need to have the light bulb ________.

① replace ② replacing ③ replaced
④ to replacing ⑤ being replaced

□ light bulb 전구
□ replace 교체하다

Answer p.36

Point 051 한 지루한 프랑스 영화가 나를 지루하게 만들었다.

A boring French movie made me bored.

- 감정을 나타내는 동사는 분사 형태로 자주 쓰인다. 주어나 명사가 감정의 원인이 되어 '~한 감정을 일으키는'의 의미일 때는 현재분사로, 감정의 대상이 되어 '~한 감정을 느끼는'의 의미일 때는 과거분사로 나타낸다.
- 감정을 나타내는 분사

exciting(흥분되게 하는) – excited(흥분한)
amazing(놀랄 만한) – amazed(놀란)
interesting(흥미로운) – interested(흥미로워하는)
surprising(놀라게 하는) – surprised(놀란)
annoying(짜증나게 하는) – annoyed(짜증이 난)
boring(지루한) – bored(지루해 하는)
disappointing(실망스러운) – disappointed(실망한)
shocking(충격적인) – shocked(충격 받은)
tiring(피곤하게 하는) – tired(피곤한)
depressing(우울하게 하는) – depressed(우울한)

The news was **surprising**. / We were **surprised** at the news.

STEP 1 다음 괄호 안에서 알맞은 말을 고르시오.

1 They were (tiring, tired) after the long journey.
2 The instructions were (confusing, confused).
3 The (touching, touched) audience broke into loud applause.
4 The trip was such an (amazing, amazed) experience to me.
5 My parents were (disappointing, disappointed) with my grades.

□ journey 여행, 여정
□ instruction 설명, 지시
□ touch 감동시키다
□ audience 청중, 관중
□ break into applause 박수갈채를 보내다

STEP 2 다음 괄호 안의 단어를 빈칸에 알맞은 형태로 쓰시오.

1 Mike is ____________ in sports. (interest)
2 The result of the contest was very ____________. (shock)
3 I was really ____________ during the flight. (bore)
4 John's loud music is ____________ to his neighbors. (annoy)
5 He became ____________ after walking for many miles. (exhaust)

□ contest 대회, 시합
□ flight 비행
□ annoy 짜증나게 하다
□ exhaust 기진맥진하게 만들다

STEP 3 다음 빈칸에 들어갈 말이 순서대로 짝지어진 것은? 

- The soccer match was really __________.
- Are you __________ with your job?

① excite – satisfy
② exciting – satisfied
③ exciting – satisfying
④ excited – satisfied
⑤ excited – satisfying

□ match 경기, 시합

Answer p.36

Point 052 뱀을 보자, 그 남자는 도망갔다.

Seeing the snake, the man ran away.

- 분사구문: 부사절(접속사+주어+동사)을 분사가 이끄는 부사구(동사원형+-ing ~)의 형태로 간단히 줄여 쓴 구문을 말한다.
- 분사구문 만드는 법

After he took the medicine, he felt sleepy. (부사절의 주어 = 주절의 주어)
① ② ③

→ Taking the medicine, he felt sleepy.

① 접속사를 없앤다. ② 주절과 부사절의 주어가 같은 경우, 부사절의 주어를 없앤다.

③ 부사절의 동사를 「동사원형+-ing」의 형태로 바꾼다.

TIP 분사구문의 부정을 나타낼 때는 분사 바로 앞에 부정어 not이나 never를 붙인다.

STEP 1 다음 괄호 안에서 알맞은 말을 고르시오.

□ far 훨씬, 많이
□ behind 뒤에, 뒤떨어져
□ shout 소리치다
□ advice 조언, 충고

1 (To start, Starting) now, you won't be too far behind.

2 (Listen, Listening) to music, he did his homework.

3 (Being, Be) angry, he started to shout at the boys.

4 (Got, Getting) too much stress, he decided to change his job.

5 (Knowing not, Not knowing) what to do, I asked her for advice.

STEP 2 다음 문장을 분사구문을 이용하여 바꿔 쓰시오.

□ although (비록) ~이긴 하지만
□ miss 놓치다

1 When he entered the room, he found the child sleeping.
→ ______________________, he found the child sleeping.

2 If you turn to the right, you will find the bank.
→ ______________________, you will find the bank.

3 Although she had many friends, she was lonely.
→ ______________________, she was lonely.

4 Because we were late, we missed the train.
→ ______________________, we missed the train.

STEP 3 다음 밑줄 친 부분을 분사구문으로 바르게 고친 것은? 내신

When we arrived at the beach, we saw the sun rising.

① Arrived at the beach
② Arriving at the beach
③ We arrived at the beach
④ We arriving at the beach
⑤ When we arriving at the beach

Answer p.36

Point 053 길을 걷다가, 나는 옛 친구를 만났다.

Walking down the street, I met my old friend.

- 때를 나타내는 분사구문: '~할 때'(when, as), '~한 후에'(after), '~하는 동안'(while)의 의미를 가진다.
  Opening the envelope, he found two concert tickets.
  (= When he opened the envelope, he found two concert tickets.)

STEP 1 자연스러운 문장이 되도록 다음을 연결하시오.

1 Washing her hands •
2 Trying to lift the piano •
3 Changing into his pajamas •
4 Tidying up the drawers •
5 Putting on a life jacket •

• ⓐ he hurt his back.
• ⓑ he went to bed.
• ⓒ she started to cook.
• ⓓ I jumped into the pool.
• ⓔ she found an old photo.

□ hurt 다치게 하다
□ pajamas 잠옷
□ tidy up 정리하다
□ drawer 서랍

STEP 2 다음 두 문장이 같은 뜻이 되도록 괄호 안의 접속사를 이용하여 문장을 완성하시오.

1 Hearing the doorbell, I rushed to the door. (when)
= ______________________, I rushed to the door.

2 Getting home, he took a shower. (after)
= ______________________, he took a shower.

3 Watching the movie, he fell asleep. (while)
= ______________________, he fell asleep.

4 Crossing the road, you should look both ways. (when)
= ______________________, you should look both ways.

5 Finishing his homework, he went out to play. (after)
= ______________________, he went out to play.

□ doorbell 초인종
□ rush 급히 움직이다
□ fall asleep 잠이 들다

STEP 3 다음 문장의 밑줄 친 부분과 바꿔 쓸 수 있는 것은? 내신

Riding a bike, he always wears his helmet.

① After he rides a bike
② Since he rides a bike
③ When he rides a bike
④ Though he rides a bike
⑤ Because he rides a bike

□ ride 타다

Answer p.37

Point 054 심한 감기에 걸려서, 나는 그냥 집에 있었다.

Having a bad cold, I just stayed home.

- 이유를 나타내는 분사구문: '~ 때문에'(because, as, since)의 의미를 가진다.
  Wanting to lose weight, I'm eating less these days.
  (= Because I want to lose weight, I'm eating less these days.)

STEP 1 자연스러운 문장이 되도록 다음을 연결하시오.

1 Quitting my job last month •
2 Having a detailed map •
3 Being a strict vegetarian •
4 Starting a new business •
5 Needing French for her job •

• ⓐ he has been very busy.
• ⓑ she's studying it very hard.
• ⓒ I'm looking for a new one.
• ⓓ we were able to find the way.
• ⓔ he never eats meat.

□ quit 그만두다
□ detailed 자세한
□ strict 엄격한
□ vegetarian 채식주의자
□ look for ~을 찾다

STEP 2 다음 두 문장이 같은 뜻이 되도록 분사구문을 이용하여 문장을 완성하시오.

1 Since he was angry with her, he didn't say a word.
= ______________________, he didn't say a word.

2 Because I walked very quickly, I was able to catch the last train.
= ______________________, I was able to catch the last train.

3 Because I had an exam the next day, I spent the day in the library.
= ______________________, I spent the day in the library.

4 Since she felt comfortable with us, she wanted to stay here longer.
= ______________________, she wanted to stay here longer.

5 As he was the top basketball player, he was popular with girls.
= ______________________, he was popular with girls.

□ be able to ~할 수 있다
□ comfortable 편안한
□ popular 인기 있는

STEP 3 다음 밑줄 친 부분 중 의미가 나머지 넷과 다른 것은? 내신

① Feeling so tired, she took a rest.
② Living near the school, I go home for lunch.
③ Loving animals, she wants to become a vet.
④ Peeling potatoes, he cooked them in the oven.
⑤ Being careful about his health, he seldom gets sick.

□ vet 수의사
□ peel 껍질을 벗기다
□ careful 조심하는, 주의 깊은

Answer p.37

Point 055 그들은 쌍둥이지만, 취향이 매우 다르다.

Being twins, they have very different tastes.

- 조건을 나타내는 분사구문: '~한다면'(if)의 의미를 가진다.
  Opening the window, you will get fresh air.
  (= If you open the window, you will get fresh air.)
- 양보를 나타내는 분사구문: '~일지라도'(though, although)의 의미를 가진다.
  Living near her house, we seldom see her.
  (= Though we live near her house, we seldom see her.)

STEP 1 다음 문장을 밑줄 친 부분에 유의하여 우리말로 해석하시오.

1 Being very sick, she attended the meeting.
2 Eating a lot, he doesn't easily gain weight.
3 Refusing his offer, you will regret it.
4 Reading the newspaper, he needs his reading glasses.
5 Being a kind person, she is loved by everybody.

□ gain weight 살이 찌다
□ refuse 거절하다
□ regret 후회하다
□ reading glasses 돋보기 안경

STEP 2 다음 우리말과 일치하도록 괄호 안의 말과 분사구문을 이용하여 빈칸에 알맞은 말을 쓰시오.

1 최선을 다했지만, 그들은 결국 경기에서 졌다. (try one's best)
_____ _____ _____, they lost in the end.

2 숙제를 끝내면, 너는 컴퓨터 게임을 할 수 있다. (finish one's homework)
_____ _____ _____, you can play computer games.

3 프랑스로 여행을 가면, 우리는 그 박물관을 방문할 것이다. (travel)
_____ _____ _____, we will visit the museum.

4 그는 돈이 많지만, 작은 집에 산다. (so much money)
_____ _____ _____ _____, he lives in a small house.

□ try one's best 최선을 다하다
□ in the end 결국

STEP 3 다음 두 문장이 같은 뜻이 되도록 할 때, 빈칸에 들어갈 말로 알맞은 것은? 내신

Being very old, he never stops challenging himself.
= _____ he is very old, he never stops challenging himself.

① If ② When ③ After
④ Because ⑤ Though

□ challenge 도전하다

Answer p.38

Point 056 피자를 먹으면서, 나는 만화책을 읽었다. 분사구문의 의미 (동시동작, 연속동작)

Eating pizza, I read a comic book.

- 동시동작을 나타내는 분사구문: '~ 하면서 동시에'라는 의미를 가진다.
  Putting his hat on, he said goodbye. (= While he was putting his hat on, he said goodbye.)
- 연속동작을 나타내는 분사구문: '그리고 ~하다'의 의미를 가진다.
  We parked the car, **searching** for the ticket machine.
  (= We parked the car and searched for the ticket machine.)

TIP Being으로 시작되는 진행형의 분사구문에서 Being은 일반적으로 생략한다.
While he was taking a shower, he sang a song. → (Being) **Taking** a shower, he sang a song.

STEP 1 다음 문장을 밑줄 친 부분에 유의하여 우리말로 해석하시오.

1 He sat at a desk, beginning to do his homework.
2 Smiling happily, she opened her birthday present.
3 Eating popcorn, the boys watched the action movie.
4 Hoping for a miracle, the doctor continued the surgery.
5 We ate dinner, enjoying ice cream for dessert.

□ miracle 기적
□ surgery 수술
□ dessert 디저트, 후식

STEP 2 다음 우리말과 일치하도록 괄호 안의 말과 분사구문을 이용하여 문장을 완성하시오.

1 그녀는 손을 흔들면서, 내 쪽으로 다가왔다. (wave one's hands)
______________________, she came toward me.

2 그 개는 나를 자세히 살피더니 내게 짖어댔다. (bark at)
The dog watched me closely, ______________________.

3 문을 두드리면서, 그는 내 이름을 불렀다. (knock on)
______________________, he called my name.

4 그녀는 안경을 벗고 눈을 비볐다. (rub one's eyes)
She removed her glasses, ______________________.

□ bark 짖다
□ knock 두드리다, 노크하다
□ rub 문지르다, 비비다
□ remove (옷 등을) 벗다

STEP 3 다음 밑줄 친 부분의 의미가 보기와 같은 것은? 내신

보기 Winking at me, she handed me a note.

① Being poor, the couple were very happy.
② Listening to the radio, she prepared dinner.
③ We drove to the airport, getting on the plane.
④ He left in the morning, coming home at noon.
⑤ Containing caffeine, coffee can keep you awake.

□ wink 윙크하다
□ get on 타다
□ contain ~이 들어있다, 함유되어 있다

Answer p.38

01회 내신 적중 실전 문제

Point 049

01 다음 대화의 빈칸에 들어갈 말로 알맞은 것은?

A: Who is the boy ________ flowers?
B: He's my cousin, Jeremy.

① hold ② held ③ holds
④ holding ⑤ to holding

Point 052

02 다음 우리말과 일치하도록 할 때, 빈칸에 들어갈 말로 알맞은 것을 모두 고르면?

돈이 없어서, 나는 집으로 걸어가야만 했다.
→ ________________, I had to walk home.

① Had no money ② I had no money
③ Having no money ④ To have no money
⑤ As I had no money

[03~05] 다음 빈칸에 들어갈 말로 알맞은 것을 고르시오.

Point 051

03

He was a little __________ when the reporters asked too many questions.

① annoy ② annoys ③ annoying
④ annoyed ⑤ to annoy

Point 050

04

She found the mirror ________.

① break ② breaks ③ breaking
④ broke ⑤ broken

Point 050

05

Brian stood ________ for a taxi.

① wait ② waits ③ waiting
④ waited ⑤ to waiting

[06~07] 다음 빈칸에 들어갈 말이 순서대로 짝지어진 것을 고르시오.

Point 047, 049

06

• The woman ________ a green dress was beautiful.
• Mom is ________ a picture on the wall.

① wears – hanging
② worn – hanging
③ worn – hung
④ wearing – hung
⑤ wearing – hanging

Point 049, 050

07

• The umbrella ________ at the bus stop belongs to John.
• Did you hear the phone ________?

① found – rung ② found – rang
③ finding – rung ④ found – ringing
⑤ finding – ringing

Point 051

08 다음 밑줄 친 부분 중 어법상 틀린 것을 모두 고르면?

① His behavior is disappointing.
② She was satisfying with her work.
③ The action movie was really excited.
④ When he saw the accident, he was shocked.
⑤ They heard some depressing news from their dad.

Point 052, 054

09 다음 밑줄 친 부분을 분사구문으로 바르게 바꿔 쓴 것은?

> Because I didn't get any message from her, I just waited there.

① Not getting any message from her
② Getting not any message from her
③ Don't getting any message from her
④ I don't getting any message from her
⑤ Having not gotten any message from her

[10~11] 다음 밑줄 친 부분의 쓰임이 보기 와 같은 것을 고르시오.

Point 053

10

> 보기 Taking off her shoes, she walked into the house.

① Wearing light clothes, she felt cold.
② Writing a note, Jason passed it to me.
③ Having nothing left to do, he went home.
④ Visiting our website, you can get a discount.
⑤ The bomb exploded, leaving ten people dead.

Point 055

11

> 보기 Climbing to the top of the mountain, you can see the port.

① Crying loudly, she left the room.
② Feeling hungry, I ate some snacks.
③ The bus leaves at seven, arriving at ten.
④ Working with him, you will find him reliable.
⑤ Waiting for the bus, my sister and I chatted.

고난도 Point 052

12 다음 중 어법상 틀린 것은?

① Being rainy, we canceled our picnic.
② She opened her bag, taking out a book.
③ Driving on the highway, you must be careful.
④ Finding out the truth, he couldn't help laughing.
⑤ Leaning against the wall, he was reading a book.

서술형

Point 051

13 다음 괄호 안의 단어를 빈칸에 알맞은 형태로 쓰시오.

> • Sam is ⓐ ________ in making movies. (interest)
> • History is a ⓑ ________ subject to Sam. (bore)

ⓐ ____________ ⓑ ____________

Point 049

14 다음 우리말과 일치하도록 괄호 안의 말을 바르게 배열하시오.

> 이것은 아이들에 의해 지어진 모래성이다.
> (built, this, the kids, is, the sand castle, by)

→ ______________________________

Point 052, 053

15 다음 밑줄 친 부분을 분사구문으로 바꿔 쓰시오.

> When I travel in Europe, I always stay in youth hostels.

→ ____________________, I always stay in youth hostels.

고난도 Point 052, 054

16 다음 대화의 상황을 분사구문을 이용하여 한 문장으로 나타낼 때 빈칸에 알맞은 말을 쓰시오.

> A: Why did Katie go to bed early?
> B: She didn't feel well.

→ ____________________, Katie went to bed early.

[01~02] 다음 빈칸에 들어갈 말로 알맞은 것을 고르시오.

중요

Point 052

01

_________ hungry, I looked for something to eat in the refrigerator.

① Be ② Is ③ Was
④ Being ⑤ Been

Point 050

02

He usually keeps all the windows in his room _________ all day.

① shut ② shutting ③ are shut
④ to shut ⑤ has shut

Point 047, 050

03 다음 빈칸에 공통으로 들어갈 말로 알맞은 것은?

- I heard Lisa _________ about her situation.
- The girls were _________ about their school lunch.

① complain ② complains
③ complaining ④ complained
⑤ to complain

Point 047, 048

04 (A), (B), (C)의 괄호 안에서 알맞은 것끼리 바르게 짝지은 것은?

- Henry has (A)[eating / eaten] the last piece of pizza.
- Maria was (B)[practicing / practiced] the violin in her room.
- She gave some cookies to the (C)[crying / cried] little girl.

	(A)		(B)		(C)
①	eaten	–	practicing	–	cried
②	eating	–	practiced	–	cried
③	eaten	–	practiced	–	cried
④	eating	–	practicing	–	crying
⑤	eaten	–	practicing	–	crying

[05~06] 다음 빈칸에 들어갈 말이 순서대로 짝지어진 것을 고르시오.

Point 049

05

- There was nothing _________ on the piece of paper.
- Tom drew a bird _________ in the sky.

① writing – flying ② writing – flown
③ written – flying ④ written – flew
⑤ written – flown

Point 051

06

- The kids went to an _________ animal show.
- The _________ kids jumped up and down.

① excited – excite ② excited – excited
③ excited – exciting ④ exciting – excited
⑤ exciting – exciting

Point 053

07 다음 우리말과 일치하도록 할 때, 빈칸에 들어갈 말로 알맞은 것을 모두 고르면?

그 집으로 걸어 들어갔을 때, 나는 작고 귀여운 개를 봤다.
→ _________________, I saw a cute little dog.

① Walked into the house
② Walking into the house
③ To walk into the house
④ I walked into the house
⑤ When I walked into the house

Point 052

08 다음 중 어법상 틀린 것은?

① Angela sat reading a magazine.
② I saw the boy crossing the street.
③ The terrified children screamed for help.
④ Following not my advice, you'll get into trouble.
⑤ The woman drinking coffee at the table is my aunt.

Answer p.40

[09~10] 다음 두 문장이 같은 뜻이 되도록 할 때, 빈칸에 들어갈 말로 알맞은 것을 고르시오.

Point 055

09

Having a big test the next day, she wanted to go to the party.
= ________ she had a big test the next day, she wanted to go to the party.

① If ② As ③ After
④ Because ⑤ Although

Point 055

10

Looking to your right, you can see the palace.
= ________ you look to your right, you can see the palace.

① If ② Since ③ While
④ Though ⑤ Because

[11~12] 다음 밑줄 친 부분의 쓰임이 보기 와 같은 것을 고르시오.

Point 054

11

보기 Being very tall, he became a basketball player.

① Preparing dinner, she cut her finger.
② Waiting in the hall, Cathy heard them talk.
③ Being very old, my grandpa can still drive.
④ Doing the high jump, she twisted her ankle.
⑤ Hating to make excuses, he said nothing more.

고난도

Point 056

12

보기 Talking on the phone, he walked down the street.

① Whistling a song, he washed the dishes.
② Being a good boy, he always helps his mom.
③ Falling over a stone, he didn't give up in the race.
④ Wanting to get high grades, he decided to study hard.
⑤ Eating too much ice cream, you will get a stomachache.

서술형

[13~14] 다음 우리말과 일치하도록 괄호 안의 말을 빈칸에 알맞은 형태로 쓰시오.

Point 052, 053

13

집에 돌아오셨을 때, 아빠는 매우 피곤해 보이셨다. (come)

→ ________ back home, Dad looked very tired.

Point 051

14

그의 태도가 돌변해서 나는 당혹스러웠다. (confuse)

→ I got ________ by his sudden change of attitude.

Point 051

15 다음 문장에서 어법상 틀린 부분을 찾아 바르게 고쳐 쓰시오.

I love Jack's jokes. His amused jokes always make me laugh.

________ → ________

Point 052, 054

16 다음 두 문장을 분사구문을 이용하여 한 문장으로 바꿔 쓰시오.

He had poor eyesight. So, he could not see clearly.

→ ________

Grammar Review 핵심 정리

1 현재분사와 과거분사

분사는 동사원형에 -ing나 -ed를 붙여 동사를 형용사처럼 쓸 수 있게 변형한 것으로 분사에는 현재분사와 과거분사가 있다.

Point

Look at the **flying** birds. 047

☞ 현재분사: 「동사원형+-ing」의 형태로 '능동(~하는), 진행(~하고 있는)'의 의미를 갖는다.

The **fallen** trees blocked the road. 048

☞ 과거분사: 「동사원형+-ed」의 형태로 '수동(~된, ~당한), 완료(~되어 있는)'의 의미를 갖는다.

2 분사의 쓰임

Who is that pretty girl **standing** at the door? 049

☞ 명사 수식: 분사는 형용사처럼 명사를 수식한다. 분사가 단독으로 명사를 수식할 때는 명사 앞에, 구를 이루어 명사를 수식할 때는 명사 뒤에 온다.

She stood **smiling** at me. 050

☞ 보어 역할: 분사는 형용사처럼 주격 보어 또는 목적격 보어로 쓰여 주어나 목적어의 상태나 행동을 보충 설명하는 역할을 한다.

3 감정을 나타내는 분사

A **boring** French movie made me **bored**. 051

☞ 주어나 명사가 감정의 원인이 되어 '~한 감정을 일으키는'의 의미일 때는 현재분사로, 감정의 대상이 되어 '~한 감정을 느끼는'의 의미일 때는 과거분사로 나타낸다.

4 분사구문 만드는 법

Seeing the snake, the man ran away. 052

☞ 분사구문: 부사절(접속사+주어+동사)을 분사가 이끄는 부사구(동사원형+-ing~)의 형태로 간단히 줄여 쓴 구문

☞ 분사구문 만드는 법: 접속사를 없애고, 주절과 부사절의 주어가 같은 경우, 부사절의 주어를 없앤 후 동사를 「동사원형+-ing」의 형태로 바꾼다.

5 분사구문의 의미

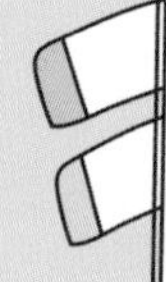

Walking down the street, I met my old friend. 053

☞ 때를 나타내는 분사구문: '~할 때'(when, as), '~한 후에'(after), '~하는 동안'(while)의 의미를 가진다.

Having a bad cold, I just stayed home. 054

☞ 이유를 나타내는 분사구문: '~때문에'(because, as, since)의 의미를 가진다.

Being twins, they have very different tastes. 055

☞ 조건을 나타내는 분사구문: '~한다면'(if)의 의미를 가진다.

☞ 양보를 나타내는 분사구문: '~일지라도'(though, although)의 의미를 가진다.

Eating pizza, I read a comic book. 056

☞ 동시동작을 나타내는 분사구문: '~하면서 동시에'라는 의미를 가진다.

☞ 연속동작을 나타내는 분사구문: '그리고 ~하다'라는 의미를 가진다.

LESSON 07

수동태

Point 057 쌀은 많은 나라에서 재배된다.

Rice is grown in many countries.

• 능동태와 수동태

능동태	수동태
'(주어가) ~하다'	'(주어가) ~당하다, ~받다'
주어가 동작을 하는 주체	주어가 동작을 받는 대상
My mom **makes** special soup.	Special soup **is made** by my mom.

• 수동태의 기본 형태: 「**be동사 + 과거분사(+ by + 행위자)**」

TIP 수동태의 행위자가 일반인일 때, 혹은 중요하지 않거나 불분명할 때 「by + 행위자」를 생략할 수 있다.

STEP 1 다음 괄호 안에서 알맞은 말을 고르시오.

1 Her storybook (loves, is loved) by many children.

2 The classroom (cleans, is cleaned) every day.

3 The mechanic (checks, is checked) the elevator regularly.

4 His pictures and videos (post, are posted) by his assistant.

5 The mother kangaroo (carries, is carried) her baby in her pouch.

□ mechanic 정비공
□ post (웹사이트에 사진 등을) 올리다[게시하다]
□ assistant 조수
□ pouch 주머니

STEP 2 다음 우리말과 일치하도록 괄호 안의 말을 바르게 배열하시오.

1 이달의 영화는 Grand Hall에서 상영된다.
(is, in the Grand Hall, played, the movie of the month)

____

2 이 궁은 많은 관광객들에 의해 방문된다. (by, is, many, this palace, tourists, visited)

____

3 많은 돈이 교육에 쓰인다. (on education, is, a lot of money, spent)

____

4 그 꽃들에게 일주일에 두 번씩 물을 준다. (watered, the flowers, twice a week, are)

____

□ palace 궁전, 궁
□ tourist 관광객
□ water (물을) 주다

STEP 3 다음 우리말과 일치하도록 할 때, 빈칸에 들어갈 말로 알맞은 것은? 내신

내 자전거는 나의 아빠에 의해서 수리된다.
→ My bike ________ by my father.

① repairs ② repaired ③ repairing
④ is repaired ⑤ is repairing

□ repair 수리하다, 고치다

Point 058 그 캐릭터는 많은 아이들에 의해 사랑받는다.

The character is loved by many children.

• 수동태를 만드는 방법

We follow the rule. (능동태)
주어 동사 목적어

The rule is followed by us. (수동태)
주어 be동사+과거분사 by+행위자

① 능동태의 목적어를 수동태의 주어로 쓴다.
② 능동태의 동사를 「be동사+과거분사」의 형태로 바꾸고 시제는 능동태 시제에 일치시킨다.
③ 능동태의 주어를 「by+행위자」의 형태로 문장 마지막에 쓴다. 능동태의 주어가 대명사이면 목적격으로 쓴다.

TIP 목적어를 취하지 않는 자동사(happen, look, appear, disappear, exist 등)와 상태나 소유를 나타내는 타동사(become, have, resemble 등)는 수동태로 바꿀 수 없다.

STEP 1 다음 괄호 안에서 알맞은 말을 고르시오.

1 The girl (resembles, is resembled) her mother.
2 Her picture (took, was taken) without her permission.
3 The magician suddenly (disappeared, was disappeared).
4 The table for dinner is set by (I, me).
5 Your bag (looks, is looked) heavy.

□ resemble ~을 닮다
□ permission 허락
□ magician 마술사

STEP 2 다음 문장을 수동태 문장으로 바꿔 쓰시오.

1 Tony feeds the dog.
→ The dog ________________________________.

2 A famous poet wrote this poem.
→ This poem ________________________________.

3 Diane packed the bags.
→ The bags ________________________________.

4 We trust our new leader.
→ Our new leader ________________________________.

□ feed ~에게 먹이를 주다 (-fed-fed)
□ poet 시인
□ pack (짐 등을) 싸다
□ trust 신뢰하다, 믿다

STEP 3 다음 중 수동태로 바꿀 수 없는 것은? 내신

① He threw the ball.
② The girls sang a song.
③ They built the houses.
④ She enjoyed the party.
⑤ She became an actress.

□ actress 여배우

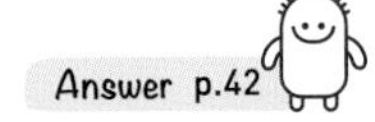

Point 059 전화는 Bell에 의해 발명되었다.

The telephone was invented by Bell.

- 과거시제 문장의 수동태는 「was/were + 과거분사(+ by + 행위자)」의 형태로 쓴다.
  The cat **was hit by** a car. (← A car hit the cat.)
  The cookies **were baked by** the volunteers. (← The volunteers baked the cookies.)

STEP 1 다음 밑줄 친 부분을 바르게 고치시오.

1 The buildings of the town was destroyed by the earthquake.
2 The invitations are made a few days ago.
3 The parcel delivered to the customer last Friday.
4 The light bulb is invented by Edison.
5 The oak tree in front of his house were planted in 2003.

□ earthquake 지진
□ invitation 초대장
□ parcel 소포
□ plant 심다

STEP 2 다음 우리말과 일치하도록 괄호 안의 말을 이용하여 빈칸에 알맞은 말을 쓰시오.

1 그 소년은 개에 물렸다. (bite)
The boy ________ ________ ________ the dog.

2 그 두 군인은 적에게 발견되었다. (discover)
The two soldiers ________ ________ ________ the enemy.

3 그 차는 경찰에 의해 세워졌다. (stop)
The car ________ ________ ________ the police officer.

4 그 회사는 Sam Walton에 의해 설립되었다. (found)
The company ________ ________ ________ Sam Walton.

5 첫 번째 패스트푸드 가게는 1916년에 미국에서 개점되었다. (open)
The first fast food restaurant ________ ________ in the USA in 1916.

□ bite 물다(-bit-bitten)
□ soldier 군인
□ enemy 적
□ found 설립하다

STEP 3 다음 두 문장이 같은 뜻이 되도록 할 때, 빈칸에 들어갈 말로 알맞은 것은? 내신

Many people loved the actress.
= The actress ________ many people.

① was loving
② is loved by
③ was loved by
④ was loving by
⑤ were loved by

Answer p.42

Point 060 그 영화는 다음 주에 개봉될 것이다.

The movie will be released next week.

- 미래시제 문장의 수동태는 「**will be + 과거분사(+ by + 행위자)**」의 형태로 쓴다.
  You **will be paid** next Friday.
  Today's debate **will be watched by** many people.

STEP 1 다음 밑줄 친 부분을 바르게 고치시오.

1 His car will be repair in a few hours.
2 A new shopping center will build in town next year.
3 The classroom will decorated by the students tomorrow.
4 The project was completed by the end of next month.
5 The problem will being solved within a week.

□ decorate 장식하다
□ complete 완료하다, 끝마치다
□ within ~내에

STEP 2 다음 문장을 수동태 문장으로 바꿔 쓰시오.

1 A new doctor will check the patients.
→ ______________________

2 The company will hire many workers this year.
→ ______________________

3 Millions of people will visit the museum.
→ ______________________

4 Mr. and Mrs. Brown will open a bakery next month.
→ ______________________

5 The manager will sign the contract tonight.
→ ______________________

□ check 살피다, 검사하다
□ patient 환자
□ millions of 수백만의
□ contract 계약(서)

STEP 3 다음 빈칸에 들어갈 말로 알맞은 것은? 내신

The furniture ____________ to you tomorrow.

① delivers ② will deliver ③ was delivered
④ will be delivering ⑤ will be delivered

□ furniture 가구

Answer p.43

Point 061 소풍은 취소되었나요?

Was the picnic canceled?

- 수동태의 부정문: 「**be동사 + not + 과거분사(+ by + 행위자)**」 형태로 쓴다.
  The streets **were not cleaned** yet.
- 수동태의 의문문: 「**be동사 + 주어 + 과거분사(+ by + 행위자)~?**」 형태로 쓴다.
  Was this report **written by** Annie?

STEP 1 다음 밑줄 친 부분을 바르게 고치시오.

□ replace 교체하다

1 The window didn't break by Tom.
2 Did the song sung by Elvis?
3 Was the dog be taken to the vet?
4 The problem was didn't solved by Janet.
5 Were the computers replace with new ones?

STEP 2 다음 우리말과 일치하도록 괄호 안의 말을 이용하여 빈칸에 알맞은 말을 쓰시오.

□ move 옮기다
□ upstairs 위층으로
□ mop (바닥을) 닦다
□ produce 생산하다

1 의자는 위층으로 옮겨졌나요? (move)
______ the chairs ______ upstairs?

2 조식은 가격에 포함되어 있지 않습니다. (include)
The breakfast ______ ______ ______ in the price.

3 바닥은 Andy에 의해 닦였나요? (mop)
______ the floor ______ ______ Andy?

4 소포는 정확한 주소로 배송되지 않았다. (deliver)
The package ______ ______ ______ to the right address.

5 이 차들은 한국에서 생산되나요? (produce)
______ these cars ______ in Korea?

STEP 3 다음 대화의 빈칸에 공통으로 들어갈 말로 알맞은 것은? 내신

□ Japanese 일본어

A: Is Japanese ______ in Indonesia?
B: No, it's not ______ there.

① speak ② spoke ③ speaking
④ spoken ⑤ to speak

Answer p.43

Point 062 그 그림들은 조심스럽게 다뤄져야 한다.

The paintings should be handled carefully.

- 조동사의 수동태: 「**조동사 + be + 과거분사(+ by + 행위자)**」 형태로 쓴다.
  Many kinds of birds **can be watched** in the area.
  – 부정문: 「**조동사 + not + be + 과거분사**」
  The items in the exhibit **must not be touched**.
  – 의문문: 「**조동사 + 주어 + be + 과거분사 ~?**」
  Will the seminar room **be cleaned** tomorrow?

STEP 1 다음 밑줄 친 부분을 바르게 고치시오.

1 The password may forget easily.
2 Children must are protected from danger.
3 Should these plants watered every day?
4 The problem can be not solved by us.
5 The bills will not pay by us.

□ protect 보호하다
□ danger 위험
□ solve 해결하다
□ bill 청구서, 계산서

STEP 2 다음 우리말과 일치하도록 괄호 안의 말을 이용하여 빈칸에 알맞은 말을 쓰시오.

1 케첩 얼룩은 즉시 제거되어야 한다. (must, remove)
Ketchup stains ________ ________ ________ immediately.

2 팩스는 내일 아침에 보내질 것이다. (will, send)
The fax ________ ________ ________ tomorrow morning.

3 중국의 만리장성이 우주에서 보일 수 있을까? (can, see)
________ the Great Wall of China ________ ________ from space?

4 그들의 이야기는 믿겨지지 않을지도 모른다. (may, believe)
Their stories ________ ________ ________ ________.

□ stain 얼룩
□ remove 제거하다
□ immediately 즉시

STEP 3 다음 우리말과 일치하도록 할 때, 빈칸에 들어갈 말로 알맞은 것은? 내신

이 제품은 13세 미만의 어린이에 의해서 사용되면 안 된다.
→ This product ________ by children under the age of 13.

① should not use
② should be not used
③ not should be used
④ should be used not
⑤ should not be used

□ product 제품
□ under the age of ~ 의 나이 미만의

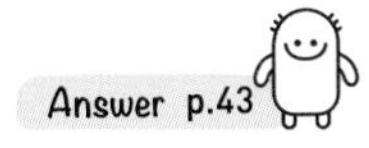

Point 063 나는 그에게 그 책을 받았다. 4형식 문장의 수동태

I was given the book by him.

- 4형식 문장은 목적어가 두 개(간접목적어와 직접목적어)이므로, 각각의 목적어를 주어로 하는 두 가지 형태의 수동태 문장을 만들 수 있다.

  They sent their customers(간접목적어) Christmas cards(직접목적어).

  → Their customers **were sent** Christmas cards (by them). (간접목적어를 주어로 하는 수동태)

  → Christmas cards **were sent** *to* their customers (by them). (직접목적어를 주어로 하는 수동태)

- 직접목적어를 주어로 할 경우에는 간접목적어 앞에 전치사를 쓴다. 전치사는 보통 to를 쓰지만 동사가 make, buy, get, cook 등의 경우는 for를 쓴다.

  TIP buy, make, get, sell, write와 같은 동사는 간접목적어를 주어로 하는 수동태로는 쓰지 않는다.

STEP 1 다음 괄호 안에서 알맞은 말을 고르시오.

1 A pretty hat was bought (to, for) the girl by her mom.

2 Interesting stories were told (to, for) the students by the teacher.

3 After he died, his will (handed, was handed) to his son.

4 His report card was shown (his parents, to his parents).

5 He (taught, was taught) the basic rules of chess by his father.

□ will 유언장
□ hand 건네주다, 넘겨주다
□ report card (학교의) 성적표, 통지표

STEP 2 다음 문장을 수동태 문장으로 바꿔 쓰시오.

1 They gave the participants snacks and drinks.
→ The participants ______________________.

2 Tom passed me the note.
→ The note ______________________.

3 The chef cooked the couple a special dish.
→ A special dish ______________________.

4 We will send you the result within 14 days.
→ The result ______________________ within 14 days.

5 The editor of *The New York Times* offered him a job.
→ He ______________________ the editor of *The New York Times*.

□ participant 참가자
□ note 쪽지
□ chef 요리사
□ dish 요리
□ editor 편집장

STEP 3 다음 빈칸에 들어갈 말로 알맞은 것은? 내신

A special desk was made ________ the boy by his grandpa.

① to ② for ③ of ④ by ⑤ of

Answer p.44
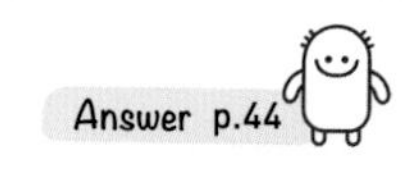

Point 064 그는 친한 친구들에게 '대장'이라고 불렸다.

He was called *Captain* by his close friends.

- 5형식 문장(주어 + 동사 + 목적어 + 목적격 보어)의 수동태를 만들 때, 능동태의 목적어는 수동태의 주어로 쓰고, 동사는 「be동사 + 과거분사」의 형태로 바꾼다. 능동태의 목적격 보어로 쓰인 명사, 형용사, to부정사는 동사 뒤에 그대로 쓴다.

His parents named him Alexander. (목적격 보어가 명사인 경우)
→ He **was named** *Alexander* by his parents.
The doctor advised him to exercise regularly. (목적격 보어가 to부정사인 경우)
→ He **was advised** *to exercise* regularly by the doctor.

STEP 1 다음 밑줄 친 부분을 바르게 고치시오.

1 The door kept open during the day.
2 Jason was told changing his plan.
3 He elected the representative by his classmates.
4 The man was forced leave the country.
5 She taught to be kind to others.

□ elect 뽑다, 선출하다
□ representative 대표
□ classmate 급우, 반 친구
□ force 강요하다

STEP 2 다음 문장을 수동태 문장으로 바꿔 쓰시오.

1 They considered Dr. Martin a great leader.
→ ______________________________
2 The manager asked me to wipe the tables.
→ ______________________________
3 They don't allow visitors to take pictures in the museum.
→ ______________________________
4 The case made the lawyer famous.
→ ______________________________

□ wipe 닦다
□ allow 허락하다
□ case 소송 (사건)

STEP 3 다음 문장을 수동태로 바르게 바꾼 것은? 내신

The teacher encouraged us to express our ideas.

① We were encouraged express our ideas by the teacher.
② To express our ideas was encouraged us by the teacher.
③ We were encouraged to express our ideas by the teacher.
④ We were encouraged expressing our ideas by the teacher.
⑤ To express our ideas was encouraged to us by the teacher.

□ encourage 격려하다
□ express 표현하다

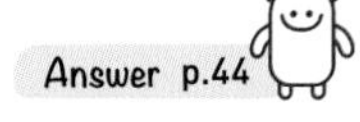
Answer p.44

Point 065 그 회의는 상사에 의해서 연기되었다.

The meeting was put off by the boss.

• 타동사 역할을 하는 동사구는 하나의 단어처럼 함께 묶어서 수동태로 바꾼다. 이때 전치사를 빠뜨리지 않도록 주의한다.

- laugh at	~을 비웃다[놀리다]	- put off	~을 미루다[연기하다]
- run over	(차가) ~을 치다	- hand in	~을 제출하다
- pay for	~을 지불하다	- deal with	~을 다루다[처리하다]
- bring up	~을 기르다	- look up to	~을 존경하다
- look after	~을 돌보다(= take care of)	- look down on	~을 얕보다[멸시하다]

A truck ran over the dog. → The dog **was run over** by a truck.

STEP 1 다음 괄호 안에서 알맞은 말을 고르시오.

1 The deer was (run, run over) by a car.

2 The bird (was taken care, was taken care of) by Maria.

3 Violence should (dealt be with, be dealt with) severely.

4 The homework (was not handed in, not was handed in) on time.

5 Will the soccer match (put off, be put off) due to the bad weather?

□ violence 폭행, 폭력
□ severely 심하게, 엄격하게
□ on time 시간을 어기지 않고, 정각에
□ due to ~때문에

STEP 2 다음 우리말과 일치하도록 괄호 안의 말을 이용하여 빈칸에 알맞은 말을 쓰시오.

1 그 강아지는 내 여동생에 의해 돌봐졌다. (look after)
The puppy ______________________ by my sister.

2 추장은 모든 마을 사람들에게 존경을 받았다. (look up to)
The chief ______________________ by all villagers.

3 깨진 유리창은 그 소년의 엄마가 변상할 것이다. (pay for)
The broken window ______________________ by the boy's mom.

4 Harry는 그의 고모에 의해 양육되었다. (bring up)
Harry ______________________ by his aunt.

5 Rudolf는 그의 빨간 코 때문에 놀림을 당했다. (laugh at)
Rudolf ______________________ because of the red nose.

□ villager 마을 사람
□ aunt 고모

STEP 3 다음 중 어법상 틀린 것은? 내신

① The trial was put off to another day.
② He was looked up to by his children.
③ He was brought up in a royal family.
④ Joseph was looked down by his brothers.
⑤ The complaint was dealt with by the manager.

□ trial 재판
□ royal 왕실의
□ complaint 불평, 항의

Answer p.45

I am interested in pop songs.

• 수동태의 행위자는 보통 by를 써서 나타내지만, in, with, at 등 다른 전치사가 쓰이기도 한다.

- be interested in	~에 관심이 있다	- be surprised at	~에 놀라다
- be covered with	~로 덮여 있다	- be scared of	~을 두려워하다
- be satisfied with	~에 만족하다	- be tired of	~에 싫증이 나다
- be made of[from]	~로 만들어지다	- be known for	~로 유명하다
- be filled with	~로 가득 차다(= be full of)	- be known to	~에게 알려지다

STEP 1 다음 괄호 안에서 알맞은 말을 고르시오.

□ smoke 연기
□ scenery 경치

1 The room was filled (of, with) smoke.
2 Some people are not interested (in, with) sports.
3 Ann was surprised (at, of) the news.
4 California is known (to, for) its beautiful scenery.
5 Her pink dress is made (of, with) silk.

STEP 2 다음 우리말과 일치하도록 괄호 안의 말을 이용하여 빈칸에 알맞은 말을 쓰시오.

□ talent 재능

1 산봉우리는 눈으로 덮여 있었다. (cover)
The mountain peak ____________ ____________ ____________ snow.

2 언젠가 너의 재능은 세상에 알려질 것이다. (know)
Someday, your talent __________ __________ __________ __________ the world.

3 Ron은 거미를 무서워한다. (scare)
Ron ____________ ____________ ____________ spiders.

4 당신은 그 결과에 만족하십니까? (satisfy)
____________ you ____________ ____________ the result?

5 나는 TV보는 것에 싫증이 난다. (tire)
I ____________ ____________ ____________ watching TV.

STEP 3 다음 빈칸에 들어갈 말이 순서대로 짝지어진 것은? 내신

□ Belgium 벨기에
□ adventure 모험

• Belgium is known ________ its chocolate.
• My life is full ________ adventures.

① to – of ② for – with ③ of – of
④ for – of ⑤ to – with

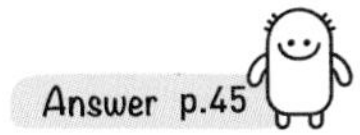

[01~02] 다음 빈칸에 들어갈 말로 알맞은 것을 고르시오.

Point 059

01

The action movie was ________ by many boys.

① see ② saw ③ seeing
④ seen ⑤ to see

Point 060

02

His name will ________ forever.

① remember ② remembers
③ remembering ④ to remember
⑤ be remembered

Point 057

03 다음 빈칸에 들어갈 말이 순서대로 짝지어진 것은?

• My mother ________ the muffins.
• The school ________ in 1988.

① baked – was building
② baked – was built
③ was baked – was built
④ was baked – was building
⑤ was baking – built

Point 057

04 다음 밑줄 친 부분 중 생략할 수 있는 것은?

① The letter was written by Dave.
② The trees were cut down by the farmer.
③ Your bags will be carried by the bell boy.
④ The buildings were destroyed by the bomb.
⑤ The painting was stolen by someone yesterday.

[05~06] 다음 우리말을 영어로 바르게 옮긴 것을 고르시오.

Point 059

05

그 하얀 말을 Victoria가 탔다.

① The white horse rides Victoria.
② Victoria is ridden by the white horse.
③ The white horse is ridden by Victoria.
④ Victoria was ridden by the white horse.
⑤ The white horse was ridden by Victoria.

Point 061

06

옥수수는 너의 삼촌에 의해 재배되니?

① Did corns grew by your uncle?
② Are corns grew by your uncle?
③ Do corns grown by your uncle?
④ Are corns grown by your uncle?
⑤ Are corns are grown by your uncle?

Point 058

07 다음 대화의 빈칸에 들어갈 말로 알맞은 것을 모두 고르면?

A: What happened in Mexico?
B: There was a strong earthquake, so many people ________.

① died ② were died
③ killed ④ were killed
⑤ were killing

Point 066

08 다음 빈칸에 공통으로 들어갈 말로 알맞은 것은?

• The table was covered ________ dust.
• I'm satisfied ________ my life.

① at ② on ③ by
④ from ⑤ with

고난도
Point 065
09 다음 문장을 수동태로 바르게 바꾼 것은?

Many students looked up to the teacher.

① The teacher was looked up many students.
② The teacher was looked up to many students.
③ The teacher was looked up by many students.
④ The teacher was looked up to by many students.
⑤ The teacher was looked up by to many students.

Point 063
10 다음 중 수동태로의 전환이 바르지 않은 것은?

① My sister cooked me lunch.
→ Lunch was cooked for me by my sister.
② Dad made me a doll house.
→ A doll house was made for me by Dad.
③ I showed him my photo album.
→ My photo album was shown to him by me.
④ She handed me the credit card.
→ I was handed the credit card by her.
⑤ We didn't give him another chance.
→ Another chance wasn't given for him by us.

[11~12] 다음 중 어법상 틀린 것을 고르시오.

Point 063
11 ① The invitation was sent to me.
② He was bought the car by his dad.
③ The poem was read to the students by Mr. Park.
④ I was given a present by my family on Christmas.
⑤ Mike was taught to think twice before doing something.

Point 064
12 ① The baby was named Amy.
② The vegetables are kept fresh.
③ I was allowed use the computer.
④ He was elected the president by his members.
⑤ She was warned to escape to another country.

서술형

Point 063
13 다음 문장을 주어진 말로 시작하는 수동태 문장으로 바꿔 쓰시오.

Jason told us the good news.

(1) We ______________________.
(2) The good news ______________________.

[14~15] 다음 문장을 수동태 문장으로 바꿔 쓰시오.

Point 061
14 Did Mr. Brown deliver the letter?

→ ______________________

Point 061
15 I didn't open the door.

→ ______________________

Point 062
16 (A)와 (B)에서 알맞은 단어를 각각 하나씩 골라 다음 우리말과 일치하도록 문장을 완성하시오. (단, 필요하면 형태를 바꿀 것)

(A)	(B)
will	recycle
can	hand in
should	break

(1) 신문지는 여러 가지 방식으로 재활용될 수 있다.
Newspapers ______________ in many ways.
(2) 이 유리는 쉽게 깨지지 않을 것이다.
This glass ______________ easily.
(3) 너의 보고서는 4월 30일까지 제출되어야 한다.
Your report ______________ by April 30.

중요

Point 057

01 다음 우리말과 일치하도록 할 때, 빈칸에 들어갈 말로 알맞은 것은?

> 지구의 날은 매년 4월 22일에 기념된다.
> → Earth Day _________ on April 22 every year.

① celebrates ② celebrating
③ celebrated ④ is celebrated
⑤ is celebrating

[02~04] 다음 문장을 수동태로 바르게 바꾼 것을 고르시오.

Point 061

02

> Most Indians don't eat beef.

① Beef is not ate by most Indians.
② Beef doesn't eat by most Indians.
③ Beef is not eaten by most Indians.
④ Beef is eaten not by most Indians.
⑤ Beef doesn't eaten by most Indians.

Point 061

03

> Did he follow you?

① Was he followed you?
② Were you follow by him?
③ Was he followed by you?
④ Were you followed by him?
⑤ Were you following by him?

중요

Point 064

04

> They advised me to start my own business.

① I was advised start my own business.
② I was advised to start my own business.
③ I was advised started my own business.
④ I was advised starting my own business.
⑤ I was advised to starting my own business.

Point 063

05 다음 빈칸에 들어갈 말이 순서대로 짝지어진 것은?

> • A soccer ball was bought _________ the children.
> • The camera was lent _________ me by my brother.

① to – to ② for – to ③ for – for
④ to – for ⑤ of – for

Point 062

06 다음 빈칸에 들어갈 말로 알맞지 않은 것은?

> This project _________ be done by the day after tomorrow.

① can ② may ③ has
④ must ⑤ should

Point 057

07 다음 밑줄 친 부분 중 어법상 옳은 것은?

① The Eiffel Tower built in 1889.
② Did the room cleaned by Mom?
③ Peter was made a house for his dog.
④ The treasures were found by the captain.
⑤ The bench painted yellow by the students.

Point 066

08 (A), (B), (C)의 괄호 안에서 알맞은 것끼리 바르게 짝지은 것은?

> • The desk is made (A)[of/by] wood.
> • The jar was filled (B)[of/with] cookies.
> • Kevin was tired (C)[in/of] eating the same thing.

	(A)		(B)		(C)
①	of	–	of	–	of
②	by	–	with	–	of
③	of	–	with	–	in
④	by	–	of	–	in
⑤	of	–	with	–	of

Point 063

09 다음 문장을 수동태로 바르게 바꾼 것을 모두 고르면?

Fred gave Lilly the flowers.

① Lilly was given the flowers by Fred.
② Lilly was given to the flowers by Fred.
③ Lilly was given for the flowers by Fred.
④ The flowers were given to Lilly by Fred.
⑤ The flowers were given for Lilly by Fred.

[10~12] 다음 중 어법상 틀린 것을 고르시오.

Point 058

10 ① He was found dead.
② It was happened yesterday.
③ The rain was expected to stop soon.
④ The new sneakers were bought for him.
⑤ The money was passed to him by his uncle.

Point 065

11 ① The trip should be put off.
② She was advised to get some rest.
③ I was ordered to pay a fine by the judge.
④ The boy is called a genius by his friends.
⑤ My grandma was taken care by my mom.

고난도 Point 066

12 ① Larry is scared for heights.
② Are you interested in magic?
③ Everyone seemed to be full of hope.
④ The durian is known for its strong smell.
⑤ His classmates were surprised at his grades.

서술형

Point 060, 064

13 다음 우리말과 일치하도록 괄호 안의 말을 이용하여 빈칸에 알맞은 말을 쓰시오.

담요가 너를 따뜻하게 유지해 줄 것이다. (keep, warm)

→ You will ____________________ the blanket.

Point 064

14 다음 문장을 수동태 문장으로 바꿔 쓰시오.

My parents persuaded me to take part in the contest.

→ ______________________________________

[15~16] 다음 대화의 흐름에 맞도록 괄호 안의 말을 이용하여 빈칸에 알맞은 말을 쓰시오.

Point 061

15

A: Did you get the invitation to the party? B: No, I ________ ________ ________ to the party. (invite)

Point 062

16

A: This story ________ ________ ________ ________ to anybody else. (must, tell) B: Okay. I'll keep it to myself.

Grammar Review 핵심 정리

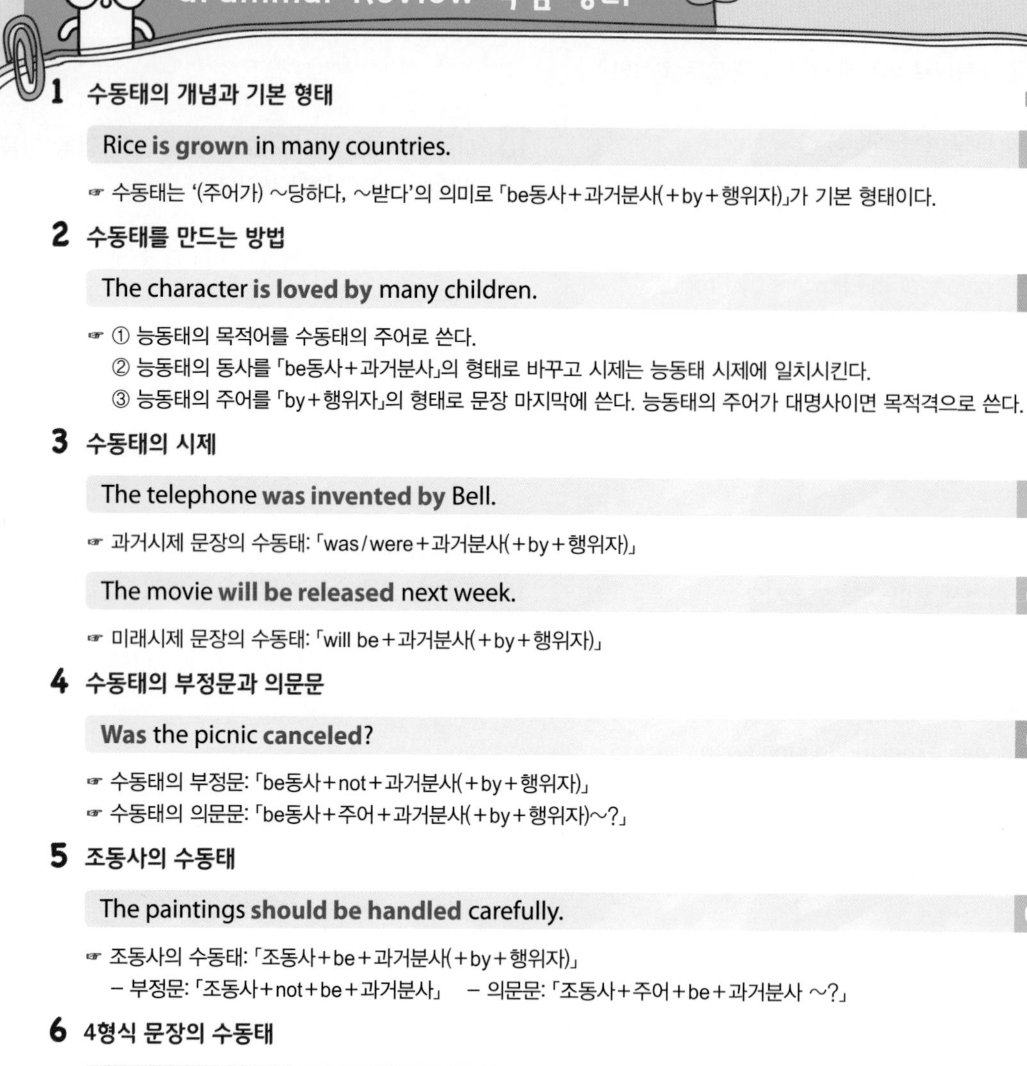

Point

1 수동태의 개념과 기본 형태

Rice **is grown** in many countries. 057

☞ 수동태는 '(주어가) ~당하다, ~받다'의 의미로 「be동사+과거분사(+by+행위자)」가 기본 형태이다.

2 수동태를 만드는 방법

The character **is loved by** many children. 058

☞ ① 능동태의 목적어를 수동태의 주어로 쓴다.
② 능동태의 동사를 「be동사+과거분사」의 형태로 바꾸고 시제는 능동태 시제에 일치시킨다.
③ 능동태의 주어를 「by+행위자」의 형태로 문장 마지막에 쓴다. 능동태의 주어가 대명사이면 목적격으로 쓴다.

3 수동태의 시제

The telephone **was invented by** Bell. 059

☞ 과거시제 문장의 수동태: 「was/were+과거분사(+by+행위자)」

The movie **will be released** next week. 060

☞ 미래시제 문장의 수동태: 「will be+과거분사(+by+행위자)」

4 수동태의 부정문과 의문문

Was the picnic **canceled**? 061

☞ 수동태의 부정문: 「be동사+not+과거분사(+by+행위자)」
☞ 수동태의 의문문: 「be동사+주어+과거분사(+by+행위자)~?」

5 조동사의 수동태

The paintings **should be handled** carefully. 062

☞ 조동사의 수동태: 「조동사+be+과거분사(+by+행위자)」
– 부정문: 「조동사+not+be+과거분사」 – 의문문: 「조동사+주어+be+과거분사 ~?」

6 4형식 문장의 수동태

I **was given** the book by him. 063

☞ 간접목적어와 직접목적어를 사용하는 두 가지 형태의 수동태 문장을 만들 수 있다.
☞ 직접목적어를 주어로 할 경우 간접목적어 앞에 쓰는 전치사에 유의한다. 보통 to를 쓰지만, 동사가 make, buy, get, cook 등의 경우에는 for를 쓴다.

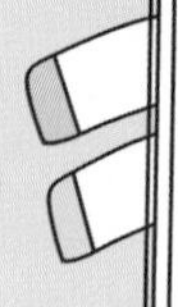

7 5형식 문장의 수동태

He **was called** *Captain* by his close friends. 064

☞ 목적어와 목적격 보어가 있는 5형식 문장은 수동태를 만들 때, 목적격 보어를 동사 뒤에 그대로 둔다.

8 동사구의 수동태

The meeting **was put off** by the boss. 065

☞ 타동사 역할을 하는 동사구를 하나의 단어처럼 함께 묶어서 수동태로 바꾼다.

9 by 이외의 전치사를 사용하는 수동태

I **am interested in** pop songs. 066

☞ be filled with, be scared of, be surprised at, be covered with, be tired of, be satisfied with 등이 있다.

LESSON 08

대명사

Point 067 나는 손목시계를 잃어버려서, 하나 사야 한다.

I lost my watch, so I have to buy one.

- 부정대명사: 정해지지 않은 불특정의 사람이나 사물을 가리키는 대명사로 another, all, both, each 등 일부 부정대명사는 명사와 함께 쓰여 형용사 역할을 하기도 한다.
- one은 앞에 나온 명사와 같은 종류의 사람이나 사물을 가리킨다. 복수형은 ones로 나타낸다.
  A: Is there a bank around here? B: Yes, there's **one** around the corner. (one = a bank)
  I like these pants. Are there bigger **ones**? (ones = pants)
- one 앞에 형용사가 올 경우 「**a(n)/the + 형용사 + one**」의 형태로 쓴다.
  My father sold his old car, and bought **a new one.**

TIP it은 앞에 나온 특정한 대상을 가리킨다.
I like your new shirt. Where did you buy **it**? (it = your new shirt)

STEP 1 다음 밑줄 친 부분을 바르게 고치시오.

□ ruler 자

1 I need a ruler. Do you have it?
2 This tea is too hot. I can't drink one.
3 The bus is full. Let's wait for the next it.
4 I saw a movie. One was boring.
5 My shoes were too small, so my mom bought me new one.

STEP 2 다음 빈칸에 one, ones, it 중 알맞은 말을 쓰시오.

□ dirty 더러운
□ clean 깨끗한
□ work 작동하다

1 This towel is dirty. Please give me a clean ____________.
2 I can't find my key. Did you see ____________?
3 This computer doesn't work. Can I use that ____________?
4 I like her earrings. I want to have the same ____________.
5 Can I borrow a pen? I'll return ____________ by tomorrow.

STEP 3 다음 대화의 빈칸에 들어갈 말로 알맞은 것은? 내신

A: Would you like to have a sandwich?
B: No, thanks. I've already had ________.

① it ② one
③ any ④ ones
⑤ another

Answer p.49

Point 068 Mike는 햄버거 하나를 먹고 또 하나를 주문했다.

Mike ate a hamburger and ordered another.

- another는 an과 other가 결합된 말로 '또 (다른) 하나(의)'라는 뜻이다. 앞에 나온 명사와 같은 종류의 또 다른 것을 가리킬 때 쓴다. 대명사와 형용사로 모두 쓰인다.
  This umbrella is broken. Please give me **another**. (대명사)
  How about **another** cup of coffee? (형용사)

TIP '앞에 나온 명사와 같은 종류의 또 다른 것'을 나타낼 때는 another를 쓰고, '막연한 다른 것들'을 나타낼 때는 others를 쓴다.

STEP 1 다음 괄호 안에서 알맞은 말을 고르시오.

1 Saying something is one thing but doing it is (one, another).
2 If you don't like this plan, I have (one, another).
3 Can you exchange this pen for (another, other) one?
4 Don't speak ill of (another, others) behind their backs.
5 The music ended, but the musician began to play (another, others) song.

□ exchange 교환하다
□ speak ill of ~ ~를 험담하다
□ back 등, 뒤
□ end 끝나다
□ musician 음악가

STEP 2 다음 우리말과 일치하도록 괄호 안의 말을 바르게 배열하시오.

1 주스를 한 잔 더 마실 수 있을까요? (another, juice, glass, have, of)
Can I ______________________________?

2 우리가 보려던 영화는 상영을 하고 있지 않아서, 우리는 또 다른 영화를 봤다.
(another, we, movie, watched)
The movie we wanted to see was not showing, so ____________________.

3 이 수학 문제를 푸는 또 다른 방법을 아니? (to, this, another, solve, way, math problem)
Do you know ______________________________?

4 이 장난감 자동차는 너무 비싸요. 다른 것을 보여주세요. (me, another, show)
This toy car is too expensive. ____________________.

5 그는 이 일을 그만두고 다른 회사로 옮겨갔다. (another, company, to, moved)
He quit the job, and ____________________.

□ show (영화를) 상영하다
□ toy 장난감

STEP 3 다음 중 빈칸에 another가 들어갈 수 없는 것은? 내신

① There is ________ door on the left side.
② My father wants to live in ________ country.
③ I used up all the paper. Get me ________ piece of paper.
④ After the exhibition, the artist is going to hold ________.
⑤ You have so many magazines in your bag. Can I read ________?

□ use up 다 써버리다
□ exhibition 전시회
□ hold 개최하다, 열다
□ magazine 잡지

Answer p.49

Point 069 그들 둘 다 내 친구들이다. 부정대명사 all, both

Both of them *are* my friends.

- all과 both는 대명사와 형용사로 모두 쓰인다. all은 단 · 복수 모두 가능한 반면, both는 항상 복수 취급한다.
- all이 사람을 나타낼 때는 복수, 사물이나 상황을 나타낼 때는 단수 취급한다. 「**all + (of) + 명사**」로 쓰인 경우에는 동사를 명사의 수에 일치시킨다.

all	모두, 모든(것, 사람들)	**All** *were* excited at the news. **All** (of) the people *look* happy.
both	둘 다, 양쪽(의) – 복수 취급	**Both** *are* mine. **Both** (of) her sons *are* doctors.

STEP 1 다음 괄호 안에서 알맞은 말을 고르시오.

1 Don't worry. (All, Both) is going to be okay.
2 All the famous movie stars (was, were) at the awards ceremony.
3 Both of the seats (is, are) empty.
4 I have two older sisters. (All, Both) of them are flight attendants.
5 (All, Both) the people in the building were rescued.

□ worry 걱정하다
□ awards ceremony 시상식
□ flight attendant 승무원
□ rescue 구출하다

STEP 2 다음 우리말과 일치하도록 괄호 안의 말을 바르게 배열하시오.

1 모두가 그 새로운 계획에 동의했다. (on, agreed, new, all, the, plan)
____

2 나는 그 영화 두 편을 다 봤다. (I, the movies, watched, both, of)
____

3 그는 자기 방의 모든 책을 다 읽었다. (he, in his room, all, the books, read)
____

4 우리 둘 다 네 비밀을 알고 있다. (both, of, secret, know, us, your)
____

5 우물 속의 모든 물이 오염되었다. (in, was, the water, the, well, all, polluted)
____

□ agree 동의하다
□ secret 비밀
□ well 우물
□ pollute 오염시키다

STEP 3 다음 중 어법상 틀린 것은? 내신

① I love both my parents.
② All my money were stolen.
③ All dancers went up on the stage.
④ Both of these books are best sellers.
⑤ All the students in my class like art class.

□ steal 훔치다(-stole-stolen)

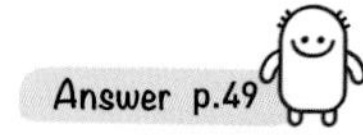

Each of us *has* our own role.

- each는 「**each + 단수 명사**」 또는 「**each of + 복수 명사**」의 형태로 쓰이며 동사는 단수 취급한다.
- every는 「**every + 단수 명사**」 형태로 쓰이며 동사는 단수 취급한다.

each	각각(의), 각자(의)	**Each** of the toys *has* a different shape. **Each** family member *has* a different schedule.
every	모든	**Every** country *has* its own traditional culture.

TIP 「**every** + 숫자 + 기간」은 '~마다'의 의미이다.
The World Cup is held **every four years**.

STEP 1 다음 괄호 안에서 알맞은 말을 고르시오.

1 (All, Every) dog has its day.
2 Each student (have, has) his own computer.
3 Each of the group (member, members) has great musical talent.
4 (Each, Every) of you should do your best.
5 Each of the flowers (have, has) a unique scent.

□ do one's best 최선을 다하다
□ unique 독특한, 고유의
□ scent 향기

STEP 2 다음 우리말과 일치하도록 괄호 안의 말을 바르게 배열하시오.

1 모든 규칙에는 예외가 있다. (rule, has, an exception, every)

____

2 각 개인은 자신의 일이 있다. (has, person, his own job, each)

____

3 기차는 매 십 분마다 떠난다. (every, the train, ten minutes, leaves)

____

4 각각의 가능한 답변들이 문제 아래에 제시되어 있다.
(is, each, the possible answers, of, below, the questions, shown)

____

□ exception 예외
□ possible 가능한
□ below ~아래에

STEP 3 다음 중 어법상 틀린 것은? 내신

① Every bus were full of passengers.
② Each of them improved their grades.
③ Each language has its own grammar.
④ Each of the children is wearing a cap.
⑤ Her family travels abroad every five years.

□ passenger 승객
□ improve 향상시키다
□ grade 성적
□ grammar 문법

Answer p.50

Point 071 몇몇 사람들은 굶주림에 죽어가고 있다.

Some are dying of hunger.

• some과 any는 모두 대명사와 형용사 둘 다로 쓰이며, 다음과 같은 의미를 가진다.

some	몇몇(의), 약간(의)	**Some** are still working in the office. There is **some** water in the bottle.
any	약간(의), 조금(의)	It's not **any** of your business. If you have **any** questions, please ask me.

• some은 주로 긍정문에, any는 주로 부정문, 의문문, 조건문에 쓰인다.

TIP some이 의문문에 쓰이면 권유나 요청의 의미를 나타내고, any가 긍정문에 쓰이면 '어떤 ~라도' 라는 의미이다.

STEP 1 다음 괄호 안에서 알맞은 말을 고르시오.

1 There are (any, some) people in the room.
2 I don't need (any, some) of your help.
3 Would you like (any, some) more cake?
4 Are there (any, some) trains leaving for Busan?
5 (Any, Some) of the food is left.

STEP 2 다음 우리말과 일치하도록 괄호 안의 말을 바르게 배열하시오.

□ prepare 준비하다
□ vacation 휴가, 방학

1 두 시 이후면 어떤 시간이라도 괜찮다. (after, is, any, fine, 2 o'clock, time)

____

2 내가 약간의 파스타를 준비했다. (prepared, I, pasta, some)

____

3 경연 대회에 대한 어떤 정보가 필요하니?
(you, any, do, about, information, the, need, contest)

____

4 운동을 좀 하는 게 어떠니? (do, why, some, you, don't, exercise)

____

5 나는 휴가 계획이 전혀 없다. (plans, for, I, the, don't, any, have, vacation)

____

STEP 3 다음 빈칸에 들어갈 말이 나머지 넷과 다른 것은? 내신

□ chat 담소를 나누다, 수다 떨다

① Will you have ________ snacks?
② I had ________ gimbap for lunch.
③ I have ________ time to chat with you.
④ There are ________ music files on my cell phone.
⑤ I don't have ________ money to buy the camera.

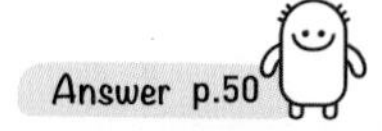

Point 072 어떤 사람들은 봄을 좋아하고, 다른 사람들은 가을을 좋아한다.

Some like spring, and others like fall.

• 「one ~ the other …」는 두 사람[사물]을 차례로 가리킬 때 쓰고, 「some ~ others …」는 불특정한 수의 사람[사물]을 대조할 때 쓴다.

one ~ the other …	(둘 중의) 하나는 ~, 나머지 하나는 …	**One** of her two sons is a lawyer, and **the other** is a doctor.
some ~ others …	어떤 것[사람]들은 ~, 다른 어떤 것[사람]들은 …	**Some** played soccer, and **others** watched.

TIP 셋 이상일 경우 하나는 one, 다른 하나는 another, 나머지는 the other(s)로 지칭한다.

STEP 1 다음 괄호 안에서 알맞은 말을 고르시오.

1 Some people were killed and (the other, others) were wounded in the war.

2 Among my club members, some join the camp and (others, the others) don't.

3 I have two aunts. One lives in Canada, and (another, the other) lives in New Zealand.

4 I have two after-school lessons. (One, Some) is dance and the other is badminton.

5 She can play three musical instruments. One is the piano, (another, other) is the cello, and the other is the guitar.

□ war 전쟁
□ wounded 부상을 입은, 다친
□ musical instrument 악기

STEP 2 다음 우리말과 일치하도록 빈칸에 알맞은 대명사를 쓰시오.

1 어떤 동물들은 털이 있지만, 다른 동물들은 그렇지 않다.
______ animals have hair, but ______ don't.

2 민지는 두 개의 선물을 받았다. 하나는 인형이고, 나머지 하나는 가방이었다.
Minji got two presents. ______ was a doll and ______ was a bag.

3 서류 중 일부는 캐비닛 안에 있고, 나머지는 책상 위에 있다.
______ of the documents are in the cabinet, and ______ are on the desk.

□ hair 털
□ doll 인형
□ document 문서, 서류

STEP 3 다음 빈칸에 들어갈 말이 순서대로 짝지어진 것은? 내신

I bought four pens. One is a red, ______ is a blue, and ______ are black.

① some – others
② the other – others
③ another – others
④ another – the others
⑤ the other – another

Answer p.51

Point 073 소라와 민수는 서로 좋아한다.

Sora and Minsu like each other.

- each other와 one another는 둘 다 '서로'의 뜻으로 두 사람 이상의 행동이나 감정이 서로 연관되어 있을 때 쓰는 표현이다.

each other	서로 (둘 일 때)	The two teams are facing **each other**.
one another	서로 (셋 이상 일 때)	We should be polite to **one another**.

STEP 1 다음 괄호 안에서 알맞은 말을 고르시오.

1 All my classmates are friendly with (each other, one another).
2 Both of us need to help (each other, one another).
3 The two cars crashed into (each other, another)
4 People use e-mail to keep in touch with (one another, another)
5 How did the couple meet (each other, one another)?

□ friendly 친절한, 우호적인
□ crash into ~와 충돌하다
□ keep in touch with ~와 연락하다

STEP 2 다음 우리말과 일치하도록 괄호 안의 말을 이용하여 빈칸에 알맞은 말을 쓰시오.

1 나의 형과 나는 많은 면에서 서로 다르다. (differ from)
My brother and I ______________________ in many ways.

2 동물들은 서로 의사소통 할 수 있다. (communicate with)
Animals can ______________________.

3 나의 세 마리 햄스터들은 항상 서로 싸운다. (fight with)
My three hamsters always ______________________.

4 그 팀의 구성원들은 서로를 만나본 적이 없다. (meet)
The team members haven't ______________________.

5 두 명의 권투 선수들은 오랫동안 서로를 쳐다보았다. (look at)
The two boxers ______________________ for a long time.

□ differ from ~와 다르다
□ communicate 의사소통하다
□ boxer 권투 선수

STEP 3 다음 빈칸에 공통으로 들어갈 말로 알맞은 것은? 내신

- Two people walked into ________ other.
- ________ of the children was satisfied with their gifts.

① one[One] ② all[All]
③ each[Each] ④ another[Another]
⑤ every[Every]

□ walk into (걸어가다가) ~에 부딪치다

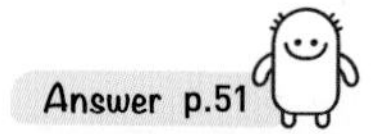

Point 074 그녀는 거울 속의 자신을 보았다.

She looked at herself in the mirror.

- 재귀대명사는 인칭대명사의 소유격이나 목적격에 -self(단수)나 -selves(복수)를 붙인 형태로 '~ 자신' 이라는 뜻이다.
- 동사나 전치사의 목적어가 주어와 같은 사람이나 사물을 지칭할 때, 즉 주어가 주어 자신에게 행위를 할 때 목적어로 재귀대명사를 쓴다. 이것을 재귀 용법이라 칭하며 재귀 용법으로 쓰인 재귀대명사는 생략할 수 없다.
  Mina made **herself** a sandwich. (동사의 목적어)
  Jason is too young to take care of **himself**. (전치사의 목적어)

STEP 1 다음 밑줄 친 부분을 바르게 고치시오.

1 Take good care of you.
2 We were not ourself for some time.
3 I'm not angry with you. I'm angry with me.
4 The interviewer asked myself about my future plans.
5 Yuna is selfish. She always puts her before others.

□ take good care of ~를 잘 돌보다
□ angry with ~에게 화가 난
□ interviewer 면접관
□ selfish 이기적인

STEP 2 다음 우리말과 일치하도록 괄호 안의 말을 이용하여 빈칸에 알맞은 말을 쓰시오.

1 그것은 네 잘못이 아니다. 스스로를 탓하지 마라. (blame)
It's not your fault. Don't ______________________.

2 그는 실수로 칼에 베였다. (cut)
______________________ with a knife by accident.

3 이 선생님은 학생들에게 자기 자신을 소개했다. (introduce)
Ms. Lee ______________________ to the students.

4 그 배우는 35살의 나이에 자살했다. (kill)
The actor ______________________ at the age of 35.

5 나의 할아버지께서는 혼잣말을 하시곤 했다. (talk to)
My grandfather would ______________________.

□ blame 탓하다, 비난하다
□ by accident 실수로, 우연히

STEP 3 다음 빈칸에 들어갈 말이 나머지 넷과 다른 것은? 내신

① The artists called ________ Romantics.
② Heaven helps those who help ________.
③ The clouds spread ________ over the sky.
④ The party members argued among ________.
⑤ They got lost, but there was nobody to help ________.

□ spread 펼치다
□ party 정당
□ argue 말다툼하다
□ get lost 길을 잃다

Answer p.51

Point 075 내가 직접 피자를 만들었다.

I myself made a pizza.

- 재귀대명사가 주어, 목적어, 보어와 동격으로 쓰여 그 말을 강조할 때 강조 용법이라 하며, 이때 재귀대명사를 생략해도 문장이 성립된다.

  The teacher (**herself**) spoke to me. (주어 강조)
  I wrote the report (**itself**). (목적어 강조)
  The dirty beggar was the king (**himself**). (보어 강조)

  TIP 주어를 강조하는 재귀대명사는 주어 다음이나 문장의 끝에 올 수 있다.

STEP 1 다음 문장에서 생략 가능한 부분에 밑줄을 긋고, 문장을 해석하시오.

□ handle 다루다, 처리하다
□ knit 짜다, 뜨개질하다
□ scarf 목도리

1 I myself designed and built the building.
2 I shook hands with the President himself.
3 I think he can handle the problem himself.
4 Let's clean the classroom ourselves.
5 My mother knitted the scarf herself.

STEP 2 다음 우리말과 일치하도록 괄호 안의 말을 바르게 배열하시오.

□ cook 요리사
□ recipe 요리법, 조리법
□ customer 고객

1 저 자신도 이곳이 처음이라 안내를 해드릴 수가 없습니다. (here, myself, new)
I can't take you on a tour because I am ______________________.

2 그 요리사는 바로 그 비밀 요리법을 나에게 말해주었다. (itself, me, the secret recipe)
The cook told ______________________.

3 너는 직접 그 프로젝트를 끝낼 수 있다. (the project, finish, yourself)
You can ______________________.

4 그 고객은 가게 지배인과 직접 이야기하기를 원했다.
(the store manager, to, speak, himself)
The customer wanted to ______________________.

5 나는 뮤지컬 자체는 좋지 않았지만, 음악이 마음에 들었다. (didn't, the musical, I, like, itself)
______________________, but I liked the music.

STEP 3 다음 밑줄 친 부분 중 쓰임이 나머지 넷과 다른 것은? 내신

□ genius 천재
□ cause 일으키다
□ accident 사고

① He thinks himself a genius.
② Did you write the poem yourself?
③ A bus driver caused the accident itself.
④ We ourselves will take care of the problem.
⑤ The special guest was the famous actor himself.

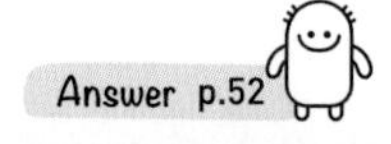

Point 076 문이 저절로 열렸다.

The door opened of itself.

- 재귀대명사를 포함한 관용적인 표현에는 다음과 같은 것들이 있다.

- by oneself	혼자서 (= alone)	- beside oneself	제정신이 아닌
- for oneself	스스로	- behave oneself	바르게 처신하다
- in itself	본래, 그 자체가	- enjoy oneself	즐거운 시간을 보내다
- of oneself	저절로	- help oneself	(~을) 마음대로 먹다
- between ourselves	우리끼리 이야기지만	- make oneself at home	편안히 있다

STEP 1 다음 괄호 안에서 알맞은 말을 고르시오.

□ polite 공손한, 예의바른

1 Minho is eating lunch (by, for) himself.
2 I made some cake. Help (itself, yourself).
3 We enjoyed (us, ourselves) at the party.
4 I finished the homework (of, for) myself.
5 Sujin is polite. She always behaves (her, herself).

STEP 2 다음 우리말과 일치하도록 빈칸에 알맞은 말을 쓰시오.

□ anger 분노
□ make it 성공하다, 해내다

1 그 어린 소녀는 스스로 옷을 갈아입었다.
The little girl changed her clothes ___________ ___________.

2 그는 홀로 전국을 여행했다.
He traveled around the world ___________ ___________.

3 그녀는 분노로 제정신이 아니었다.
She was ___________ ___________ with anger.

4 우리끼리 얘기지만, 그는 성공하지 못할 것이다.
___________ ___________, he won't make it.

5 계획 자체는 나쁘지 않다.
The plan ___________ ___________ is all right.

STEP 3 다음 빈칸에 들어갈 말이 순서대로 짝지어진 것은? 내신

□ take off (옷을) 벗다

- Take off your coat and _________ yourself at home.
- Please _________ yourself to anything you'd like.

① make – help
② help – enjoy
③ make – behave
④ help – make
⑤ enjoy – behave

Answer p.52

Point 067, 072

01 다음 빈칸에 공통으로 들어갈 말로 알맞은 것은?

- I lost my cell phone. I have to buy ________.
- I have two sisters. ________ is tall, and the other is short.

① one[One] ② any[Any] ③ each[Each] ④ another[Another] ⑤ some[Some]

중요

Point 075

02 다음 밑줄 친 부분의 쓰임이 보기 와 같은 것은?

보기 Let's solve this problem ourselves.

① I taught myself how to swim.
② You should believe in yourself.
③ He said to himself, "I can do it."
④ I decorated the Christmas tree myself.
⑤ Can you introduce yourself in English?

Point 071

03 다음 빈칸에 들어갈 말이 나머지 넷과 다른 것은?

① I don't have ________ money.
② Why don't we get ________ rest?
③ If there is ________ problem, I'll let you know.
④ Are there ________ tickets left for tonight's show?
⑤ Sora just looked around, and didn't buy ________ clothes.

Point 070

04 다음 우리말을 영어로 바르게 옮긴 것은?

각 나라마다 자신의 국기를 가지고 있다.

① All country has its own flag.
② Each country has its own flag.
③ Every country has its own flag.
④ Each countries have their own flags.
⑤ All the countries have their own flags.

Point 069

05 다음 우리말과 일치하도록 할 때, 빈칸에 들어갈 말로 알맞은 것은?

왕들은 매일 모든 종류의 맛있는 음식을 먹었다.
→ Kings ate ________ kinds of delicious food every day.

① all ② every ③ each ④ both ⑤ some

Point 074

06 다음 우리말을 영작할 때, 어법상 틀린 것은?

그녀는 겨우 다섯 살이지만 매일 아침 혼자 옷을 입는다.
→ She is only five years old, but she dresses her every morning.

① years ② but ③ dresses ④ her ⑤ every

[07~08] 다음 빈칸에 들어갈 말로 알맞은 것을 고르시오.

Point 067

07

The black sneakers don't belong to me. The white ________ are mine.

① one ② ones ③ those ④ others ⑤ the others

Point 072

08

Some students like English and ________ like math.

① any ② all ③ every ④ others ⑤ the other

Answer p.52

[09~10] 다음 대화의 빈칸에 들어갈 말로 알맞은 것을 고르시오.

Point 069

09

A: Which pen will you take, the red one or the blue one?
B: I'll take _________ of them.

① one ② any ③ another
④ both ⑤ some

Point 068

10

A: I don't think this blue sweater goes well with me.
B: Don't worry. We have this sweater in _________ color.

① it ② others ③ one
④ the other ⑤ another

Point 070

11 다음 중 어법상 틀린 것은?

① Both girls are my nieces.
② Every moment is precious.
③ All the fans were happy to see the singer.
④ Each student is wearing a school uniform.
⑤ Each of my brothers have their own room.

Point 076

12 다음 두 문장이 같은 뜻이 되도록 할 때, 빈칸에 들어갈 말로 알맞은 것은?

Mike makes his study plans on his own.
= Mike makes his study plans _________ himself.

① in ② for ③ of
④ beside ⑤ between

서술형

Point 069

13 다음 문장을 바르게 고쳐 쓰시오.

All of us has a duty to protect the environment.

→ ______________________________

Point 076

14 우리말과 일치하도록 괄호 안의 말을 이용하여 빈칸에 알맞은 말을 쓰시오.

우리는 그 콘서트에서 좋은 시간을 보냈다. (enjoy)

→ We _________ _________ at the concert.

[15~16] 다음은 한 부부의 자녀들의 직업을 나타낸 표이다. 다음 표를 보고 물음에 답하시오.

first daughter	teacher
second daughter	teacher
first son	vet
second son	banker

Point 069

15

조건 1 both로 시작할 것
조건 2 총 4단어로 쓸 것

A: What do their daughters do?
B: ______________________________

Point 072

16

조건 1 one으로 시작할 것
조건 2 총 10단어로 쓸 것

A: What do their sons do?
B: ______________________________

02회 내신 적중 실전 문제

Point 069

01 다음 빈칸에 들어갈 말이 순서대로 짝지어진 것은?

- All the students ________ wearing glasses.
- All the money ________ in the safe.

① are – is ② is – is ③ are – are ④ is – are ⑤ are – were

Point 069

02 다음 우리말을 영어로 바르게 옮긴 것은?

그녀의 개는 두 마리 다 푸들이다.

① Both her dog is a poodle.
② Both her dogs are poodles.
③ Both her dogs is poodles.
④ Both of her dog is a poodle.
⑤ Both of her dog are poodles.

고난도 Point 075

03 다음 밑줄 친 부분 중 쓰임이 나머지 넷과 다른 것은?

① I myself painted the picture.
② She burnt herself on the stove.
③ Socrates said, "Know yourself."
④ The actor killed himself yesterday.
⑤ You are old enough to look after yourself.

Point 069

04 다음 빈칸에 들어갈 말이 나머지 넷과 다른 것은?

① Every person ________ unique.
② All ________ well that ends well.
③ Each girl ________ carrying a backpack.
④ All the people ________ equal before the law.
⑤ Each of us ________ in charge of one part of the work.

Point 076

05 다음 대화의 빈칸에 들어갈 말로 알맞은 것은?

A: Help ________ to some more cake.
B: No, thanks. I'm full.

① me ② you ③ myself ④ yourself ⑤ ourselves

Point 067

06 다음 빈칸에 들어갈 말이 순서대로 짝지어진 것은?

I bought a pencil yesterday, but I lost ________. I need to buy ________.

① one – one ② it – one ③ one – another ④ it – another ⑤ another – one

[07~08] 다음 빈칸에 들어갈 말로 알맞은 것을 고르시오.

Point 070

07

Korea elects the president ________ five years.

① any ② all ③ every ④ each ⑤ both

Point 071

08

I'm going to have ice cream. Do you want ________, too?

① any ② one ③ all ④ each ⑤ some

Answer p.54

Point 068, 073

09 다음 빈칸에 공통으로 들어갈 말로 알맞은 것은?

- This T-shirt is a little tight for me. Can you show me ________?
- All the members of the family are so different from one ________.

① it ② both ③ each
④ another ⑤ others

중요

Point 072

10 다음 밑줄 친 부분 중 쓰임이 잘못된 것은?

① There are some fruits in the refrigerator.
② Both of my hands are frozen from the cold.
③ I didn't buy red roses. I bought the yellow ones.
④ One of my two uncles has a job, but other doesn't.
⑤ I dropped my spoon. Could you get me another?

Point 074

11 다음 밑줄 친 부분 중 생략할 수 없는 것은?

① She is the beauty itself.
② The reporter interviewed me myself.
③ We planted the apple tree ourselves.
④ Have you yourself seen the actress?
⑤ My parents bought themselves an apartment.

Point 068

12 다음 두 문장이 같은 뜻이 되도록 할 때, 빈칸에 들어갈 말로 알맞은 것은?

Can I have one more piece of cake?
= Can I have ________ piece of cake?

① one ② other ③ another
④ the other ⑤ others

서술형

[13~14] 다음 문장을 조건에 맞게 바꿔 쓰시오.

Point 070

13

조건 1 every로 시작할 것
조건 2 총 6단어로 쓸 것

All the audiences are enjoying the concert.

→ ________________________________

Point 069

14

조건 1 both로 시작할 것
조건 2 총 6단어로 쓸 것

My father is a dentist. My mother is a dentist, too.

→ ________________________________

Point 073

15 다음 우리말과 일치하도록 괄호 안의 말을 바르게 배열하시오.

현대인들은 이메일을 통해 서로 의사소통을 한다. (communicate, people, with, e-mail, by, modern, one another)

→ ________________________________

Point 072

16 다음 밑줄 친 우리말과 일치하도록 주어진 조건을 이용하여 영작하시오.

There are 30 students in my class. 어떤 학생들은 음악 감상을 좋아하고, 다른 학생들은 독서를 좋아한다.

조건 1 총 12단어로 쓸 것
조건 2 listening to music, reading books를 사용할 것

→ ________________________________
____

Grammar Review 핵심 정리

1 부정대명사

부정대명사: 정해지지 않은 불특정의 사람이나 사물을 가리키는 대명사이다.

Point

I lost my watch, so I have to buy one. 067

☞ one: 앞에 나온 명사와 같은 종류의 사람이나 사물을 가리킨다. 복수형은 ones로 나타낸다.

Mike ate a hamburger and ordered another. 068

☞ another: '또 (다른) 하나(의)'라는 뜻으로 앞에 나온 명사와 같은 종류의 또 다른 것을 가리킬 때 쓴다.

Both of them are my friends. 069

☞ all, both: all과 both는 대명사와 형용사로 모두 쓰인다. all은 단수와 복수 모두 가능한 반면, both는 항상 복수 취급한다.

Each of us has our own role. 070

☞ each는 「each+단수 명사」 또는 「each of+복수 명사」의 형태로 쓰이며 동사는 단수 취급한다. every는 「every+단수 명사」 형태로 쓰이며 동사는 단수 취급한다.

Some are dying of hunger. 071

☞ some, any: some과 any는 모두 대명사와 형용사 둘 다로 쓰이며, some은 주로 긍정문에, any는 주로 부정문, 의문문, 조건문에 쓰인다.

Some like spring, and others like fall. 072

☞ 「one ~ the other …」는 두 사람[사물]을 차례로 가리킬 때 쓰고, 「some ~ others …」는 불특정한 수의 사람[사물]을 대조할 때 쓴다.

Sora and Minsu like each other. 073

☞ each other과 one another은 둘 다 '서로'의 뜻으로 each other는 둘 일 때, one another는 셋 이상일 때 사용한다.

2 재귀대명사

재귀대명사는 인칭대명사의 소유격이나 목적격에 -self(단수)나 -selves(복수)를 붙인 형태로 '~ 자신'이라는 뜻이다.

She looked at herself in the mirror. 074

☞ 재귀 용법: 재귀대명사가 동사나 전치사의 목적어로 쓰인 경우로 생략할 수 없다.

I myself made a pizza. 075

☞ 강조 용법: 재귀대명사가 주어, 목적어, 보어와 동격으로 쓰여 그 말을 강조하는 경우이며, 재귀대명사를 생략해도 문장이 성립된다.

The door opened of itself. 076

☞ 재귀대명사의 관용적 표현

by oneself	혼자서 (= alone)	beside oneself	제정신이 아닌
for oneself	스스로	behave oneself	바르게 처신하다
in itself	본래, 그 자체가	enjoy oneself	즐거운 시간을 보내다
of oneself	저절로	help oneself	(~을) 마음대로 먹다
between ourselves	우리끼리 이야기지만	make oneself at home	편안히 있다

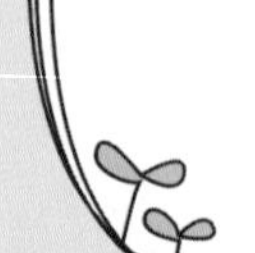

LESSON 09

비교 구문

Point 077 그는 그의 형만큼 키가 크다.

He is as tall as his brother.

- 원급 비교는 「**as + 형용사/부사의 원급 + as ~**」의 형태로 쓰며 '~만큼 …한[하게]'의 뜻이다. 두 대상의 동등함을 나타낼 때 사용한다.
  Kelly speaks Korean **as well as** I do.
- 「**not + as[so] + 형용사/부사의 원급 + as ~**」는 '~만큼 …하지 않은[않게]'의 뜻이다.
  Jane is **not as[so] young as** he is.

TIP 「**as** + 원급 + **as possible**」은 '가능한 ~한[하게]'의 뜻으로 「**as** + 원급 + **as** + 주어 + **can[could]**」로 바꿔 쓸 수 있다.
Please call me back **as soon as possible**. = Please call me back **as soon as you can**.

STEP 1 다음 괄호 안에서 알맞은 말을 고르시오.

□ light 가벼운

1 This suitcase is (as, so) light as that one.
2 Seoul is not (so, that) hot as Daegu today.
3 Ben eats as (much, more) as Ted.
4 My room is as large as (you, yours).
5 Please do it as quickly as (possible, possibly).

STEP 2 다음 우리말과 일치하도록 괄호 안의 말을 이용하여 빈칸에 알맞은 말을 쓰시오.

□ thoughtful 사려 깊은, 배려심 있는
□ bullet 총알
□ heavy 무거운
□ clearly 분명하게

1 Jina는 Sumi만큼 사려 깊다. (thoughtful)
Jina is ______________ Sumi.

2 그는 총알만큼 빨리 달렸다. (fast)
He ran ______________ a bullet.

3 이 상자는 저 상자만큼 무겁지 않다. (heavy)
This box is ______________ that one.

4 나는 가능한 분명히 말하려고 노력했다. (clearly)
I tried to speak ______________ possible.

STEP 3 다음 우리말을 영어로 바르게 옮긴 것은? 내신

오늘은 어제만큼 춥다.

① Today is cold as yesterday.
② Today is as cold yesterday.
③ Today is so cold as yesterday.
④ Today is as cold as yesterday.
⑤ Today is colder than yesterday.

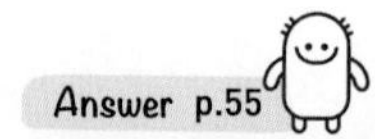
Answer p.55

Which is bigger, the sun or the earth?

• 비교급, 최상급 만드는 법

대부분의 단어	+-er/-est	small – smaller – smallest
-e로 끝나는 단어	+-r/-st	wise – wiser – wisest
「자음+-y」로 끝나는 단어	y를 i로 고치고 +-er/-est	easy – easier – easiest
「단모음+단자음」으로 끝나는 단어	자음을 한 번 더 쓰고 +-er/-est	big – bigger – biggest
-ful, -ous, -ing, -ive 등으로 끝나는 대부분의 2음절 단어와 3음절 이상의 단어	단어 앞에 more/most	famous – more famous – most famous

STEP 1 다음 단어의 비교급과 최상급을 괄호 안에 쓰시오.

1 hot – ( ) – ( )
2 cheap – ( ) – ( )
3 nice – ( ) – ( )
4 pretty – ( ) – ( )
5 amazing – ( ) – ( )
6 difficult – ( ) – ( )

STEP 2 다음 우리말과 일치하도록 빈칸에 들어갈 말을 보기에서 골라 알맞은 형태로 쓰시오.

□ thin 날씬한
□ coin 동전
□ toilet 변기, 화장실

보기 fast thin dirty popular

1 이것이 공항으로 가는 가장 빠른 길이다.
This is the ____________ way to the airport.

2 한국에서는 야구가 축구보다 더 인기가 많다.
Baseball is ____________ than soccer in Korea.

3 미나는 우리 반에서 가장 날씬하다.
Mina is the ____________ in my class.

4 동전이 변기보다 더 더럽다.
Coins are ____________ than a toilet.

STEP 3 다음 밑줄 친 부분 중 어법상 틀린 것은? 내신

□ elephant 코끼리
□ hippo 하마
□ expect 예상하다, 기대하다

① Minho is smarter than I am.
② My cat is fatter than my dog.
③ Elephants are heavyer than hippos.
④ My little brother studies harder than I do.
⑤ The pie was more delicious than I expected.

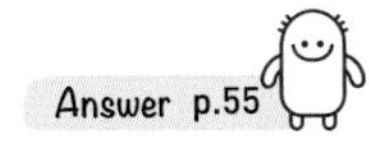
Answer p.55

Point 079 수지는 나보다 노래를 더 잘한다.

Suji sings better than I do.

원급	비교급	최상급
good / well	better	best
bad / badly	worse	worst
many / much	more	most
little	less	least

TIP 같은 단어여도 의미에 따라 비교급과 최상급이 달라지기도 한다.

late	(시간) 늦은	later	latest
	(순서) 나중인	latter	last
far	(거리) 먼	farther	farthest
	(정도) 심한	further	furthest
old	(나이) 많은	older	oldest
	(순서) 손위의	elder	eldest

STEP 1 다음 밑줄 친 부분을 바르게 고치시오.

1 My dog is my goodest friend.
2 The room condition was badder than I heard.
3 The bed is the eldest furniture that I have.
4 My father earns much money than my mother does.
5 If you want to lose weight, try to eat little flour than before.

□ condition 상태, 조건
□ furniture 가구
□ earn (돈을) 벌다

STEP 2 다음 우리말과 일치하도록 괄호 안의 단어를 빈칸에 알맞은 형태로 쓰시오.

1 Hana는 Yujin보다 영어를 더 잘한다. (well)
Hana speaks English ____________ than Yujin.

2 나는 너무 지쳤기 때문에 더 멀리 갈 수가 없었다. (far)
I couldn't go ____________ because I was too tired.

3 나의 언니는 나보다 잠을 덜 잔다. (little)
My sister sleeps ____________ than I do.

4 그것은 한국 역사에서 최악의 재난이었다. (bad)
It was the ____________ disaster in Korean history.

□ disaster 재난, 재해

STEP 3 다음 빈칸에 들어갈 말로 알맞은 것은? 내신

I finished my homework ________ than I expected.

① late ② later ③ latter ④ last ⑤ latest

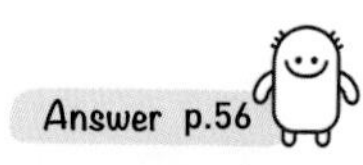

Point 080 내 여동생은 나보다 키가 더 크다.

My sister is taller than me.

- 비교급을 이용한 비교는 「**형용사/부사의 비교급 + than ~**」의 형태로 쓰며 '~보다 더 …한[하게]'의 뜻이다.
  「**not + as[so] + 형용사/부사의 원급 + as ~**」로 바꿔 쓸 수 있다.
  My sister is **more careful than** I am. = I am **not as[so] careful as** my sister.
- much, still, even, far, a lot 등은 비교급 앞에 쓰여 '훨씬'의 뜻으로 비교급을 강조한다.
  My father is **much** older than my mother.
  TIP very(매우)는 원급을 강조하며, 비교급 앞에는 쓸 수 없다.

STEP 1 다음 괄호 안에서 알맞은 말을 고르시오.

1 Your bag is heavier (as, than) mine.
2 Jake came to school (very, much) earlier than usual.
3 Yuna is (very, much) good at dancing.
4 Sejin is not as active (as, than) Jinho.
5 I feel much (happy, happier) now than before.

□ active 활동적인

STEP 2 다음 우리말과 일치하도록 괄호 안의 말을 바르게 배열하시오.

1 그는 내가 예상했던 것보다 훨씬 더 키가 컸다. (he, taller, a lot, than, expected, I, was)

____

2 내 남동생은 나보다 더 늦게 잠자리에 들었다.
(went to bed, I, later, my brother, than, did)

____

3 지하철을 타는 것이 운전하는 것보다 더 빠르다.
(driving, is, taking, than, faster, the subway)

____

4 금은 은보다 훨씬 더 값이 비싸다. (is, than, gold, valuable, silver, more, still)

____

5 신용카드가 현금보다 더 편리하다. (cash, more, than, credit cards, are, convenient)

____

□ subway 지하철
□ valuable 값비싼, 가치가 큰
□ credit card 신용카드
□ convenient 편리한
□ cash 현금

STEP 3 다음 빈칸에 들어갈 말로 알맞지 않은 것은? 내신

It was cold yesterday, but it's ________ colder today.

① much ② still ③ very ④ even ⑤ a lot

Answer p.56

Point 081 너의 방은 내 방보다 두 배 더 크다.

Your room is twice as big as mine.

- '~배 만큼 …하다'는 의미를 나타내기 위해 「**배수사 + as + 원급 + as**」를 쓴다.
- 「**배수사 + as + 원급 + as**」는 「**배수사 + 비교급 + than**」으로 바꿔 쓸 수 있다.
  I work **three times as hard as** my boss. = I work **three times harder than** my boss.
  TIP twice(두 배)의 경우 「**배수사 + as + 원급 + as**」의 형태로만 쓴다.

STEP 1 다음 밑줄 친 부분을 바르게 고치시오.

□ dumbbell 아령
□ full moon 보름달
□ bright 밝은

1 My mother is twice as older as me.
2 These dumbbells are four times heavy than those ones.
3 Sumi's smartphone is three times more expensive as mine.
4 The full moon is twice so bright as the half moon.
5 This building is five taller than that building.

STEP 2 다음 우리말과 일치하도록 괄호 안의 말을 바르게 배열하시오.

□ previous 이전의

1 그는 평소보다 두 배는 더 빨리 걸었다. (fast, he, usual, as, twice, walked, as)

____

2 이번 시험은 지난번 시험보다 열 배는 더 어려웠다.
(ten times, than, this exam, difficult, was, the previous one, more)

____

3 우리는 그 일을 예상보다 두 배는 더 빨리 끝냈다.
(we, the work, as, quickly, we, expected, as, finished, twice)

____

4 수민이의 점수는 지수의 점수보다 세 배 더 높다.
(higher, than, Sumin's score, Jisu's, is, three times)

____

STEP 3 다음 우리말을 영어로 바르게 옮긴 것은? 내신

내 새 컴퓨터는 오래된 컴퓨터보다 두 배 더 좋다.

① My new computer is twice better as the old one.
② My new computer is twice good than the old one.
③ My new computer is as twice good as the old one.
④ My new computer is twice as good as the old one.
⑤ My new computer is twice as better as the old one.

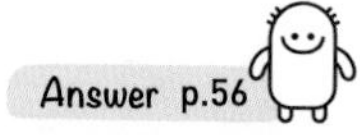

Point 082 우리는 더 많이 가질수록 더 많이 원한다.

The more we have, the more we want.

- 「**the+비교급, the+비교급**」은 '~하면 할수록 더 …한[하게]'의 뜻으로 한 가지의 변화에 비례하여 다른 것이 변화할 때 쓰는 표현이다.

  The older she grew, **the more beautiful** she became.

  TIP 「the+비교급」이 명사를 꾸미는 경우, 꾸밈을 받는 명사를 비교급 바로 뒤에 쓴다.

  The more you eat, **the more weight** you will gain.

STEP 1 다음 문장을 밑줄 친 부분에 유의하여 우리말로 해석하시오.

1 The more you read, the wiser you will be.
2 The harder you try, the more successful you will be.
3 The higher we climbed, the thinner the air was.
4 The earlier you order, the sooner your food will arrive.
5 The colder it gets, the more people catch a cold.

□ climb 오르다, 올라가다
□ thin 산소가 희박한
□ order 주문하다
□ catch a cold 감기에 걸리다

STEP 2 다음 우리말과 일치하도록 괄호 안의 말을 바르게 배열하시오.

1 많이 운동하면 할수록, 너는 더 건강해질 것이다. (you, be, the, healthier, will)
The more you exercise, ______________________.

2 더 많은 돈을 벌수록, 너는 더 많이 소비한다. (more, the, make, you, money)
______________________, the more you spend.

3 날이 어두워질수록, 아이들은 더 무서워졌다. (the children, the, scared, felt, more)
The darker it grew, ______________________.

4 많이 허우적거릴수록, 그는 점점 더 깊이 진흙 속으로 빠져들었다.
(the mud, deeper, he, the, got into)
The more he struggled, ______________________.

5 음악을 오래 들을수록, 나는 점점 더 평화로움을 느꼈다.
(listened, I, longer, the, to the music)
______________________, the more peaceful I felt.

□ scared 무서워하는, 겁먹은
□ mud 진흙
□ struggle 허우적거리다, 몸부림치다

STEP 3 다음 빈칸에 공통으로 들어갈 말로 알맞은 것은? 내신

__________ more you get to know her, __________ more you'll like her.

① So[so] ② As[as] ③ Then[then]
④ The[the] ⑤ Than[than]

Answer p.57

Point 083 날씨가 점점 더 추워지고 있다.

The weather is getting colder and colder.

- 「비교급+and+비교급」은 '점점 더 ~한[하게]'의 뜻으로 점진적인 변화를 나타낼 때 쓰는 표현이다.
  More and more people are living alone.
  TIP 「비교급 + and + 비교급」은 주로 상태가 변화되는 동사 get, become, grow, turn 등과 함께 쓰인다.

STEP 1 다음 문장을 밑줄 친 부분에 유의하여 우리말로 해석하시오.

1 Everything will get better and better.
2 More and more children are using smartphones.
3 The river ran faster and faster.
4 The trees are becoming greener and greener.
5 The birds flew lower and lower.

□ fly 날다
□ low 낮게, 아래로

STEP 2 다음 우리말과 일치하도록 괄호 안의 말을 바르게 배열하시오.

1 하늘이 점점 더 어두워지고 있다. (darker, the, is, sky, and, getting, darker)
____

2 수지는 점점 더 날씬해지고 있다. (is, slimmer, Suji, and, getting, slimmer)
____

3 그녀의 건강 상태는 점점 더 악화되었다.
(became, her, worse, health, and, condition, worse)
____

4 가격이 점점 더 올랐다. (higher, the, got, and, price, higher)
____

5 일꾼들은 점점 더 갈증이 나고 있었다.
(the, were, workers, thirstier, and, growing, thirstier)
____

□ slim 날씬한
□ price 가격
□ thirsty 목이 마른, 갈증 나는

STEP 3 다음 우리말을 영어로 바르게 옮긴 것은? 내신

나는 점점 더 빨리 걷기 시작했다.

① I began to walk the fastest.
② I began to walk fast and fast.
③ I began to walk fast and faster.
④ I began to walk faster and fast.
⑤ I began to walk faster and faster.

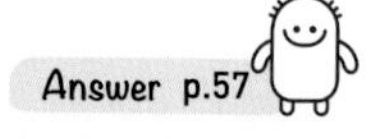

Point 084 나일강은 세상에서 가장 긴 강이다.

The Nile is the longest river in the world.

- 최상급 표현은 「the+형용사/부사의 최상급」의 형태로 쓰며 '가장 ~한[하게]'의 뜻이다. 보통 최상급 뒤에 비교 범위를 한정해 주는 in이나 of가 함께 온다.
  I am **the shortest** in my family.

TIP in 뒤에는 장소나 범위를 나타내는 단수 명사가 오며, of 뒤에는 비교 대상이 되는 명사가 오는데, 주로 복수 명사가 온다.
The actor is the most famous **in** Korea. / Minsu is the funniest **of** my friends.

STEP 1 다음 괄호 안에서 알맞은 말을 고르시오.

1 Jaemin is (a, the) tallest student in my class.
2 This is the (cheaper, cheapest) dish in this restaurant.
3 I made the (bad, worst) mistake in my life.
4 It was the (better, best) scene in the movie.
5 Yujin is the smartest (in, of) the students.

□ make a mistake 실수를 하다
□ scene 장면

STEP 2 다음 우리말과 일치하도록 괄호 안의 말을 이용하여 빈칸에 알맞은 말을 쓰시오.

1 서울은 한국에서 가장 붐비는 도시이다. (crowded)
Seoul is ________________ in Korea.

2 8월은 일 년 중 가장 더운 달이다. (hot)
August is ________________ of the year.

3 세호는 남자아이들 중에서 가장 빠르다. (fast)
Seho is ________________ of the boys.

4 나는 생애 가장 행복한 생일을 맞았다. (happy)
I had ________________ in my life.

5 세상에서 가장 높은 산은 무엇인가? (high)
What is ________________ in the world?

□ crowded 붐비는, 복잡한

STEP 3 다음 빈칸에 들어갈 말이 나머지 넷과 다른 것은? 내신

① It was ________ funniest story in the book.
② My family is ________ most precious to me.
③ She is ________ most famous star in her town.
④ The bench is not ________ comfortable as the sofa.
⑤ The giraffe has ________ longest neck of the animals.

□ precious 귀중한, 소중한
□ comfortable 편안한, 안락한
□ giraffe 기린

Answer p.57

Point 085 한라산은 한국에서 가장 높은 산들 중 하나이다.

Mt. Halla is one of the highest mountains in Korea.

- 「**one of the + 최상급 + 복수 명사**」는 '가장 ~한 것들 중 하나'라는 뜻으로 가장 ~한 것들이 여럿 존재할 때 쓸 수 있는 완화된 최상급 표현이다.
  King Sejong was **one of the greatest kings** in Korean history.
- 「**the + 최상급 + (that) + 주어 + have ever p.p.**」는 '지금까지 ~한 것 중 가장 …한'의 뜻으로 자신의 경험과 관련하여 최상급을 표현할 때 쓴다.
  It was **the worst** movie **(that) I've ever seen.**

STEP 1 다음 괄호 안에서 알맞은 말을 고르시오.

1 This is one of the (good, best) restaurants in the city.
2 The ring is the (more, most) expensive item I have ever bought.
3 Beethoven is one of the (greater, greatest) musicians in the world.
4 Yubin is one of the smartest (student, students) in his class.
5 His joke was the funniest one that I have ever (hear, heard).

□ item 물건, 물품
□ musician 음악가
□ joke 농담

STEP 2 다음 우리말과 일치하도록 괄호 안의 말을 바르게 배열하시오.

1 스위스는 내가 지금까지 방문한 곳들 중 가장 아름다운 나라이다.
(that, country, ever, I have, the most beautiful, visited)
Switzerland is ______________________________.

2 캐나다는 세계에서 가장 추운 나라들 중 하나이다.
(countries, in the world, one, the coldest, of)
Canada is ______________________________.

3 그것은 내가 지금까지 겪었던 가장 나쁜 경험들 중 하나였다.
(one, I've ever had, experiences, of, the worst)
It was ______________________________.

4 그는 한국에서 가장 유명한 영화감독들 중 하나이다.
(movie directors, of, in Korea, one, the most famous)
He is ______________________________.

□ Switzerland 스위스
□ movie director 영화감독

STEP 3 다음 밑줄 친 부분 중 어법상 틀린 것은? 내신

This scarf is <u>one</u> <u>of</u> <u>the</u> <u>best</u> <u>thing</u> I have.
① ② ③ ④ ⑤

Answer p.58

Point 086 다른 어떤 선생님도 김 선생님만큼 친절하지 않다.

No other teacher is as kind as Ms. Kim.

• 원급과 비교급을 이용하여 최상급을 표현할 수 있다.

No (other) ~ as+원급+as	어떤 ~도 …만큼 ~하지 않는
No (other) ~ 비교급+than	어떤 ~도 …보다 더 ~하지 않는
비교급+than+any other+단수 명사	다른 어떤 ~보다도 더 …한
비교급+than+all the other+복수 명사	다른 모든 ~보다도 더 …한

STEP 1 다음 괄호 안에서 알맞은 말을 고르시오.

□ subject 과목

1 (No, Not) other boy in my school is as strong as Sehun.
2 No comedian in Korea is funnier (as, than) him.
3 Science is more difficult than any (other, another) subject.
4 This is more interesting than all the other (book, books).
5 Roses are more beautiful than any other (flower, flowers).

STEP 2 다음 우리말과 일치하도록 괄호 안의 말을 바르게 배열하시오.

1 어떤 다른 경기도 야구만큼 흥미진진하지 않다.
(as, is, no, baseball, other, exciting, as, sport)

____

2 이것은 가게의 다른 어떤 가방보다 더 비싸다.
(is, in the shop, more, any, this, than, bag, expensive, other)

____

3 그 어떤 산도 에베레스트 산보다 높지 않다.
(other, is, than, Mt. Everest, higher, no, mountain)

____

4 그녀는 한국의 다른 모든 여배우들보다 더 매력적이다.
(more, she, in Korea, all, than, other, attractive, actresses, is, the)

____

STEP 3 다음 중 의미가 나머지 넷과 다른 것은? 내신

① No dessert is as delicious as cheese cake.
② Cheese cake is the most delicious dessert.
③ No dessert is less delicious than cheese cake.
④ Cheese cake is more delicious than any other dessert.
⑤ Cheese cake is more delicious than all the other desserts.

Answer p.58

Point 077

01 다음 중 어법상 틀린 것은?

① Judy is older than Kate.
② Her hair is as long as me.
③ The river is getting drier and drier.
④ The more you eat, the fatter you'll become.
⑤ The game was the most exciting game I've ever watched.

중요

Point 086

02 다음 중 보기 의 문장과 의미가 다른 것은?

> 보기 No singer in Korea is as popular as him.

① He is the most popular singer in Korea.
② No singer in Korea is more popular than him.
③ He is not as popular as other singers in Korea.
④ He is more popular than any other singer in Korea.
⑤ He is more popular than all the other singers in Korea.

Point 082

03 다음 우리말과 일치하도록 할 때, 빈칸에 공통으로 들어갈 말로 알맞은 것은?

> 더 많이 일할수록, 우리는 더 많이 스트레스를 받는다.
> ➜ The ________ we work, the ________ stressed we get.

① better ② more ③ most
④ best ⑤ much

중요

Point 080

04 다음 빈칸에 들어갈 말로 알맞지 않은 것은?

> There are ________ more people on the street than yesterday.

① far ② still ③ much
④ very ⑤ even

Point 078

05 다음 밑줄 친 부분 중 어법상 틀린 것은?

① Jinho is creativer than I am.
② Kate looks prettier than before.
③ Susan is slimmer than her sister.
④ The bank is closer than the post office from here.
⑤ The Internet can be more dangerous than we think.

Point 083

06 다음 우리말과 일치하도록 할 때, 빈칸에 들어갈 말로 알맞은 것은?

> 비가 점점 더 거세지고 있다.
> ➜ The rain is getting ________________.

① heavily ② more heavy
③ heaviest ④ heavy and heavier
⑤ heavier and heavier

[07~08] 다음 빈칸에 들어갈 말로 알맞은 것을 고르시오.

Point 084

07

> Health is ________ most important thing in life.

① a ② the ③ as
④ much ⑤ than

Point 086

08

> Alex is lazier than ________ other boy in his school.

① an ② any ③ many
④ all ⑤ some

[09~10] 다음 빈칸에 공통으로 들어갈 말로 알맞은 것을 고르시오.

Point 081

09

The playground is twice ________ large ________ the gym.

① as ② so ③ very
④ more ⑤ than

Point 083

10

The prisoner grew ________ and ________.

① thin ② old ③ elder
④ thinner ⑤ oldest

고난도

Point 079

11 다음 중 밑줄 친 부분이 내용상 어색한 것은?

① My elder sister goes to university.
② The former is better than the latter.
③ We need to discuss the problem farther.
④ Her condition got worse because of the rain.
⑤ These days, I sleep less than 6 hours a day.

Point 086

12 다음 빈칸에 들어갈 말이 순서대로 짝지어진 것은?

A hummingbird is ________ than any other ________ on earth.

① small – bird ② smaller – bird
③ small – birds ④ smaller – birds
⑤ smallest – bird

서술형

Point 081

13 다음 두 문장을 주어진 조건에 맞게 한 문장으로 바꿔 쓰시오.

조건 1 Jisu's bag을 주어로 쓸 것
조건 2 twice, expensive를 사용하여 총 8단어로 쓸 것

My bag is 5,000 won. Jisu's bag is 10,000 won.

→ ________________

Point 085

14 다음 우리말과 일치하도록 괄호 안의 말을 이용하여 영작하시오.

곰은 세상에서 가장 위험한 동물들 중 하나이다. (bears, dangerous)

→ ________________

[15~16] 다음 표를 보고 아래 질문에 완전한 문장으로 답하시오.

Name	Height	Weight
Yubin	170 cm	60 kg
Minho	165 cm	55 kg
Namsu	180 cm	80 kg

Point 080

15 Who is taller, Yubin or Minho? (5 words)

→ ________________

Point 084

16 Who is the heaviest of them? (6 words)

→ ________________

Point 084
01 다음 빈칸에 들어갈 말이 순서대로 짝지어진 것은?

• Suji is the prettiest girl ________ my friends.
• Chile is the longest country ________ the world.

① in – in ② in – of ③ of – of
④ of – in ⑤ in – to

Point 080
02 다음 중 보기 의 문장과 의미가 같은 것은?

보기 My room is not as large as hers.

① My room is larger than hers.
② My room is smaller than hers.
③ Her room is smaller than mine.
④ Her room is not as large as mine.
⑤ Her room is not larger than mine.

[03~04] 다음 두 문장이 같은 뜻이 되도록 할 때, 빈칸에 들어갈 말로 알맞은 것을 고르시오.

Point 086
03

Volleyball is the most exciting sport of all.
= ________ is more exciting than volleyball.

① No sport ② Any sport
③ All sports ④ Some sports
⑤ Every sport

Point 079, 085
04

I've never seen such a bad movie.
= That's the ________ movie I've ever seen.

① best ② better ③ worse
④ worst ⑤ most

Point 085
05 다음 우리말을 영어로 바르게 옮긴 것은?

뉴욕은 세계에서 가장 붐비는 도시들 중 하나이다.

① New York is the busiest city in the world.
② New York is one of the busiest city in the world.
③ New York is busier than any other city in the world.
④ New York is one of the busiest cities in the world.
⑤ New York is as busy as all the other cities in the world.

Point 080
06 다음 중 두 문장의 의미가 서로 다른 것은?

① I like pizza better than spaghetti.
= I prefer pizza to spaghetti.
② I can't speak English as well as Jessy.
= Jessy speaks English better than I do.
③ This is the most boring book I've ever read.
= No book is as boring as this book.
④ This exam was not as hard as the previous one.
= This exam was harder than the previous one.
⑤ No one in my school can play the piano better than Yuna.
= Yuna plays the piano the best in my school.

[07~08] 다음 빈칸에 들어갈 말로 알맞은 것을 고르시오.

Point 078
07

Alex is the most ________ student in my class.

① tall ② strong ③ funny
④ smart ⑤ popular

Point 081
08

His car is three times as ________ as mine.

① bigger ② smaller ③ faster
④ cheaper ⑤ expensive

Answer p.60

[09~10] 다음 빈칸에 들어갈 말로 알맞지 않은 것을 고르시오.

Point 078

09

This is more ________ than that.

① easy ② famous ③ boring
④ useful ⑤ interesting

Point 086

10

No one in my family is as ________ as Uncle Joe.

① rich ② fat ③ wiser
④ active ⑤ intelligent

고난도

Point 080

11 다음 빈칸에 들어갈 말이 나머지 넷과 다른 것은?

① Tom is taller ________ Ben.
② Judy is older ________ Frank.
③ My ruler is longer ________ yours.
④ Math is more difficult ________ English.
⑤ This building is ________ higher than that one.

중요

Point 083

12 다음과 같이 우리말을 영작할 때 옳지 않은 것은?

봄이 옴에 따라, 날씨가 점점 따뜻해지고 있다.
→ As spring comes, it is getting warm and warm.

① As ② comes ③ it
④ is getting ⑤ warm and warm

서술형

Point 082

13 다음 문장을 조건에 맞게 바꿔 쓰시오.

조건 1 The more로 시작할 것
조건 2 총 8단어로 쓸 것

As you exercise more, you become healthier.
→ ________________

Point 086

14 다음 우리말과 일치하도록 괄호 안의 말을 이용하여 빈칸에 알맞은 말을 쓰시오.

달팽이는 지구상의 다른 어떤 동물보다 더 느리다. (slow)

→ A snail is ________ ________ ________ ________ ________ on earth.

[15~16] 다음 표를 보고 아래 질문에 답하시오.

Dokdo	Seoul	Gangneung	Jejudo
10℃	22℃	14℃	22℃

Point 077

15

조건 1 Seoul을 주어로 쓸 것
조건 2 warm을 사용할 것

Compare the temperature of Seoul and Jejudo.
→ ________________

Point 086

16

조건 1 colder, any other를 사용할 것
조건 2 총 9단어로 쓸 것

Which region is the coldest in Korea?
→ ________________

Grammar Review 핵심 정리

Point

1 as ~ as 구문

He is as tall as his brother. 077

☞ 원급 비교는 「as+형용사/부사의 원급+as ~」의 형태로 쓰며 '~만큼 …한[하게]'의 뜻이다.

2 비교급, 최상급 만드는 법

Which is **bigger**, the sun or the earth? 078

☞ 규칙 변화
대부분의 단어: +-er/-est, -e로 끝나는 단어: +-r/-st, 「자음+-y」로 끝나는 단어: y를 i로 고치고 +-er/-est, 「단모음+단자음」으로 끝나는 단어: 자음을 한 번 더 쓰고 +-er/-est, 대부분의 2음절 단어(-ful, -ous, -ing, -ive 등으로 끝나는 단어)와 3음절 이상의 단어: 단어 앞에 more/most

Suji sings **better** than I do. 079

☞ 불규칙 변화
good/well – better – best, bad – worse – worst, many/much – more – most, little – less – least

3 비교급+than

My sister is **taller than** me. 080

☞ 비교급을 이용한 비교는 「형용사/부사의 비교급+than」의 형태로 쓰며 '~보다 더 …한[하게]'의 뜻이다.
☞ much, still, even, far, a lot 등은 비교급 앞에 쓰여 '훨씬'의 뜻으로 비교급을 강조한다.

4 비교 구문을 이용한 표현

Your room is **twice as big as** mine. 081

☞ '~배 만큼 …하다'는 의미를 나타내기 위해 「배수사+as+원급+as」를 쓴다.

The more we have, **the more** we want. 082

☞ 「the+비교급, the+비교급」은 '~하면 할수록 더 …한[하게]'의 뜻이다.

The weather is getting **colder and colder**. 083

☞ 「비교급+and+비교급」은 '점점 더 ~한[하게]'의 뜻으로 점진적인 변화를 나타낼 때 쓰는 표현이다.

5 the+최상급

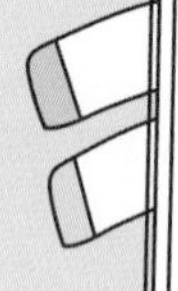

The Nile is **the longest** river in the world. 084

☞ 최상급 표현은 「the+형용사/부사의 최상급」의 형태로 쓰며 '가장 ~한[하게]'의 뜻이다.

6 최상급을 이용한 표현

Mt. Halla is **one of the highest mountains** in Korea. 085

☞ 「one of the+최상급+복수 명사」는 '가장 ~한 것들 중 하나'라는 뜻이다.
☞ 「the+최상급+(that)+주어+have ever p.p.」는 '지금까지 ~한 것 중 가장 ~한'의 뜻이다.

7 원급, 비교급을 이용한 최상급 표현

No other teacher is **as kind as** Ms. Kim. 086

☞ 원급, 비교급을 이용한 최상급 표현에는 No (other) ~ as+원급+as (어떤 ~도 …만큼 ~하지 않는), No (other) ~ 비교급+than (어떤 ~도 …보다 더 ~하지 않는), 비교급+than+any other+단수 명사 (다른 어떤 ~보다도 더 …한), 비교급+than+all the other+복수 명사 (다른 모든 ~보다도 더 …한)가 있다.

LESSON

10

관계사

Point 087 나는 암을 낫게 할 수 있는 의사가 되고 싶다.

I want to be a doctor who can cure cancer.

- 관계대명사는 접속사와 대명사의 역할을 하며, 관계대명사가 이끄는 절은 앞에 나온 명사(선행사)를 수식한다.
  This is the man. + He sang at my wedding.
  → This is the man **who** sang at my wedding.
- 선행사가 사람이고 관계대명사절 안에서 주어 역할을 할 때, 주격 관계대명사 who를 쓴다. 주격 관계대명사절의 동사는 선행사의 인칭과 수에 일치시킨다.
  I met a girl **who** was very pretty.

STEP 1 다음 문장을 우리말로 해석하시오.

□ photographer 사진작가

1 She has a son who is a famous artist.
2 A photographer is a person who takes pictures.
3 Do you see the lady who is wearing sunglasses?
4 The girl who is riding a bike is my little sister.
5 Who is the boy who is talking with Jenny?

STEP 2 다음 두 문장을 관계대명사 who를 이용하여 한 문장으로 바꿔 쓰시오.

□ carry a cane 지팡이를 짚고 다니다
□ several 몇몇의
□ gym 체육관
□ neighbor 이웃 사람

1 Ms. Park is the teacher. She teaches us history.
→ ____________________

2 The gentleman is my grandfather. He is carrying a cane.
→ ____________________

3 There are several students. They are playing basketball in the gym.
→ ____________________

4 John is the boy. He broke the window.
→ ____________________

5 The woman is kind to the neighbors. She lives next door.
→ ____________________

STEP 3 다음 밑줄 친 부분 중 쓰임이 나머지 넷과 다른 것은? 내신

□ laugh 웃다
□ rob 도둑질하다
□ relative 친척

① The man who laughs last laughs best.
② The news didn't say who robbed the bank.
③ There are many people who want to get jobs.
④ My relative who lives in Canada sent me a present.
⑤ The tall man who is standing next to the door is my uncle.

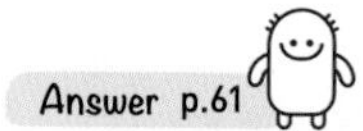

Point 088 내게는 별명이 걸어 다니는 사전인 반 친구가 있다.

I have a classmate **whose** nickname is a walking dictionary.

- 관계대명사절 안에서 소유격 역할을 할 때, 선행사가 사람이면 소유격 관계대명사 whose를, 사람이 아니면 소유격 관계대명사 whose나 of which를 쓴다.
  I have a friend. + His[Her] father is a famous actor.
  → I have a friend **whose** father is a famous actor.
- 어순: 「**선행사 + whose/of which + 명사**」 / 「**선행사 + 명사 + of which**」
  There are many houses **whose roofs[of which the roofs / the roofs of which]** are red.

STEP 1 다음 괄호 안에서 알맞은 말을 고르시오.

1 A giraffe is an animal (who, whose) neck is very long.
2 I read a book of which the title (was, were) interesting.
3 The person (whose, who) taught me English is my older sister.
4 Minho is a baseball player (whose, his) position is a pitcher.
5 My mom bought a bag (who, of which) the price was very high.

□ giraffe 기린
□ position 위치, 자리
□ pitcher 투수

STEP 2 다음 우리말과 일치하도록 괄호 안의 말을 바르게 배열하시오.

1 벽이 분홍색인 그 방이 내 방이다. (the wall, pink, of which, is)
The room ______________________ is my room.

2 우리 이모는 목소리가 부드러운 남자와 데이트를 하고 있다.
(voice, a man, is, whose, soft)
My aunt is dating ______________________.

3 이곳은 소유주가 인기 있는 가수인 식당이다. (whose, is, a popular singer, owner)
This is the restaurant ______________________.

4 나는 쓰기 능력을 향상시키는 것이 목표인 수업을 듣고 있다.
(the aim, to develop, is, of which, writing skills)
I am taking a course ______________________.

□ owner 소유주
□ aim 목표
□ develop 향상시키다

STEP 3 다음 빈칸에 들어갈 말이 나머지 넷과 다른 것은? 내신

① I have a dog ________ fur is white.
② You can't use the table ________ leg is broken.
③ There lived a king ________ name was Midas.
④ Susan is the girl ________ is known for her beauty.
⑤ Tom is my friend ________ favorite sport is soccer.

□ fur (동물의) 털

Answer p.62

Point 089 수지는 내가 가장 좋아하는 여자아이이다.

목적격 관계대명사 whom

Suji is the girl whom I like most.

- 선행사가 사람이고 관계대명사절 안에서 동사나 전치사의 목적어 역할을 할 때, 목적격 관계대명사 who(m)을 쓴다.

Yesterday I ran into the boy. + I met him at the science camp.
→ Yesterday I ran into the boy **who(m)** I met at the science camp. (동사의 목적어 역할)

I respect the people **who(m)** I work **with**.
= I respect the people **with whom** I work. (전치사의 목적어 역할)

TIP 관계대명사가 전치사의 목적어 역할을 할 때 전치사를 관계대명사 앞으로 옮길 수 있는데, 이때 who 대신 whom을 써야 한다.

STEP 1 다음 문장에서 who(m)가 들어갈 부분에 V 표시를 하시오.

1 The politician many people support is giving a speech.
2 Sumin is the boy with I went to the flea market yesterday.
3 Ryan has a girlfriend he has dated for a long time.
4 My schoolmate I fought with the other day apologized to me.
5 The baby to my aunt gave birth is so cute.

□ politician 정치가
□ support 지지하다
□ flea market 벼룩시장
□ apologize 사과하다

STEP 2 다음 우리말과 일치하도록 괄호 안의 말을 이용하여 빈칸에 알맞은 말을 쓰시오.

1 우리가 홍콩에서 만난 여행 가이드는 영어를 유창하게 했다. (meet, Hong Kong)
The tour guide ______________________ spoke English fluently.

2 내가 지난주에 너에게 소개해 준 여자를 기억하니? (introduce to)
Do you remember the woman ______________________?

3 나와 같이 일했던 동료들 중 대부분은 매우 똑똑했다. (work, with)
Most of the colleagues ______________________ were very smart.

4 나에게는 패션 감각이 상당히 좋은 친구가 있다. (sense of fashion, quite)
I have a friend ______________________.

□ fluently 유창하게
□ introduce 소개하다
□ colleague (직장) 동료
□ quite 상당히

STEP 3 다음 중 어법상 틀린 것은? 내신

① Here are some of the people whom I am close with.
② Do you know anyone who can translate French into Korean?
③ I met the person whom you mentioned before.
④ We are looking for a lawyer who we can trust.
⑤ The boy with who the principal is shaking hands is the student president.

□ translate 번역하다
□ mention 언급하다
□ trust 믿다
□ principal 교장

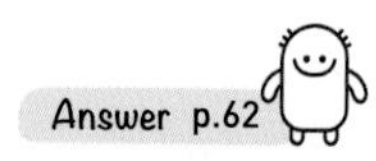

Point 090 나는 특수효과가 많은 영화를 봤다.

I watched a movie which had lots of special effects.

- 선행사가 사물 · 동물이고 관계대명사절 안에서 주어나 목적어 역할을 할 때, 주격 · 목적격 관계대명사 which를 쓴다.
  This is the swing **which** my father made in the backyard.
  Do you like the club **which** you belong **to**?
  = Do you like the club **to which** you belong?

STEP 1 다음 괄호 안에서 알맞은 말을 고르시오.

1 This is a book (who, which) is about the Vietnam War.
2 I have a younger sister (who, which) is majoring in computer science.
3 The best seller (who, which) my favorite author wrote is sold out.
4 I have a beautiful homeland (which, of which) I'm proud.
5 We talked about the topic (whom, which) the article dealt with.

□ author 작가
□ homeland 조국
□ article 기사
□ deal with ~를 다루다, 처리하다

STEP 2 다음 우리말과 일치하도록 괄호 안의 말을 바르게 배열하시오.

1 상자 안에 있는 앨범은 내 것이다. (is, which, in the box, mine, is)
The album ______________________________.

2 네가 나에게 추천해 준 호텔은 매우 좋았다.
(to me, was, which, recommended, very nice, you)
The hotel ______________________________.

3 이곳은 위험한 동물들이 많이 살고 있는 동물원이다.
(which, live, dangerous, many, animals)
This is the zoo in ______________________________.

4 내가 듣고 있는 음악은 평화롭다. (I'm, which, is, listening to, peaceful)
The music ______________________________.

□ recommend 추천하다
□ peaceful 평화로운

STEP 3 다음 밑줄 친 부분 중 쓰임이 나머지 넷과 다른 것은? 내신

① There are many problems which I can't deal with.
② The company for which my father worked went bankrupt.
③ Do you know which way the post office is?
④ The book which you lent me was very interesting.
⑤ The washing machine which we bought needs to be repaired.

□ go bankrupt 파산하다
□ washing machine 세탁기
□ repair 수리하다

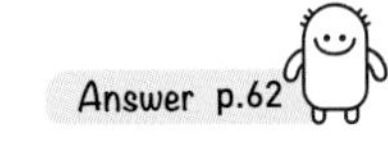
Answer p.62

Point 091 나는 주머니가 많은 가방을 샀다.

I bought a bag that had many pockets.

- 관계대명사 that은 선행사의 성격(사람 · 사물 · 동물 등)과 상관없이 주격 · 목적격 관계대명사 who(m), which와 바꿔 쓸 수 있다.
  I ate the potatoes **that** my grandfather grew.
- 관계대명사 that 앞에는 전치사를 쓸 수 없다.
  I can't understand anything **about that** Mr. Johnson is talking. (×)
  → I can't understand anything **that** Mr. Johnson is talking **about**.

STEP 1 다음 괄호 안에서 알맞은 말을 모두 고르시오.

1 Have you ever watched the movies (who, which, that) Tim Burton made?
2 We need a person (who, which, that) is good at math.
3 Michael lives in a house (who, which, that) has no heating system.
4 The passenger (who, which, that) I was carrying told me to drive more carefully.
5 Ms. White is the teacher to (who, whom, that) I wrote a thank-you card.

□ heating system 난방 설비
□ passenger 승객

STEP 2 다음 두 문장을 관계대명사 that을 이용하여 한 문장으로 바꿔 쓰시오.

1 This is the garden. My grandmother takes care of it.
→ ____________________

2 He is the only witness to the car accident. It happened last night.
→ ____________________

3 I helped the old lady with her baskets. She lived upstairs.
→ ____________________

4 What do you think of the woman? You met her yesterday.
→ ____________________

□ witness 목격자
□ upstairs 위층에

STEP 3 다음 우리말을 영어로 바르게 옮긴 것은? 내신

Linda가 존경하는 사람은 그녀의 아버지이다.

① The person to who Linda looks up is her father.
② The person to that Linda looks up is her father.
③ The person whose Linda looks up to is her father.
④ The person which Linda looks up to is her father.
⑤ The person that Linda looks up to is her father.

□ look up to ~을 존경하다

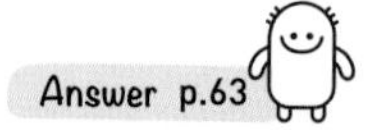

Point 092 내가 네 돈을 훔친 그 남자를 모른다는 것은 사실이다. 관계대명사 that vs. 접속사 that

It's true that I don't know the man that stole your money.

- 관계대명사 that은 선행사를 수식하는 형용사절을 이끈다.
- 접속사 that은 '~라는 것'으로 해석하며, 문장에서 주어, 목적어, 보어 역할을 하는 명사절을 이끈다.
  It was surprising **that** my team won the game. (주어 역할)
  I think **that** he is honest. (목적어 역할) / The fact is **that** she can't swim. (보어 역할)

STEP 1 다음 밑줄 친 that이 관계대명사면 '관', 접속사면 '접'이라고 쓰고, 문장을 우리말로 해석하시오.

□ Mars 화성
□ salty (맛이) 짠

1 The Eiffel Tower is the tower that brings many tourists to Paris.
2 Do you believe that there is life on Mars?
3 It was a comedy show that was popular before I was born.
4 The hot dog that I ate for lunch was salty.
5 The truth is that the service at the restaurant was terrible.

STEP 2 다음 우리말과 일치하도록 괄호 안의 말을 바르게 배열하시오.

□ vet 수의사
□ driver's license 운전면허증

1 수의사는 아픈 동물들을 돌보아 주는 사람이다.
(a person, takes care of, a vet, that, is, sick animals)
____

2 우리는 Amy가 운전면허증을 땄다는 것을 믿을 수 없었다.
(couldn't, Amy, that, her driver's license, we, got, believe)
____

3 흡연이 건강에 해롭다는 것은 사실이다. (true, is, it, that, smoking, bad, is, for health)
____

4 그것은 내가 지금껏 들은 것 중에서 가장 웃긴 이야기이다.
(the funniest, that, I've, it, story, is, ever heard)
____

STEP 3 다음 밑줄 친 부분 중 쓰임이 나머지 넷과 다른 것은? 내신

□ curly 곱슬곱슬한

① I don't think that the witness is telling the truth.
② Did you see the watch that I put on the table?
③ That's the same scarf that I bought on the street.
④ How did you like the spaghetti that I made for you?
⑤ The girl that has long curly hair is my older sister.

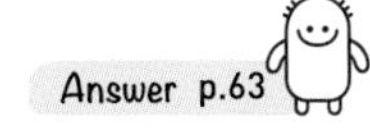
Answer p.63

Point 093 나는 아직도 네가 나에게 했던 말을 기억한다.

I still remember what you said to me.

- what은 선행사를 포함하는 관계대명사로, 「the thing(s) which[that]」으로 바꿔 쓸 수 있다.
  What I want now is water. = **The thing which[that]** I want now is water.
- 관계대명사 what은 '~하는 것'으로 해석하며, 문장에서 주어, 목적어, 보어 역할을 하는 명사절을 이끈다.
  The parcel was **what** I waited for.

STEP 1 다음 괄호 안에서 알맞은 말을 고르시오.

1 Let's see (what, that) you have done.
2 I will do anything (what, that) you ask me to do.
3 Make sure to review (what, that) you learned today.
4 Here are the plants (what, which) you should water.
5 Don't tell others (what, who) I told you.

□ make sure to 반드시 ~해라
□ review 복습하다

STEP 2 다음 우리말과 일치하도록 빈칸에 알맞은 말을 쓰시오.

1 너는 내가 말하고 있는 것을 이해하니?
Do you understand ________ ________ ________ ________?

2 그림을 그리는 것은 나를 행복하게 만들어 주는 일이다.
Painting pictures is ________ ________ ________ ________.

3 그것이 수미가 기다리고 있는 것이다.
That's ________ ________ ________ ________ ________.

4 Ben이 가장 즐기는 것은 요리이다.
________ ________ ________ ________ is cooking.

5 나는 내가 읽고 있는 것에 집중할 수가 없다.
I can't concentrate on ________ ________ ________ ________.

□ concentrate on ~에 집중하다

STEP 3 다음 빈칸에 들어갈 말이 순서대로 짝지어진 것은? 내신

- I don't have a watch ________ has a leather band.
- I didn't hear ________ you whispered to me.

① which – which
② what – which
③ which – what
④ what – what
⑤ which – that

□ leather 가죽
□ whisper 속삭이다

Answer p.64

Point 094 이것은 내가 처음으로 만든 영화이다.

This is the first film I've ever made.

- 동사의 목적어로 쓰인 목적격 관계대명사 who(m), which, that은 생략할 수 있다.
  I need a friend **(who[whom])** I can call anytime.
  Did you see the building **(which[that])** the architect built?

STEP 1 다음 문장에서 생략 가능한 부분에 밑줄을 긋고, 문장을 우리말로 해석하시오.

□ bake 굽다
□ praise 칭찬하다

1 I don't remember anything that she told me.
2 Try some cookies which I baked for you.
3 The old man who you helped yesterday is my grandfather.
4 The jeans which I bought need to be washed.
5 Yuna is the student whom every teacher praises.

STEP 2 다음 우리말과 일치하도록 괄호 안의 말을 바르게 배열하시오.

□ rent 빌리다
□ complain 항의하다
□ admire 존경하다

1 이것이 내가 빌리고 싶은 스포츠카이다. (is, the, I, to, this, sports car, want, rent)

____

2 우리 아버지께서 가장 좋아하시는 영화는 'Ben-Hur'이다.
(my father, most, is, the movie, likes, *Ben-Hur*)

____

3 너는 내가 학교에서 잃어버린 열쇠를 어떻게 찾았니?
(I, find, at school, lost, how, the key, did, you)

____

4 저는 지난주에 산 이 가방에 대해 항의하고 싶어요.
(this bag, I, last week, want to, about, I, complain, bought)

____

5 내가 가장 존경하는 미국인은 Barack Obama이다.
(I, is, admire, the American, most, Barack Obama)

____

STEP 3 다음 밑줄 친 부분 중 생략할 수 없는 것은? 내신

□ prisoner 죄수
□ court 법정

① This is not the book which I lent you the other day.
② I didn't like the movie which we watched together.
③ Is there anything else that you would like to order?
④ Everything that the prisoner said in court was true.
⑤ There are lots of students that want to join the science camp.

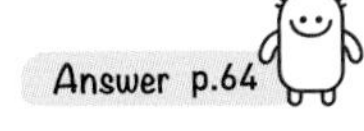
Answer p.64

Point 095 나는 쓸 종이가 한 장 필요하다.

I need a piece of paper I can write on.

- 전치사의 목적어로 쓰인 목적격 관계대명사 who(m), which, that은 생략할 수 있다.
  I know the girl **(who[whom])** John is talking with.
  This is the house **(which[that])** I grew up in.
- 전치사가 관계대명사 앞에 올 경우 관계대명사를 생략할 수 없다.
  Baseball is the sport **at** Tom is good. (×) → Baseball is the sport **at which** Tom is good.

STEP 1 다음 문장에서 관계대명사가 생략된 부분에 V 표시를 하시오.

□ common 흔한

1 I don't have a pen I can write with.
2 He has a daughter he is very proud of.
3 That is the dog my little brother is scared of.
4 Emily finally found the memo she was looking for.
5 Love is a common topic most writers write about.

STEP 2 다음 우리말과 일치하도록 괄호 안의 말을 바르게 배열하시오.

□ located 위치한
□ go out 사귀다
□ share 나누다, 공유하다
□ sorrow 슬픈 일, 슬픔

1 내가 호텔에서 잠을 잔 침대는 매우 편안했다.
(I, at, in, slept, the hotel, the bed)
____________________________ was very comfortable.

2 로마는 콜로세움이 위치한 도시이다. (in, the city, is, the Colosseum, located)
Rome is ____________________________.

3 그녀는 초대받은 파티에 갈 수 없었다. (she, to, invited, was, the party, to)
She couldn't go ____________________________.

4 Mike는 사귀고 있는 여자를 정말 좋아한다. (he, with, is, the girl, going out)
Mike really likes ____________________________.

5 그는 기쁜 일과 슬픈 일을 나와 함께 나눈 친구이다.
(have shared, a friend, with, I, joys and sorrows)
He is ____________________________.

STEP 3 다음 중 어법상 틀린 것은? 내신

□ belong to ~에 속하다
□ rely on ~에 의지하다
□ physical education 체육
□ source (자료의) 출처

① The soccer club is the club to which I belong.
② My parents are the people on I can rely.
③ Physical education is the subject Tyler is most interested in.
④ Dictionaries are the sources that I get information from.
⑤ My grandmother is the person by whom I was raised.

Answer p.64

Point 096 나무에서 노래하는 새들을 봐.

Look at the birds singing in the tree.

- 「주격 관계대명사 + be동사 + 형용사구/분사구」 구문에서 「**주격 관계대명사 + be동사**」는 생략할 수 있다.
  I want to marry a man **(who[that] is)** close to my age. (주격 관계대명사 + be동사 + 형용사구)
- 「주격 관계대명사 + be동사」가 생략된 후 뒤에 남은 형용사구[분사구]는 앞에 있는 명사를 수식하는 관계가 된다.
  The song **(which[that] was)** written in the 1990s is my favorite. (주격 관계대명사 + be동사 + 분사구)

STEP 1 다음 문장에서 생략 가능한 부분에 밑줄을 그으시오. (생략 가능한 부분이 없으면 × 표시를 할 것)

1 Confidence is a factor which is important in recovery from failures.
2 The car that was parked here was towed away by the police.
3 The company is looking for those who majored in law.
4 Do you know the girls who are singing on the stage?
5 We bought the things which are the main ingredients of cake.

□ confidence 자신감
□ factor 요인
□ recovery 회복
□ tow 견인하다

STEP 2 다음 우리말과 일치하도록 관계대명사와 괄호 안의 말을 이용하여 빈칸에 알맞은 말을 쓰시오. (생략 가능한 부분에는 밑줄을 그을 것)

1 다리를 절뚝거리고 있는 저 남자를 봐. (limping)
Look at ________________________.

2 도서관에는 책을 읽고 있는 학생들이 많이 있다. (a lot of, in the library)
There are ________________________.

3 우리는 학교에서 삶의 유용한 지식을 배운다. (knowledge, useful, at school)
We learn ________________________.

4 예술에 관심이 있는 사람은 누구나 전시회에 올 수 있다. (anyone, interested in)
________________________ can come to the exhibition.

5 세탁소에서 드라이클리닝이 된 옷은 새 옷 같아 보였다. (dry-cleaned, at the laundry)
________________________ looked like new ones.

□ limp 다리를 절뚝거리다
□ exhibition 전시회
□ dry-clean 드라이클리닝 하다
□ laundry 세탁소

STEP 3 다음 문장에서 공통으로 생략된 말로 알맞은 것은? 내신

- The old man smoking a cigarette is my grandfather.
- The water boiling on the stove is for ramyeon.

① who ② that ③ which is
④ who is ⑤ that is

□ cigarette 담배
□ boil 끓다
□ stove 난로

Answer p.65

Point 097 2002년은 한국에서 월드컵이 열린 해였다.

2002 was the year when the World Cup was held in Korea.

- 관계부사는 접속사와 부사구의 역할을 하며, 관계부사가 이끄는 절은 선행사를 수식한다. 관계부사는 「전치사 + which」로 바꿔 쓸 수 있다.
- 선행사가 시간 · 때(the time, the day, the month, the year 등)를 나타낼 때 관계부사 when을 쓴다. 관계부사 when은 「in/at/on + which」로 바꿔 쓸 수 있다.
  I will never forget the day. + I first met you on the day[then].
  → I will never forget the day **when[on which]** I first met you.

STEP 1 다음 문장을 우리말로 해석하시오.

1 April 5 is the day when we plant trees.
2 May is the month in which there are many holidays.
3 2015 was the year in which my nephew was born.
4 Now is the time when we have to pray for his safe return.
5 Many people still remember the day when the 9/11 attacks took place.

□ nephew (남자) 조카
□ pray 기도하다
□ attack 공격
□ take place 발생하다

STEP 2 다음 두 문장을 관계부사 when을 이용하여 한 문장으로 바꿔 쓰시오.

1 March is the month. The new school year begins in Korea in March.
→ ______________________________

2 Yesterday was the day. My father came back from a business trip yesterday.
→ ______________________________

3 Seven o'clock is the time. I leave home for work at seven o'clock.
→ ______________________________

4 Spring is the season. Lots of flowers blossom in spring.
→ ______________________________

□ school year 학년
□ blossom (꽃이) 피다

STEP 3 다음 빈칸에 들어갈 말이 순서대로 짝지어진 것은? 내신

- Do you remember the day on ________ the Korean soccer team advanced to the semifinals?
- Let me know the time ________ the meeting will start.

① which – where
② which – when
③ who – where
④ that – when
⑤ that – where

□ advance 진출하다
□ semifinal 4강, 준결승

Answer p.65

Point 098 서울은 내가 거주하는 도시이다.

Seoul is the city **where I live.**

- 선행사가 장소(the place, the house, the country, the city 등)를 나타낼 때 관계부사 where을 쓴다. 관계부사 where는 「in/at/on/to + which」로 바꿔 쓸 수 있다.

This is the park. + I lost my dog in the park[there].

→ This is the park **where[in which]** I lost my dog.

STEP 1 다음 괄호 안에서 알맞은 말을 고르시오.

1 New York is the city (when, where) the Statue of Liberty is.

2 A nursing home is a place (where, which) the elderly can rest.

3 A playing field is a place (in, for) which people can play sports.

4 There was a man in the airplane (who, where) looked like a wealthy businessman.

5 Gyeongbok Palace is the palace in (where, which) kings lived in the Joseon Dynasty.

□ the Statue of Liberty 자유의 여신상
□ nursing home 양로원
□ palace 궁
□ the Joseon Dynasty 조선 왕조

STEP 2 다음 우리말과 일치하도록 괄호 안의 말을 이용하여 빈칸에 알맞은 말을 쓰시오.

1 그 음식점은 어제 우리 가족이 외식을 한 장소이다. (place, where, eat out)
The restaurant is ______________________________.

2 Sandwich는 Sandwich 백작이 살았던 마을의 이름이다.
(town, in which, the Earl of Sandwich)
Sandwich is the name ______________________________.

3 스위스는 우리가 자연의 아름다움을 발견할 수 있는 나라이다.
(country, where, find, natural beauty)
Switzerland is ______________________________.

4 파리는 Monet가 태어난 도시이다. (city, in which, Monet, born)
Paris is ______________________________.

□ earl 백작
□ Switzerland 스위스
□ natural 자연의

STEP 3 다음 빈칸에 들어갈 말이 나머지 넷과 다른 것은? 내신

① I went to the village ________ my father used to live.
② This is the season ________ many tourists visit Jeju Island.
③ The Louvre is the museum ________ the famous painting, *Mona Lisa*, hangs.
④ They are going to move to a country________ the air is clean.
⑤ This is the wedding hall ________ my parents got married.

□ village 마을
□ used to ~하곤 했다
□ hang 걸리다, 매달리다

Answer p.66

Point 099 나는 그녀가 나를 떠난 이유를 모른다.

I don't know the reason why she left me.

- 선행사가 이유(the reason)를 나타낼 때 관계부사 why를 쓴다. 관계부사 why는 「for + which」로 바꿔 쓸 수 있다.

Tell me the reason. + You were late for that reason.

→ Tell me the reason **why[for which]** you were late.

STEP 1 다음 밑줄 친 부분을 바르게 고치시오.

1 I can't think of any reason when he is angry with me.

2 There is a certain reason which I cannot speak about it.

3 They are waiting for the result why will be announced soon.

4 She quit her job with a reason why I couldn't understand.

5 The reason for that they broke up is simple.

□ certain 어떤
□ announce 발표하다
□ quit 그만두다
□ break up 헤어지다

STEP 2 다음 우리말과 일치하도록 괄호 안의 말을 바르게 배열하시오.

1 나는 그가 여기에 오지 못한 이유가 있다고 확신해.
(there is, why, I'm sure, he didn't, a reason, come here)

____

2 그녀가 나를 피하고 있는 이유가 있니?
(some reason, she is, is there, for which, avoiding me)

____

3 내가 이 식당을 좋아하는 한 가지 이유는 적당한 가격이다.
(I like, one reason, its reasonable prices, is, why, this restaurant)

____

4 그 영화가 대성공이었던 데에는 이유가 있다.
(a reason, the movie, a big hit, there's, was, for which)

____

□ avoid 피하다
□ reasonable 적당한
□ big hit 대성공

STEP 3 다음 빈칸에 들어갈 말이 순서대로 짝지어진 것은? 내신

- The reason ________ she attends church is to find peace.
- John finally told me the reason ________ which he left me.

① why – for ② where – for ③ why – with
④ where – with ⑤ why – in

□ attend (~에) 다니다

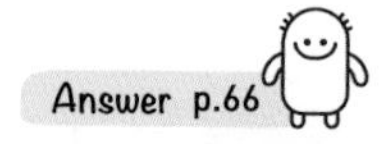

Point 100 당신이 나를 향해 미소 짓던 모습을 기억해요.

I remember how you smiled at me.

- 선행사가 방법(the way)을 나타낼 때 관계부사 how를 쓴다. 관계부사 how는 「in + which」로 바꿔 쓸 수 있다.
- 선행사 the way와 관계부사 how는 함께 쓸 수 없고, 둘 중 하나만 써야 한다.

  We learned about the way. + Egyptians made mummies in that way.

  → We learned about **the way** Egyptians made mummies.

  = We learned about **how** Egyptians made mummies.

  = We learned about **the way in which** Egyptians made mummies.

STEP 1 다음 괄호 안에서 알맞은 말을 고르시오.

1 Do you know (what, how) the machine works?

2 Sam showed Laura the way (which, in which) she can use chopsticks.

3 Let me know (which, how) you fixed the computer.

4 I like the way (how, in which) you dressed up.

5 He is kind to everyone. It's the (reason, way) he treats people.

□ chopstick 젓가락
□ fix 고치다
□ dress up 옷을 입다
□ treat (특정한 태도로) 대하다

STEP 2 다음 우리말과 일치하도록 괄호 안의 말을 이용하여 빈칸에 알맞은 말을 쓰시오.

1 나는 그가 행동하는 방식이 마음에 들지 않았다. (way, act)

I didn't like ______________________________.

2 사람들이 의사소통하는 방식은 많이 바뀌었다. (way, communicate)

______________________________ has changed a lot.

3 네가 그 로봇을 어떻게 만들었는지 나에게 알려 줘. (how, make, robot)

Let me know ______________________________.

4 그것이 그녀가 일을 처리하는 방식이다. (how, handle, things)

That's ______________________________.

5 아기를 어떻게 재울 수 있는지 나에게 말해 줘. (how, put the baby to sleep)

Tell me ______________________________.

□ communicate 의사소통하다
□ handle 처리하다
□ put ~ to sleep ~를 재우다

STEP 3 다음 중 어법상 틀린 것은? 내신

① You are just fine the way you are.

② That's how I memorize words.

③ Don't judge a person by the way he looks.

④ I love the way she smiles at me.

⑤ The way how Daniel speaks French is funny.

□ memorize 암기하다
□ judge 판단하다

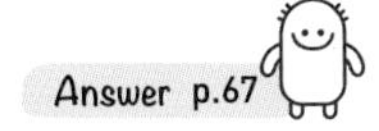
Answer p.67

Point 090

01 다음 밑줄 친 부분 중 쓰임이 나머지 넷과 다른 것은?

① The pet which I'm raising is a parrot.
② I can't decide which one I should wear.
③ Do you like the perfume which I bought for you?
④ Can you pass me the salt which is on the table?
⑤ Camels are animals which have humps on their backs.

Point 087, 088

02 다음 빈칸에 들어갈 말이 나머지 넷과 다른 것은?

① The car ________ window is broken is my father's.
② I have a little brother ________ has many nicknames.
③ Have you read the novel ________ title is *The Giver*?
④ The woman ________ hair is blond is my new English teacher.
⑤ An international movie star ________ name was well-known came to Korea.

Point 095

03 다음 밑줄 친 부분 중 생략할 수 없는 것은?

① Art is the subject at which I am poor.
② This is the book that I bought at the bookstore.
③ The boy who I went traveling with is from Kenya.
④ Look at the cat which is sleeping under the car.
⑤ There are a few children who are playing soccer.

Point 089

04 다음 빈칸에 공통으로 들어갈 말로 알맞은 것은?

- Jake is not the person ________ you can trust.
- What's the name of the girl to ________ Tom is sitting next?

① who ② what ③ which
④ that ⑤ whom

Point 099

05 다음 두 문장을 한 문장으로 바꿀 때, 빈칸에 들어갈 말로 알맞은 것은?

Can you explain the reason? You didn't hand in your homework for the reason.
→ Can you explain the reason ________ you didn't hand in your homework?

① why ② how ③ when
④ which ⑤ where

Point 088

06 다음 밑줄 친 부분 중 어법상 틀린 것은?

She has taught(①) Korean to(②) students that(③) native(④) language is(⑤) not Korean.

[07~08] 다음 빈칸에 들어갈 말로 알맞은 것을 고르시오.

Point 087

07

They are looking for the ________ who parked in the no parking zone.

① car ② truck ③ person
④ bus ⑤ vehicle

Point 091

08

The phone number ________ I wrote down was wrong.

① who ② what ③ whose
④ that ⑤ whom

Answer p.67

[09~10] 다음 대화의 빈칸에 들어갈 말로 알맞은 것을 고르시오.

Point 093

09

A: What do you want for dinner?
B: __________ I want for dinner is sushi.

① That ② How ③ What
④ Which ⑤ Who

Point 100

10

A: Have you ever watched __________ ants carry their food?
B: Yes. They work together to move food.

① how ② that ③ when
④ which ⑤ where

고난도

Point 092

11

다음 밑줄 친 부분의 쓰임이 보기 와 같은 것은?

보기 Vincent van Gogh is an artist that is still loved by many people.

① Some people believe that there are UFOs.
② I cannot forget the sunset that I saw from the beach.
③ Did you know that Ms. Lee moved to another school?
④ It is shocking that such a thing happens in modern society.
⑤ My hope is that I can convey something of value to the readers.

Point 096

12

다음 중 어법상 옳은 것은?

① I know a girl which can speak German.
② Luke is wearing pants made of cotton.
③ There are many people are waiting for the train.
④ A crocodile is an animal of which has a big mouth.
⑤ This is an area with I have been familiar since childhood.

서술형

Point 087, 091

13

다음 보기 와 같이 괄호 안의 말을 이용하여 단어의 정의를 묻는 질문에 답하시오.

보기 A: Who is a pilot?
B: A pilot is a person who flies airplanes.
(fly, airplanes)

A: Who is a firefighter?
B: ______________________________
(put out, fires)

Point 094, 095

14

다음 문장에서 공통으로 생략된 말을 쓰시오.

• The professor I interviewed is known for her work on the brain.
• The hotel they stayed at was four-star.

➜ ______________

[15~16] 메모를 참고하여, 다음 우리말과 일치하도록 주어진 조건을 이용하여 영작하시오.

I invite you to my birthday party.
When: My birthday (February 18)
Where: John's Pizza
From Mira

Point 097

15

조건 관계부사와 born을 사용할 것

2월 18일은 미라가 태어난 날이다.

➜ ______________________________

Point 098

16

조건 관계부사와 place, will, be held를 사용할 것

John's Pizza는 미라의 생일 파티가 열릴 장소이다.

➜ ______________________________

Point 087

01 다음 밑줄 친 부분의 쓰임이 보기 와 같은 것은?

보기 I have a cousin who lives in New Zealand.

① Who is she waiting for?
② Do you know who the tall man is?
③ I can tell you who took your umbrella.
④ Who do you think is the best dancer in Korea?
⑤ I visited a teacher who taught me in elementary school.

중요

Point 091, 093

02 다음 밑줄 친 부분 중 어법상 틀린 것은?

① I always like what my mom makes for me.
② Tell me anything what comes to your mind.
③ My teacher teaches me what I need to know.
④ What I want for my birthday is a new camera.
⑤ Try to be content with what you already have.

Point 097

03 다음 밑줄 친 부분 중 쓰임이 나머지 넷과 다른 것은?

① You can call me when you need help.
② Fall is the season when the sky is blue.
③ It is the time when strawberries taste most delicious.
④ I still remember the day when I graduated from high school.
⑤ December is the month when we share presents with loved ones.

Point 098

04 다음 중 빈칸에 where가 들어갈 수 없는 것은?

① The village ________ I grew up is very small.
② France is the country ________ Jina met her fiancé.
③ The cafe ________ we ate ice cream closes at 11 p.m.
④ This is the house ________ my father built ten years ago.
⑤ The building ________ many firms are located looks modern.

Point 089

05 다음 밑줄 친 부분 중 어법상 틀린 것은?

Jack is the person(①) from(②) who(③) I heard(④) the unbelievable(⑤) story.

Point 099

06 다음 두 문장이 같은 뜻이 되도록 할 때, 빈칸에 들어갈 말로 알맞은 것은?

I don't know the reason for which the meeting was delayed.
= I don't know the reason ________ the meeting was delayed.

① why ② how ③ when
④ who ⑤ where

[07~08] 다음 빈칸에 들어갈 말로 알맞은 것을 고르시오.

Point 088

07

The book ________ cover is red sells well.

① who ② that ③ what
④ which ⑤ whose

Point 093

08

Do you understand ________ you learned today?

① what ② who ③ when
④ where ⑤ whose

[09~10] 다음 빈칸에 공통으로 들어갈 말로 알맞은 것을 고르시오.

Point 092

09

- I like movies ________ are based on true stories.
- The rumor is ________ a Hollywood star visited the small village.

① who ② what ③ which
④ that ⑤ whom

Point 090, 100

10

- A submarine is a ship ________ can go under the water.
- Please tell me the way in ________ you lost ten kilograms.

① why ② how ③ what
④ which ⑤ that

Point 100

11 다음 중 어법상 틀린 것은?

① Let's meet at the place where we first met.
② Noon is the time when I have lunch at school.
③ Barcelona is the city in which Gaudi's buildings exist.
④ Nobody knows the way how the prisoner escaped.
⑤ Chuseok is the day on which we eat songpyeon.

Point 094, 095

12 다음 문장에서 공통으로 생략된 말로 알맞은 것은?

- I finally found the document I required.
- My mom bought an armchair she can rest in.

① why ② what ③ whom
④ where ⑤ which

서술형

Point 091

13 다음 우리말과 일치하도록 괄호 안의 말을 바르게 배열하시오.

내가 표를 사 둔 콘서트가 취소됐어.
(was, for, I, that, bought, the concert, a ticket, canceled)

→ ________________________________

Point 100

14 다음 우리말을 괄호 안의 말을 이용하여 영작하시오.

나는 세종대왕이 한글을 발명한 방법을 알기를 원한다.
(know, how, King Sejong, invent, Hangeul)

→ ________________________________

[15~16] 다음 두 문장을 주어진 조건에 맞게 한 문장으로 바꿔 쓰시오.

Point 094

15

조건 1 관계대명사를 생략할 것
조건 2 총 8단어로 쓸 것

Susan was wearing the sunglasses. She took them off.

→ ________________________________

Point 096

16

조건 1 관계대명사를 생략할 것
조건 2 총 7단어로 쓸 것

I bought a pen. It was made in Japan.

→ ________________________________

Grammar Review 핵심 정리

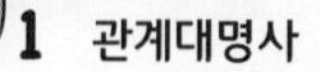

1 관계대명사

관계대명사는 접속사와 대명사의 역할을 하며, 관계대명사절은 선행사를 수식한다.

선행사 \ 격	주격	소유격	목적격
사람	who	whose	who(m)
동물 · 사물	which	whose / of which	which
사람 · 동물 · 사물	that	—	that

Point

I want to be a doctor **who** can cure cancer. 087

I have a classmate **whose** nickname is a walking dictionary. 088

Suji is the girl **whom** I like most. 089

I watched a movie **which** had lots of special effects. 090

I bought a bag **that** had many pockets. 091

It's true **that** I don't know the man **that** stole your money. 092

☞ 관계대명사 that은 형용사절을 이끄는 반면, 접속사 that은 '~라는 것'의 의미로 명사절을 이끈다.

2 관계대명사 what

I still remember **what** you said to me. 093

☞ what은 선행사를 포함하는 관계대명사로, '~하는 것'으로 해석하며 명사절을 이끈다.

3 관계대명사의 생략

This is the first film I've ever made. 094

I need a piece of paper I can write on. 095

☞ 동사나 전치사의 목적어로 쓰인 목적격 관계대명사 who(m), which, that은 생략할 수 있다.

Look at the birds singing in the tree. 096

☞ 「주격 관계대명사+be동사」는 뒤에 형용사구[분사구]가 올 때 생략할 수 있다.

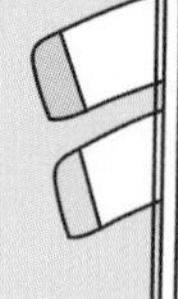

4 관계부사

관계부사는 접속사와 부사구의 역할을 하며, 관계부사절은 선행사를 수식한다.

2002 was the year **when** the World Cup was held in Korea. 097

Seoul is the city **where** I live. 098

I don't know the reason **why** she left me. 099

I remember **how** you smiled at me. 100

☞ 선행사가 시간을 나타낼 때는 관계부사 when을, 선행사가 장소를 나타낼 때는 관계부사 where를, 선행사가 the reason일 때는 관계부사 why를, 선행사가 the way일 때는 관계부사 how를 쓴다.

LESSON 11

가정법

Point 101 만약 네가 더 쉰다면 기분이 더 나아질 텐데.

If you got more rest, you would feel better.

- 가정법 과거: '만약 ~하다면[이라면] …할 텐데'의 뜻으로, 현재의 사실을 반대로 가정하거나 실현 가능성이 희박한 일을 가정할 때 사용한다. 「**If + 주어 + 동사의 과거형~, 주어 + 조동사의 과거형 + 동사원형…**」의 형태이다.
- if절의 be동사는 주어의 인칭과 수에 관계없이 were를 쓴다.

TIP 가정법 과거 문장은 직설법 현재 문장으로 바꿔 쓸 수 있다.
If I were rich, **I could travel** all around the world.
→ **As I am not** rich, **I can't travel** all around the world.

STEP 1 다음 괄호 안에서 알맞은 말을 고르시오.

□ enter (대회 등에) 참가하다
□ marathon 마라톤

1 If I (was, were) a bird, I would fly to you.
2 If they (had, have) more time, they could finish the project.
3 If he were healthy, he (will, would) enter the marathon.
4 If I (knew, know) her address, I would visit her.
5 If she lived in London, she (can, could) see Big Ben.

STEP 2 다음 우리말과 일치하도록 빈칸에 알맞은 말을 쓰시오.

□ win first place 1등을 하다
□ forgive 용서하다

1 만약 그녀가 정답을 찾아낸다면, 그녀는 1등을 할 텐데.
_______ _______ _______ _______ _______, she would win first place.

2 만약 Tom이 아프지 않다면, 그는 소풍을 갈 수 있을 텐데.
_______ _______ _______ _______ _______, he could go on a picnic.

3 만약 사람들이 진실을 안다면, 그들은 그녀를 용서하지 않을 텐데.
_______ _______ _______ _______ _______, they wouldn't forgive her.

4 만약 나에게 충분한 돈이 있다면, 나는 그 카메라를 살 수 있을 텐데.
If I had enough money, _______ _______ _______ _______ _______.

5 만약 네가 나이가 더 많다면, 너는 이 책을 이해할 텐데.
If you were older _______ _______ _______ _______ _______.

STEP 3 다음 중 어법상 틀린 것은? 내신

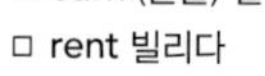

□ earn (돈을) 벌다
□ rent 빌리다

① If it were a fine day, we would take a walk.
② If you helped me, I could do anything.
③ If she studied hard, she could pass the test.
④ If the bag were a little cheaper, I would buy it.
⑤ If he got a job, he can earn enough to rent the house.

Point 102 만약 내가 더 일찍 일어났다면 버스를 잡을 수 있었을 텐데.

If I had got up earlier, I could have caught the bus.

- 가정법 과거완료: '만약 ~했다면[였다면] …했을 텐데'의 뜻으로, 과거의 사실을 반대로 가정할 때 사용한다. 「**If + 주어 + had p.p.~, 주어 + 조동사의 과거형 + have p.p.…**」의 형태이다.

TIP 가정법 과거완료 문장은 직설법 과거 문장으로 바꿔 쓸 수 있다.

If you hadn't lent me the book, **I couldn't have done** my homework.
→ **As you lent** me the book, **I was able to do** my homework.

STEP 1 다음 밑줄 친 부분을 바르게 고치시오.

1 If she hurried, she would not have been late.
2 If you had come to the party, you could meet him.
3 If I had not been sick, I will have gone on the school trip.
4 If he had not give me advice, I would have failed.
5 If John had have a car, he might have given me a ride.

□ school trip 수학여행
□ advice 충고
□ fail 실패하다
□ give a ride (차를) 태워 주다

STEP 2 다음 우리말과 일치하도록 괄호 안의 말을 바르게 배열하시오.

1 만약 내가 바쁘지 않았다면 콘서트에 갔을 텐데. (if, not, had, been, I, busy)
______________________, I would have gone to the concert.

2 만약 네가 그 소식을 들었다면 매우 놀랐을 텐데. (had, you, the news, if, heard)
______________________, you would have been very surprised.

3 만약 내가 잠을 더 잤다면 피곤함을 느끼지 않았을 텐데.
(would, felt, I, have, tired, not)
If I had slept more, ______________________.

4 만약 네가 그 영화를 봤다면 눈물을 흘렸을 텐데. (have, might, you, tears, shed)
If you had seen the movie, ______________________.

□ shed (눈물을) 흘리다

STEP 3 다음 중 보기와 의미가 같은 것은? 내신

보기 As I didn't have my phone, I couldn't call you.

① If I have my phone, I can call you.
② If I had my phone, I could call you.
③ If I didn't have my phone, I couldn't call you.
④ If I had had my phone, I could have called you.
⑤ If I hadn't had my phone, I couldn't have called you.

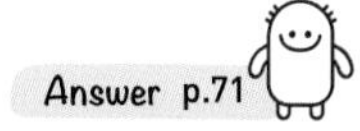

Point 103 내가 지금보다 키가 더 크다면 좋을 텐데.

I wish I were **taller than now.**

- '~하면[이라면] 좋을 텐데'의 뜻으로, 실현 불가능하거나 실현 가능성이 희박한 현재의 소망을 나타낼 때 사용한다. 「**I wish + (that) + 주어 + 동사의 과거형~**」의 형태이다.

TIP 「I wish + 가정법 과거」 문장은 직설법 현재 문장으로 바꿔 쓸 수 있다.
I wish I could speak Japanese. → **I'm sorry (that) I can't speak** Japanese.

STEP 1 다음 문장을 밑줄 친 부분에 유의하여 우리말로 해석하시오.

1 I wish it snowed heavily.
2 I wish I had wings like a bird.
3 I wish you were staying here.
4 I wish they got along with each other.
5 I wish there were an easy way to solve this.

□ heavily 아주 많이, 심하게
□ wing 날개
□ get along with ~와 잘 지내다

STEP 2 다음 주어진 문장을 가정법을 이용하여 바꿔 쓰시오.

1 I'm sorry that I am too shy.
→ I wish I ________________.

2 I'm sorry that you can't understand me.
→ I wish you ________________.

3 I'm sorry that I can't run as fast as Usain Bolt.
→ I wish I ________________.

4 I'm sorry that I don't have magical powers.
→ I wish I ________________.

5 I'm sorry that my grandmother doesn't live in the countryside.
→ I wish my grandmother ________________.

□ shy 수줍음을 많이 타는
□ magical 마법의
□ countryside 시골

STEP 3 다음 빈칸에 들어갈 말로 알맞은 것은? 내신

I already have two pairs of sunglasses. I wish I ________ a pair of brown sunglasses, too.

① have ② has ③ had
④ having ⑤ have had

□ a pair of 한 쌍의 ~

Answer p.71

Point 104 내가 그녀의 충고를 따랐다면 좋았을 텐데.

I wish I had followed her advice.

- '~했다면[였다면] 좋았을 텐데'의 뜻으로, 과거에 이루어지지 못했던 일에 대한 아쉬움이나 후회를 나타낼 때 사용한다. 「I wish + (that) + 주어 + had p.p.~」의 형태이다.

TIP 「I wish + 가정법 과거완료」 문장은 직설법 현재 문장으로 바꿔 쓸 수 있다.
I wish I had learned how to swim. → **I'm sorry (that) I didn't learn** how to swim.

STEP 1 다음 우리말과 일치하도록 괄호 안의 단어를 알맞은 형태로 고치시오.

1 내가 그곳에 있었다면 좋았을 텐데.
I wish I (be) there.

2 네가 그 상을 받았다면 좋았을 텐데.
I wish you (get) the prize.

3 그 사고가 일어나지 않았다면 좋았을 텐데.
I wish the accident (happen).

4 그들이 제시간에 왔다면 좋았을 텐데.
I wish they (come) in time.

□ accident 사고
□ happen 일어나다, 발생하다
□ in time 제시간에

STEP 2 다음 우리말과 일치하도록 괄호 안의 말을 이용하여 빈칸에 알맞은 말을 쓰시오.

1 네가 그렇게 말하지 않았다면 좋았을 텐데. (say, so)
I wish ______________________.

2 우리의 계획이 성공했다면 좋았을 텐데. (plan, succeed)
I wish ______________________.

3 그 문이 열려 있지 않았다면 좋았을 텐데. (be, open)
I wish ______________________.

4 내가 너를 더 일찍 만났다면 좋았을 텐데. (meet, earlier)
I wish ______________________.

□ plan 계획
□ succeed 성공하다

STEP 3 다음 중 보기와 의미가 같은 것은? 내신

보기 I wish I had taken the job.

① I'm glad I took the job.
② I'm glad I didn't take the job.
③ I'm sorry I won't take the job.
④ I'm sorry I didn't take the job.
⑤ I'm sorry I'm not taking the job.

Answer p.72

Point 105 그는 마치 모든 것을 아는 것처럼 말한다.

He speaks as if he knew everything.

- '마치 ~인[하는] 것처럼'의 뜻으로, 실제와 다른 상황을 나타낼 때 사용한다. 「**as if + 주어 + 동사의 과거형~**」의 형태이다.
- 주절의 시제가 현재든 과거든 상관없이, as if가 이끄는 절은 주절과 같은 시점의 내용을 나타낸다.
  He **looks** as if he **were** from a different world.
  He **looked** as if he **were** from a different world.

TIP 「as if + 가정법 과거」 문장은 직설법 문장으로 바꿔 쓸 수 있다.
She behaves **as if she liked** animals. → **In fact, she doesn't like** animals.

STEP 1 다음 문장을 밑줄 친 부분에 유의하여 우리말로 해석하시오.

1 I feel as if I were dreaming.
2 It seems as if they were close friends.
3 Lucy smiled as if she welcomed me.
4 It sounded as if he were yelling at someone.
5 Don't talk to me as if you were my mom.

□ seem ~처럼 보이다
□ welcome 환영하다
□ yell 고함을 지르다

STEP 2 다음 우리말과 일치하도록 괄호 안의 말을 바르게 배열하시오.

1 그는 마치 백만장자인 것처럼 생활한다. (lives, he, a millionaire, were, as if, he)
____

2 나는 마치 공기 중에 떠 있는 것 같은 기분이 들었다.
(I, in the air, were, I, felt, as if, floating)
____

3 Mark는 마치 어느 누구에게도 주의를 기울이지 않는 것처럼 행동했다.
(to anyone, didn't pay, as if, acted, he, attention, Mark)
____

4 엄마는 마치 내가 아기인 것처럼 나를 대하신다. (treats, Mom, as if, a baby, were, I, me)
____

□ millionaire 백만장자
□ float (가라앉지 않고) 뜨다
□ pay attention 주의를 기울이다
□ treat 대하다, 다루다

STEP 3 다음 빈칸에 들어갈 말로 알맞은 것은? 내신

He talks as if ______________________. In fact, he doesn't know him.

① he knows my uncle
② he knew my uncle
③ he doesn't know my uncle
④ he didn't know my uncle
⑤ he hadn't known my uncle

Answer p.72

Point 106 그녀는 마치 전에 나를 만난 적이 없던 것처럼 행동했다.

She acted as if she hadn't met me before.

- '마치 ~였던[했던] 것처럼'의 뜻으로, 실제와 다른 상황을 나타낼 때 사용한다. 「**as if + 주어 + had p.p.~**」의 형태이다.
- 주절의 시제가 현재든 과거든 상관없이, as if가 이끄는 절은 주절보다 더 과거 시점의 내용을 나타낸다.
  The gentleman **speaks** as if he **had been** poor in his youth.
  The gentleman **spoke** as if he **had been** poor in his youth.

TIP 「as if + 가정법 과거완료」 문장은 직설법 문장으로 바꿔 쓸 수 있다.
It sounds **as if you had studied** hard last night. → **In fact, you didn't study** hard last night.

STEP 1 다음 문장을 밑줄 친 부분에 유의하여 우리말로 해석하시오.

1 He behaved as if nothing had happened.
2 You eat as if you had not eaten breakfast.
3 Robin hurriedly left the room as if he were angry.
4 Jack talked as if he had visited New York.
5 Carol looks blank as if she didn't know anything.

□ behave 행동하다
□ hurriedly 황급히
□ look blank 멍해 보이다

STEP 2 다음 우리말과 일치하도록 가정법을 이용하여 빈칸에 알맞은 말을 쓰시오.

1 너는 마치 지난밤에 잠을 잘 못 잔 것처럼 보인다.
You look _______ _______ _______ _______ _______ well last night.

2 Henry는 마치 자기가 유명 인사였던 것처럼 행동했다.
Henry behaved _______ _______ _______ _______ _______ a celebrity.

3 소라는 마치 전생에 공주였던 것처럼 보였다.
Sora looked _______ _______ _______ _______ _______ a princess in her previous life.

4 그들은 마치 싸웠던 것처럼 보인다.
It seems _______ _______ _______ _______ _______.

□ celebrity 유명 인사
□ previous 이전의
□ fight 싸우다

STEP 3 다음 주어진 문장을 가정법을 이용하여 바꿀 때, 빈칸에 들어갈 말로 알맞은 것은? 내신

In fact, Paul was not in Japan.
→ Paul talks as if _______________.

① he is in Japan
② he was in Japan
③ he were in Japan
④ he would be in Japan
⑤ he had been in Japan

Answer p.72

내신 적중 실전 문제

Point 101

01 다음 중 보기 와 의미가 같은 것은?

보기 As I don't have money, I can't lend any to you.

① If I had money, I can lend some to you.
② If I have money, I can lend some to you.
③ If I had money, I could lend some to you.
④ If I had had money, I could have lent some to you.
⑤ If I didn't have money, I couldn't have lent some to you.

Point 104

02 다음 중 어법상 틀린 것은?

① I wish I have apologized to Michael then.
② I wish we could get rid of all the old furniture.
③ If you were in my shoes, you would do the same.
④ If it had not rained, we could have played soccer.
⑤ She told me about the accident as if she had seen it herself.

Point 101, 105

03 다음 빈칸에 공통으로 들어갈 말로 알맞은 것은?

• If it ________ winter now, I would go skiing.
• She speaks English as if she ________ American.

① be ② is ③ were
④ has been ⑤ had been

Point 103

04 다음 우리말을 영어로 바르게 옮긴 것은?

내가 그 문제에 대한 답을 안다면 좋을 텐데.

① I wish I knew the answer to that question.
② I wish I know the answer to that question.
③ I wish I had known the answer to that question.
④ I wish I have known the answer to that question.
⑤ I wish I could have known the answer to that question.

Point 102

05 다음 대화의 빈칸에 들어갈 말이 순서대로 짝지어진 것은?

A: I bought a vacuum cleaner at the store yesterday. It was quite expensive.
B: If you ________ it online, you ________ a discount.

① bought – can get
② buy – could have got
③ had bought – could get
④ have bought – could get
⑤ had bought – could have got

Point 106

06 다음 우리말과 일치하도록 할 때, 빈칸에 들어갈 말로 알맞은 것은?

그는 마치 그 캠프에 갔던 것처럼 말한다. (사실, 그는 캠프에 가지 않았음)
→ He talks as if he ________ to the camp.

① goes ② went ③ has gone
④ had gone ⑤ have gone

[07~08] 다음 빈칸에 들어갈 말로 알맞은 것을 고르시오.

Point 101

07

What would you do if you ________ very rich?

① be ② are ③ were
④ had been ⑤ have been

Point 105

08

He acts as if he ________ my boss. In fact, he isn't.

① is ② were ③ be
④ has been ⑤ had been

Point 102

09 다음 밑줄 친 부분 중 어법상 틀린 것은?

Jake felt(①) as if his heart stopped(②) when he saw(③) a thief. If he had been(④) brave, he could catch(⑤) the thief.

Point 106

10 다음 두 문장이 같은 뜻이 되도록 할 때, 빈칸에 들어갈 말로 알맞은 것은?

The athlete stopped running as if he had sprained his ankle.
= In fact, ________________.

① he sprained his ankle
② he didn't want to run
③ he wanted to run faster
④ he didn't sprain his ankle
⑤ he had sprained his ankle before

Point 103

11 다음 대화의 빈칸에 들어갈 말로 알맞은 것은?

A: I wish I ________ a ticket for the rock band's concert. All of the tickets sold out.
B: Me, too. I really want to see it.

① have ② had
③ have had ④ had had
⑤ would have had

고난도

Point 102

12 다음 빈칸에 들어갈 말이 나머지 넷과 다른 것은?

① I miss her. I wish she ________ here.
② Minji walks as if she ________ a model.
③ If you ________ there, you would have enjoyed yourself.
④ If my father ________ free, he could spend time with me.
⑤ If the movie ________ not scary, I would watch it with you.

서술형

Point 104

13 다음 주어진 문장을 가정법을 이용하여 바꿔 쓰시오.

I'm sorry that I didn't tell you sooner.

→ ________________

Point 105

14 다음 우리말과 일치하도록 주어진 조건을 이용하여 영작하시오.

조건 1 as if와 가정법을 사용할 것
조건 2 총 8단어로 쓸 것

너는 마치 그를 믿는 것처럼 말하고 있다.

→ ________________

[15~16] 다음 일기를 보고 아래 질문에 답하시오.

Yesterday was the worst day in my life. ⓐ I fell down in front of my friends. I wasn't careful. After that, I broke my glasses. What an idiot! ⓑ 어제로 다시 되돌아갈 수 있다면 좋을 텐데.

Point 102

15 밑줄 친 ⓐ를 가정법을 이용하여 한 문장으로 바꿔 쓰시오.

→ ________________
____

Point 103

16 밑줄 친 ⓑ를 괄호 안의 말을 이용하여 영작하시오.

→ ________________
(go back to)

Point 101, 102

01 다음 빈칸에 들어갈 말이 순서대로 짝지어진 것은?

> • I would rescue people in danger if I ________ Superman.
> • If I had taken the advice, I ________ succeeded.

① am – would
② was – would
③ were – would
④ were – would have
⑤ had been – would have

Point 103

02 다음 중 보기 와 의미가 같은 것은?

> 보기 I wish I had a dog.

① I'm glad that I have a dog.
② I was glad that I had a dog.
③ I'm sorry that I don't have a dog.
④ I'm sorry that I didn't have a dog.
⑤ I was sorry that I didn't have a dog.

Point 105

03 다음 밑줄 친 부분 중 어법상 틀린 것은?

> She behaves(①) as if(②) she is(③) a movie star. In fact, she is(④) just a normal(⑤) girl.

중요 Point 101

04 다음 중 어법상 옳은 것은?

① If she were kind, she will be popular.
② If I had the book, I could lend it to you.
③ If I saw your email, I would have called you.
④ If you had been there, you will enjoy the show.
⑤ If the camera had been cheaper, I could buy it.

고난도 Point 102

05 다음 중 두 문장의 연결이 내용상 어색한 것은?

① I don't have a sister. I wish I had one.
② The movie is only for adults. If I were older, I could see it.
③ He acts as if he were my teacher. In fact, he is my classmate.
④ I'm sorry that I didn't attend my yoga class yesterday. I wish I had gone to the class.
⑤ If I didn't miss the school bus, I could get to school with ease. I had to go to school on foot.

Point 105

06 다음 중 보기 의 속뜻을 바르게 표현한 것은?

> 보기 He pretended as if he were not interested in her.

① In fact, he is interested in her.
② In fact, he was interested in her.
③ In fact, he is not interested in her.
④ In fact, he was not interested in her.
⑤ In fact, he has been interested in her.

[07~08] 다음 빈칸에 들어갈 말로 알맞은 것을 고르시오.

Point 103

07

> I'm too busy these days. I wish I ________ free.

① am ② be ③ were
④ have been ⑤ had been

Point 102

08

> If the weather had been fine, I ________ hiking.

① go ② went
③ would go ④ will go
⑤ would have gone

[09~10] 다음 두 문장이 같은 뜻이 되도록 할 때, 빈칸에 들어갈 말로 알맞은 것을 고르시오.

Point 104

09

I'm sorry Jiho was not chosen for the leader.
= I wish Jiho ________ chosen for the leader.

① is ② was ③ were
④ has been ⑤ had been

Point 102

10

As my father was on a business trip, he couldn't come to my graduation.
= If my father ________ on a business trip, he could have come to my graduation.

① were ② were not ③ has not been
④ had been ⑤ had not been

[11~12] 다음 대화의 빈칸에 들어갈 말로 알맞은 것을 고르시오.

Point 101

11

A: ______________ if you won a lottery?
B: I would donate the money to charity.

① What do you do
② What can you do
③ What will you do
④ What would you do
⑤ What are you going to do

Point 104

12

A: Why didn't you hand in your homework on time?
B: Actually, I started my homework late at night.
________________.

① I wish I started it earlier.
② I'm glad I started it earlier.
③ I wish I had started it earlier.
④ I'm sorry I don't start it earlier.
⑤ I'm sorry you didn't start it earlier.

서술형

Point 103

13 다음 우리말과 일치하도록 괄호 안의 말을 빈칸에 알맞은 형태로 쓰시오.

우리 아파트에 운동 시설이 있다면 좋을 텐데. (have)

→ I wish my apartment ________ an exercise facility.

Point 106

14 다음 글의 흐름에 맞도록 괄호 안의 말을 이용하여 빈칸에 알맞은 말을 쓰시오.

You talk ______________________
__________. (as if) In fact, you were not right all the time.

Point 101

15 다음 대화의 밑줄 친 부분을 조건에 맞게 바꿔 쓰시오.

조건 1 "If I were you ~"로 시작할 것
조건 2 총 13단어로 쓸 것

A: My classmate always shakes his leg, and it bothers me.
B: Why don't you ask him to stop shaking his leg?
→ ______________________

Point 105

16 다음 대화의 흐름에 맞도록 주어진 조건에 따라 빈칸에 알맞은 말을 쓰시오.

조건 1 look과 as if를 사용할 것
조건 2 총 8단어로 쓸 것

A: Mom, look at me. I dressed up like a fire fighter.
B: Wow! You ______________________.

Grammar Review 핵심 정리

1 가정법 과거

Point

If you got more rest, **you would feel** better. 101

☞ 현재의 사실을 반대로 가정하거나 실현 가능성이 희박한 일을 가정할 때 사용한다.
☞ 「If+주어+동사의 과거형~, 주어+조동사의 과거형+동사원형…」의 형태로, '만약 ~하다면[이라면] …할 텐데'로 해석한다.

2 가정법 과거완료

If I had got up earlier, **I could have caught** the bus. 102

☞ 과거의 사실을 반대로 가정할 때 사용한다.
☞ 「If+주어+had p.p.~, 주어+조동사의 과거형+have p.p.…」의 형태로, '만약 ~했다면[였다면] …했을 텐데'로 해석한다.

3 I wish + 가정법

I wish I were taller than now. 103

☞ 「I wish+(that)+주어+동사의 과거형~」은 '~하면[이라면] 좋을 텐데'로 해석한다.
☞ 실현 불가능하거나 실현 가능성이 희박한 현재의 소망을 나타낸다.

I wish I had followed her advice. 104

☞ 「I wish+(that)+주어+had p.p.~」는 '~했다면[였다면] 좋았을 텐데'로 해석한다.
☞ 과거에 이루어지지 못했던 일에 대한 아쉬움이나 후회를 나타낸다.

4 as if + 가정법

He speaks **as if he knew** everything. 105

☞ 「as if+주어+동사의 과거형~」은 '마치 ~인[하는] 것처럼'으로 해석한다.
☞ 주절과 같은 시점에서 실제와 다른 상황을 나타낼 때 사용한다.

She acted **as if she hadn't met** me before. 106

☞ 「as if+주어+had p.p.~」는 '마치 ~였던[했던] 것처럼'으로 해석한다.
☞ 주절보다 더 과거 시점에서 실제와 다른 상황을 나타낼 때 사용한다.

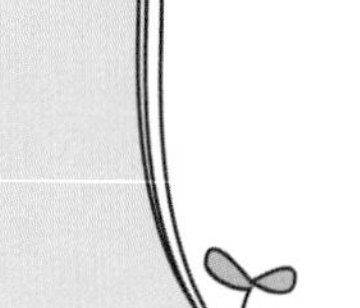

LESSON

12

접속사

Point 107 나는 동시에 슬프고 행복했다.

I felt sad and happy at the same time.

- 등위접속사는 형태와 문법적 역할이 대등한 단어와 단어, 구와 구, 절과 절을 연결하는 접속사로 and, but, or, so 등이 있다.
- and는 '~와', '그리고', '그래서' 등의 뜻으로 앞뒤 내용이 순조롭게 이어질 때 쓰거나, 대등한 것을 연결한다.
  I bought a shirt **and** a pair of pants.
- but은 '그러나', '그런데'의 뜻으로 서로 상반되거나 대조되는 내용을 연결한다.
  The food was expensive, **but** delicious.

TIP (1) and로 연결된 단어가 하나의 사물이나 개념을 나타낼 때는 단수 취급한다. Bread **and** butter is my favorite breakfast.
(2) 「**not A but B**」는 'A가 아니라 B'의 뜻이다. I am **not** sick **but** tired.

STEP 1 다음 괄호 안에서 알맞은 말을 고르시오.

1 I am cold (and, but) hungry.
2 John was sick (and, but) he came to school yesterday.
3 You can develop reading (and, but) writing skills through this book.
4 He lifted the box (and, but) put it down carefully.
5 The exam was difficult, (and, but) I managed to pass it.

□ develop 개발하다
□ manage to 겨우 ~하다

STEP 2 다음 우리말과 일치하도록 괄호 안의 말을 이용하여 빈칸에 알맞은 말을 쓰시오.

1 도서관은 9시에 열고 6시에 닫는다. (close)
The library opens at 9 ______________________.

2 경주는 쉽지 않았으나, 그는 포기하지 않았다. (give up)
The race was challenging, ______________________.

3 삼촌은 기술자가 아니라 수의사이다. (vet)
My uncle is not an engineer ______________________.

4 나는 배가 아파서 약을 먹었다. (take some medicine)
I had a stomachache ______________________.

□ challenging 쉽지 않은, 도전적인
□ give up 포기하다
□ engineer 기술자
□ vet 수의사
□ stomachache 복통

STEP 3 다음 중 어법상 틀린 것은? 내신

① Trial and error is a great teacher.
② I was very sick but didn't go see a doctor.
③ The audience was laughing and crying at the same time.
④ She likes playing the piano and take pictures in her free time.
⑤ I am not good at sports but good at playing musical instruments.

□ audience 관중
□ musical instrument 악기

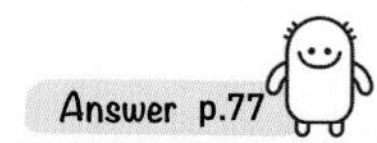

Point 108 너는 학교에 버스로 가니 아니면 자전거로 가니?

Do you go to school by bus or by bike?

- or은 '또는,' '아니면'의 뜻으로 둘이나 그 이상의 대상 중에서 선택할 때 쓴다.
  Which do you prefer, tea **or** coffee?
- so는 '그래서,' '그러므로'의 뜻으로 인과관계를 연결할 때 쓴다. 앞 내용에 대한 결과를 나타내기도 한다.
  He is not honest, **so** I don't trust him.

STEP 1 다음 괄호 안에서 알맞은 말을 고르시오.

1 You can stay (or, so) leave now.
2 He lost the key, (or, so) he couldn't enter the room.
3 Which do you like better, soccer, baseball (or, so) basketball?
4 Does your father work at a radio station (or, so) at a fire station?
5 I had a terrible headache, (or, so) I went to see a doctor.

□ stay 머무르다
□ radio station 라디오 방송국
□ fire station 소방서

STEP 2 다음 우리말과 일치하도록 괄호 안의 말을 바르게 배열하시오.

1 줄무늬 셔츠는 서랍 속이나 장롱 속에 있을 것이다. (the, or, in, closet)
The striped shirt might be in the drawer ______________________.

2 어두워서, 나는 그의 얼굴을 보지 못했다. (didn't, I, face, his, so, see)
It was dark, ______________________.

3 아무도 회의에 오지 않아서, 회의가 취소되었다. (it, so, canceled, was)
Nobody came to the meeting, ______________________.

4 너는 책, 잡지, 또는 일간지를 읽을 수 있다. (the, or, newspaper, daily)
You can read the books, the magazines, ______________________.

5 이 물고기들은 살아있니 아니면 죽었니? (dead, are, or, they)
Are those fish alive ______________________?

□ striped 줄무늬가 있는
□ drawer 서랍
□ cancel 취소하다
□ alive 살아있는

STEP 3 다음 빈칸에 들어갈 말이 나머지 넷과 다른 것은? 내신

① Is the story fact ________ fiction?
② You can call him now ________ later.
③ I broke the vase, ________ my mom got angry.
④ Which do you like better, pizza ________ spaghetti?
⑤ You can eat ________ drink only things that are liquid.

□ fact 사실
□ fiction 허구

Answer p.77

Point 109 내가 열 살 때, 우리 가족은 캐나다로 이주했다. 시간 접속사 when, as, while

When I was 10, my family moved to Canada.

- when은 '~할 때'의 뜻으로 특정한 때를 나타낸다.
  Stop writing **when** the bell rings.
- as는 '~하면서', '~할 때', '~함에 따라'의 뜻이다.
  As we got far away from the city, the roads got narrower.
- while은 '~하는 동안'의 뜻으로 특정 길이가 있는 기간을 나타낸다.
  Please take care of my dog **while** I'm away.
  TIP while은 '~인 데 반하여'의 뜻으로 둘 사이의 대조를 나타내기도 한다.

STEP 1 다음 문장을 밑줄 친 부분에 유의하여 우리말로 해석하시오.

1 When I have a cold, I have a sore throat.
2 As time went by, it got darker.
3 While he was taking a shower, he sang a song.
4 My father was abroad when I was born.
5 Try not to talk while you are eating.

□ sore throat 인후염
□ time goes by 시간이 지나다
□ abroad 해외에

STEP 2 다음 우리말과 일치하도록 괄호 안의 말을 바르게 배열하시오.

1 나는 눈이 오면 항상 눈사람을 만든다. (it, when, snows)
I always make a snowman ______________.

2 아기가 자는 동안 시끄럽게 하지 마라. (the, baby, is, while, sleeping)
Don't make any noise ______________.

3 내가 컴퓨터를 켰을 때, 엄마가 들어오셨다. (turned, on, I, as, the, computer)
______________, Mom came in.

4 그가 공원에서 조깅을 할 때, 비가 오기 시작했다. (he, jogged, when)
______________ in the park, it started to rain.

□ snowman 눈사람
□ prepare a meal 식사를 준비하다

STEP 3 다음 빈칸에 공통으로 들어갈 말로 알맞은 것은? 내신

- ________ I got there, the play started.
- ________ I drive, I listen to the radio.
- ________ time passed by, his illness got worse.

① As ② When ③ Once
④ While ⑤ Since

□ illness 병

Answer p.77
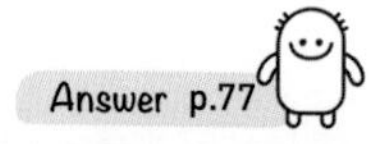

Please wait until the water boils.

- before는 '~하기 전에, ~하기에 앞서서'라는 뜻이다.
  I turned off the light **before** I went out.
- after는 '~한 후에'라는 뜻이다.
  It began to rain **after** I left home.
- until[till]은 '~할 때까지'의 뜻이다.
  I didn't wake up **until[till]** my mom came in my room.

TIP 시간·조건을 나타내는 부사절에서는 미래의 일이라도 현재시제를 쓴다.

STEP 1 다음 문장을 밑줄 친 부분에 유의하여 우리말로 해석하시오.

1 We took a walk after we had lunch.
2 Before I took the test, I took a deep breath.
3 I won't go to bed until my mom comes back.
4 They shook hands after the match was over.
5 People waited at the platform till the subway stopped.

□ take a walk 산책하다
□ take a deep breath 심호흡을 하다
□ shake hands 악수하다

STEP 2 다음 우리말과 일치하도록 빈칸에 알맞은 말을 쓰시오.

1 나는 숙제를 한 후에 TV를 보았다.
I watched TV ____________ I did my homework.

2 아이들은 해가 질 때까지 놀이터에서 놀았다.
The children played at the playground ____________ the sun set.

3 저녁식사를 하기 전에 손을 씻어라.
Wash your hands ____________ you have dinner.

4 Kim 선생님께서는 강의를 하기 전에 자기소개를 하셨다.
Mr. Kim introduced himself ____________ he started the lecture.

5 우리는 영화를 본 후에 쇼핑을 하러 갔다.
____________ we watched the movie, we went shopping.

□ set (해, 달이) 지다
□ introduce 소개하다
□ lecture 강의, 강연

STEP 3 다음 중 어법상 틀린 것은? 내신

① Before the bell rang, I finished the test.
② I'll call you after the concert will be over.
③ We have to get home before it starts raining.
④ He won't tell you anything until he makes up his mind.
⑤ Jisu saved her allowance until she could buy a new cell phone.

□ make up one's mind 결심하다
□ allowance 용돈

Answer p.78

Point 111 나는 아팠기 때문에 학교에 갈 수 없었다. 이유 접속사 because, as, since

I couldn't go to school because I was sick.

- because, as, since는 '~ 때문에'라는 뜻으로 이유의 부사절을 이끄는 접속사이다.

  I took a taxi **because** I was late.

  As he was very hungry, he ate a big lunch.

  Since there was no water, I couldn't take a shower.

  TIP because 뒤에는 '주어+동사'가 오고, because of 뒤에는 '명사(구)'가 온다.

STEP 1 다음 문장을 밑줄 친 부분에 유의하여 우리말로 해석하시오.

1 I was late for school because I got up late.

2 Since she didn't feel well, she left school early.

3 As he is only 5 years old, he can't get on the roller coaster.

4 Since you are new here, I'll give you a tour.

5 Susan was very happy because she got many presents.

□ feel well 몸 상태가 좋다
□ roller coaster 롤러코스터
□ give a tour 안내하다

STEP 2 다음 우리말과 일치하도록 괄호 안의 말을 이용하여 빈칸에 알맞은 말을 쓰시오.

1 나는 샤워하는 중이었기 때문에 전화를 받을 수 없었다. (because, take a shower)
I couldn't answer the phone ________________.

2 Lisa는 사려 깊기 때문에, 친구가 많다. (as, thoughtful)
________________, she has many friends.

3 밖이 추우니, 코트를 입어라. (since, cold outside)
________________, wear a coat.

4 민수는 여동생을 돌봐야 해서 콘서트에 갈 수 없었다. (because, take care of)
Minsu couldn't go to the concert ________________ his little sister.

5 그는 피곤했기 때문에, 휴식을 취했다. (because, tired)
________________, he took a rest.

□ thoughtful 사려 깊은
□ take care of ~을 돌보다
□ take a rest 쉬다

STEP 3 다음 빈칸에 들어갈 말이 나머지 넷과 다른 것은? 내신

① She isn't popular ________ she is selfish.
② We hurried ________ there wasn't enough time.
③ The plane couldn't take off ________ the heavy rain.
④ I went to see my grandmother ________ she was sick.
⑤ Fans were excited ________ the Korean soccer team won the game.

□ selfish 이기적인
□ take off 이륙하다

Answer p.78

Point 112 영화가 너무 지루해서 나는 잠이 들었다.

The movie was so boring that I fell asleep.

- 「so + 형용사/부사 + that …」은 '너무[매우] ~해서 …하다'의 뜻으로 that절에는 「**so + 형용사/부사**」로 인한 결과가 나온다. 「**형용사/부사 + enough + to부정사**」로 바꿔 쓸 수 있다.
  She practiced speaking English **so** hard **that** she was able to do well in the contest.
  = She practiced speaking English hard **enough to** do well in the contest.

  TIP 「so + 형용사 + that …」은 「such (a/an) + 형용사 + 명사 + that …」으로 바꿔 쓸 수 있다.
  The cake was **so** delicious **that** everyone liked it. = It was **such** a delicious cake **that** everyone liked it.

STEP 1 다음 괄호 안에서 알맞은 말을 고르시오.

□ attract 마음을 끌다
□ solve (문제를) 풀다
□ thirsty 목이 마른

1 The weather was (so, such) nice that we went on a picnic.
2 She was beautiful enough (that, to) attract many people.
3 The puzzle was so difficult (how, that) nobody solved it.
4 I was thirsty (so, enough) to drink three glasses of water.
5 I was (so, enough) hungry that I ate all the food on the table.

STEP 2 다음 우리말과 일치하도록 빈칸에 알맞은 말을 쓰시오.

□ put down 내려놓다
□ take a nap 낮잠자다

1 그 책은 너무 재미있어서 나는 그것을 내려놓을 수가 없었다.
The book was ____________ interesting ____________ I couldn't put it down.

2 경기에서 이길만큼 충분히 그들은 열심히 연습했다.
They practiced hard ____________ ____________ win the game.

3 그 수프는 너무 매워서 John은 그것을 다 먹을 수 없었다.
The soup was ____________ spicy ____________ John couldn't finish it.

4 그녀는 낮잠을 잘만큼 충분히 졸렸다.
She was sleepy ____________ ____________ take a nap.

5 나는 너무 놀라서 아무 말도 할 수가 없었다.
I was ____________ surprised ____________ I couldn't say anything.

STEP 3 다음 중 보기와 의미가 같은 것은? 내신

보기	He is strong enough to move the box.

① He is so strong that he can move the box.
② He is so strong that he can't move the box.
③ He is such strong that he can move the box.
④ He is not so strong that he can move the box.
⑤ He is not so strong that he could move the box.

Answer p.78

Point 113 피자를 너무 많이 먹는다면, 넌 살이 찔 것이다.

조건 접속사 if, unless

If you eat too much pizza, you'll get fat.

- if는 '만일 ~라면(한다면)'의 뜻으로 어떤 사건이나 행동이 일어날 수 있는 조건을 제시한다.
  If you keep the secret, I'll tell you everything.
- unless는 '만일 ~하지 않는다면'의 뜻으로 「**if ~ not**」으로 바꿔 쓸 수 있다. 그 자체에 부정적 의미가 포함되어 있으므로 unless 뒤에는 보통 부정어가 오지 않는다.
  I want to join the team **unless** it's late.

STEP 1 다음 괄호 안에서 알맞은 말을 고르시오.

1 (If, Unless) you finish your homework, you can go out.
2 (If, Unless) you don't hurry, you'll miss the bus.
3 Anyone can lose weight (if, unless) they exercise regularly.
4 (If, Unless) I am too busy, I'll help you finish your work.
5 It's difficult to find the place (if, unless) you have a map.

□ lose weight 살을 빼다
□ regularly 규칙적으로

STEP 2 다음 우리말과 일치하도록 괄호 안의 말을 이용하여 빈칸에 알맞은 말을 쓰시오.

1 너에게 돈이 좀 있다면, 나에게 빌려줘라. (if)
______________________, please lend it to me.

2 네가 약속을 지키지 않는다면, 나는 너에게 기회를 주지 않겠다. (unless)
______________________, I won't give you an opportunity.

3 비가 오지 않는다면, 우리는 등산을 하러 갈 것이다. (unless)
We are going to go hiking ______________________.

4 그가 우리 팀에 합류한다면, 우리는 우승할 것이다. (if)
We will win the game ______________________.

5 네가 나를 도와주지 않는다면, 나는 이 프로젝트를 끝낼 수 없다. (unless)
______________________, I can't finish the project.

□ lend 빌려주다
□ keep a promise 약속을 지키다
□ opportunity 기회

STEP 3 다음 빈칸에 들어갈 말이 나머지 넷과 다른 것은? 내신

① ________ you feel cold, drink this tea.
② ________ you're tired, let's go to the movies.
③ ________ you meet her, you'll see why I like her.
④ ________ you know her address, please let me know.
⑤ ________ you leave now, you can catch the first train.

□ address 주소
□ catch (버스, 기차 등을 시간 맞춰) 타다

Answer p.79

Point 114 나는 공부를 열심히 했음에도 불구하고 시험에 떨어졌다. 양보 접속사 though[although]

Although[Though] I studied hard, I failed the test.

- though와 although는 '비록 ~이지만' '~임에도 불구하고'의 뜻으로, 의미를 강조하기 위해 even though로도 쓴다.

Though[Although] I was full, I ate the dessert.

TIP despite와 in spite of는 전치사(구)로 '…에도 불구하고'의 의미이다.

STEP 1 다음 문장을 밑줄 친 부분에 유의하여 우리말로 해석하시오.

1 Although the traffic was heavy, we arrived on time.

2 The children went for a walk despite the heavy rain.

3 Although my family is not rich, we are happy.

4 Even though he lied to me, I can forgive him.

5 The actress is attractive although she is not that kind.

□ traffic 교통
□ heavy (차가) 막히는
□ on time 제 시간에
□ attractive 매력적인

STEP 2 다음 우리말과 일치하도록 괄호 안의 말을 바르게 배열하시오.

1 그는 키가 작음에도 불구하고 힘이 세다. (although, short, is, he)
_______________, he is strong.

2 해가 비침에도 불구하고 날씨가 춥다. (is, though, the, sun, shining)
_______________, it is cold.

3 우리 팀이 경기에서 졌음에도 불구하고 우리는 최선을 다했다.
(although, lost, our, the, team, game)
_______________, we did our best.

4 그것은 사실이었음에도 불구하고 사람들은 그것을 믿지 않았다. (though, was, true, it)
_______________, people didn't believe it.

5 우리 할머니는 비록 연세가 많으시지만 아직도 일을 하신다.
(although, grandmother, old, my, is)
_______________, she still works.

□ shine 빛나다, 반짝이다
□ do one's best 최선을 다하다

STEP 3 다음 중 어법상 틀린 것은? 내신

① Despite it was true, I didn't believe it.
② Although it was hot, he wore winter clothes.
③ I am healthy even though I usually skip breakfast.
④ She wants to be a singer although she doesn't sing well.
⑤ Although the restaurant is popular, its food is not that good.

□ skip 거르다

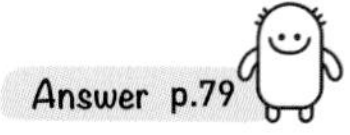

Point 115 수지는 예쁠 뿐만 아니라 친절하기까지 하다.

both A and B/
not only A but also B

Suji is not only pretty but also kind.

- 「both A and B」는 'A와 B 둘 다'라는 뜻으로 복수 취급한다.
  Both Eric **and** Ben *are* professional basketball players.
- 「not only A but (also) B」는 'A뿐만 아니라 B도'라는 뜻으로 주어로 쓰일 경우 B에 동사의 수를 일치시킨다.
  Not only the driver **but also** the passengers *were* hurt in the accident.

TIP 「not only A but (also) B」와 의미가 같은 표현으로 「B as well as A」가 있다.

STEP 1 다음 괄호 안에서 알맞은 말을 고르시오.

1 (All, Both) Minsu and his brother are English teachers.
2 Not only Koreans (and, but) also Japanese respect the elderly.
3 The soup was not (both, only) hot but also bitter.
4 The book is both interesting (and, but) educational.
5 (No, Not) only I but also you have to attend the meeting.

- □ respect 공경하다
- □ bitter (맛이) 쓴
- □ educational 교육적인
- □ attend 참석하다

STEP 2 다음 우리말과 일치하도록 빈칸에 알맞은 말을 쓰시오.

1 Tom은 기타와 피아노를 둘 다 연주할 수 있다.
Tom can play ______________________.

2 우리는 중국 뿐만 아니라 베트남도 방문할 계획이다.
We are going to visit ______________________.

3 그는 잘생겼을 뿐만 아니라 키도 크다.
He is ______________________.

4 Linda 뿐만 아니라 그의 남동생도 스페인어를 말할 수 있다.
______________________ can speak Spanish.

5 Matt와 John은 둘 다 운동을 잘한다.
______________________ are good at sports.

- □ Spanish 스페인어
- □ be good at ~을 잘하다

STEP 3 다음 중 어법상 틀린 것은? 내신

① Both soccer and baseball are popular sports.
② Ms. Kim is not only kind but also intelligent.
③ We felt both sadness and anger at the news.
④ She as well as her mother is allergic to peanuts.
⑤ Not only I but also my brother are a big fan of the player.

- □ intelligent 지적인
- □ sadness 슬픔
- □ anger 분노
- □ allergic 알레르기가 있는
- □ peanut 땅콩

Answer p.79

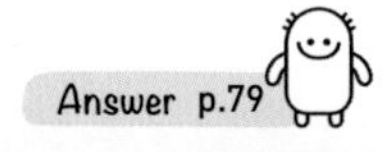

Point 116 너는 커피 또는 주스를 마실 수 있다.

You can drink either coffee or juice.

- 「**either A or B**」는 'A와 B 둘 중 하나'라는 뜻으로 주어로 쓰일 경우 B에 동사의 수를 일치시킨다.
  Either Susan **or** I *have* to take care of the baby.
- 「**neither A nor B**」는 'A도 B도 아닌'의 뜻으로 두 가지 이상을 동시에 부정할 때 쓴다. 주어로 쓰일 경우 B에 동사의 수를 일치시킨다.
  Neither Tom **nor** his team members *were* satisfied with the result.

STEP 1 다음 괄호 안에서 알맞은 말을 고르시오.

□ genius 천재
□ idiot 바보

1 (Either, Neither) you or I am wrong.
2 Helen Keller could (either, neither) see nor hear.
3 You can have (either, neither) Italian food or Indian food here.
4 Neither Minho (or, nor) Changmin was chosen for the soccer team.
5 He is either a genius (or, nor) an idiot.

STEP 2 다음 우리말과 일치하도록 빈칸에 알맞은 말을 쓰시오.

1 나는 키가 크지도 작지도 않다.
I am ______________________.

2 우리 점심으로 피자나 스파게티를 먹자.
Let's have ______________________ for lunch.

3 그는 글을 읽을 줄도 쓸 줄도 모른다.
He can ______________________.

4 Lisa도 나도 둘 다 수영을 잘하지 못한다.
______________________ good at swimming.

5 너와 Minji 둘 중 한 명은 거짓말을 하고 있다.
______________________ lying.

STEP 3 다음 빈칸에 들어갈 말이 순서대로 짝지어진 것은? 내신

□ be to blame 책임이 있다
□ be responsible for ~ 에 책임이 있다
□ matter 문제

- Either I or you ________ to blame.
- Neither I nor you ________ responsible for that matter.

① am – are ② am – am ③ are – am
④ are – are ⑤ is – are

Answer p.80

Point 117 나는 그가 진실을 말하고 있다는 것을 알고 있었다.

I knew that he was telling the truth.

- that은 '~이라는 것'의 의미로 명사절을 이끌며 문장에서 주어, 목적어, 보어 역할을 한다.
  That he lost the election was shocking. (주어)
  I think **that** she is fashionable. (목적어)
  The fact is **that** he is a liar. (보어)
- that절이 문장에서 주어 역할을 할 경우 일반적으로 그 자리에 가주어 it을 쓰고 진주어 that절은 뒤로 보낸다.
  That he is smart is not true. = **It** is not true **that** he is smart.

TIP that절이 목적어 역할을 할 때 that은 생략 가능하다.

STEP 1 다음 문장을 밑줄 친 부분에 유의하여 우리말로 해석하고, that절의 역할을 쓰시오.

1 That blood is thicker than water is true. (   )
2 I know that I am funny. (   )
3 The problem is that we don't have enough time. (   )
4 It is a pity that you can't come to the camp. (   )
5 The key point is that we can control the matter. (   )

□ blood 피
□ thick 진한, 두꺼운
□ pity 유감
□ key 핵심적인
□ control 통제하다

STEP 2 다음 우리말과 일치하도록 괄호 안의 말을 바르게 배열하시오.

1 어떤 사람들은 돈이 가장 중요하다고 생각한다. (that, is, money, important, most)
Some people think ______________________________.

2 사실은 우리가 출구를 찾을 수 없다는 것이다. (we, the, way, out, can't, that, find)
The fact is ______________________________.

3 그녀가 겨우 9살이라는 것은 놀랍다. (she, only, is, that, 9, years, old)
______________________________ is surprising.

4 나는 네가 미국으로 떠난다고 들었다. (are, that, the United States, leaving, you, for)
I heard ______________________________.

□ way out 출구

STEP 3 다음 중 어법상 틀린 것은? 내신

① I don't think that I did anything wrong.
② It is disappointing that you lied to me.
③ She is the only child is not surprising.
④ The important thing is that we are happy together.
⑤ The news that the musician passed away was shocking.

□ disappointing 실망스러운
□ pass away 죽다
□ shocking 충격적인

Answer p.80

Point 118 너는 그녀가 올지 안 올지 알고 있니?

Do you know **whether** she will come or not?

- 명사절을 이끄는 if는 '~인지 아닌지'의 뜻으로 목적어나 진주어로 쓰인다.
  I want to know **if** Mike loves me. (목적어)
  It doesn't matter **if** we are late. (진주어)
- 명사절을 이끄는 whether은 '~인지 아닌지'의 뜻으로 주어, 목적어, 보어 역할을 하고 뒤에 or not이 붙기도 한다.
  It really matters **whether** we can raise the funds **or not**. (주어)
  I wonder **whether** he is at home. (목적어)
  The question is **whether** it still exists. (보어)

STEP 1 다음 괄호 안에서 알맞은 말을 고르시오.

□ decide 결정하다
□ matter 중요하다

1 Do you know (while, whether) she is sick?
2 (If, Whether) you like it or not is not important.
3 I can't decide (if, until) I will go there.
4 It doesn't matter (if, when) we win or lose.
5 The problem is (because, whether) we can stay at the hotel or not.

STEP 2 다음 우리말과 일치하도록 괄호 안의 말을 바르게 배열하시오.

□ in style 유행하는

1 나는 그것이 유행이 아니라도 상관하지 않는다. (if, not, in, style, it, is)
I don't care ______________________.

2 너는 그녀가 곧 돌아올지 아닐지 알고 있니? (soon, if, come, she, will, back)
Do you know ______________________?

3 비가 올지 안 올지는 중요하지 않다. (not , whether, or, it, will, rain)
______________________ doesn't matter.

4 그는 다른 도시로 이사갈지 말지 생각 중이다. (he, move, will, to, city, if, another)
He is thinking ______________________.

STEP 3 다음 빈칸에 공통으로 들어갈 말로 알맞은 것은? 내신

□ recover 회복되다
□ illness 병

- Nobody knows ________ she will recover from her illness.
- I can't finish my homework ________ you don't help me.

① if ② that ③ which
④ whether ⑤ unless

Answer p.81

Point 119 지금 떠나라, 그러면 너는 버스를 탈 수 있을 것이다. 명령문+and / 명령문+or

Leave now, and you'll catch the bus.

- 「**명령문, and ~**」는 '…해라, 그러면 ~할 것이다'의 뜻으로 if절로 바꿔 쓸 수 있다.
  Help each other, **and** you'll save time. (= *If* you help each other, you'll save time.)
- 「**명령문, or ~**」은 '…해라, 그렇지 않으면 ~할 것이다'의 뜻으로 if ~ not이나 unless로 바꿔 쓸 수 있다.
  Keep the deadline, **or** you'll lose points.
  (= *If* you *don't* keep the deadline, you'll lose points. / *Unless* you keep the deadline, you'll lose points.)

STEP 1 다음 괄호 안에서 알맞은 말을 고르시오.

□ catch a cold 감기 걸리다
□ stay in shape 건강(몸매)을 유지하다

1 Wear a jacket, (and, or) you will catch a cold.
2 Call your mom, (and, or) she'll worry about you.
3 Take some medicine, (and, or) you'll feel much better.
4 Take an umbrella, (and, or) you won't get wet.
5 Exercise regularly, (and, or) you will stay in shape.

STEP 2 다음 우리말과 일치하도록 빈칸에 알맞은 말을 쓰시오.

□ honest 정직한

1 공부를 열심히 해라, 그렇지 않으면 너는 시험에 합격할 수 없다.
Study hard, ____________ you won't pass the exam.

2 조심해라, 그렇지 않으면 너는 다칠 것이다.
Be careful, ____________ yo will get hurt.

3 부모님께 솔직해라, 그러면 부모님께서 너를 이해하실 것이다.
Be honest with your parents, ____________ they will understand you.

4 수업 시간에 자지 마라, 그렇지 않으면 너의 선생님께서 화를 낼 것이다.
Don't sleep in class, ____________ your teacher will get angry.

STEP 3 다음 빈칸에 들어갈 말이 나머지 넷과 다른 것은? 내신

□ achieve 성취하다

① Go to bed early, _________ you will feel tired.
② Study hard, _________ you will get good grades.
③ Do your best, _________ you won't achieve your goal.
④ Don't eat too much, _________ you will have a stomachache.
⑤ Practice English more, _________ you won't be able to speak English well.

Answer p.81

Point 107, 115

01 다음 빈칸에 공통으로 들어갈 말로 알맞은 것은?

• I am so sleepy ________ tired.
• She can speak both English ________ French.

① and ② but ③ or
④ so ⑤ as

고난도 Point 109

02 다음 밑줄 친 부분의 의미가 나머지 넷과 다른 것은?

① He is short while his brother is very tall.
② While I was sleeping, it snowed heavily.
③ Somebody broke into my house while I was out.
④ While I was washing the dishes, I broke a cup.
⑤ You should not use your cell phone while you are driving.

[03~04] 다음 중 어법상 틀린 것을 고르시오.

Point 107

03 ① My room is not large, but it is cozy.
② The movie was very long but interest.
③ I met both Susan and Kathy yesterday.
④ Have you been to Hong Kong or Taiwan?
⑤ There was not enough time, so I asked for help.

Point 111

04 ① As it is getting cold, we should go home.
② Because she was sick, she didn't go to work.
③ She moved to Dallas because she got a new job.
④ Since it's raining outside, we should stay home.
⑤ Because of the traffic was terrible, we were late.

Point 112

05 다음 두 문장이 같은 뜻이 같도록 할 때, 빈칸에 들어갈 말이 순서대로 짝지어진 것은?

The gentleman was ________ kind that he showed me the way.
= The gentleman was kind ________ to show me the way.

① so – though ② so – enough
③ so – unless ④ such – though
⑤ such – enough

Point 114

06 다음 우리말과 일치하도록 할 때, 빈칸에 들어갈 말로 알맞은 것은?

그는 걸을 수 없었음에도 불구하고, 그는 경주를 포기하지 않았다.
→ ________ he couldn't walk, he didn't give up the race.

① Since ② While ③ Until
④ After ⑤ Although

[07~10] 다음 빈칸에 들어갈 말로 알맞은 것을 고르시오.

Point 113

07

________ you feel tired, take a rest.

① Until ② If ③ That
④ Whether ⑤ Or

Point 116

08

I felt neither sad ________ happy at the news.

① or ② so ③ nor
④ for ⑤ also

Answer p.81

09

Point 117

People say ________ health is most important.

① when ② while ③ that
④ if ⑤ whether

10

Point 119

Stop talking, ________ your teacher will be mad at you.

① or ② and ③ so
④ but ⑤ till

11

Point 117

다음 밑줄 친 부분 중 쓰임이 나머지 넷과 다른 것은?

① We knew that we were in trouble.
② Did you hear that he won the election?
③ I was watching TV at home at that time.
④ It is interesting that she has a twin sister.
⑤ The problem was that nobody had money.

12

Point 110

다음 두 문장이 같은 뜻이 되도록 할 때, 빈칸에 들어갈 말로 알맞은 것은?

I took a shower. And then, I ate some cookies.
= ________ I took a shower, I ate some cookies.

① Before ② Until ③ When
④ As ⑤ After

서술형

13

Point 113

다음 문장을 unless를 이용하여 바꿔 쓰시오.

If you don't clean your room, your mom will scold you.

→ ________________________________

14

Point 118

다음 우리말과 일치하도록 주어진 조건을 이용하여 영작하시오.

조건 1 whether를 사용할 것
조건 2 총 10단어로 쓸 것

너는 내일 비가 올지 안 올지 알고 있니?
→ ________________________________

[15~16] 다음 Jisu의 스케줄 표를 보고 아래 질문에 답하시오.

	Wed.	Fri.
Morning	Meet Kevin	Have lunch
Afternoon	Go swimming	Go to the library

15

Point 110

What will Jisu do on Wednesday? (after를 사용)
→ She will ________________________________.

16

Point 013

What will Jisu do on Friday? (before를 사용)
→ She will ________________________________.

Point 113, 118

01 다음 중 보기 의 밑줄 친 부분과 의미가 같은 것은?

보기 I can't decide if I will take the job.

① I will lend you my notebook if you need it.
② Please contact me if you have any questions.
③ I don't know if she still lives in this neighborhood.
④ If I have a time, I will hang out with my friends.
⑤ You can't go out if you don't finish your homework.

Point 119

02 다음 빈칸에 들어갈 말이 나머지 넷과 다른 것은?

① Set an alarm, ________ you will get up late.
② Water the plants regularly, ________ they will die.
③ Stop eating late at night, ________ you will lose weight.
④ Clean the mess, ________ you parents will be angry.
⑤ Wear gloves, ________ your hands will freeze.

중요

Point 117

03 다음 밑줄 친 부분 중 성격이 나머지 넷과 다른 것은?

① That the earth is round is true.
② Everyone knows that she loves music.
③ Many people say that the man is diligent.
④ The fact is that nobody wants that position.
⑤ Look at that man standing next to the tree.

고난도

Point 116

04 다음 중 어법상 틀린 것은?

① Neither Sumi nor I has the key.
② Eric as well as Amy likes cooking.
③ Either you or I have to stay here.
④ Both you and your friend are welcome.
⑤ Not only Juho but also his brother was absent.

Point 108, 112

05 다음 빈칸에 공통으로 들어갈 말로 알맞은 것은?

• It was warm, ________ I took off my jacket.
• The tea was ________ hot that I couldn't drink it.

① so ② as ③ too
④ very ⑤ and

Point 117

06 다음 문장에서 접속사 that이 들어가야 할 곳은?

It was (①) surprising (②) the baseball player (③) caught and threw (④) the ball with (⑤) only one hand.

[07~10] 다음 빈칸에 들어갈 말로 알맞은 것을 고르시오.

Point 110

07

He kept waiting ________ the door opened.

① as ② while ③ whether
④ if ⑤ until

Point 113

08

________ you read this book, you can't write a report about it.

① And ② But ③ Or
④ Unless ⑤ That

Point 119

09

> Wear a helmet, __________ you will be safe.

① as ② but ③ and
④ if ⑤ so

Point 114

10

> The baby slept sound __________ the room was noisy.

① if ② that ③ whether
④ after ⑤ although

Point 109, 111

11 다음 밑줄 친 부분 중 의미가 나머지 넷과 다른 것은?

① As he works, he listens to classical music.
② As I don't have money, I can't go shopping.
③ As the bus has already left, we'll have to wait.
④ As you're under 14, you can't watch the movie.
⑤ As my music teacher is kind, students like her.

Point 109, 110

12 다음 대화의 빈칸에 들어갈 말이 순서대로 짝지어진 것은?

> A: Can you look after your little sister __________ I'm making a cake this afternoon?
> B: Of course, I will come home __________ school is over.

① when – till ② while – until
③ when – until ④ while – after
⑤ until – after

서술형

Point 116

13 다음 두 문장을 주어진 조건에 맞게 한 문장으로 바꿔 쓰시오.

> **조건 1** neither를 사용할 것
> **조건 2** 총 7단어로 쓸 것

My father doesn't like hiking. He doesn't like fishing.

→ ______________________________

Point 119

14 다음 우리말과 일치하도록 주어진 조건을 이용하여 영작하시오.

> **조건 1** 명령문을 사용할 것
> **조건 2** 총 8단어로 쓸 것

서둘러라, 그렇지 않으면 너는 버스를 놓칠 것이다.

→ ______________________________

[15~16] 다음 표를 보고 아래 질문에 답하시오.

	Height	Personality
Emily	short	outgoing, friendly
Amy	tall	

Point 109

15 Emily와 Amy의 키를 비교하는 문장을 쓰시오.

> **조건 1** while로 시작하여 Emily부터 언급할 것
> **조건 2** 총 7단어로 쓸 것

→ ______________________________

Point 115

16 Emily와 Amy의 성격을 서술하시오.

> **조건 1** both A and B를 사용하여 Emily부터 언급할 것
> **조건 2** 총 8단어로 쓸 것

→ ______________________________

Grammar Review 핵심 정리

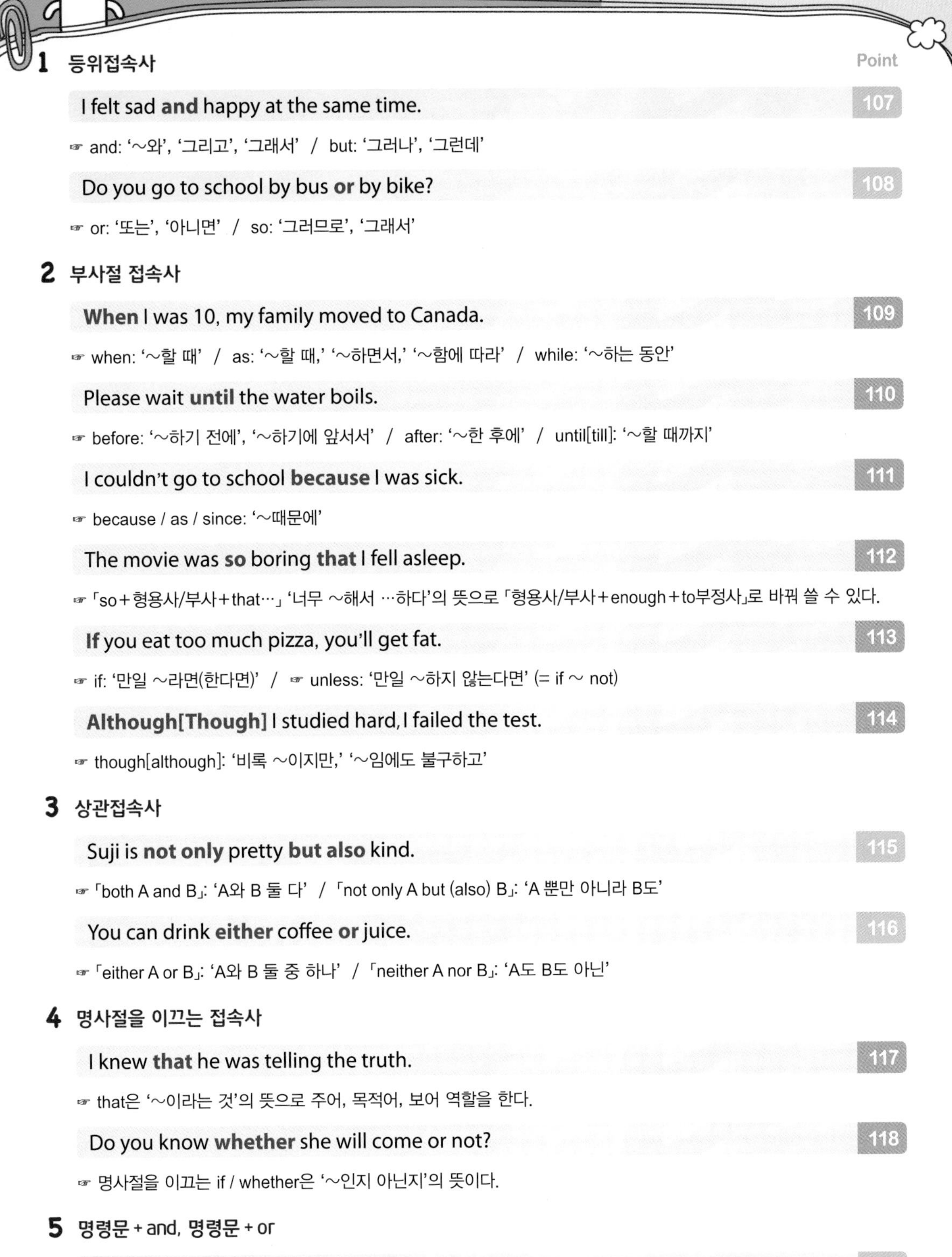

1 등위접속사

Point

I felt sad **and** happy at the same time. 107

☞ and: '~와', '그리고', '그래서' / but: '그러나', '그런데'

Do you go to school by bus **or** by bike? 108

☞ or: '또는', '아니면' / so: '그러므로', '그래서'

2 부사절 접속사

When I was 10, my family moved to Canada. 109

☞ when: '~할 때' / as: '~할 때,' '~하면서,' '~함에 따라' / while: '~하는 동안'

Please wait **until** the water boils. 110

☞ before: '~하기 전에', '~하기에 앞서서' / after: '~한 후에' / until[till]: '~할 때까지'

I couldn't go to school **because** I was sick. 111

☞ because / as / since: '~때문에'

The movie was **so** boring **that** I fell asleep. 112

☞ 「so+형용사/부사+that…」 '너무 ~해서 …하다'의 뜻으로 「형용사/부사+enough+to부정사」로 바꿔 쓸 수 있다.

If you eat too much pizza, you'll get fat. 113

☞ if: '만일 ~라면(한다면)' / ☞ unless: '만일 ~하지 않는다면' (= if ~ not)

Although[Though] I studied hard, I failed the test. 114

☞ though[although]: '비록 ~이지만,' '~임에도 불구하고'

3 상관접속사

Suji is **not only** pretty **but also** kind. 115

☞ 「both A and B」: 'A와 B 둘 다' / 「not only A but (also) B」: 'A 뿐만 아니라 B도'

You can drink **either** coffee **or** juice. 116

☞ 「either A or B」: 'A와 B 둘 중 하나' / 「neither A nor B」: 'A도 B도 아닌'

4 명사절을 이끄는 접속사

I knew **that** he was telling the truth. 117

☞ that은 '~이라는 것'의 뜻으로 주어, 목적어, 보어 역할을 한다.

Do you know **whether** she will come or not? 118

☞ 명사절을 이끄는 if / whether은 '~인지 아닌지'의 뜻이다.

5 명령문 + and, 명령문 + or

Leave now, **and** you'll catch the bus. 119

☞ 「명령문, and ~」: '…해라, 그러면 ~할 것이다' / 「명령문, or ~」: '…해라, 그렇지 않으면 ~할 것이다'

숨마 주니어® 중학 영문법 매뉴얼 119

FINISH

10 minutes

마무리 10분 TEST

Lesson 01 문장의 형태

[01~04] 다음 괄호 안에서 알맞은 말을 고르시오.

01 Dad looked (angry, angrily).

02 I advised her (staying, to stay) active.

03 I'd like to have my photo (taken, take).

04 I saw a man (sleeping, sleeps) on the bench.

[05~08] 다음 4형식 문장을 3형식 문장으로 바꿔 쓰시오.

05 I bought her a beautiful dress.

→ I ______________________________.

06 He asked them an important question.

→ He ______________________________.

07 Jimmy cooked his friends dinner that evening.

→ Jimmy ______________________________.

08 Can you lend me your dictionary?

→ Can you ______________________________?

[09~12] 다음 우리말과 일치하도록 괄호 안의 단어를 빈칸에 알맞은 형태로 쓰시오.

09 장교는 그들에게 출발하라고 명령했다. (leave)

The officer ordered them ________.

10 Tom은 밖에서 사람들이 이야기하는 소리를 들을 수 있었다. (talk)

Tom could hear people ________ outside.

11 그의 손녀는 그를 항상 미소 짓게 한다. (smile)

His granddaughter always makes him ________.

12 Jessica는 아들이 그 공포 영화를 보도록 허락하지 않았다. (watch)

Jessica didn't let her son ________ the horror movie.

[13~16] 다음 밑줄 친 부분을 바르게 고치시오.

13 That doesn't sound <u>an apology</u>.

14 She asked a favor <u>to her sister</u>.

15 He <u>kept calmly</u> during the competition.

16 Her parents <u>allowed her go</u> to the concert.

[17~20] 다음 우리말과 일치하도록 괄호 안의 말을 바르게 배열하시오.

17 네 여동생을 혼자 있게 내버려 두지 마. (your, alone, sister, leave)
Don't ________________________.

18 내가 여행 가방을 싸는 것 좀 도와줄래? (me, suitcase, help, my, pack)
Can you ________________________?

19 제가 당신의 반지를 당신에게 찾아 줄게요. (your, you, ring, find, for)
I'll ________________________.

20 Maria는 아들에게 부엌을 청소하도록 시켰다. (her son, clean up, got, to, the kitchen)
Maria ________________________.

[21~25] 다음 우리말과 일치하도록 괄호 안의 말을 이용하여 빈칸에 알맞은 말을 쓰시오.

21 그들은 우리에게 즉시 팩스를 보낼 것이다. (send, a fax)
They will immediately ________________ us.

22 나는 그가 나를 쳐다보고 있음을 알아차렸다. (notice, look)
I ________________ at me.

23 우리 엄마는 내게 커다란 케이크를 만들어 주셨다. (make, a huge cake)
My mom ________________ me.

24 내가 그들에게 이 상자를 다락방으로 옮기도록 시킬게요. (have, move)
I'll ________________ these boxes to the attic.

25 우리 부모님은 내가 최선을 다할 것이라고 기대하셨다. (expect, do my best)
My parents ________________.

Lesson 02

동사의 시제

[01~05] 다음 밑줄 친 부분을 바르게 고치시오.

01 Peter is having breakfast at 7 every morning.

02 A baby slept! Please, be quiet now!

03 When you called me, I am preparing dinner.

04 The Korean War breaks out in 1950.

05 Seoul was the capital city of Korea.

[06~09] 다음 우리말과 일치하도록 빈칸에 알맞은 말을 쓰시오.

06 내가 그에게 전화를 걸었을 때, 그는 운전 중이었다.

When I called him, he ___________ ___________.

07 나의 할아버지는 매일 신문을 읽는다.

My grandfather ___________ the newspaper every day.

08 나는 너에게 10분 전에 전화를 걸었는데, 너는 받지 않았어.

I ___________ you ten minutes ago, but you didn't answer.

09 말보다 행동이 중요하다.

Actions ___________ louder than words.

[10~13] 다음 우리말과 일치하도록 괄호 안의 말을 이용하여 빈칸에 알맞은 말을 쓰시오.

10 그는 세 달 동안 그 카메라를 사용해 왔다. (use)

He ___________ ___________ the camera ___________ for three months.

11 그는 평생 해외여행을 해 본 적이 없다. (travel)

He ___________ ___________ ___________ abroad in his life.

12 나는 오늘 아침부터 그를 보지 못했다. (see)

I ___________ ___________ him ___________ this morning.

13 너희들은 얼마나 오랫동안 알고 지냈니? (know)

How long ___________ ___________ ___________ each other?

[14~17] 다음 밑줄 친 부분을 바르게 고쳐 문장을 다시 쓰시오.

Answer p.85

14 Maggie has written the report last night.

15 He hasn't been at work since a week.

16 I used this cell phone for two years.

17 I haven't seen him for last year.

[18~21] 다음 문장을 현재완료를 이용하여 바꿔 쓰시오.

18 I moved to Suwon three years ago, and I still live here.

→ I ________________________________.

19 The boy lost his favorite toy car, and he can't find it.

→ The boy ________________________________.

20 I got this medal in 2002, and I still have it.

→ I ________________________________.

21 Cathy went to London. She doesn't live here now.

→ Cathy ________________________________.

[22~25] 다음 우리말과 일치하도록 괄호 안의 말을 바르게 배열하시오.

22 그녀는 지금 막 돌아왔다. (just, has, come, back)

She ________________________________.

23 그는 아직 꽃을 사지 못했다. (yet, bought, hasn't, the, flowers)

He ________________________________.

24 나는 이미 그 소설을 읽었다. (read, the, novel, have, already)

I ________________________________.

25 너는 태국 음식을 먹어본 적이 있니? (eaten, you, have, ever)

________________________________ Thai food?

Lesson 03

조동사

[01~04] 다음 밑줄 친 부분을 바르게 고치시오.

01 He can <u>fixing</u> his bike.

02 I <u>can't</u> understand her at that time.

03 You <u>not must</u> make a single mistake.

04 I <u>have to</u> attend the meeting yesterday.

[05~08] 다음 우리말과 일치하도록 빈칸에 알맞은 말을 쓰시오.

05 그는 그가 본 것을 믿을 수가 없었다.
He ________ ________ ________ his eyes.

06 운전 면허증을 볼 수 있을까요?
________ ________ ________ your driver's license?

07 우리는 종종 저녁을 먹고 보드게임을 하곤 했었다.
we ________ often ________ board games after dinner.

08 그는 그의 약속을 어기지 않을 거라고 말했다.
He said he ________ ________ ________ his promise.

[09~13] 다음 우리말과 일치하도록 괄호 안의 말을 이용하여 빈칸에 알맞은 말을 쓰시오.

09 그녀는 내 생일파티에 못 올지도 모른다. (come)
She ____________________ to my birthday party.

10 계산서에 착오가 있는 것이 틀림없다. (be)
There ____________________ a mistake in the bill.

11 그는 배고플 리가 없다. (be)
He ____________________ hungry.

12 너는 이 돈을 필요로 할지 모른다. (need)
You ____________________ this money.

13 그들은 서로 알고 있는 사이임이 분명하다. (know)
They ____________________ each other.

학습 일자 : 월 일 | 맞은 개수 : /25

[14~17] 다음 문장에서 틀린 부분을 바르게 고치시오.

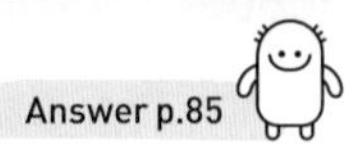
Answer p.85

14 I would like going home.

15 You had better not to park here.

16 He used to staying up late at night.

17 Would you like to eating some ice cream?

[18~21] 다음 우리말과 일치하도록 괄호 안의 말을 바르게 배열하시오.

18 너는 매일 머리를 감을 필요가 없다. (wash, to, you, have, your, hair, don't, every day)

____

19 그녀는 그 퍼즐을 풀 수 있었다. (able, was, she, the, puzzle, solve, to)

____

20 그는 정말로 많은 책을 읽는다. (read, a lot of, he, does, books)

____

21 그녀는 아침마다 커피를 마시곤 했다. (coffee, to, she, drink, used, every morning)

____

[22~25] 다음 우리말과 일치하도록 괄호 안의 말을 이용하여 빈칸에 알맞은 말을 쓰시오.

22 그는 집으로 걸어와야만 했다. (have to, walk)

____

23 너는 그 버튼을 누르지 않는 게 좋겠어. (had better, touch)

____

24 우리는 그에 대해 걱정할 필요가 없었다. (have to)

____

25 이것 좀 입어보실래요? (would like)

____

Lesson 04 to부정사

[01~04] 다음 밑줄 친 부분을 바르게 고치시오.

01 I need a friend <u>to travel</u>.

02 She decided <u>going</u> back to college.

03 It's difficult <u>for she</u> to make decisions.

04 I have <u>exciting something</u> to tell you.

[05~09] 다음 두 문장이 같은 뜻이 되도록 할 때, 빈칸에 알맞은 말을 쓰시오.

05 He didn't know whom he should help first.
= He didn't know ________ ________ ________ first.

06 He saved some money to buy a house.
= He saved some money so ________ ________ buy a house.

07 My students were clever enough to solve that.
= My students were ________ ________ ________ they were able to solve that.

08 To learn a foreign language is not easy.
= It ________ ________ ________ ________ ________ a foreign language.

09 The chance was too good for her to miss.
= The chance was so ________ ________ ________ ________ ________ it.

[10~13] 다음 우리말과 일치하도록 괄호 안의 말을 이용하여 빈칸에 알맞은 말을 쓰시오.

10 파스타는 만들기 쉽다. (easy, make)
Pasta is ________ ________ ________.

11 그들은 일본으로 여행 가기로 계획했다. (plan, travel)
They ________ ________ ________ to Japan.

12 내 가방을 들어 주다니 너는 친절하구나. (kind, carry)
It is ________ ________ ________ ________ ________ my bag.

13 그에게는 농구를 하는 것이 즐겁다. (fun, play)
It is ________ ________ ________ ________ ________ basketball.

[14~17] 다음 문장에서 틀린 부분을 바르게 고치시오.

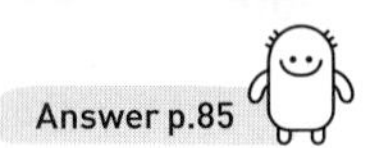

14 There is fun nothing to do.

15 He tried to run away, to only fail.

16 It was silly for you to speak to him like that.

17 The boy was enough smart to solve the problem.

[18~21] 다음 우리말과 일치하도록 괄호 안의 말을 바르게 배열하시오.

18 그 스프는 너무 짜서 먹을 수가 없다. (salty, to, is, too, eat)
The soup ______________________.

19 아이들은 뛰어 놀 마당이 필요하다. (in, a yard, to, need, play)
The children ______________________.

20 엉망인 상태를 보면 그녀는 화낼 것이다. (to, be, the mess, upset, would, see)
She ______________________.

21 그는 잠에서 깨어 자신이 혼자라는 것을 깨달았다. (himself, alone, find, to)
He woke up ______________________.

[22~25] 다음 두 문장을 to부정사를 이용하여 한 문장으로 바꿔 쓰시오.

22 I was foolish. I believed the story.
→ ______________________

23 He told me the truth. He must be honest.
→ ______________________

24 They practiced very hard. But they lost the game.
→ ______________________

25 She got so much support from her fans. She was happy.
→ ______________________

Lesson 05 동명사

[01~04] 다음 괄호 안에서 알맞은 말을 고르시오.

01 (Listen, Listening) to music makes me relaxed.

02 The kids were excited about (going, to go) to the zoo.

03 I lost weight by (not eating, eating not) at night.

04 Spending time with your family (is, are) very important.

[05~08] 다음 괄호 안의 단어를 빈칸에 알맞은 형태로 쓰시오. (두 개가 가능한 경우, 둘 다 쓸 것)

05 He just smiled and left without ____________ my questions. (answer)

06 They decided ____________ her offer. (refuse)

07 The boy started ____________ excuses. (make)

08 Avoid ____________ too much money on games. (spend)

[09~13] 다음 우리말과 일치하도록 괄호 안의 말을 빈칸에 알맞은 형태로 쓰시오.

09 내게 답장하는 것을 기억해. (write)
Remember ____________ me back.

10 나는 그 문을 한번 열어 보았으나 그것은 잠겨 있었다. (open)
I tried ____________ the door, but it was locked.

11 학생들은 교수님이 들어오시자 이야기하던 것을 멈췄다. (talk)
The students stopped ____________ when the professor came in.

12 나는 Sally에게 내 비밀을 이야기한 것을 후회한다. 이제 모두가 내 비밀을 안다. (tell)
I regret ____________ Sally my secret. Now everyone knows my secret.

13 Brian은 종종 문을 잠그는 것을 잊는다. (lock)
Brian often forgets ____________ the door.

[14~17] 다음 두 문장이 같은 뜻이 되도록 할 때, 빈칸에 알맞은 말을 쓰시오.

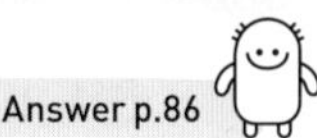

14 He began running toward the door.
= He began ________ toward the door.

15 As soon as she heard the news, she burst into tears.
= On ________ the news, she burst into tears.

16 We are sorry we have to inform you that your flight has been canceled.
= We regret ________ you that your flight has been canceled.

17 He doesn't remember that he read the article.
= He doesn't remember ________ the article.

[18~21] 다음 우리말과 일치하도록 괄호 안의 말을 바르게 배열하시오.

18 나는 그 영화를 보는 것을 기대한다. (look, watching, to, forward)
I ________________ the movie.

19 나는 너를 사랑하지 않을 수 없다. (you, cannot, loving, help)
I ________________.

20 나는 기타를 연주하고 싶다. (like, playing, feel, the guitar)
I ________________.

21 Herbert는 신문을 계속 읽었다. (reading, kept, the newspaper, on)
Herbert ________________.

[22~25] 다음 우리말과 일치하도록 괄호 안의 말을 이용하여 빈칸에 알맞은 말을 쓰시오.

22 여종업원은 주문을 받느라고 바빴다. (busy, take orders)
The waitress ________________.

23 미래에 대해 걱정해봤자 소용없다. (use, worry)
It ________________ about the future.

24 나의 할머니는 작은 글씨를 읽는 데 어려움이 있으시다. (trouble, read)
My grandma ________________ small print.

25 그 우정은 지킬 만한 가치가 있다. (worth, keep)
The friendship ________________.

분사

[01~05] 다음 괄호 안에서 알맞은 말을 고르시오.

01 The (disappointing, disappointed) crowd left the square.

02 The students found his lecture so (boring, bored).

03 This question is so (confusing, confused) that I can't understand it.

04 There were many cans (throwing, thrown) near the vending machine.

05 The cute little boy (singing, sung) in the choir is my cousin, Joe.

[06~09] 다음 괄호 안의 단어를 빈칸에 알맞은 형태로 쓰시오.

06 We have some ___________ news for you. (excite)

07 I was very ___________ to sing in front of our class. (embarrass)

08 The sudden appearance of the star made everyone ___________. (surprise)

09 He felt his heart ___________ when his name was called. (beat)

[10~13] 다음 두 문장을 한 문장으로 바꿀 때 빈칸에 알맞은 말을 쓰시오.

10 The kids were terrified by the noise. The noise was frightening.
→ The kids were terrified by ___________ ___________ ___________.

11 The problems were discussed in class. They will be on your final exam.
→ The problems ___________ ___________ ___________ will be on your final exam.

12 Would you like some bread? It is freshly baked.
→ Would you like some ___________ ___________ bread?

13 I saw some children in the playground. They were playing hide-and-seek.
→ I saw ___________ ___________ ___________ hide-and-seek in the playground.

[14~17] 다음 우리말과 일치하도록 괄호 안의 말을 바르게 배열하시오.

Answer p.86

14 코치는 선수들에게 둘러싸인 채 서 있었다. (surrounded, by, stood, the players)

The coach ______________________________.

15 미세먼지 때문에, 우리는 창문을 닫은 채로 두어야 했다. (we, closed, the windows, keep, had to)

Because of the fine dust, ______________________________.

16 그들은 건물이 10초 정도 흔들리는 것을 느꼈다. (shaking, they, the building, felt)

______________________________ for about ten seconds.

17 집 밖에서 기다리고 있는 남자는 Susie의 남자친구이다. (waiting, the man, is, outside)

______________________________ Susie's boyfriend.

[18~21] 다음 두 문장이 같은 뜻이 되도록 분사구문을 이용하여 문장을 완성하시오.

18 After he graduated from college, he got a job at a bank.

= ______________________________, he got a job at a bank.

19 Because she got the lead in the school play, she was excited.

= ______________________________, she was excited.

20 If you go out without a jacket, you can catch a cold.

= ______________________________, you can catch a cold.

21 He heard someone knocking at the door and rushed to answer it.

= He heard someone knocking at the door, ______________________________.

[22~25] 다음 두 문장이 같은 뜻이 되도록 괄호 안의 접속사를 이용하여 문장을 완성하시오.

22 Being a foreigner, he can speak Korean well. (though)

= ______________________________, he can speak Korean well.

23 Booking the tickets in advance, we were able to enter the museum. (because)

= ______________________________, we were able to enter the museum.

24 Taking a taxi, you will get caught in heavy traffic. (if)

= ______________________________, you will get caught in heavy traffic.

25 Looking in her bag, she found her phone missing. (when)

= ______________________________, she found her phone missing.

Lesson 07 수동태

[01~04] 다음 괄호 안에서 알맞은 말을 고르시오.

01 Alice (solved, was solved) the puzzle easily.

02 Dollars (use, are used) all over the world.

03 The book (disappeared, was disappeared).

04 Stars can (see, be seen) at night.

[05~08] 다음 우리말과 일치하도록 괄호 안의 말을 이용하여 빈칸에 알맞은 말을 쓰시오.

05 그 열쇠는 침대 아래서 발견되었다. (find)

The key ___________ ___________ under the bed.

06 많은 돈이 로봇을 개발하는 데 쓰인다. (spend)

A lot of money ___________ ___________ on developing robots.

07 이 편지는 Jerry에 의해서 쓰이지 않았다. (write)

This letter ___________ ___________ ___________ by Jerry.

08 그 차는 심하게 손상되었나요? (damage)

___________ the car badly ___________?

[09~12] 다음 문장을 수동태 문장으로 바꿀 때 빈칸에 알맞은 말을 쓰시오.

09 You should carry this box carefully.

→ This box ___________ ___________ ___________ by you carefully.

10 Pregnant women must not take this medicine.

→ This medicine ___________ ___________ ___________ ___________ by pregnant women.

11 Tony told me the good news.

→ The good news ___________ ___________ ___________ ___________ by Tony.

12 My parents bought me a laptop.

→ A laptop ___________ ___________ ___________ ___________ by my parents.

Answer p.86

[13~17] 다음 밑줄 친 부분을 바르게 고치시오.

13 I was allowed leave school because I was sick.

14 Korean was taught for Bob by Minho.

15 The balloons were given for the children.

16 Lunch and dinner will are cooked for you.

17 His word should be not trusted.

[18~21] 다음 우리말과 일치하도록 괄호 안의 말을 바르게 배열하시오.

18 Paul은 운동과 식이요법으로 살을 빼라는 권고를 받았다. (advised, weight, was, lose, to)
Paul ______________ by exercising and dieting.

19 그 소녀는 그녀의 할머니에 의해 양육되었다. (up, her grandma, brought, was, by)
The girl ______________.

20 그 배는 Titanic이라고 이름이 지어졌다. (Titanic, was, the ship, named)
______________.

21 아이들은 부모에 의해 보살핌을 받아야 한다. (must, care, be, taken, by, of)
Children ______________ the parents.

[22~25] 다음 우리말과 일치하도록 괄호 안의 말을 이용하여 빈칸에 알맞은 말을 쓰시오.

22 그는 과학에 관심이 있다. (interest)
He ______________ science.

23 우리는 그 큰 소음에 놀랐다. (surprise)
We ______________ the loud noise.

24 그 바구니는 과일로 가득하다. (fill)
The basket ______________ fruits.

25 그 무덤은 풀로 덮여 있었다. (cover)
The grave ______________ grass.

Lesson 08 대명사

[01~04] 다음 밑줄 친 부분을 바르게 고치시오.

01 I don't have some time to go out with my friends.

02 Every person have unique fingerprints.

03 My old printer doesn't work. I have to buy a new it.

04 I don't like this scarf. Please show me the other.

[05~08] 다음 우리말과 일치하도록 빈칸에 알맞은 말을 쓰시오.

05 나는 돈이 전혀 없어서 그 책을 살 수 없다.
I can't buy the book because I don't have ________ ________.

06 나에게는 형제가 두 명 있다. 둘 다 고등학생이다.
I have two brothers. ________ ________ ________ are high school students.

07 학생들 각자가 사물함을 가지고 있다.
________ ________ has his own locker.

08 내 돈은 모두 은행에 있다.
________ my money ________ in the bank.

[09~12] 다음 밑줄 친 부분을 재귀대명사를 이용하여 바꾸고, 문장을 다시 쓰시오.

09 Tom is listening to music under the tree alone.
→ ________________________________

10 I made the robot dog without any help.
→ ________________________________

11 After his wife died, he was out of his mind with grief.
→ ________________________________

12 I had a great time in Hong Kong.
→ ________________________________

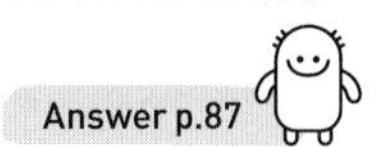

[13~17] 다음 문장에서 틀린 부분을 바르게 고치시오.

13 Each of us have to follow the rules.

14 Would you like any more cake?

15 All the people was shocked at the scene.

16 I finally finished the project. I am proud of me.

17 Both drivers was hurt in the car accident.

[18~21] 다음 우리말과 일치하도록 괄호 안의 말을 바르게 배열하시오.

18 냉장고 안에 과일이 있니? (any, in the refrigerator, there, fruit, is)

____

19 Wilson 선생님은 학교의 모든 학생들을 아신다. (in her school, student, Ms. Wilson, every, knows)

____

20 우리 둘 다 학교에 걸어온다. (walk, of, us, school, both, to)

____

21 책 두 권 중 한 권은 내 것이지만, 다른 하나는 아니다. (is, but, not, the other, one, mine, is, of the two books)

____

[22~25] 다음 우리말과 일치하도록 괄호 안의 말을 이용하여 빈칸에 알맞은 말을 쓰시오.

22 어떤 사람들은 액션 영화를 좋아하고, 다른 사람들은 공포 영화를 좋아한다. (scary movies)
Some like action movies, and ______________________________.

23 나는 내 공책을 잃어버렸다. 새 것을 살 필요가 있다. (need, new)
I lost my notebook. ______________________________.

24 칼을 조심해라. 베일 수도 있다. (might, hurt, yourself)
Be careful with the knife. ______________________________.

25 나는 문을 열지 않았다. 그것은 저절로 열렸다. (open, itself)
I didn't open the door. ______________________________.

Lesson 09

비교 구문

[01~05] 다음 밑줄 친 부분을 바르게 고치시오.

01 I woke up as earlier as my mother this morning.

02 Science is easyer than math to me.

03 The sun is very brighter than other stars.

04 London is one of the busiest city in the world.

05 Jim is taller than any other boys in his class.

[06~09] 다음 우리말과 일치하도록 빈칸에 알맞은 말을 쓰시오.

06 내 카메라는 너의 것만큼 비싸다.

My camera is __________ expensive __________ yours.

07 이 티셔츠는 저것보다 두 배 더 비싸다.

This T-shirt is __________ __________ expensive as that one.

08 연습을 더 많이 할수록, 너는 축구를 더 잘할 것이다.

__________ __________ you practice, the better you'll play soccer.

09 이 꽃은 가게의 어떤 꽃보다도 더 아름답다.

This flower is more beautiful than __________ __________ flower in the shop.

[10~13] 다음 주어진 문장을 지시에 맞게 바꿔 쓰시오.

10 I am 160cm tall. Mina is 160cm tall. (as를 사용한 원급 비교 표현으로)

→ ____

11 I weigh 50 kg. Dongsu weighs 60 kg. (heavy를 사용한 비교급 표현으로)

→ ____

12 Chicken is the most delicious food. (No other food, as를 사용한 표현으로)

→ ____

13 Cheetahs are the fastest animals in the world. (than all the other를 사용한 표현으로)

→ ____

[14~17] 다음 문장에서 틀린 부분을 바르게 고치시오.

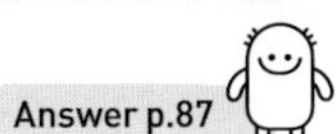

14 The first lady is famouser than the president in that country.

15 Today is the colder day of the year.

16 Everyone is getting old and old.

17 League of Legends is more exciting than all the other game.

[18~21] 다음 우리말과 일치하도록 괄호 안의 말을 바르게 배열하시오.

18 Susan은 Clara만큼 예쁘지 않다. (is, Susan, so, pretty, as, not, Clara)

____

19 늑대는 개보다 훨씬 더 빠르다. (are, than, still, wolves, dogs, faster)

____

20 제네바는 세상에서 가장 멋진 도시들 중 하나이다. (one, is, the finest, Geneva, of, in the world, cities)

____

21 잠을 많이 잘수록, 너는 더 피곤해진다. (the more, you, tired, sleep, the more, feel, you)

____

[22~25] 다음 우리말과 일치하도록 괄호 안의 말을 이용하여 빈칸에 알맞은 말을 쓰시오.

22 낮이 점점 더 길어지고 있다. (long)
The days are getting _______________________________________.

23 더 오래 기다릴수록, 나는 점점 더 화가 났다. (angry, become)
The longer I waited, _______________________________________.

24 내 휴대폰은 네 것보다 네 배 더 무겁다. (four times, as, heavy)
My cell phone is _______________________________________.

25 한국어는 세상에서 가장 어려운 언어들 중 하나이다. (difficult, language)
Korean is _______________________________________.

Lesson 10

관계사

[01~04] 다음 밑줄 친 부분을 바르게 고치시오.

01 I have a friend <u>who</u> mother is a lawyer.

02 James was the man for <u>who</u> Linda was waiting.

03 I wrote down <u>which</u> my teacher said in my notebook.

04 Busan is one of the cities in <u>that</u> the famous singer held concerts.

[05~08] 다음 우리말과 일치하도록 빈칸에 알맞은 말을 쓰시오.

05 나는 색이 빨간 스포츠카를 가지고 싶다.

I want to have a sports car ________ ________ is red.

06 이곳은 우리 이모가 사시는 아파트이다.

This is the apartment ________ ________ my aunt lives.

07 9월은 새 학기가 시작되는 달이다.

September is the ________ ________ a new semester starts.

08 지금 그 선수들에게 필요한 것은 국민들의 격려이다.

________ the players need now ________ the people's encouragement.

[09~12] 다음 두 문장을 관계대명사나 관계부사를 이용하여 한 문장으로 바꿔 쓰시오.

09 I am riding the bicycle. I borrowed it from John.

→ ________________________________

10 Yujin can read the books. They are written in Chinese.

→ ________________________________

11 This is the hospital. My little sister works there as a nurse.

→ ________________________________

12 The news reported the way. The people on the ship were rescued in that way.

→ ________________________________

[13~16] 다음 문장에서 틀린 부분을 바르게 고치시오.

Answer p.87

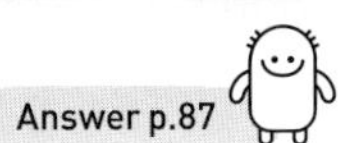

13 Nobody believed that the boy said.

14 I liked the hotel when I stayed in London.

15 Winter is the season where we can enjoy skiing.

16 The reason which I called you was to ask you about the homework.

[17~20] 다음 우리말과 일치하도록 괄호 안의 말을 바르게 배열하시오.

17 나는 우리 엄마가 나를 위해 만들어 주신 그 드레스를 입을 것이다.
(the dress, for me, made, I will, my mom, wear)

____

18 내가 너에게 이 기계를 작동시키는 방법을 알려 줄게.
(show you, I will, operate, you can, how, the machine)

____

19 컴퓨터 공학은 내가 관심 있어 하는 학문이다.
(in, I, is, am, computer technology, interested, the study)

____

20 우리 아버지가 찍으신 사진이 벽에 걸려 있다.
(is, on, the wall, the picture, by my father, taken, hanging)

____

[21~25] 다음 우리말과 일치하도록 괄호 안의 말을 이용하여 빈칸에 알맞은 말을 쓰시오.

21 오고자 하는 사람은 누구나 환영합니다. (who, want)
Anyone ______________ is welcome.

22 내가 이번 주말에 하고 싶은 일은 영화를 보러 가는 것이다. (what, want)
______________ is going to the movies.

23 우리는 서비스가 훌륭한 식당에서 식사를 했다. (whose, great)
We ate at a restaurant ______________.

24 나는 오스트리아에서 Mozart가 살았던 집을 방문했다. (where, live)
I visited the house ______________ in Austria.

25 저쪽에 우리 할아버지에 의해 심어진 사과나무가 있다. (which, plant)
There is an apple tree ______________ over there.

Lesson 11

가정법

[01~04] 다음 밑줄 친 부분을 바르게 고치시오.

01 I wish I <u>can</u> read other people's minds.

02 If I had a lot of money, I <u>will</u> buy a house.

03 If the weather <u>were</u> fine, I would have gone on a hike.

04 He treats me as if I <u>am</u> younger than him. In fact, I'm older than him.

[05~09] 다음 우리말과 일치하도록 빈칸에 알맞은 말을 쓰시오.

05 내가 아침을 먹었다면 좋았을 텐데.
I wish I ________ ________ breakfast.

06 그녀는 마치 자기가 의사인 것처럼 행동한다. (사실, 그녀는 의사가 아님)
She acts ________ ________ she ________ a doctor.

07 만약 우리 할머니가 한국에 계신다면 나를 돌봐 주실 텐데.
If my grandmother ________ in Korea, she ________ look after me.

08 만약 나에게 전화기가 있었다면 그에게 전화를 했을 텐데.
If I ________ ________ a phone, I ________ ________ called him.

09 그의 프랑스어는 마치 그가 프랑스에서 수년간 살았던 것처럼 들린다. (사실, 그는 프랑스에서 산 적이 없음)
His French sounds ________ ________ he ________ ________ in France for many years.

[10~13] 다음 주어진 문장을 가정법을 이용하여 바꿔 쓰시오.

10 I'm sorry I don't have an older brother.
→ ________________________________

11 I'm sorry you didn't come to the audition.
→ ________________________________

12 I couldn't pick you up as I didn't have a car.
→ ________________________________

13 As I don't know his address, I can't write a letter to him.
→ ________________________________

[14~17] 다음 문장에서 <u>틀린</u> 부분을 바르게 고치시오.

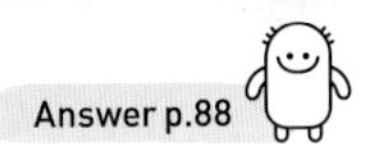
Answer p.88

14 I wish I studied yesterday.

15 I wish I am in New York now.

16 Don't talk to me as if you are my boss.

17 They looked at each other as if they never met before.

[18~21] 다음 우리말과 일치하도록 괄호 안의 말을 바르게 배열하시오.

18 만약 내가 한가하다면 여행을 갈 텐데. (I, go on a trip, would, were, if, I, free)

____

19 그때 나에게 돈이 좀 있었다면 좋았을 텐데. (had, I, wish, at that time, some money, I, had)

____

20 Mina의 말은 마치 그녀가 런던에 가 봤던 것처럼 들렸다. (Mina, as if, had been, she, sounded, to London)

____

21 만약 그가 아프지 않았다면 회의에 왔을 텐데.
(if, had not, he, to the meeting, would, he, have come, been sick)

____

[22~25] 다음 우리말과 일치하도록 괄호 안의 말을 이용하여 빈칸에 알맞은 말을 쓰시오.

22 네가 나와 함께 불꽃놀이를 볼 수 있다면 좋을 텐데. (see the fireworks)
I wish ______________________________.

23 그들은 마치 그 소식에 충격을 받은 것처럼 보였다. (be shocked at the news)
They looked ______________________________.

24 내가 어젯밤에 일찍 잠자리에 들었다면 좋았을 텐데. (go to bed early last night)
I wish ______________________________.

25 만약 나에게 열쇠가 있었다면 그 방에 들어갈 수 있었을 텐데. (enter the room)
If I had got the key, ______________________________.

Lesson 12 접속사

[01~04] 다음 밑줄 친 부분을 바르게 고치시오.

01 It is cold but sun.

02 I was sick and I went to school.

03 Be kind to others, or they will be nice to you.

04 Both Jim and I am good at math.

[05~09] 다음 우리말과 일치하도록 빈칸에 알맞은 말을 쓰시오.

05 나는 아버지가 오실 때까지 저녁을 먹지 않을 것이다.
I won't have dinner ______ my father comes.

06 Brown 씨는 미국 사람이 아니라 캐나다 사람이다.
Mr. Brown is not American ______ Canadian.

07 우리가 높이 올라감에 따라, 점점 더 추워졌다.
______ we went higher, it became colder.

08 나는 축구 동아리나 농구 동아리에 가입할 것이다.
I'm going to join ______ a soccer club or a basketball club.

09 그녀는 나이가 많음에도 불구하고 여전히 에너지가 넘친다.
______ she is old, she is still energetic.

[10~13] 다음 두 문장을 괄호 안의 접속사를 이용하여 한 문장으로 바꿔 쓰시오.

10 I didn't study hard. I failed the test. (so)
→ ______

11 She can't ski. She can't skate. (neither)
→ ______

12 I love roses. My mom loves roses. (both)
→ ______

13 The book was boring. I couldn't finish it. (so ~ that)
→ ______

[14~17] 다음 문장에서 틀린 부분을 찾아 바르게 고치시오.

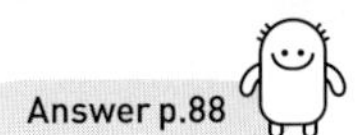

14 It is strange whether nobody knows the news.

15 She practiced very hard that she could win the contest.

16 Either Paul or Sam have to carry the bag.

17 Get some fresh air, or you will feel better.

[18~21] 다음 우리말과 일치하도록 괄호 안의 말을 바르게 배열하시오.

18 그는 키가 크지도 않고 잘생기지도 않았다. (nor, is, tall, he, neither, handsome)

→ ______________________________

19 집에 오기 전에 우유를 좀 사라. (home, some, you, buy, milk, come, before)

→ ______________________________

20 회의실이 비어있어서 나는 불을 껐다. (the, lights, I, empty, the, meeting, room, turned, off, since, was)

→ ______________________________

21 수프는 차가울 뿐만 아니라 짜기까지 했다. (was, cold, the, soup, but, also, salty, not, only)

→ ______________________________

[22~25] 다음 우리말과 일치하도록 괄호 안의 말을 이용하여 빈칸에 알맞은 말을 쓰시오

22 누군가 벨을 눌렀다, 그래서 나는 문을 열었다. (open)

Someone rang the door bell, ______________________________.

23 그녀가 양파를 자르는 동안 나는 감자를 씻었다. (cut)

I washed the potatoes ______________________________.

24 엄마가 동의하지 않으신다면 나는 캠프에 가지 않을 것이다. (agree)

I won't go to the camp ______________________________.

25 최선을 다해라, 그러면 너는 목표를 이룰 것이다. (achieve)

Do your best, ______________________________.

Memo

Memo

쎄듀 주니어®

119 개 대표 문장으로 끝내는

중학 영문법

MANUAL

2

중학 2학년 영어 교과서 **핵심 문법** 119개 30일 **완성!!**

총 2,000여 **개 문항** 3단계 반복 학습으로 **기초 탄탄! 내신 만점!**

SUB NOTE 정답 및 해설

쏠마 주니어®

119 개 대표 문장으로 끝내는

중학 영문법 MANUAL 119

중학2학년 영어 교과서 **핵심 문법 119**개 30일 **완성!!**

총 2,000여 개 문항 3단계 반복 학습으로 **기초 탄탄! 내신 만점!**

2

SUB NOTE 정답 및 해설

Lesson 01 | 문장의 형태

Point 001 1형식 · 2형식 문장

본문 14쪽

STEP 1
1 2형식 2 1형식 3 2형식 4 2형식 5 1형식

STEP 2
1 became, a great artist
2 rises, in the east
3 cried, all day long
4 stayed, awake all night

STEP 3 ③

• 모든 사람들은 언젠가는 죽는다.
• 그녀의 얼굴이 창백해졌다.

STEP 1
1 나의 시력은 나쁘다.
2 우리는 모두 진심으로 기도했다.
3 날이 매우 어두워졌다.
4 우리는 항상 역사 수업 시간에 지루해지곤 한다.
5 그들은 자정에 역에 도착했다.

STEP 3
① 그들은 침묵을 지켰다.
② 이 우유는 상했다.
③ 그녀는 잠을 아주 깊이 잤다.
④ 그의 꿈은 실현되었다.
⑤ 아기는 마침내 잠이 들었다.

③은 「주어+동사+부사구」로 이루어진 1형식 문장이며, 나머지는 모두 「주어+동사+주격보어」로 이루어진 2형식 문장이다.

Point 002 감각동사+형용사

본문 15쪽

STEP 1
1 beautiful 2 sweet 3 hungry
4 lovely 5 like an angel

STEP 2
1 smell 2 looks 3 felt 4 taste 5 sounded

STEP 3 ②

• 이 향수는 향이 좋다.
• 실크는 부드럽게 느껴진다.

STEP 1
1 그 음악은 아름답게 들린다.
2 이 초콜릿 케이크는 맛이 너무 달다.
3 그 남자아이들은 배고픔을 느꼈다.
4 네가 그 드레스를 입으니 사랑스러워 보인다.
5 그 소녀는 천사처럼 보인다.

STEP 3
그녀는 ________ 보인다.
① 신이 난 ② 피곤하게 ③ 불안해하는
④ 다정한 ⑤ 여왕처럼

감각동사 look의 주격보어 자리에는 형용사가 와야 하는데, tiredly는 부사이므로 빈칸에 들어갈 수 없다.

Point 003 3형식 · 4형식 문장

본문 16쪽

STEP 1
1 간접목적어, 직접목적어
2 직접목적어, 부사구
3 간접목적어, 직접목적어, 부사구
4 직접목적어, 부사구
5 간접목적어, 직접목적어, 부사구

STEP 2
1 Ms. Wilson teaches us science. 4형식
2 He ate a hamburger for lunch. 3형식
3 His dad bought him a new bike. 4형식
4 I saw Jenny in the hallway. 3형식

STEP 3 ③

• 그녀에게는 약간의 휴식이 필요하다.
• Tom은 자신의 여자친구에게 꽃다발을 보내 주었다.

STEP 1
1 선생님은 우리에게 짧은 비디오를 보여 주셨다.
2 학생들은 조용히 시험을 치렀다.
3 나는 그에게 답을 여러 차례 말해 주었다.
4 Fred는 학교에 자전거를 타고 간다.
5 그는 내게 간식으로 마늘빵을 만들어 주었다.

STEP 3

① 나는 TV에서 뉴스를 들었다.
② 그들은 매일 축구를 연습한다.
③ 그녀는 자신의 아들에게 편지를 보냈다.
④ 우리 형은 내게 돈을 좀 빌려 주었다.
⑤ 우리 아빠는 내게 인형을 사 주셨다.

③ 4형식 문장의 어순은 「주어+수여동사+간접목적어+직접목적어」이므로, She sent her son a letter.로 고쳐야 한다.

Point 004 4형식 문장 → 3형식 문장 전환

본문 17쪽

STEP 1

1 to 2 for 3 for 4 of 5 to

STEP 2

1 found a personal trainer for the marathoner
2 get some water for me
3 gave a five-dollar tip to the waiter
4 asked me a favor
5 read her children bedtime stories

STEP 3 ①

• 아빠는 우리에게 버섯 수프를 요리해 주셨다.

STEP 1

1 Umika는 내게 일본어를 가르쳐 주었다.
2 Peter는 자신의 여동생에게 딸기 아이스크림을 사 주었다.
3 나의 조카는 자신의 남자친구에게 생일 케이크를 만들어 주었다.
4 팬들은 그 가수에게 많은 질문을 했다.
5 Alex는 Lizzy에게 감사 카드를 보내 주었다.

STEP 2

1 그는 그 마라톤 선수에게 개인 트레이너를 찾아 주었다.
2 내게 물 좀 가져다 줄 수 있니?
3 Smith 씨는 그 웨이터에게 5달러의 팁을 주었다.
4 Tony는 내게 부탁을 하나 했다.
5 그녀는 아이들에게 잠자기 전에 동화를 읽어 주었다.

STEP 3

할머니는 그 아이들에게 책을 ________.
① 사 주셨다 ② 보내 주셨다 ③ 주셨다
④ 보여 주셨다 ⑤ 가져다주셨다

4형식 문장을 3형식 문장으로 전환할 때, 동사 buy는 전치사 for를 사용한다.

Point 005 5형식 문장의 목적보어 I

본문 18쪽

STEP 1

1 warmly → warm
2 we → us
3 to their son → their son
4 sadly → sad
5 for a world star → a world star

STEP 2

1 named the doll Pinocchio
2 leave the door open
3 elected Joe their president
4 painted her room white
5 keeps the kitchen clean

STEP 3 ③

• 우리는 우리의 개를 Max라고 불렀다.
• 카페인은 당신을 계속 깨어 있게 한다.

STEP 1

1 그 코트는 너를 따뜻한 상태로 유지시켜 줄 거야.
2 너무나 많은 일은 우리를 피곤하게 했다.
3 그들은 아들의 이름을 David라고 지었다.
4 그 나쁜 소식은 나를 슬프게 했다.
5 그 영화는 그녀를 세계적인 스타로 만들었다.

STEP 3

5형식 문장의 어순은 「주어+동사+목적어+목적보어」이다.

Point 006 5형식 문장의 목적보어 II (to부정사)

본문 19쪽

STEP 1

1 to wait 2 write 3 to sell
4 to try 5 to pay

STEP 2

1 advised him to stop smoking
2 expect me to believe you
3 asked them to be quiet
4 wanted Lily to understand me

5 help me find my seat

STEP 3 ④

• 부모님은 내가 캠핑 가는 것을 허락하셨다.
• Harry는 나에게 자신과 결혼해 달라고 청했다.

STEP 1

1 그의 비서는 우리에게 기다리라고 말했다.
2 누군가가 네가 이 보고서를 쓰는 것을 도와주었니?
3 Mac 씨는 그에게 집을 팔라고 충고했다.
4 우리 부모님은 항상 내게 새로운 것을 시도해 보라고 격려하신다.
5 법원은 그에게 5만 달러의 벌금을 내라고 명령했다.

STEP 3

우리 엄마는 내게 남동생을 돌보라고 말씀하셨다.

주어진 문장은 5형식 문장으로, tell은 to부정사를 목적보어로 취하는 동사이다.

Point 007 5형식 문장의 목적보어 Ⅲ (사역동사)

본문 20쪽

STEP 1

1 help 2 to leave 3 shiver
4 to read 5 washed

STEP 2

1 use 2 installed 3 to take
4 stop 5 to look

STEP 3 ④

• Jane은 정비공이 브레이크를 점검하게 했다.
• Tom은 내게 자신의 새 차를 운전하게 해 주었다.
• 나는 그에게 식탁을 치우도록 시켰다.

STEP 1

1 내가 그로 하여금 널 도와주도록 할게.
2 우리는 그에게 떠나 달라고 요청해야만 했다.
3 차가운 물이 그를 떨게 만들었다.
4 어떻게 부모가 아이들에게 독서를 더 많이 하게 할 수 있을까?
5 이 재킷을 세탁해 주실 수 있나요?

STEP 2

1 그녀는 학생들이 시험을 보는 동안 사전을 사용하도록 허락해 주었다.
2 너는 히터가 설치되도록 했니?
3 Helen은 아들에게 약을 먹게 했다.
4 Dylan은 아이들이 밤에 TV를 그만 보게 했다.
5 우리 이모는 내가 자신의 개를 일주일간 돌봐 주기를 원하셨다.

STEP 3

① 그 소리는 아기를 울게 만들었다.
② 그녀는 내가 개를 목욕시키도록 했다.
③ 나는 그가 우리 팀에 들어오기를 기대했다.
④ 그녀는 내가 집에 일찍 가도록 해 주었다.
⑤ 엄마는 내가 TV를 끄게 하셨다.

④ 사역동사 let은 목적보어로 동사원형을 쓴다. (to go → go)

Point 008 5형식 문장의 목적보어 Ⅳ (지각동사)

본문 21쪽

STEP 1

1 burning 2 shake[shaking]
3 knock[knocking] 4 climb[climbing]
5 make

STEP 2

1 I heard someone call my name.
2 Nobody saw him come in.
3 We watched the kids play in the sand.
4 He felt a snake crawl over his shoulder.
5 They noticed him leaving the room.

STEP 3 ①

• 엄마는 우리가 수영장에서 수영하는 것을 지켜보셨다.
• 나는 개가 사납게 짖어대는 소리를 들었다.

STEP 1

1 나는 부엌에서 뭔가가 타고 있는 것을 알아차렸다.
2 그녀는 약 1분 동안 땅이 흔들리는 것을 느꼈다.
3 그 교수는 누군가가 문을 두드리는 것을 들었다.
4 나는 몇 명의 소년들이 울타리를 넘어가는 것을 보았다.
5 우리는 그녀가 참치 샌드위치를 만드는 것을 처음부터 끝까지 지켜보았다.

STEP 3

A: 내가 나갈 때 창문을 닫았니?
B: 응, 닫았어. 나는 네가 창문을 닫는 것을 봤어.

지각동사 see는 목적보어로 동사원형이나 v-ing를 쓴다.

01회 내신 적중 실전 문제

본문 22쪽

01 ④ 02 ③ 03 ② 04 ③ 05 ②
06 ② 07 ③, ④ 08 ④ 09 ①, ③ 10 ①
11 ③, ⑤ 12 ④
13 called him a genius
14 made me rewrite the report
15 to clean the stable first
16 (1) lent Sally (2) made some cookies for
(3) taught math to (4) cooked spaghetti for

01

Simpson씨는 ________ 느꼈다.
① 외로운 ② 어리석은
③ 어지러운 ④ 형편없이
⑤ 생기가 넘치는

감각동사 feel의 주격보어 자리에는 형용사가 온다. terribly는 부사이므로 빈칸에 들어갈 수 없다.

Words lonely 외로운 silly 어리석은 dizzy 어지러운 terribly 형편없이 lively 생기가 넘치는

02

Mike는 내게 그 카메라를 ________.
① 빌려 주었다 ② 주었다 ③ 찾아 주었다
④ 보여 주었다 ⑤ 갖다 주었다

4형식 문장을 3형식 문장으로 바꿔 쓸 때, 동사가 find이면 간접목적어 앞에 전치사 for를 쓴다.

03

• 나는 그가 오후 1시쯤 도착하리라고 예상했다.
• Sam은 자신의 오래된 차를 내게 주었다.

동사 expect는 목적보어로 to부정사를 쓴다. 문장을 4형식에서 3형식으로 바꿔 쓸 때, 동사가 give이면 간접목적어 앞에 전치사 to를 쓴다.

Words expect 예상하다 arrive 도착하다

04

보기 갑자기 그의 눈이 더 커졌다.
① Brian은 수업 중에 절대 떠들지 않는다.
② 영화는 11시에 시작된다.
③ 그는 그 소식을 듣고 창백해졌다.
④ 그녀는 파티에서 크게 웃었다.
⑤ 그 사고는 어젯밤에 일어났다.

보기 와 ③은 2형식 문장으로 「주어+동사+주격보어」 형태이다. 나머지는 모두 「주어+동사」로 이루어진 1형식 문장이다.

Words suddenly 갑자기 pale 창백한 laugh 웃다 accident 사고 happen 일어나다

05

① 나는 그 영화가 지루하다고 생각했다.
② 그녀는 우리에게 사회를 가르쳐 주신다.
③ 스트레스는 나를 짜증나게 했다.
④ 그는 항상 자신의 방을 깔끔하게 유지한다.
⑤ 눈이 산을 하얗게 만들었다.

②는 「주어+수여동사+간접목적어+직접목적어」로 이루어진 4형식 문장이다. 나머지는 모두 「주어+동사+목적어+목적보어」로 이루어진 5형식 문장이다.

Words find 생각하다 social studies (교과로서의) 사회 irritated 짜증난 tidy 깔끔한, 정돈된

06

• 나는 그가 가도록 허락하지 않았다.
• 그녀는 우리가 밖에서 놀기를 원했다.

사역동사 let은 동사원형을 목적보어로 취하고, 동사 want는 to부정사를 목적보어로 취한다.

07

나는 그 소녀가 엄마와 이야기하고 있는 것을/음악에 맞춰 춤추는 것을 보았다.

지각동사 see는 목적보어로 동사원형 또는 v-ing를 취한다.

08

A: 제가 Lisa와 통화할 수 있을까요?
B: 그녀는 지금 여기에 없어요. 그녀가 당신에게 전화를 다시 걸게 할게요.

목적보어로 동사원형을 취하는 동사는 사역동사 have뿐이다. 나머지는 모두 목적보어로 to부정사를 취하는 동사이다.

Words at the moment 지금

09

수여동사 ask를 사용한 4형식 문장은 「주어+수여동사+간접목적어+직접목적어」 형식이며, 이를 전치사 of를 사

용해 3형식 문장으로 전환할 수 있다.

Words interesting 흥미로운

10

① 너는 물에 젖은 쥐처럼 보이는구나!
② Smith 씨는 나에게 팩스를 보냈다.
③ 나는 그가 나를 집까지 차로 태워 주도록 했다.
④ 그녀는 내게 돈을 저축하라고 충고했다.
⑤ 그는 3년 전에 한국에 왔다.

①의 빈칸에는 전치사 like를 넣어 「look like+명사구」와 같은 어구를 만들어야 알맞다. 나머지 빈칸에는 모두 to가 들어가야 한다.

Words wet 젖은 rat 쥐 fax 팩스 save 저축하다

11

① 나는 그가 내 차를 고치도록 하겠다.
② 나는 어제 머리카락을 잘랐다.
③ 누가 Rachel을 파티에 가게 해 주었나요?
④ 그의 엄마는 그가 중국어를 공부하도록 시켰다.
⑤ 그녀는 자신의 남편이 설거지를 하는 것을 도왔다.

① 동사 get은 사역의 의미를 지니지만 목적보어로 to부정사를 취한다. (fix → to fix)
② 사역동사 have의 목적어가 사물일 경우, 목적보어로 수동의 의미를 가진 p.p.를 쓴다. (cutting → cut)
④ 사역동사 make는 목적보어로 동사원형을 취한다. (to study → study)

Words fix 고치다 Chinese 중국어

12

① 나는 누군가가 나를 쳐다보고 있는 것을 느꼈다.
② 그의 엄마는 그가 춤추는 것을 보았다.
③ 나는 Joe가 거리를 걸어 내려가는 것을 보았다.
④ 나는 내 남동생이 노래를 부르는 소리를 들었다.
⑤ 그녀는 그가 이상하게 행동하고 있는 것을 알아차렸다,.

지각동사 hear는 목적보어로 동사원형이나 v-ing를 취한다. (sings → sing[singing])

Words act 행동하다 strangely 이상하게

13

동사 call을 이용해 '~를 …로 부르다'라는 뜻의 문장을 표현하려면, 목적어와 목적보어가 필요하다. a genius는 목적보어의 역할을 한다.

Words genius 천재

14

사역동사 make는 「주어+사역동사+목적어+목적보어」 어순의 5형식 문장을 구성한다. 이때 목적보어 자리에는 동사원형이 온다.

Words rewrite 다시 쓰다, 고쳐 쓰다 professor 교수

15

신데렐라: 제가 파티에 가도 될까요?
계모: 너는 먼저 마구간을 청소해야 해.
→ 신데렐라는 파티에 가기를 원했지만, 그녀의 계모는 그녀에게 마구간을 먼저 청소하라고 말했다.

동사 tell을 이용해 '~에게 …하라고 말하다'라는 뜻의 문장을 표현하려면, 목적보어로 to부정사를 써야 한다.

Words stepmother 계모 stable 마구간

16

(1) Kevin은 Sally에게 자신의 카메라를 빌려 주었다.
(2) Sally는 Kevin에게 쿠키를 좀 만들어 주었다.
(3) Mina는 Tony에게 수학을 가르쳐 주었다.
(4) Tony는 Mina에게 스파게티를 요리해 주었다.

(1)은 수여동사 lend를 사용한 4형식 문장이다. (2), (4)는 각각 동사 make와 cook을 사용한 3형식 문장으로 전치사 for가 필요하다. (3)은 동사 teach를 사용한 3형식 문장으로 전치사 to가 필요하다.

Words spaghetti 스파게티

02회 내신 적중 실전 문제

본문 24쪽

01 ②	02 ⑤	03 ①	04 ③	05 ①	06 ④
07 ①	08 ④	09 ②	10 ②	11 ①	12 ④

13 felt drops of rain falling on my head
14 expect you to like
15 (1) He bought a necklace for his girlfriend.
(2) Becky sent her brother a text message.
16 (1) let Semin[him] play video games
(2) wants Semin[him] to help her clean the floor

01

그녀는 ________였다.
① 친절한 ② 슬프게 ③ 다정한 ④ 내 사촌 ⑤ 작가

be동사는 2형식 문장을 구성하는 동사로, 주격보어로 형용사나 명사가 온다. ②의 sadly는 부사이므로 빈칸에 들어갈 수 없다.

Words cousin 사촌 writer 작가

02

그는 내가 그 책을 읽도록 ________.

① 해 주었다 ② 보았다 ③ 시켰다

④ 시켰다 ⑤ 허용했다

주어진 문장의 목적보어 자리에는 동사원형(read)이 왔는데, 동사 allow는 목적보어로 to부정사를 쓰므로, ②는 빈칸에 들어갈 수 없다.

Words allow 허용하다

03

그의 할머니는 그가 집안일을 하도록 시키셨다.

사역동사 make는 동사원형을 목적보어로 취한다. 따라서 빈칸에 들어갈 말은 do이다.

Words housework 집안일

04

나는 그 소년이 무대에서 춤추고 있는 것을 보았다.

see는 지각동사로 동사원형 또는 v-ing를 목적보어로 취한다.

Words stage 무대

05

① 그는 많은 재산을 남겼다.

② 엄마의 손은 따뜻하다.

③ 너는 파란색이 무척 잘 어울리는구나.

④ 그녀는 헤어 디자이너가 되었다.

⑤ 그 소년은 몸집이 더 커지고 키가 더 자랐다.

①은 3형식 문장으로 「주어+동사+목적어」의 형태이다. 나머지는 모두 「주어+동사+주격보어」의 형태로 2형식 문장이다.

Words fortune 재산, 행운

06

그의 가족 모두가 축구 경기를 보러 가서 그가 헤딩슛으로 득점을 하는 것을 보았다.

지각동사 see는 목적보어로 동사원형이나 v-ing를 취한다. 따라서 scored는 score 또는 scoring으로 고쳐야 한다.

Words score a goal 득점하다, 골을 넣다

07

① Tom은 우리에게 재미있는 이야기를 들려주었다.

② 내게 빨간색 모자를 찾아 주겠니?

③ 아기에게 우유를 좀 가져다주세요.

④ 내게 감자 수프를 만들어 줄 수 있니?

⑤ 엄마는 내게 새 신발을 한 켤레 사 주셨다.

동사 find, get, make, buy는 3형식으로 쓸 때 전치사 for를 사용하지만, tell은 전치사 to를 사용한다.

Words a pair of 한 켤레[쌍]의

08

보기 이곳의 볶음밥은 맛이 약간 짜다.

① 나는 지구가 움직이는 것을 느낄 수 없다.

② 나는 그 커피의 맛을 좋아한다.

③ 제게 길을 알려 주시겠어요?

④ 이 치즈는 너무 이상한 냄새가 난다.

⑤ 그들은 함께 밤하늘을 보았다.

보기 와 ④는 감각동사가 사용된 2형식 문장이다. ①은 5형식, ②는 3형식, ③은 4형식, ⑤는 1형식 문장이다.

Words fried rice 볶음밥 a bit 약간 salty 짠 Earth 지구

09

• 그 노인은 우리가 양에게 먹이를 주게 했다.
• Jordan은 나를 자신의 동아리에 가입하게 했다.
• 나는 내 딸에게 상을 차리도록 시켰다.

사역동사 let과 have는 목적보어로 동사원형을 쓴다. 동사 get은 목적보어로 to부정사를 쓴다.

Words feed 먹이를 주다 sheep 양

10

• 그녀는 내게 자신을 따라오라고 지시했다.
• 나는 그가 집을 청소하게 했다.
• 나는 그들이 조심하기를 원했다.
• 그는 내게 자신의 파트너가 되어 달라고 요청했다.
• 그녀는 그가 컴퓨터를 사용하도록 허락했다.

어법상 옳은 문장은 두 번째 문장과 네 번째 문장이다. 나머지 문장 모두 목적보어로 to부정사가 와야 한다.

Words order 지시하다, 명령하다 follow 따라가다[오다]

11

① 그들은 아기의 이름을 Joseph이라고 지었다.

② 우리 삼촌은 내게 피자를 사 주셨다.

③ 냉장고는 채소를 신선하게 유지시킨다.

④ Bob은 그 의자가 매우 편안하다는 것을 알게 되었다.

⑤ 그 선생님은 학생들에게 숙제를 너무 많이 내 주신다.

② for를 없애서 4형식 문장으로 고치거나, for me와 a pizza의 순서를 서로 바꿔 3형식 문장으로 고친다.

③ 5형식 문장이므로 목적보어 자리에 부사 freshly 대신 형용사 fresh가 와야 한다.

④ that을 없애서 5형식 문장을 만든다.

⑤ with를 없애서 4형식 문장을 만든다.

Words refrigerator 냉장고 comfortable 편안한

12

① 네게 부탁 하나 해도 될까?

② 나는 너에게 그의 그림을 보여 줄 것이다.

③ Dave는 아이들에게 영어를 가르쳐 준다.

④ 그는 내게 사과 편지를 써 주었다.

⑤ 너는 그에게 신문을 가져다주었니?

④ 동사 write는 3형식 문장으로 쓸 때 전치사 to를 사용한다. (for → to)

Words ask a favor 부탁을 하다 apology 사과

13

지각동사 feel은 「주어+지각동사+목적어+목적보어」로 이루어진 5형식 문장을 구성한다. 이때 목적보어로 동사원형이나 v-ing가 온다.

14

동사 expect는 목적보어로 to부정사를 취한다. 「expect+목적어+to부정사」의 어순으로 쓴다.

Words expect 예상하다 suggestion 제안

15

(1) 그는 자신의 여자 친구에게 목걸이를 사 주었다.

(2) Becky는 자신의 남동생에게 문자 메시지를 보냈다.

(1)은 수여동사 buy가 사용된 4형식 문장으로, 이를 3형식 문장으로 전환할 때는 「수여동사+직접목적어+for+간접목적어」의 어순으로 쓴다.

(2)는 동사 send가 사용된 3형식 문장으로, 이를 4형식 문장으로 전환할 때는 「수여동사+간접목적어+직접목적어」의 어순으로 쓴다.

Words necklace 목걸이 text message 문자 메시지

16

세민: 엄마, 저 비디오 게임해도 돼요?

엄마: 미안하지만 안 돼. 너는 내가 마루를 닦는 것을 도와줘야 해.

→ 세민이의 엄마는 세민이가[그가] 비디오 게임을 하게 허락하지 않는다. 그녀는 세민이가[그가] 마루를 닦는 것을 돕기를 원한다.

엄마는 세민이가 게임을 하는 것을 허락하지 않고, 자신이 마루 닦는 것을 세민이가 도와주길 원하는 상황이다. 이를 「let+목적어+동사원형」, 「want+목적어+to부정사」로 표현한다.

Lesson 02 | 동사의 시제

Point 009 현재시제와 현재진행 시제

본문 28쪽

STEP 1

1 has 2 is using 3 take 4 rises 5 is always

STEP 2

1 collects 2 Are you watching
3 is not working 4 goes

STEP 3 ④

• 그는 지금 기분이 좋다.
• 빛은 소리보다 더 빨리 이동한다.
• 그 소년은 지금 춤추고 있다.
• Julia는 이번 학기에 열심히 공부하고 있다.

STEP 1

1 Joe는 매일 정오에 점심을 먹는다.
2 나는 지금 컴퓨터를 사용할 수 없다. 나의 형이 그것을 사용하고 있다.
3 올림픽 경기는 4년마다 개최된다.
4 해는 매일 아침 동쪽에서 뜬다.
5 그녀는 언제나 약속 시간을 잘 지킨다.

STEP 3

욕조 밖으로 물이 흐르고 있어. 당장 수도 꼭지를 잠가!

현재 진행 중인 동작 또는 상태는 현재진행 시제로 나타낸다.

Point 010 과거시제와 과거진행 시제

본문 29쪽

STEP 1

1 David는 어제 아침 10시에 자전거를 타고 있었다.
2 Cathy는 지난 주 토요일에 쇼핑을 갔다.
3 30분 전에 그 형제들은 야구 경기를 보고 있었다.
4 Henry는 축구를 하다가, 그의 무릎을 다쳤다.
5 내가 집에 왔을 때, 엄마는 설거지를 하고 계셨다.

STEP 2

1 read 2 were you doing
3 was 4 was waiting, arrived

STEP 3 ⑤

• 우리는 지난 주말에 하이킹을 갔다.
• 제2차 세계 대전은 1945년에 끝났다.
• 나는 어젯밤 10시에 컴퓨터 게임을 하고 있었다.

TIP 그가 사과 껍질을 깎는 중에, 그는 그의 손가락을 베었다.

STEP 3

TV를 보던 중에 잠들었던 것이므로 진행 중이었던 일은 과거진행 시제 was watching으로 나타내고, 도중에 일어난 일은 과거시제 fell로 나타낸다.

Point 011 미래시제

본문 30쪽

STEP 1

1 will get 2 going to play
3 Are you going to stay 4 is not going to make
5 Will you be

STEP 2

1 Air pollution will be a huge problem in the future.
2 The English test will not be easy.
3 The movie is going to start soon.
4 Are you going to cook bulgogi and bibimbap for dinner?

STEP 3 ⑤

• 나는 약속을 지키겠다.
• 나는 그녀에게 특별한 선물을 줄 것이다.

STEP 1

1 Nancy는 내일 그곳에 도착할 것이다.
2 나는 이번 주 토요일에 축구를 할 것이다.
3 당신은 내일도 여기에 머물 것 인가요?
4 그는 그녀를 위해 케이크를 만들지 않을 것이다.
5 당신은 오늘밤에 집에 있을 건가요?

STEP 3

A: 이번 주말에 무엇을 할 거니?
B: 나는 자전거를 타려고 해.
① 나는 축구를 했어.
② 나는 영화를 봤어.
③ 나는 엄마랑 이야기하고 있었어.
④ 나는 숙제를 하고 있었어.

「be going to+동사원형」은 '~할 것이다'의 의미로 이미 계획한 일을 나타낸다.

Point 012 현재완료의 개념

본문 31쪽

STEP 1

1 happened 2 has taken 3 has lived
4 worked 5 have been

STEP 2

1 have known 2 has worked
3 didn't go skiing 4 Have you seen

STEP 3 ⑤

• Jane은 아침 이후로 Chris를 보지 못했다.
• 배로 여행한 적이 있나요?

STEP 1

1 그 교통사고는 지난주 금요일에 일어났다.
2 Tylor는 3년 동안 바이올린 수업을 들어왔다.
3 Jenny는 Los Angeles에 산다. 그녀는 평생 동안 그곳에서 살아왔다.
4 나의 삼촌은 2016년에 그 은행에서 일했다.
5 나는 한 시간 동안 카페에 있었다.

STEP 3

Jim은 작년부터 테니스 강습을 받고 있다.

과거부터 현재까지 계속 강습을 받고 있는 것이므로 현재완료 「have[has]+p.p.」로 나타낸다.

Point 013 현재완료의 용법 (경험)

본문 32쪽

STEP 1

1 Has she ever tried 2 has been
3 have met 4 has never eaten
5 Have you ever seen

STEP 2

1 Henry has visited the museum several times.
2 Have you ever met him?
3 She has never been to Spain.
4 Has he ever run a marathon?

STEP 3 ③

• 나는 전에 그 영화를 본 적이 있다.
• 나는 달팽이 요리를 먹어 본 적이 없다.
• 너는 아일랜드에 가 본 적이 있니?

STEP 1

1 그녀는 번지점프를 해 본 적이 있나요?
2 그는 런던에 한 번 가본 적이 있다.
3 나는 Tom을 네 번 만난 적이 있다.
4 그 소녀는 전에 바닷가재를 먹어 본 적이 없다.
5 너는 '바람과 함께 사라지다'라는 영화를 본 적이 있니?

STEP 3

① 나는 Rachel을 두 번 만난 적이 있다.
② 그는 이탈리아를 방문한 적이 있니?
③ 나는 그 배우를 전에 본 적이 있다.
④ 그리스 음식 먹어본 적 있니?
⑤ 그는 오르세 미술관에 간 적이 있다.

현재완료 용법의 경험은 '~한 적이 있다'로 해석하며, 「have[has]+p.p.」의 형태이므로 ③의 have see는 have seen이 되어야 한다.

Point 014 현재완료의 용법 (완료)

본문 33쪽

STEP 1

1 우리는 방금 집에 도착했다.
2 그는 이미 새 집으로 이사 왔다.
3 나는 지금 막 과학 보고서를 끝냈다.
4 그들은 아직 해결책을 찾지 못했다.
5 나는 이미 나의 가족과 저녁을 먹었다.

STEP 2

1 have just had
2 haven't told them yet
3 have just got[gotten]
4 have already done

STEP 3 ②

• 나는 아직 숙제를 다 하지 못했다.

STEP 2

1 A: 너 배고프니?
B: 아니, 나는 방금 점심을 먹었어.
2 A: 너의 부모님은 너의 계획에 대해 어떻게 생각하시니?
B: 사실은, 아직 그것들에 대해서 말씀 못 드렸어.
3 A: Tony가 너에게 전화했니?
B: 응, 방금 그로부터 전화를 받았어.
4 A: 가스 잠그는 것 잊지 마.
B: 걱정하지 마. 내가 이미 했어.

STEP 3

① 비가 아직 그치지 않았다.

② 나는 지금 막 너에게 이메일을 보냈다.

③ 나는 아직 그로부터 편지를 받지 못했다.

④ 나는 그렇게 아름다운 드레스를 본 적이 없다.

⑤ 버스가 아직 버스 정류장에 도착하지 않았다.

just는 주로 have[has]와 p.p. 사이에 온다. 따라서 ②는 I have just sent you an e-mail.이 되어야 한다.

Point 015 현재완료의 용법 (계속)

본문 34쪽

STEP 1

1 for 2 since 3 has had
4 have you known 5 lately

STEP 2

1 has been sick since
2 has loved music since
3 have been friends for
4 has wanted to be a pilot since

STEP 3 ③

• 나는 이 휴대전화를 2년 동안 사용해왔다.
• 통증이 얼마나 오래 되었나요?

STEP 1

1 Smith 선생님은 3년 동안 영어를 가르쳐왔다.
2 우리는 지난 달부터 그에게서 소식을 못 들었다.
3 Kevin은 그가 5살 때부터 개를 길렀다.
4 너희는 얼마나 오랫동안 서로 알고 지냈니?
5 요새 살기가 힘들다.

STEP 2

보기 나는 7년 전에 피아노를 치기 시작했다. 나는 여전히 피아노를 친다. → 나는 7년 동안 피아노를 쳐왔다.

1 Amy는 일요일에 아프기 시작했다. 그녀는 여전히 아프다. → Amy는 일요일부터 아팠다.
2 그는 그 때 음악을 좋아하기 시작했다. 그는 여전히 그것을 좋아한다. → 그는 그때부터 음악을 좋아한다.
3 Kevin과 Jenny는 10년 전에 친구가 되었다. 그들 여전히 친구이다. → Kevin과 Jenny는 10년째 친구이다.
4 Peter는 어렸을 때 조종사가 되고 싶었다. 그는 여전히 조종사가 되고 싶어 한다. → Peter는 어렸을 때부터 조종사가 되고 싶어 했다.

STEP 3

• Sarah는 작년 이래로 간호사로 일해 오고 있다.
• Green 선생님은 2년 동안 영어를 가르쳐 왔다.

현재완료 문장에서 since 뒤에는 과거 시점이 오고, for 뒤에는 기간이 온다.

Point 016 현재완료의 용법 (결과)

본문 35쪽

STEP 1

1 can't 2 tidy 3 isn't
4 have been to 5 can't

STEP 2

1 My sunglasses have disappeared.
2 Katie has lost her ring.
3 I have left my math homework at home.
4 Cathy has gone to the library.

STEP 3 ④

• 그는 밖으로 나갔다. (= 그는 밖으로 나가서 지금 여기에 없다.)

STEP 1

1 나는 자동차 열쇠를 잃어버렸다. 나는 차 안에 들어갈 수 없다.
2 그는 그의 방을 청소했다. 지금 그의 방은 깨끗하다.
3 그녀는 아프리카로 가 버렸다. 그래서 그녀는 지금 여기에 없다.
4 나는 아빠의 사무실에 가 본 적이 있다.
5 Michael은 그의 다리가 부러졌다. 그래서 지금 그는 걸을 수가 없다.

STEP 2

보기 그는 깊은 구덩이에 빠졌다. 그는 아직도 그 안에 있다. → 그는 깊은 구덩이에 빠졌다.

1 내 선글라스가 사라졌다. 그것은 지금 여기에 없다. → 내 선글라스가 사라져서 없다.
2 Katie는 그녀의 반지를 잃어 버렸다. 그래서 그녀는 지금 그것을 갖고 있지 않다. → Katie는 그녀의 반지를 잃어 버렸다.
3 나는 내 수학 숙제를 집에 두고 왔다. 그래서 나는 지금 그것이 없다. → 나는 내 수학 숙제를 집에 두고 왔다.
4 Cathy는 도서관에 갔다. 그래서 그녀는 지금 여기에 없다. → Cathy는 도서관에 가고 없다.

STEP 3

누군가 내 커피는 마셔버렸다. 그 컵이 비어있다.

현재완료의 용법 중 결과를 나타내므로, 과거분사 형태인 ③ drunk가 알맞다.

01회 내신 적중 실전 문제

본문 36쪽

01 ⑤	02 ④	03 ⑤	04 ③	05 ⑤	06 ③
07 ①	08 ②	09 ④	10 ②	11 ③	12 ①

13 The girls were playing with dolls.
14 have already eaten lunch
15 has worked, since
16 have forgotten

01
그가 집에 도착했을 때, 그의 형은 TV를 보고 있었다.
진행 중이었던 일인 '그의 형이 TV를 보고 있었던 것'은 과거진행 시제를, 도중에 일어난 일인 '내가 도착한 일'은 과거시제를 사용하여 나타낸다.

02
Peter는 지난달부터 스페인어를 공부해왔다.
「has+p.p.」 형태로 현재완료 시제가 쓰였으므로, '~이래로'의 뜻인 「since+과거 시점」이 들어가는 것이 알맞다.
Words Spanish 스페인어

03
A: Erica는 병원에 있어.
B: 알아. 나는 내일 그녀를 방문하려고 해.
tomorrow라는 단서를 바탕으로 「be going to+동사원형」의 형태를 답으로 찾는다.

04
A: Judy는 어디 있어?
B: 그녀는 이미 사업차 뉴욕에 갔어. 일주일 전에 떠났어.
'가버리고 없다'는 현재완료의 형태 「has gone to」를 이용하므로 빈칸에는 ③ gone이 알맞다.
Words already 이미, 벌써 ago ~전에

05
A: 당신은 여기 얼마 동안 머무르셨어요?
B: 저는 이 주일 동안 머물러 왔어요.
부사구 for two weeks로 보아 현재완료 시제가 들어가야 하므로 ⑤ been이 알맞다.
Words stay 머무르다

06
그는 시계를 잃어버렸다. 그는 아직도 그것을 찾지 못한다.
→ 그는 그의 시계를 잃어버렸다.
열쇠를 잃어버렸고, 지금도 찾지 못한 상태이므로 현재완료 용법의 결과이다. 따라서 ③ has lost가 들어가야 한다.
Words still 여전히

07
• 그는 삼일 동안 아무것도 먹지 못하고 있다.
• 그녀는 지난 주 화요일부터 수업에 참석하지 않고 있다.
현재완료 시제는 「for+기간」, 「since+시점」과 함께 사용한다.
Words attend 참석하다

08
• 서둘러! 모두가 널 기다리고 있어.
• 시간은 아무도 기다려주지 않는다.
첫 번째 문장은 화자가 말하는 시점에서 진행 중인 동작 또는 상태이므로 현재진행 시제로 나타낸다. 두 번째 문장은 일반적인 사실이나 진리이므로 현재시제로 나타낸다.
Words hurry up 서두르다

09
과거에 시작해서 현재까지 영향을 주고 있으므로 현재완료 「have+p.p.」로 나타낸다. 기간을 나타내는 two days 앞에는 for를 사용한다.
Words science 과학

10
① Tony는 그의 자전거를 잃어버렸다.
② 그[그녀]는 영국에 가버렸다.
③ 나는 일본에 두 번 가본 적이 있다.
④ 나는 그 영화를 전에 본 적이 있다.
⑤ 그는 이미 공항에 도착했다.
「has gone to」는 '~로 가버렸다(지금은 여기에 없다)'는 뜻이므로 3인칭 주어와 사용 가능하다. 따라서 ②의 주어 I를 He나 She로 바꿔야 한다.
Words arrive 도착하다

11
① 나는 그를 한 번 만난 적이 있다.
② 그는 이탈리아에 가본 적이 없다.
③ 1년 전에 비가 많이 내렸다.
④ 엄마는 지금 막 쿠키를 만들었다.

⑤ 누군가 내 수프를 먹어버렸다.

현재완료는 a year ago와 같은 명백한 과거와 쓰이지 않는다. 따라서 ③의 a year ago는 「since+과거 시점」, 「for+기간」의 표현으로 고쳐야 한다.

Words once 한 번 Italy 이탈리아

12

보기 Jason은 3년 전에 시카고로 이사 갔다. 그는 아직도 거기에 산다.

② Jason은 3년 동안 시카고에서 살고 있다.

3년 전에 시카고로 이사 가서 현재까지 살고 있다는 의미이므로 현재완료 「has+p.p.」의 형태로 나타낸다. '~동안'을 의미하는 for와 함께 쓴다.

13

'~하고 있는 중이었다'는 과거진행 시제를 사용한다. 주어가 복수이므로 「were+v-ing」을 쓴다.

14

A: 점심 먹자. 배고프다.

B: 미안해, 하지만 난 이미 점심을 먹었어.

현재완료와 부사 already가 함께 쓰일 경우 「have+already+p.p.」의 형태가 된다.

15

Diana는 2012년부터 은행에서 일하기 시작했다. 그녀는 아직도 거기서 일한다.

→ Diana는 2012년부터 은행에서 일해 왔다.

과거에서 시작해서 현재까지 계속되고 있으므로 현재완료 「has+p.p.」로 나타내고, since 뒤에는 과거 시점이 온다.

16

나는 온라인 뱅킹 비밀번호를 잊었다. 나는 내 계정에 접속할 수 없다.

→ 나는 온라인 뱅킹 비밀번호를 잊어버렸다.

과거에 행한 동작이 현재 결과로 나타나고 있으므로 현재완료 결과 「have+p.p.」로 표현한다.

Words password 비밀번호 account 계정

02회 내신 적중 실전 문제

본문 38쪽

01 ④	02 ③	03 ③	04 ④	05 ③	06 ④
07 ①	08 ③	09 ⑤	10 ③	11 ①	12 ④

13 (1) I haven't met her before.
(2) Has he finished his report?

14 He has used the computer for 5 years.

15 I have left my umbrella on the bus.

16 (1) have already done it
(2) haven't finished it yet

01

Kelly는 보통 저녁 8시부터 9시까지 숙제를 한다. 지금은 8시 20분이다. 그녀는 지금 숙제를 하는 중이다.

반복적인 일에는 현재형을 쓰고, 지금 진행 중인 동작에는 현재진행형을 쓴다.

Words do one's homework 숙제를 하다

02

• Jessica는 어제 그 편지를 보냈다.

• 나는 작년 이후로 그로부터 연락을 받지 못했다.

첫 번째 문장은 과거시제로 특정 시점을 나타내는 last Friday, yesterday 등과 함께 쓰인다. 두 번째 문장은 현재완료로 for, since 등의 표현과 함께 쓰인다.

03

A: 네가 돌아왔을 때 Tony는 공부를 하고 있었니?

B: 아니, 그는 그때 컴퓨터 게임을 하고 있었어.

과거에 어떤 일이 진행 중인 도중에 다른 일이 일어나면, 진행 중이었던 일은 과거진행 시제를 사용하고 도중에 일어난 일은 과거시제를 사용한다.

Words come back 돌아오다

04

A: 너 하와이에 가 본 적 있니?

B: 응, 난 거기 두 번 가 봤어.

'하와이에 가본 적 있니?'라는 표현은 경험을 물어보는 것으로 현재완료의 경험 용법인 have been이 어울린다. 그에 대한 대답 역시 have been으로 답변해야 한다.

05

그녀는 1년 전에 그를 좋아했다.

a year ago라는 명백한 과거표현은 과거시제와 함께 사용한다.

06

나는 2012년 이후로 일본어를 공부해왔다.

현재완료 시제에서 since 뒤에는 과거 시점이 온다. 현재완료는 과거의 특정 시점을 나타내는 부사구와 함께 쓸 수 없다.

Words Japanese 일본어

07

나는 보통 아침식사로 씨리얼을 먹는다.

현재시제에 자주 쓰이는 빈도부사 usually는 보통 일반동사 앞에 온다.

08

과거의 일이 현재까지 영향을 주고 있으므로 현재완료 「has+p.p.」로 나타낸다. 기간을 나타내는 a week 앞에는 for를 사용한다.

09

과거부터 현재까지 계속 머무르고 있는 것이므로 현재완료 「has+p.p.」로 나타낸다.

10

보기 나는 그 영화를 본 적이 있다.

① 그녀는 파리로 가버렸다.
② 그는 지금 막 상자를 열어보았다.
③ 너는 큰 물고기를 잡은 적이 있니?
④ 너는 얼마나 오랫동안 이 컴퓨터를 사용해 왔니?
⑤ 나는 내 책을 잃어버렸다. 그래서 그것을 읽을 수 없다.

보기 와 ③은 현재완료의 경험 용법으로 쓰였다.

11

① 나는 차를 운전해 본 적이 없다.
② 그녀는 몇 년 동안 커피를 마시지 않아왔다.
③ 너는 네 애완동물을 얼마나 오랫동안 길러왔니?
④ 너는 내가 마지막으로 너를 봤을 때 이후로 쭉 컸구나.
⑤ 그는 어린 아이였을 때부터 축구를 좋아해왔다.

현재완료는 「have[has]+p.p.」의 형태이므로 ①의 drove는 driven이 되어야 한다.

12

① 너는 전에 말을 탄 적이 있니?
② Henry는 일주일 간 계속 바빴다.
③ 나는 2년 전에 뉴욕에 갔었다.
④ 우리는 이 규칙을 10년 넘게 지켜왔다.
⑤ 그녀는 오늘 아침부터 아무것도 먹지 못했다.

① Do you have ridden ~? → Have you ridden ~?
② have been → has been
③ have been to → went to 또는 two years ago 삭제
⑤ didn't have → hasn't had

Words ride a horse 말을 타다 rule 규칙

13

(1) 나는 전에 그녀를 만난 적이 있다.
→ 나는 전에 그녀를 만난 적이 없다.
(2) 그는 그의 보고서를 끝냈다.
→ 그는 그의 보고서를 끝냈니?

현재완료의 부정은 「haven't+p.p.」의 형태로 나타낸다. 현재완료의 의문문은 「Has+주어+p.p. ~?」의 형태로 나타낸다.

Words report 보고서

14

그는 5년 전에 그 컴퓨터를 쓰기 시작했다. 그는 아직도 그 컴퓨터를 사용하고 있다.
→ 그는 5년 동안 그 컴퓨터를 사용해왔다.

「has+p.p.」의 형태로 현재완료의 계속을 나타낸다. 기간을 나타내는 5 years 앞에는 for를 사용한다.

Words use 사용하다

15

나는 버스에 우산을 놓고 내렸다. 나는 지금 그것이 없다.
→ 나는 버스에 우산을 놓고 내려버렸다.

과거에 행한 동작이 현재 결과로 나타나고 있으므로 「have+p.p.」의 형태로 현재완료의 결과를 나타낸다.

Words leave ~을 두고 오다[가다]

16

A: 너는 과학 숙제를 끝냈니?
B: 네, 저는 이미 그것을 다 했어요.
A: 수학 숙제는 어때? 너는 그것을 다 했니?
B: 아니오, 저는 아직 그것을 다 못했어요.

현재완료의 완료 용법을 이용하여 문장을 완성한다. already는 have와 p.p. 사이에 위치하고, yet은 문장 맨 뒤에 위치한다.

Words subject 과목 done 다 끝난, 완료된

Lesson 03 | 조동사

Point 017 can, could

본문 42쪽

STEP 1

1 부탁 2 능력 3 허가 4 능력 5 허가

STEP 2

1 Can, play 2 Can[Could], pass
3 Can[Could], stay 4 can make

STEP 3 ④

- 나의 아이는 수영을 매우 잘한다.
- 너는 지금 가도 좋다.
- 나[저]를 역까지 태워줄래[주시겠어요]?

STEP 1

1 문 좀 열어주실 수 있으세요?
2 나는 너무 졸려서 나는 집중할 수 없었다.
3 내 펜을 빌리고 싶으면 빌려도 돼.
4 나의 할아버지는 3개의 국어를 할 수 있으셨다.
5 당신의 사진을 봐도 되나요?

STEP 3

A: 너는 피곤해보여.
B: 응, 나는 어젯밤에 잠을 제대로 잘 수 없었어.

빈칸에는 '(과거에) ~할 수 없었다'라는 뜻의 ④ couldn't 가 알맞다.

Point 018 may, might

본문 43쪽

STEP 1

1 허가 2 추측 3 추측 4 추측 5 허가

STEP 2

1 May I close 2 You may[might] miss
3 may borrow 4 may[might] be

STEP 3 ④

- 제가 들어가도 되나요?
- 그녀는 학교에 있을지도 모른다.
- 그것은 사실이 아닐지도 모른다.

STEP 1

1 제가 화장실에 가도 될까요?
2 오늘 오후에 비가 내릴지도 모른다.
3 그는 지금 샤워를 하고 있을지도 모른다.
4 나는 그 회의에 약간 늦을지도 모른다.
5 너는 둘러봐도 되지만, 아무것도 부수진 마라.

STEP 3

① 그녀는 배가 고플지도 모른다.
② 너는 이것이 필요할지도 모른다.
③ 그는 다락방에 있을지도 모른다.
④ 너는 오늘 일직 집에 가도 된다.
⑤ 그들은 네 이야기를 믿지 않을지도 모른다.

④의 may는 '~해도 좋다'는 허가를 나타내는 반면, 나머지는 모두 '~일지도 모른다'의 불확실한 추측을 나타낸다.

Point 019 will, would

본문 44쪽

STEP 1

1 will 2 wouldn't 3 won't 4 will 5 would

STEP 2

1 will be 2 will study
3 Will[Would], carry 4 would visit

STEP 3 ③

- 그들은 이번 주말에 잠옷 파티를 할 것이다.
- A: 내 파트너가 되어 줄래? B: 아니, 안 할래.
- 그녀는 우리를 지원해 주겠다고 말했다.
- 좀 더 천천히 말씀해 주시겠어요?
- Peter는 화가 날 때마다, 걷곤 했다.

STEP 1

1 나는 내일 춤추러 갈 것이다.
2 나는 그녀가 제 시간에 나타나지 않을 것을 알고 있었다.
3 비가 오고 있다. 나는 밖으로 나가지 않을 것이다.
4 난 지금 도서관에 있어. 내가 나중에 전화할게.
5 내가 군대에 있을 때, 나는 새벽 5시 30분에 일어나곤 했다.

STEP 2

1 여동생은 내년에는 10살이 될 것이다.
2 나는 내일 시험이 있다. 나는 오늘밤 늦게까지 공부할 것이다.
3 나를 위해 이 가방 좀 옮겨 주겠니[주시겠어요]?
4 나는 어렸을 때 주말마다 조부모님 댁을 방문하곤 했다.

STEP 3

• 저랑 금요일에 같이 저녁 먹을래요?
• 나는 그녀가 나를 기다릴 것이라고 생각했다.
• 내가 어렸을 때, 나는 방학을 할머니 집에서 보내곤 했다.

정중한 부탁, will의 과거형, 과거의 습관을 나타내는 말은 ③ would[Would]이다.

Point 020 must

본문 45쪽

STEP 1

1 must not 2 can't 3 must 4 must 5 must

STEP 2

1 must not use 2 must keep 3 must be
4 cannot[can't] be 5 must know

STEP 3 ③

• 너는 12시 전에 돌아와야 한다.
• 너는 늦어서는 안 된다.
• 그렇게 많이 걸었으니 넌 배가 고픔이 틀림없다.

STEP 1

1 너는 빗속에서 자전거를 타면 안 된다. 그것은 위험하다.
2 Ted는 이미 교실을 떠났다. 그는 학교에 있을 리가 없다.
3 너는 도서관에서 조용히 해야 한다.
4 너는 Julie의 여동생임이 분명하구나. 너는 그녀와 꼭 닮았다.
5 Sarah는 오늘 결석했다. 그녀는 아픈 것이 틀림없다.

STEP 3

Lisa는 울고 있다. 그녀는 슬픈 것이 틀림없다.

빈칸에는 '~임이 틀림없다'라는 의미의 강한 추측을 나타내는 말인 ③ must가 알맞다.

Point 021 have to

본문 46쪽

STEP 1

1 우리는 길게 줄을 서서 기다릴 필요가 없다.
2 그가 내일 일을 해야 합니까?
3 제가 회사에 정장을 입고 가야 합니까?
4 그녀는 욕실을 청소할 필요가 없다.
5 그들은 학교로 돌아가야 했다.

STEP 2

1 have to 2 don't have to
3 had to 4 Do, have to

STEP 3 ⑤

• 나는 오늘 밤 늦게까지 일해야 한다.
• 너는 서두를 필요가 없다.
• 내가 병원에 가야 할까?
• 그는 스스로 저녁밥을 해야 했다.

STEP 3

빈칸에는 '~할 필요가 없다'라는 뜻의 불필요를 나타내는 ⑤ don't have to가 알맞다.

Point 022 should

본문 47쪽

STEP 1

1 shouldn't 2 should 3 should
4 shouldn't 5 should

STEP 2

1 We should protect the environment.
2 Should I bring something to the party?
3 You should not break the promise.
4 Should I wear sunscreen indoors?
5 He should listen to his parents.

STEP 3 ③

• 너는 좀 쉬는 것이 좋겠다.
• 너는 너무 늦게 자면 안 된다.
• 내가 그녀에게 사과해야 할까?

STEP 1

1 너는 너무 많이 먹으면 안 된다. 너는 다이어트 중이다.
2 너는 런던에 가야 한다. 대단한 도시이다.
3 너는 그녀의 감정을 상하게 했다. 내 생각에는 너는 그녀에게 사과하는 것이 좋겠다.
4 너는 신호등이 빨간 불일 때 길을 건너면 안 된다.
5 너는 피곤해 보인다. 너는 며칠 동안 쉬는 게 좋겠다.

STEP 3

조용히 해! 너는 도서관에서 떠들면 안 돼!

빈칸에는 '~하면 안 된다'는 뜻의 ③ shouldn't가 알맞다.

Point 023 had better

본문 48쪽

STEP 1
1 had better 2 had better
3 had better not 4 had better not be
5 had better

STEP 2
1 had better not throw
2 had better go
3 had better not pack
4 had better book
5 had better not eat

STEP 3 ①

• 너는 빨리 떠나는 것이 좋겠다, 그렇지 않으면 기차를 놓칠 것이다.
• 너는 이런 악천후에 밖으로 나가지 않는 것이 좋겠다.

STEP 1
1 그들은 수표를 받지 않는다. 우리는 현금을 마련하는 것이 좋겠다.
2 너는 네 방을 정리하는 게 좋겠다. 그렇지 않으면 너의 엄마는 화를 내실 것이다.
3 그것은 위험해 보인다. 시도하지 않는 것이 좋겠다.
4 너는 다시는 늦지 않는 것이 좋겠다. 그렇지 않으면 너는 실직할 것이다.
5 그는 집에 머무는 게 좋겠다. 비가 많이 오고 있다.

STEP 2
1 너는 그것을 버리지 않는 것이 좋겠다. 그것은 쓸모 있을지도 모른다.
2 나는 차가 막히기 전에 지금 가는 것이 좋겠다.
3 너는 공항에서 짐을 다시 빼고 싶지 않으면, 짐을 너무 많이 싸지 않는 것이 좋겠다.
4 우리는 그 표를 지금 예약하는 게 좋겠다. 내일은 표가 하나도 남지 않을 것이다.
5 너는 살을 빼고 싶다면 간식을 먹지 않는 게 좋겠다.

STEP 3
A: 오, 비가 내리고 있어!
B: 나는 내 드레스를 젖게 하고 싶지 않아. 나는 우산을 가져가는 것이 좋겠어

빈칸에는 '~하는 것이 좋겠다'라는 의미의 「had better+동사원형」이 와야 하므로 ① had better bring이 알맞다.

Point 024 would like to

본문 49쪽

STEP 1
1 나는 콜라와 함께 햄버거를 먹고 싶다.
2 나는 너에게 나의 새로운 신발을 보여주고 싶다.
3 이번 주말에 무엇을 하고 싶습니까?
4 일등석으로 하시겠어요, 일반석으로 하시겠어요?
5 당신은 그녀에 관해 무엇을 알고 싶나요?

STEP 2
1 I would like to watch
2 Would you like to go out with
3 What would you like to do
4 I would like to travel

STEP 3 ④

• 당신에게 질문을 하나 하고 싶어요.
• 무엇을 드시고 싶으신가요?
• A: 차 한 잔 하시겠어요? B: 저는 커피가 좋겠어요.

STEP 3
저와 함께 가시겠어요?

「Would you like to+동사원형」은 '~하고 싶다'라는 뜻으로 정중한 제안을 나타내므로 ④ to come이 알맞다.

Point 025 used to, would

본문 50쪽

STEP 1
1 used to, would 2 used to 3 used to
4 used to, would 5 used to

STEP 2
1 We used to go on a bike ride every Saturday.
2 My family used to live in Los Angeles when I was a kid.
3 I would get up at 6 to go to school.
4 My grandfather would tell stories about his job.

STEP 3 ⑤

• (전에는) 여기에 공원이 있었다.
• Bob은 방과 후에 축구를 하곤 했다.
• 우리는 매주 토요일에 수영하러 가곤 했다.

STEP 1
1 우리는 공원에 가서 야구를 하곤 했다.

2 이 주변에 큰 호수가 있었다.
3 나는 십 대일 때 머리가 짧았었다.
4 그는 자러가기 전에 해변을 걷곤 했다.
5 나의 고향은 매우 평화로웠다.

STEP 3
이 거리에 우체국이 있었는데, 지금은 그 자리에 있지 않다.
= 이 거리에 우체국이 있었었다.
현재에는 더 이상 지속되지 않는 과거의 상태는 「used to+동사원형」을 이용하여 나타내므로 빈칸에는 ⑤ used to be가 알맞다.

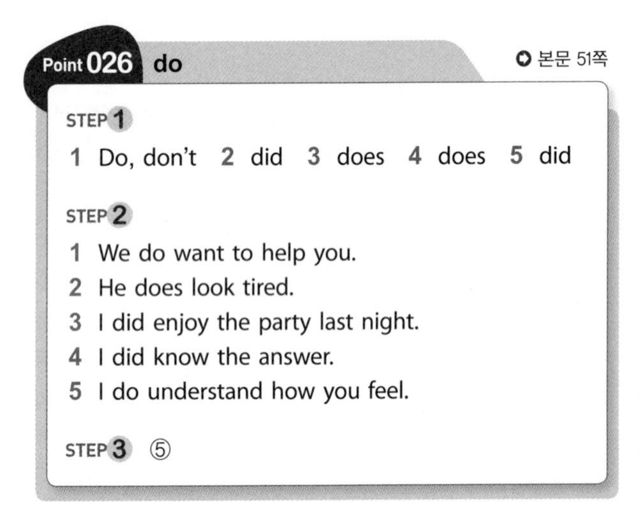

Point 026 do

본문 51쪽

STEP 1
1 Do, don't 2 did 3 does 4 does 5 did

STEP 2
1 We do want to help you.
2 He does look tired.
3 I did enjoy the party last night.
4 I did know the answer.
5 I do understand how you feel.

STEP 3 ⑤

• 너는 정답을 아니?
• 그는 나보다 글을 잘 쓴다.
• Mike는 정말 열심히 일한다.

STEP 1
1 A: 고양이들은 개들을 좋아하니?
B: 아니, 그들은 그렇지 않아.
2 A: 너는 그에게 돈을 지불해야 할 거야.
B: 난 이미 그렇게 했어.
3 A: 오, 이런. Mike가 저 노래를 또 부르고 있네.
B: 그는 정말 저 노래를 좋아해. 나는 저 노래를 오늘 열 번 들었어.
4 A: 누가 더 빨리 달리니, 너니 너의 형이니?
B: 내가 형보다 더 빨리 달려.
5 A: 너는 어젯밤에 왜 나한테 전화 안 했니?
B: 난 어젯밤에 정말 너에게 전화했어! 하지만 네가 안 받았잖아.

STEP 2
1 우리는 너를 정말 돕고 싶다.
2 그는 정말 피곤해 보인다.
3 나는 정말 어젯밤 그 파티를 즐겼다.
4 나는 정말 답을 알고 있었다.
5 나는 정말 너의 기분을 이해한다.

STEP 3
보기 나는 그가 버는 것보다 돈을 더 잘 번다.
① 그녀는 쇼핑을 좋아하니?
② 그녀가 그 드레스를 입으니 정말 멋지게 보인다.
③ 그 상자는 식탁으로 써도 괜찮을 것이다.
④ 그는 진실을 모른다.
⑤ 너는 1년 전보다 경기를 더 잘한다.
조동사 do의 용법을 묻는 문제로 보기 의 does와 ⑤의 did는 앞 문장에 나온 동사의 반복을 피하기 위한 대동사로 쓰였다. ①의 Does와 ④의 does는 의문문, 부정문을 만들 때 사용되는 조동사, ②의 does는 강조, ③은 '적절하다, 충분하다'라는 뜻의 일반동사로 쓰였다.

01회 내신 적중 실전 문제

본문 52쪽

01 ⑤	02 ③	03 ②	04 ④	05 ②
06 ②	07 ⑤	08 ⑤	09 ④	10 ②
11 ④, ⑤	12 ④			

13 I would like to have
14 I did study hard
15 used to be
16 (1) must not (2) must not (3) must

01
• 제가 당신의 카메라를 빌릴 수 있을까요?
• 그녀는 어젯밤에 잠을 잘 수 없었다.
⑤의 could[Could]는 정중한 부탁과 기능을 나타낸다.

02
• 어제 나는 중간고사를 위해 하루 종일 공부를 해야 했다.
• 내가 살이 많이 쪘기 때문에 새 옷들을 사야 했다.
빈칸에는 과거에 '~해야 했다'라는 뜻의 ③ had to가 알맞다.
Words gain[lose] weight 체중이 늘다[줄다]

03
'~하곤 했다'로 과거의 반복적인 행동을 나타낼 때는 조동사 ② would를 쓴다.

Words in those days 그 때[당시]는 draw 퍼올리다
well 우물

04

당신의 전화기를 사용해도 될까요?

may와 could는 허락이나 허가를 나타내는 조동사로 쓰이므로 ④의 could가 알맞다.

05

'~하지 않는 편이 좋겠다'는 경고성이 있는 충고는 「had better not+동사원형」으로 나타낸다.

06

A: 누가 문 앞에 와있어요.

B: 그건 Andy가 아닐 거예요. 그는 아직도 일하는 중이에요.

「may not+동사원형」은 약한 부정적 추측을 나타낸다.

07

A: 디저트를 좀 더 드실래요?

B: 아니오, 괜찮습니다. 배가 불러요.

「would you like to+동사원형」은 상대방의 의향을 정중히 물을 때 사용한다.

08

- 너무 시끄럽게 하지 마라. 우리는 아기를 깨우면 안 된다.
- 그 건물에는 승강기가 있어서, 우리는 계단을 올라갈 필요가 없다.

첫 번째 문장은 '~하지 말아야 한다'는 강한 금지를 나타내므로 must not이, 두 번째 문장은 '하지 않아도 된다'는 불필요를 나타내므로 don't have to가 알맞다.

Words make noise 시끄럽게 하다 stairs 계단

09

① 이 지도는 도움이 될지도 모른다.

② 그녀는 너의 대답을 좋아하지 않을지도 모른다.

③ 그는 너의 이름을 기억할지도 모른다.

④ 시험 때 제가 계산기를 사용해도 되나요?

⑤ 그는 우리의 새로운 영어 선생님일지도 모른다.

보기 와 ④의 may는 '~해도 좋다'는 허가를 나타내는 반면, 나머지 may는 '~일지도 모른다'의 불확실한 추측을 나타낸다.

Words map 지도 helpful 도움이 되는 calculator 계산기

10

① 나의 아버지는 담배를 많이 피우시곤 했다.

② 자기소개를 해 주시겠습니까?

③ 그는 그의 개를 매일 아침 산책시키곤 했다.

④ 나는 나의 언니를 어디든 따라 다니곤 했다.

⑤ 내가 어렸을 때 나의 아빠와 나는 낚시하러 가곤 했다.

②는 공손한 요청을 나타내고 나머지는 would는 과거의 반복적인 행동을 나타낸다.

11

① 나는 그를 정말 믿는다.

② 그는 정말 다시 왔다.

③ 그녀는 그것을 정말 많이 좋아한다.

④ 그는 오늘 정말 행복해 보인다.

⑤ 나는 그녀를 정말 복도에서 보았다.

④는 주어가 3인칭 단수, 현재이므로 does를 쓴다. ⑤ 강조의 조동사 do, does, did 뒤에는 동사원형을 써야 하므로 did see가 되어야 한다.

Words hallway (건물 안의) 복도

12

① 너는 거짓말을 하면 안 된다.

② 그녀는 그 책을 살 필요가 없다.

③ 그녀는 지금 학교에 있지 않을지도 모른다.

④ 그녀는 남동생을 돌봐야 한다.

⑤ 나는 아빠가 도착하기 전에 집으로 돌아와야만 했다.

① must not 뒤에는 동사원형이 와야 한다. (telling → tell)

② 주어가 3인칭 단수이므로 doesn't have to가 되어야 한다.

③ may의 부정은 「may not+동사원형」의 형태이다. (may be not → may not be)

⑤ have to의 과거는 had to이다. 과거 시제인 before my dad arrived로 보아 had to가 알맞다.

13

A: 주문 받을까요?

B: 네, 저는 새우 버거를 먹는 게 좋겠어요.

'~하고 싶다'라는 뜻의 「would like to+동사원형」을 이용한다.

Words shrimp 새우

14

A: 너는 수학 시험에서 또 낙제했구나. 공부는 했니?

B: 전 정말 공부 열심히 했어요. 하지만 수학 시험이 너무 어려

웠어요.

동사의 시제가 과거이므로 동사를 강조할 때는 did로 강조하고 이어지는 동사의 형태는 동사원형이다.

15

그 강은 깨끗했었지만, 지금은 더럽다.
= 그 강은 깨끗했었다.

「used to+동사원형」으로 현재에는 더 이상 지속되지 않는 과거의 상태를 나타낸다.

16

지하철에서는...
(1) 당신은 크게 이야기하면 안 됩니다.
(2) 당신은 먹거나 마시면 안 됩니다.
(3) 당신은 애완동물을 캐리어 안에 두어야 합니다.

(1), (2)는 '~하면 안 된다'라는 강한 금지의 「must not+동사원형」의 형태를 이용한다. (3)은 '~해야 한다'는 「must+동사원형」를 이용한다.

Words loudly 크게 pet 애완동물 carrier 캐리어

02회 내신 적중 실전 문제

본문 54쪽

01 ① 02 ① 03 ④ 04 ④ 05 ③
06 ③ 07 ⑤ 08 ④ 09 ③ 10 ②, ③
11 ⑤ 12 ②
13 (1) must (2) was able to
14 you had better not eat
15 You don't have to wear
16 (1) should lose (2) should not[shouldn't] eat (3) should do

01

너는 그의 새 스마트폰을 부쉈다. 그가 화를 낼지도 모른다.

'~일지도 모른다'의 의미의 약한 추측을 나타내는 조동사는 ① may이다.

02

• 그 소년들은 쌍둥이임이 틀림없다. 그들은 똑같이 생겼다.

'~임이 틀림없다'는 강한 추측을 나타내므로 ① must가 알맞다.

03

우리는 어렸을 때 시골에 살았었다. 하지만 지금 우리는 도시에 산다.

현재에는 더 이상 지속되지 않는 과거의 상태는 「used to+동사원형」으로 나타내므로 ④의 used to가 알맞다.

04

① 대부분의 새들은 날 수 있다.
② 나는 튜브 없이 수영할 수 있다.
③ 너는 Jake보다 빨리 달릴 수 있니?
④ 제가 파티에 친구 한 명을 데려와도 되나요?
⑤ 너는 그 숫자를 기억할 수 있니?

④의 can은 '~해도 좋다'의 허가를 나타내고, 나머지는 '~할 수 있다'는 뜻의 능력을 나타낸다.

Words without ~없이 tube 튜브

05

① 나는 내 일을 정말 좋아한다.
② 그녀는 정말 피곤해 보인다.
③ 신용카드를 받으시나요?
④ 나는 정말 그녀가 옳다고 믿는다.
⑤ 우리는 파티에서 정말 즐거운 시간을 보냈다.

③은 의문문을 만들 때 사용되는 do이고, 나머지는 모두 강조의 do로 쓰였다.

Words credit card 신용카드

06

A: 그는 어제 그녀에게 사과했니?
B: 응, 그는 그녀에게 정말 사과했어.

동사를 강조할 때 do/does/did를 써서 강조하는데, 과거 시제이므로 did를 써야한다. 이때 did는 조동사이므로 뒤에 동사원형이 온다.

Words apologize 사과하다

07

• 그가 어렸을 때 그의 아빠는 자기 전에 항상 그에게 책을 읽어주곤 하셨다.
• 그는 그 돈을 일주일 안에 갚겠다고 말했다.

두 문장 모두 과거 시제로 쓰였고, 빈칸에는 '~하곤 했다'는 과거의 반복적인 행동과 '~할 것이다'라는 의미의 화자의 의지를 나타내는 말이 필요하므로 공통으로 들어갈 말은 ⑤ would이다.

Words pay back (빌린 돈을) 갚다 within (특정한 기간) 이내에

08

너는 내 보고서를 도와줄 수 있니? / 도와줄 수 있나요? / 도와줄래? / 도와주시겠어요?

부탁을 할 때는 조동사 Can[could]나 Will[would]를 쓸 수 있다. ③ Should는 의무를 나타내므로 빈칸에 어울리지 않는다.

Words help A with B A가 B하는 것을 돕다

09

우리는 학교 끝나고 몇 시간씩 컴퓨터 게임을 하곤 했다.

과거의 반복적인 행동 나타낼 때는 「used to+동사원형」과 「would+동사원형」을 둘 다 쓸 수 있다.

10

그들은 (이전에) 친구였다.

① 그들은 이제 친구이다.
② 그들은 과거에는 친구였다.
③ 그들은 더 이상 친구가 아니다.
④ 그들은 과거에는 친구가 아니었다.
⑤ 그들은 오랫동안 친구였다.

「used to+동사원형」으로 현재에는 더 이상 지속되지 않는 과거의 상태를 나타낸다.

11

'~하지 않는 것이 좋겠다'라는 뜻의 경고성의 강한 충고를 나타낼 때는 「had better not」를 쓴다. '~일지도 모른다'의 뜻의 불확실한 추측을 나타낼 때는 may를 쓴다.

Words be angry with ~에게 화를 내다

12

① 저는 그 동아리에 가입하고 싶습니다.
② 차 좀 드시겠습니까?
③ 당신은 무엇을 마시고 싶으세요?
④ 나는 도움을 좀 받고 싶습니다.
⑤ 보드게임을 하시겠습니까?

②의 「would like+명사」는 '~을 원하다' 뜻으로 to를 쓰지 않는다.

13

(1) 나는 그가 스파이라는 것을 확신해.
= 그는 스파이임이 틀림없다.
(2) 그녀는 노래를 잘 불렀었다.
= 그녀는 노래를 잘 불렀었다.

(1) 빈칸에는 '~임이 틀림없다'는 뜻의 강한 확신을 나타내는 must가 알맞다. (2) 능력을 나타내는 could는 was able to로 바꿔 쓸 수 있다.

Words spy 스파이, 첩자

14

A: 나는 견과류에 알레르기가 있어.
B: 오, 너는 이 호두 파이를 안 먹는 게 좋겠다.

'~하지 않는 편이 좋겠다'는 경고성이 있는 충고는 「had better not+동사원형」으로 나타낸다.

Words nut 견과 be allergic to ~에 알레르기가 있다
walnut 호두

15

A: 밖의 날씨가 어때?
B: 따뜻해. 너는 코트를 입을 필요가 없어.

'~할 필요가 없다'라는 의미의 불필요는 「don't have to+동사원형」으로 나타낸다.

Words weather 날씨

16

A: 엄마, 저 요새 살이 쪘어요. 살을 빼야할 것 같아요.
B: 음, 밤에 간식을 먹으면 안 돼. 그리고 운동을 좀 해야 해.

(1), (3)에는 '~해야 한다'라는 뜻의 「should+동사원형」이 알맞다. (2)에는 '~하면 안 된다'라는 뜻의 「shouldn't+동사원형」이 알맞다.

Lesson 04 | to부정사

Point 027 명사적 용법 (주어, 보어)

본문 58쪽

STEP 1

1 To learn 2 to get 3 It 4 to have 5 be

STEP 2

1 It is easy to blame other people.
2 My dream is to be a science teacher.
3 It is important to read the instructions.
4 His plan is to build a house in the country.
5 To be a good parent is to be a good listener.

STEP 3 ④

• 컴퓨터 게임을 하는 것은 재미있다.
• 그의 목표는 월드컵 결승에 진출하는 것이다.

STEP 1

1 우리 역사를 배우는 것은 중요하다.
2 그녀의 임무는 폭탄을 제거하는 것이다.
3 시험에서 부정행위를 하는 것은 잘못된 일이다.
4 그녀에게는 마을에 많은 친구들이 있는 것처럼 보였다.
5 Smith 선생님은 30대 후반처럼 보였다.

STEP 3

① 인도에서 걷는 것이 안전하다.
② 빗속에서 자전거를 타는 것은 위험하다.
③ 그 개의 의무는 주인의 집을 지키는 것이다.
④ 그녀의 목소리는 나에게 음악 같이 들렸다.
⑤ 모두를 기쁘게 하는 것은 불가능하다.

④의 to는 전치사로 '~에게'를 뜻하며, 나머지 문장에서는 모두 to부정사를 만들 때 사용되는 to가 쓰였다.

Point 028 명사적 용법 (목적어)

본문 59쪽

STEP 1

1 너는 너의 문제에 대해 이야기하고 싶니?
2 너는 우리에게 이것을 설명할 필요가 있다.
3 나는 너를 여기서 보게 되리라곤 예상하지 못했다.
4 그는 의과 대학에 진학하기를 희망한다.
5 Tom은 약속을 지키지 못했다.

STEP 2

1 hope to stay 2 decided to start
3 promise to love 4 planned to go back
5 choose to accept

STEP 3 ③

• 그는 그 동아리에 가입하기로 결정했다.
• 그들은 식당을 열기로 계획했다.

STEP 3

보기 나는 스웨터를 뜨는 것을 배웠다.
① 충고를 하는 것은 쉽다.
② 그의 직업은 말을 훈련하는 것이다.
③ 그녀는 외국에서 공부하기를 바란다.
④ 여권을 소지하는 것이 필요하다.
⑤ 그의 목표는 유명한 작가가 되는 것이었다.

보기 와 ③의 to부정사는 목적어로 쓰인 반면, ①, ④의 to부정사는 주어로, ②, ⑤의 to부정사는 보어로 쓰였다.

Point 029 명사적 용법 (의문사+to부정사)

본문 60쪽

STEP 1

1 나는 내일 무엇을 입어야 할지 모르겠다.
2 너는 케이크를 굽는 법을 알고 있니?
3 그들은 어디서 살아야 할지에 관해 이야기했다.
4 우리는 우리 팀을 위해 누구를 선택해야 할지 결정해야 한다.
5 너는 내게 이탤릭체를 언제 사용해야 할지 가르쳐 줄 수 있니?

STEP 2

1 I'm not sure where to start.
2 Did you carefully pick whom to follow?
3 Please let me know when to book the hotel.
4 I asked him how to use the camera.

STEP 3 ②

• 언제 멈춰야 할지 제게 알려 주세요.
• 그는 왜 그것을 해야 하는지 설명하지 않았다. (×)

STEP 2

보기 무엇을 해야 할지 제게 알려 주세요.
1 나는 어디서 시작해야 할지 모르겠어.

2 너는 누구를 따를지 신중하게 선택했니?
3 언제 호텔을 예약해야 할지 제게 알려 주세요.
4 나는 그에게 카메라를 사용하는 법을 물어보았다.

STEP 3
• 우리는 내일 여행을 갈 것이다. 하지만 우리는 어디서 머물지 결정하지 못했다.
• 미안해. 나는 무슨 말을 해야 할지 모르겠어.

「where to부정사」는 '어디서 ~할지'라는 뜻이며, 「what to부정사」는 '무엇을 ~할지'라는 뜻이다.

Point 030 형용사적 용법

본문 61쪽

STEP 1
1 the best way to learn
2 a new dress to wear
3 no friends to hang out with
4 anything good to read
5 some paper to write on

STEP 2
1 gave us some problems to solve
2 brought a book to read on the plane
3 have any money to spend
4 like anything cold to drink
5 need a house to live in

STEP 3 ④

• 나는 앉을 의자가 필요하다. (← 의자에 앉다)

TIP 나는 맛있는 먹을거리를 원해.

STEP 1
1 영어를 배우는 최선의 방법은 무엇인가요?
2 나는 파티에서 입을 새 드레스를 사고 싶다.
3 그에게는 함께 어울려 다닐 친구가 없다.
4 나는 좋은 읽을거리를 찾을 수 없다.
5 너는 쓸 종이를 좀 갖고 와야 한다.

STEP 3
A: 내게 가지고 쓸 것 좀 줄래?
B: 물론이지. 여기 펜이 있어.

something과 to부정사를 사용해 '가지고 쓸 것'이라는 뜻을 나타낸다. 이때 수단을 의미하는 전치사 with를 반드시 붙여 준다.

Point 031 부사적 용법 (목적)

본문 62쪽

STEP 1
1 엄마는 쿠키를 굽기 위해 밀가루를 좀 사셨다.
2 나는 내일 온종일 집에 있기로 계획했다.
3 그녀는 살을 빼기 위해 매일 줄넘기를 했다.
4 우리들은 그에게 도망갈 기회를 주었다.
5 그들은 야구 경기를 보기 위해 경기장에 갔다.

STEP 2
1 to avoid 2 to ask 3 to get 4 to look

STEP 3 ①

• 그는 신선한 공기를 좀 마시기 위해 밖으로 나갔다.

STEP 3
① 나는 일찍 일어나서 첫 기차를 탔다. (결과)
②~⑤ 나는 첫 기차를 타기 위해 일찍 일어났다. (목적)

to부정사, 「in order to+동사원형」, 「so as to+동사원형」, 「so that+주어+could+동사원형」은 '~하기 위해'라는 뜻이다.

Point 032 부사적 용법 (결과)

본문 63쪽

STEP 1
1 ⓑ 2 ⓓ 3 ⓐ 4 ⓔ 5 ⓒ

STEP 2
1 to find his wallet on the desk
2 only to fail
3 to find himself late for the meeting
4 only to fall asleep
5 only to miss the last train

STEP 3 ③

TIP 그는 열심히 일했지만 (결국) 실패했다.

STEP 1
1 Diana는 집에 와서 자신의 고양이가 죽은 것을 발견했다.
2 그는 자라서 유명한 배우가 되었다.
3 우리 할머니께서는 100세까지 사셨다.
4 나는 그의 시력을 구하고자 노력했지만 (결국) 실패했다.
5 나는 서둘러서 은행에 갔지만 (결국) 문을 닫았음을 알게 되었다.

STEP 2

1 그는 집에 와서 책상 위에 자신의 지갑이 있는 것을 발견했다.
2 나는 그녀를 잊으려고 노력했지만 (결국) 실패했다.
3 그는 잠에서 깨어 자신이 회의에 늦은 것을 알게 되었다.
4 그녀는 자지 않고 깨어 있으려고 최선을 다했지만 (결국) 잠이 들었다.
5 우리는 역으로 뛰어갔지만 (결국) 마지막 열차를 놓쳤다.

STEP 3

① 그녀는 잠에서 깨어 전깃불이 켜져 있음을 알아차렸다.
② 그들은 영원히 함께 살자고 약속했지만 (결국) 이혼했다.
③ 나는 창문을 닦기 위해서 스펀지와 부드러운 천을 사용했다.
④ 그 호기심 많은 소년은 커서 전구를 발명했다.
⑤ 우리는 정상에 오르려고 노력했지만 (결국) 중간에 포기했다.

③의 to부정사는 목적을 나타내는 반면, 나머지는 모두 to부정사가 결과를 나타낸다.

Point 033 부사적 용법 (감정의 원인)

본문 64쪽

STEP 1

1 그는 그들의 이야기를 읽고 감동했다.
2 그녀는 옛 친구들을 만나서 정말 기뻐했다.
3 그는 레드카드를 받아서 화가 났다.
4 나는 생일 선물을 많이 받아서 행복했다.
5 그는 기회를 놓쳐서 실망했다.

STEP 2

1 We were glad to finish our long journey.
2 He was shocked to hear of the movie star's death.
3 They were excited to win the game.
4 She was sad to see him go away.
5 I was angry to find the door locked.

STEP 3 ②

• 저는 당신을 다시 만나게 되어서 기뻐요.

STEP 3

보기 이 시간에 당신을 귀찮게 해서 죄송해요.
① 나는 사촌동생을 봐주려고 집에 왔다.
② 나는 그 결과를 보고 놀랐다.
③ 그녀는 잠에서 깨어 자신이 하룻밤 사이에 유명해졌음을 알았다.
④ 나는 우표를 좀 사려고 우체국에 갔다.
⑤ 그녀의 자식 모두가 커서 선생님이 되었다.

보기 와 ②의 to부정사는 감정의 원인을 나타내는 반면, ①, ④의 to부정사는 목적을, ③, ⑤의 to부정사는 결과를 나타낸다.

Point 034 부사적 용법 (판단의 근거)

본문 65쪽

STEP 1

1 ⓒ 2 ⓐ 3 ⓔ 4 ⓑ 5 ⓓ

STEP 2

1 He must be clever to answer all the questions.
2 She must be angry to say not a word.
3 He was generous to give me a second chance.
4 My brother was careless to break my mom's favorite cup.
5 She was silly to tell the man her password.

STEP 3 ③

• 그렇게 많은 돈을 낭비하다니 그는 어리석었다.
• 그렇게 말하다니 그녀는 현명한 것이 틀림없다.

STEP 1

1 그렇게 엉망을 만든 것을 보니 그 소년은 말을 안 듣는구나.
2 그렇게 일찍 자러 가는 것을 보니 John은 피곤한 게 틀림없다.
3 노숙자들을 도와주는 것을 보니 그녀는 친절한 게 틀림없다.
4 법대에 들어가다니 그녀는 매우 똑똑했다.
5 그런 거짓말을 믿다니 그는 바보임이 틀림없다.

STEP 3

그는 매일 그녀에게 꽃을 보내 준다. 그는 그녀를 좋아하는 것이 틀림없다.
= 매일 그녀에게 꽃을 보내 주는 것으로 보아 그는 그녀를 좋아하는 것이 틀림없다.

'~하는 것을 보니'라는 뜻의 판단의 근거를 의미하는 to부정사를 쓴다.

Point 035 부사적 용법 (정도, 조건)

본문 66쪽

STEP 1

1 그 오토바이는 타기에 위험하다.
2 그의 질문은 답하기에 어려웠다.
3 이 믹서기는 사용하기에 편리하다.
4 그가 농구하는 것을 본다면, 너는 그가 프로라고 생각할 것이다.

5 그녀가 이야기하는 것을 들으면, 너는 그녀를 거짓 말쟁이로 여길 것이다.

STEP 2

1 safe to drink
2 easy to persuade
3 To hear her play
4 To see her dance

STEP 3 ①, ④

• 그 이론은 이해하기 어렵다.
• 우리는 당신과 함께 일한다면 매우 기쁠 것입니다.

STEP 2

1 이 물은 마시기에 안전하다.
2 그녀는 설득하기 쉽지 않다.
3 그녀가 피아노 연주하는 것을 듣는다면, 여러분은 그녀의 실력에 놀랄 것입니다.
4 그녀가 춤추는 것을 본다면, 당신은 그녀가 발레리나라고 생각할 것이다.

STEP 3

①은 가주어인 it과 진주어인 to부정사구를 사용한 문장이다. ④는 정도를 나타내는 to부정사를 사용한 문장이다.

Point 036 to부정사의 의미상의 주어

본문 67쪽

STEP 1

1 of 2 of 3 for 4 of 5 for

STEP 2

1 It was brave of him to save the child.
2 It is difficult for us to finish the project
3 It is exciting for them to play a new game.
4 It was very polite of her to give up her seat
5 It is important for children to play

STEP 3 ②

• 네가 화나는 것은 당연하다.
• 버스를 잘못 타다니 그녀는 부주의했다.

STEP 1

1 그를 믿다니 나는 어리석었다.
2 내 개를 돌봐주다니 넌 친절하구나.
3 그는 금연을 해야 할 필요가 있다.
4 선생님께 말대답을 하다니 그는 무례했다.
5 그녀가 산꼭대기에 도달하는 것은 불가능하다.

STEP 3

• 살을 빼는 것은 그녀에게 쉽지 않다.
• 비상 버튼을 누르다니 그는 어리석었다.

to부정사의 의미상의 주어를 쓸 때, 앞의 형용사가 사람의 성격을 나타내면 전치사 of를 쓰고, 사람의 성격과 무관할 때는 전치사 for를 쓴다.

Point 037 too ~ to부정사

본문 68쪽

STEP 1

1 그 파이는 너무 뜨거워서 나는 그것을 먹을 수가 없다.
2 그는 너무 아파서 퇴원할 수 없었다.
3 그녀는 너무 바빠서 휴식을 취할 수 없었다.
4 그녀는 살이 너무 쪄서 자신의 청바지를 입을 수가 없다.
5 그 반지가 내게는 너무 비싸서 살 수가 없었다.

STEP 2

1 sleepy to drive
2 too scared, move
3 late that, couldn't catch
4 so difficult, she couldn't pass

STEP 3 ⑤

• 나는 너무 피곤해서 쇼핑하러 갈 수 없다.
• 그 상자는 내게 너무 무거워서 나를 수가 없었다.

STEP 2

1 나는 너무 졸려서 운전할 수 없다.
2 그는 너무 겁이 나서 움직일 수 없었다.
3 나는 너무 늦게 일어나서 버스를 탈 수 없었다.
4 그 시험은 너무 어려워서 그녀는 통과할 수 없었다.

STEP 3

그녀는 너무 느려서 그를 따라잡을 수 없다.

「too+형용사+to부정사」는 「so+형용사+that+주어+can't/couldn't+동사원형」으로 바꿔 쓸 수 있다. 보기 문장의 시제가 현재이므로 that절의 주어 뒤에는 조동사 can't를 쓴다.

Point 038 enough+to부정사

본문 69쪽

STEP 1
1 ⓑ 2 ⓔ 3 ⓐ 4 ⓓ 5 ⓒ

STEP 2
1 strong enough to lift
2 too shy to perform
3 too late, to change
4 large enough to hold
5 too narrow, to go

STEP 3 ③

- 그는 경주에서 이길 수 있을 만큼 충분히 빠르다. = 그는 매우 빨라서 경주에서 이길 수 있다.
- 그녀는 요트를 살 수 있을 만큼 충분히 부유했다. = 그녀는 매우 부유해서 요트를 살 수 있었다.

STEP 1
1 너의 셔츠는 너무 작아서 내가 입을 수가 없다.
2 나는 맨 위 선반에 손이 닿을 정도로 충분히 키가 크다.
3 그는 너무 어려서 이 프로그램을 볼 수 없다.
4 운전면허 시험은 너무 쉬워서 그녀는 그것을 통과할 수 있었다.
5 그 피자는 모두가 나눠 먹을 수 있을 만큼 충분히 컸다.

STEP 2
1 나는 힘이 매우 세다. 나는 그 바위를 들 수 있다.
→ 나는 그 바위를 들 수 있을 만큼 충분히 힘이 세다.
2 그 소녀들은 수줍음을 많이 탔다. 그들은 연극에서 연기를 잘할 수 없었다.
→ 그 소녀들은 수줍음을 너무 많이 타서 연극에서 연기를 잘할 수 없었다.
3 너무 늦어버렸다. 우리는 계획을 변경할 수 없었다.
→ 너무 늦어버려서 우리는 계획을 변경할 수 없었다.
4 내 여행 가방은 매우 크다. 그것은 이 옷을 모두 담을 수 있다.
→ 내 여행 가방은 이 옷을 모두 담을 수 있을 만큼 충분히 크다.
5 문이 매우 좁다. 그 피아노는 안으로 들어갈 수가 없다.
→ 문이 너무 좁아서 그 피아노는 안으로 들어갈 수가 없다.

STEP 3
그 물은 걱정 없이 마실 수 있을 만큼 충분히 깨끗하다.
enough는 형용사나 부사의 뒤, to부정사의 바로 앞에 위치한다.

01회 내신 적중 실전 문제

본문 70쪽

01 ④ 02 ② 03 ③ 04 ③ 05 ① 06 ④
07 ② 08 ② 09 ③ 10 ③ 11 ① 12 ③
13 I want to be[become] a reporter.
14 where to have the party
15 small enough to fit
16 (1) sunglasses to protect my eyes
(2) snacks to eat during the hike
(3) a camera to take pictures with

01
① 나는 다른 도시로 이사를 가게 돼서 슬펐다.
② 그녀의 목표는 자신의 반에서 우등생이 되는 것이다.
③ 너는 한국의 문화에 대해 배우고 싶니?
④ 그는 병원에 있는 아이들에게 재미있는 이야기를 들려 주었다.
⑤ 내 아들은 3개 언어를 구사할 수 있을 만큼 충분히 똑똑하다.
④의 to는 전치사로 '~에게'를 뜻하는 반면, 나머지 문장에서는 모두 to부정사를 만들 때 사용되는 to가 쓰였다.
Words goal 목표 culture 문화 language 언어

02
보기 그 노래는 따라 부르기 쉬웠다.
① 나는 나를 도와줄 누군가가 필요하다.
② 오래된 습관은 고치기 어렵다.
③ 그는 에베레스트 산을 등반하기로 결심했다.
④ 나는 사용할 칫솔을 몇 개 샀다.
⑤ 우리의 계획은 그녀를 위해 깜짝 파티를 열어 주는 것이다.
보기와 ②의 to부정사는 정도를 나타내는 부사적 용법으로 쓰인 반면, ①, ④는 형용사적 용법, ③, ⑤는 명사적 용법으로 쓰였다.
Words sing along to ~을 따라 부르다 assist 돕다
habit 습관 decide 결심하다 toothbrush 칫솔
hold a surprise party 깜짝 파티를 열다

03
보기 나는 자선 캠페인에 참가하는 데 동의했다.
① 먹을 것을 주실 수 있나요?
② 그녀는 그것을 듣고 놀랐다.
③ 높은 나무에 오르는 것은 위험하다.
④ 나는 경기에서 져서 실망했다.
⑤ 누가 최초로 달에 착륙한 사람이었나요?
보기와 ③의 to부정사는 명사적 용법으로 쓰인 반면, ①, ⑤는 형용사적 용법, ②, ④는 부사적 용법으로 쓰였다.

Words disappointed 실망한 lose (시합 등에서) 지다
land 착륙하다

04

그 노인은 내게 어디로 가야 할지를 알려 주었다.

「의문사+주어+should+동사원형」은 「의문사+to부정사」로 바꿔 쓸 수 있다.

05

그는 매우 열심히 일했지만 (결국) 다시 실직했다.

'하지만 결국 ~하다'라는 뜻은 「only+to부정사」로 나타낼 수 있다.

06

보기 그녀는 너무 피곤해서 숙제를 할 수 없었다.

「too+형용사+to부정사」는 「so+형용사+that+주어+can't/couldn't+동사원형」으로 바꿔 쓸 수 있다. 보기 의 문장이 과거 시제이므로 couldn't를 쓴다.

07

보기 나는 경주에서 1위를 해서 만족스러웠다.
① 우리는 그 행진을 보고 신이 났다.
② 이 기계를 발명하다니 그는 똑똑한 것이 틀림없다.
③ 그녀는 그렇게 큰 개를 봐서 놀랐다.
④ 그 여인은 무료 표를 받아서 기뻐했다.
⑤ 그 소년은 어두운 데서 혼자 있어서 겁이 났다.

②의 to부정사는 판단의 근거를 나타내는 반면, 보기 와 나머지 문장의 to부정사는 모두 감정의 원인을 나타낸다.

Words satisfied 만족스러운 finish first 1위를 하다
invent 발명하다 machine 기계 scared 겁이 난
alone 혼자의

08

• 그가 이 프로젝트를 하는 것은 불가능하다.
• 그런 일을 하다니 너는 어리석었다.

to부정사의 의미상의 주어는 보통 「for+목적격」으로 나타낸다. stupid는 사람의 태도를 나타내는 형용사이므로, 두 번째 문장의 의미상의 주어는 「of+목적격」으로 나타낸다.

Words project 프로젝트, 일 stupid 어리석은

09

'~할 수 있을 정도로 충분히 …한'이라는 의미의 문장은 「형용사+enough+to부정사」로 표현한다.

10

보기 스포츠카를 사다니 그는 부자임이 틀림없다.
① 그녀는 그의 편지를 받아서 기뻐했다.
② 그 쌍둥이들은 돌보기 어려웠다.
③ 그와 같은 친구가 있다니 너는 운이 좋구나.
④ 나는 집으로 돌아와서 내 여동생이 울고 있는 것을 발견했다.
⑤ 그는 옷을 좀 사려고 가게에 갔다.

보기 와 ③의 to부정사는 판단의 근거를 나타낸다. 반면에 ①은 감정의 원인을, ②는 정도를, ④는 결과를, ⑤는 목적을 나타낸다.

Words receive 받다 twin 쌍둥이 take care of ~을 돌보다
lucky 운이 좋은 return 돌아오다 cry 울다

11

① 나는 함께 이야기할 친구가 정말로 필요하다.
② 그는 나에게 작성할 서식을 주었다.
③ 여기에는 너를 도와줄 사람이 아무도 없다.
④ 우리는 이 문제를 해결할 사람을 원한다.
⑤ 당신은 함께 살 룸메이트를 구하고 있나요?

① to부정사의 수식을 받는 명사가 전치사의 목적어일 때 뒤에 전치사를 써야 한다. 따라서 to talk를 to talk with로 고쳐야 한다.

Words form 서식 fill out ~를 작성하다 fix 해결하다

12

①, ② 나는 건강을 유지하기 위해서 운동을 많이 했다. (목적)
③ 나는 운동을 많이 해서 건강을 유지할 수 있었다. (결과)
④, ⑤ 나는 건강을 유지하기 위해서 운동을 많이 했다. (목적)

to부정사, 「in order to+동사원형」, 「so as to+동사원형」, 「so that+주어+could+동사원형」은 '~하기 위해'라는 뜻이다.

Words keep in shape 건강을 유지하다

13

A: 너의 꿈은 무엇이니?
B: 나는 기자가 되고 싶어.

want 뒤에 to부정사를 써서 '~하고 싶다'라는 뜻을 나타낸다.

Words reporter 기자

14

A: 너희들은 파티를 어디서 열지 정했니?
B: 응, 우리는 Julie의 집에서 파티를 열 거야.

「where to부정사」는 '어디서 ~할지'라는 뜻이다.

15

그 폰은 매우 작아서 내 주머니에 들어갈 수 있다.

「so+형용사+that+주어+can+동사원형」은 「형용사+enough+to부정사」로 바꿔 쓸 수 있다.

Words fit into ~에 들어가다, 꼭 맞다

16

(1) 나는 눈을 보호해 줄 선글라스가 필요해.
(2) 나는 하이킹하는 동안 먹을 간식이 좀 필요해.
(3) 나는 사진을 찍을 카메라가 필요해.

필요한 물건을 먼저 쓰고 to부정사를 이용해 각 물건의 용도를 설명한다. (3)의 경우 전치사 with를 반드시 써야 함에 유의하자.

Words protect 보호하다 take a picture 사진을 찍다

02회 내신 적중 실전 문제

본문 72쪽

01 ③	02 ④	03 ②	04 ②	05 ④
06 ①	07 ③	08 ③	09 ⑤	10 ⑤
11 ④	12 ②, ⑤			

13 give me something to drink
14 smart enough to understand its master's orders
15 too late to get good seats
16 to complain to his boss

01

• 새로운 것을 배우는 일은 즐겁다.
• 그가 영어로 말하는 것을 듣는다면, 너는 그가 원어민이라고 생각할 것이다.

첫 번째 빈칸에는 가주어인 It이 들어가야 알맞다. 두 번째 빈칸에는 조건을 나타내는 to부정사가 들어가야 알맞다.

Words native speaker (특정 언어를) 모국어로 하는 사람

02

A: 그는 왜 대구에 갔니?
B: 그는 자신의 삼촌을 방문하러 거기에 갔어.

빈칸에는 목적(~하기 위해)을 나타내는 to부정사가 들어가야 알맞다.

03

① 편지를 쓰는 일이 나에게는 어렵다.
② 아이를 구하다니 그는 용감했다.
③ 네가 최선을 다하는 것은 중요하다.
④ 그녀가 담을 오르는 것은 불가능했다.
⑤ 네가 이 강에서 수영하는 것은 위험하다.

② brave는 성품을 나타내는 형용사이므로, to부정사의 의미상의 주어는 「of+목적격」으로 쓴다. 나머지는 모두 빈칸에 for를 써야 한다.

Words brave 용감한 save 구하다 impossible 불가능한 wall 담, 벽

04

① 그는 너무 어려서 차를 운전할 수 없다.
② 그는 매우 어리지만 차를 운전할 수 있다.
③, ④, ⑤ 그는 너무 어려서 차를 운전할 수 없다.

「too+형용사+to부정사」와 「so+형용사+that+주어+can't+동사원형」은 '너무 ~해서 …할 수 없다'라는 의미이다.

05

빈칸에 들어갈 to부정사는 형용사적 용법으로 쓰였다. 빈칸에 들어갈 말의 어순은 「명사+to+동사원형+전치사」이다.

06

보기 그는 버스를 쫓아 매우 빠르게 달렸지만, (결국) 그것을 놓치고 말았다.

「only+to부정사」는 but의 의미를 포함하여 '하지만 (결국) ~하다[되다]'의 뜻을 나타낸다.

07

나는 그 소식을 듣고 ________였다[했다].
① 슬픈 ② 기쁜 ③ 가능한
④ 기분이 좋은 ⑤ 안타까운

주어진 문장에 사용된 to부정사는 감정의 원인을 나타내므로, 앞에는 감정을 나타내는 형용사가 나와야 한다.

Words possible 가능한

08

① 그는 일을 끝내고 휴식을 취하기 위해서 TV를 본다.
② 나는 좋은 교육을 받으려고 여기에 왔다.
③ 우리에게는 중국어를 가르쳐 줄 사람이 필요하다.
④ 그녀는 과일을 좀 사려고 시장에 갔다.
⑤ 그들은 보물을 찾기 위해서 그 섬으로 떠났다.

③의 to부정사는 형용사적 용법으로 쓰인 반면, 나머지는 모두 부사적 용법(목적)으로 쓰였다.

Words relax 휴식을 취하다 education 교육 Chinese 중국어 island 섬 treasure 보물

09

보기 일찍 일어나는 것은 쉽지 않다.
① 그는 자라서 교수가 되었다.
② 나는 그들을 다시 보게 되어 기뻤다.
③ 나는 기차에서 먹을 것이 필요하다.
④ 1등상을 탄다면 나는 기쁠 것이다.
⑤ 그의 충고를 따르는 것은 불가능해 보였다.

보기 와 ⑤의 to부정사는 명사적 용법으로 쓰였다. 반면에 ①, ②, ④는 부사적 용법으로, ③은 형용사적 용법으로 쓰였다.

Words professor 교수 prize 상 follow 따르다 advice 충고 seem ~하게 보이다

10

① 이 물은 마시기에 안전하다.
② 내게는 해야 할 중요한 일이 있다.
③ 그녀에게는 함께 놀 친구가 없다.
④ 그녀는 자신의 차를 고쳐 줄 사람을 필요로 했다.
⑤ 그 문제를 푼 것으로 보아 그는 바보일 리가 없다.

① it은 주어 This water를 가리키는 말이므로 생략한다.
② 「-thing으로 끝나는 명사+형용사+to부정사」 순으로 쓴다. (important something → something important)
③ '함께 놀 친구'를 영어로 표현하려면 '~와 함께'라는 뜻의 전치사 with가 필요하다. 따라서 play 뒤에 with를 붙여야 한다.
④ somebody를 수식하는 내용이 뒤에 이어지고 있으므로, for를 to로 고쳐서 형용사적 용법의 to부정사가 되게 한다.

Words safe 안전한 repair 고치다 fool 바보

11

① Ted는 이탈리아 음식을 먹길 원했다.
② 그는 선거에 출마하기로 선택했다.
③ 아빠는 내게 그 자전거를 사 주겠다고 약속하셨다.
④ 그녀는 이모와 함께 여행하기로 계획했다.
⑤ 그는 고국으로 돌아가기로 결심했다.

④ 동사 plan은 to부정사를 목적어로 취하는 동사이므로, traveling을 to travel로 고쳐야 한다.

Words Italian 이탈리아의 run for ~에 출마하다 election 선거 aunt 이모[고모, 숙모] country 국가

12

① 그 아이를 도와주다니 넌 친절하구나.
② 선생님께서는 내게 왜 살아야 하는지 가르쳐 주셨다. (×)
③ 오븐을 언제 꺼야 할지 나에게 알려 줘.
④ 그들은 앉을 가죽 소파를 샀다.
⑤ 그것을 이해하는 것은 그에게 어려웠다.

② 의문사 why는 to부정사와 함께 쓸 수 없다.
⑤ to부정사의 의미상의 주어는 「for+목적격」으로 나타내므로, 주격 he 대신 목적격 him을 써야 한다.

Words turn off ~를 끄다 leather 가죽 understand 이해하다

13

저는 목이 말라요. 저에게 마실 것 좀 주실 수 있으세요?

to부정사는 형용사적 용법으로 쓰여 명사를 뒤에서 수식할 수 있다.

Words thirsty 목이 마른

14

그 개는 매우 똑똑해서 주인의 명령을 이해할 수 있다.

「so+형용사+that+주어+can+동사원형」은 「형용사+enough+to부정사」로 바꿔 쓸 수 있다.

Words master 주인 order 명령, 지시

15

우리는 너무 늦어서 좋은 자리를 차지할 수 없었다.

「so+형용사+that+주어+couldn't+동사원형」은 「too+형용사+to부정사」로 바꿔 쓸 수 있다.

16

그는 자신의 상사에게 불평했다. 그는 매우 어리석었다.
→ 자신의 상사에게 불평하다니 그는 매우 어리석었다.

주어진 두 문장은 판단의 근거와 판단을 나타낸다. 첫 번째 문장에서 근거에 해당하는 동사구를 찾아 「to+동사원형」의 형태로 만든 후 두 번째 문장 뒤에 연결한다.

Words complain 불평하다

Lesson 05 동명사

Point 039 동명사의 역할 (주어, 보어)

본문 76쪽

STEP 1

1 Getting 2 saves 3 attending
4 is 5 singing

STEP 2

1 Hunting tigers is dangerous.
2 Her hobby is collecting old stamps.
3 His job is driving a school bus.
4 Learning a foreign language requires a lot of time.

STEP 3 ⑤

• 규칙적으로 운동하는 것은 당신의 건강에 중요하다.
• 그녀의 계획은 정원에 장미를 심는 것이다.

STEP 1

1 좋은 일자리를 구하는 것은 쉽지 않다.
2 컴퓨터를 사용하는 것은 당신의 시간을 절약해준다.
3 그의 의무 중의 하나는 회의에 참석하는 것이다.
4 며칠 내에 바다를 건너는 것은 불가능하다.
5 나의 삼촌의 습관은 샤워 중에 노래를 부르는 것이다.

STEP 3

동사가 문장의 주어로 쓰이려면 동명사나 to부정사 형태가 되어야 한다. 이때 동명사 또는 to부정사 주어는 단수 취급하므로 동사는 단수 동사인 makes가 되어야 한다.

Point 040 동명사의 역할 (동사의 목적어)

본문 77쪽

STEP 1

1 Susan은 판타지 소설을 읽는 것을 좋아한다.
2 당신은 물 없이 사는 것을 상상할 수 있나요?
3 대도시에 사는 것은 편리하다.
4 John은 시험에서 부정행위를 한 것을 인정했다.
5 내가 가장 좋아하는 활동은 음악을 듣는 것이다.

STEP 2

1 cleaning 2 telling 3 writing
4 painting 5 buying

STEP 3 ②

• 그는 내 질문에 답하는 것을 피했다.

STEP 3

① 목욕을 하는 것은 마음을 편안하게 해준다.
② 그 아기는 크게 울기 시작했다.
③ 걷는 것은 네가 기분이 나아지는 데 도움이 된다.
④ 그들은 계속해서 구호를 외쳤다.
⑤ 그의 직업은 고객으로부터의 전화를 받는 것이다.

began의 목적어로 쓰이려면 동사 cry는 동명사 또는 to부정사의 형태가 되어야 한다.

Point 041 동명사의 역할 (전치사의 목적어)

본문 78쪽

STEP 1

1 동사의 목적어 2 주어 3 전치사의 목적어
4 보어 5 전치사의 목적어

STEP 2

1 dreams of living
2 apologized for being late
3 for not forgetting me
4 worries about making friends
5 is interested in learning

STEP 3 ③

• 우리는 우리가 직접 영화를 만드는 것에 대해 흥분했다.

TIP 나는 제시간에 도착하지 않은 것에 대해 미안했다.

STEP 1

1 Peter는 그 시를 외우는 것을 포기했다.
2 나무로 된 장난감을 만드는 것은 내가 가장 좋아하는 취미이다.
3 나는 버스를 기다리는 것에 지쳤다.
4 중요한 것은 균형 잡힌 식사를 하는 것이다.
5 그들은 새 집을 사는 것에 대해서 이야기를 하고 있다.

STEP 3

그는 작별 인사도 하지 않고 떠났다.

전치사의 목적어는 동명사 형태가 되어야 하므로 빈칸에는 saying이 알맞다.

Point 042 동명사와 현재분사

본문 79쪽

STEP 1

1 동명사 2 현재분사 3 현재분사
4 동명사 5 동명사

STEP 2

1 (a) 춤추고 있는 소녀들을 보아라.
(b) 그 소녀들은 무용화를 신고 있었다.
2 (a) 그가 가장 좋아하는 취미는 사진을 찍는 것이다.
(b) 그 남자는 사진을 찍고 있다.
3 (a) 그 소년은 수영복을 입고 있다.
(b) 수영하고 있는 소년은 나의 오빠이다.
4 (a) Jason은 자전거를 고치고 있다.
(b) 나의 할아버지는 물건을 고치는 것을 좋아한다.

STEP 3 ④

- 내 계획은 해변을 따라 운전하는 것이다.
- 그는 트럭을 운전 중이다.

STEP 1

1 그의 습관은 손톱을 깨무는 것이다.
2 그녀는 풍선을 불고 있다.
3 그들은 그를 '걸어 다니는 사전'이라고 불렀다.
4 그녀는 새 세탁기를 샀다.
5 나의 직업에서 가장 좋은 부분은 사람들을 웃게 한다는 것이다.

STEP 3

① 흡연실 ② 지팡이 ③ 쇼핑몰 ④ 불타는 집 ⑤ 수영장

④를 제외한 나머지는 모두 목적이나 용도를 나타내는 동명사인 반면, ④는 명사를 수식하는 현재분사이다.

Point 043 동명사와 to부정사 I

본문 80쪽

STEP 1

1 to move 2 complaining 3 playing
4 to study 5 watching

STEP 2

1 reading 2 to build 3 doing
4 packing 5 to get

STEP 3 ②

STEP 1

1 나는 다른 도시로 이사 가는 것을 원하지 않는다.
2 Peter는 그의 직업에 관해 불평하는 것을 그만두었다
3 너는 매일 바이올린 연주하는 것을 연습하니?
4 John은 런던에서 경제학을 공부하기로 결심했다.
5 제 가방을 잠시 동안 봐주시겠습니까?

STEP 3

- 그녀는 금메달을 따기를 희망했다.
- 그들은 일주일 동안 하와이로 가는 것을 고려하고 있다.

hope는 to부정사를, consider는 동명사를 목적어로 취한다.

Point 044 동명사와 to부정사 II

본문 81쪽

STEP 1

1 to boil, boiling 2 getting 3 to eat, eating
4 to take 5 to watch, watching

STEP 2

1 singing 2 to teach 3 to talk
4 swimming 5 giving

STEP 3 ②

- 그들을 그 집을 청소하기 시작했다.

STEP 1

1 냄비의 물이 끓기 시작했다.
2 Thomas는 새 일자리를 구하는 것을 고려하고 있다.
3 그 소년은 당근을 먹는 것을 싫어한다.
4 아빠는 우리를 해변으로 데려가기로 약속했다.
5 그녀는 공포영화를 보는 것을 좋아하지 않는다.

STEP 2

1 그는 집에 혼자 있을 때 노래 부르는 것을 좋아한다.
2 Porter 씨는 2년 전에 영어를 가르치기 시작했다.
3 사람들은 그들 자신에 대해 이야기하는 것을 좋아한다.
4 그녀는 온 힘을 다해 수영하기를 계속했다.
5 대통령은 연설을 하기 시작했다.

STEP 3

- Cindy는 옷에 돈을 쓰는 것을 좋아한다.
- Eddie는 주말에 농구하는 것을 좋아한다.

① 계획하다 ③ 원하다 ④ 바라다 ⑤ 즐기다

like는 목적어로 동명사와 to부정사를 모두 취한다.

Point 045 동명사와 to부정사 Ⅲ
본문 82쪽

STEP 1
1 너는 너희 할머니께 전화 드리는 것을 잊어버렸니?
2 나는 내가 어린 아이였을 때 그 박물관을 방문했던 것을 기억한다.
3 그녀는 16살에 학교를 그만둔 것을 후회한다.
4 나는 너무 졸려서 쉬려고 멈췄다.
5 그는 일자리를 구하려고 노력했지만, 구할 수 없었다.

STEP 2
1 to buy 2 flying 3 drinking 4 driving

STEP 3 ④

STEP 3
- Max는 회의에 갔던 것을 후회한다. 그것은 시간 낭비였다.
- 네 수영복을 챙기는 것을 잊지 마! 그 호텔에는 멋진 수영장이 있어.

「regret+v-ing」는 '(과거에) ~했던 것을 후회하다'라는 뜻이고 「forget+to-v」는 '(앞으로) ~할 것을 잊다'라는 뜻이다.

Point 046 동명사의 관용 표현
본문 83쪽

STEP 1
1 나를 보자마자, 그는 도망쳤다.
2 엎질러진 우유를 두고 울어 봤자 소용없다.(이미 엎질러진 물이다.)
3 우리는 곧 당신을 보기를 기대한다.
4 나는 당신과 사랑에 빠지지 않을 수 없다.
5 그는 친구를 사귀는 데 어려움을 겪었다.

STEP 2
1 keep on running 2 feel like walking
3 was busy answering 4 is worth trying
5 go fishing

STEP 3 ③

STEP 3
나는 배가 고프다. 나는 간식을 먹고 싶다.

「feel like v-ing」는 '~하고 싶다'라는 의미이다.

01회 내신 적중 실전 문제
본문 84쪽

01 ④ 02 ③ 03 ④ 04 ① 05 ① 06 ③
07 ⑤ 08 ④ 09 ② 10 ② 11 ③ 12 ③
13 finding 14 to book 15 working
16 (1) try to do (2) decided to keep
(3) finished painting

01
우정을 유지하는 것은 쉬운 일이 아니다.

동사가 문장의 주어로 쓰이려면 동명사나 to부정사의 형태가 되어야 하므로 ④가 알맞다.

Words friendship 우정

02
나는 이번 달 말까지 논문을 쓰는 것을 끝낼 것이다.

finish는 동명사를 목적어로 취한다.

03
Larry는 대학에 가지 않은 것을 후회하기 시작했다.

동명사의 부정은 동명사 바로 앞에 not을 쓴다.

04
Cathy는 공포영화를 보는 것을 ___________.
① 원하다 ② 즐기다 ③ 매우 좋아하다
④ 좋아하다 ⑤ 싫어하다

① want는 to부정사만 목적어로 취하므로 빈칸에 알맞지 않다.

05
서로를 존중하는 것이 모든 성공적인 관계의 비결이다.

'존중하는 것'이라는 의미로 동사가 명사처럼 쓰이려면 동명사나 to부정사의 형태로 써야 한다. 따라서 ①의 Respect를 Respecting이나 To respect로 고쳐야 한다.

06
나는 분명히 그 문을 잠갔어요.
= 나는 그 문을 잠갔던 것을 기억해요.

「remember+v-ing」는 '(과거에) ~했던 것을 기억하다'라는 의미이다.

07
- 그는 새로운 사람들을 만나는 것을 피한다.
- 그 커플은 가능한 빨리 결혼하기로 동의했다.

avoid는 동명사를 목적어로 취하고, agree는 to부정사를 목적어로 취한다.
Words as soon as possible 가능한 빨리

08
• 이 책은 두 번 읽을 만한 가치가 있다.
• 저에게 당신의 이름을 말해 주시겠습니까?
「be worth v-ing」는 '~할 가치가 있다'라는 의미이며, mind는 동명사를 목적어로 취하는 동사이다.

09
이야기하는 것을 멈추고 조용히 해. 너는 도서관에 있어.
「stop+v-ing」는 '~하는 것을 멈추다'라는 의미이다.

10
① 그 아기는 공을 가지고 노는 것을 좋아한다.
② 너는 떨어지는 눈송이들을 볼 수 있니?
③ 영화감독이 되는 것은 나의 꿈이다.
④ 우리는 마침내 예식장에 도착했다.
⑤ 그가 가장 좋아하는 여가 활동은 테니스를 하는 것이다.
②는 명사를 꾸며주는 현재분사인 반면 나머지는 모두 동명사로 쓰였다.
Words snowflake 눈송이

11
'~하고 싶다'는 「feel like v-ing」로 표현한다.

12
① 그녀는 자신의 애완동물과 놀기를 좋아한다.
② 너는 플루트를 부는 것을 연습했니?
③ 우리는 이집트로 여행가는 것을 고려하고 있다.
④ 나는 불필요한 것을 사는 것을 그만둘 것이다.
⑤ 그 아이들은 눈사람을 만드는 것을 계속했다.
consider는 동명사를 목적어로 취한다. (to travel → traveling)
Words pet 애완동물 unnecessary 불필요한

13
당신의 진정한 사랑을 찾는 것을 포기하지 마라.
give up은 동명사를 목적어로 취한다.

14
그곳은 매우 붐비는 레스토랑이다. 자리를 예약하는 것을 잊지 마.
주어진 단어를 to부정사로 써야 한다. 「forget+to-v」는 '(앞으로) ~할 것을 잊다'라는 의미이다.
Words busy 붐비는 book 예약하다

15
나는 밤에 늦게까지 일하는 것을 싫어한다.
hate는 동명사와 to부정사를 모두 목적어로 취하는 동사이다.

16
(1) 「try+to-v」: ~하려고 노력하다
(2) decide는 to부정사를 목적어로 취한다.
(3) finish는 동명사를 목적어로 취한다.
Words do one's best 최선을 다하다
keep a journal 일기를 쓰다

02회 내신 적중 실전 문제

본문 86쪽

01 ④ **02** ④ **03** ②, ③ **04** ②, ⑤ **05** ③
06 ③ **07** ⑤ **08** ② **09** ② **10** ③, ⑤
11 ⑤ **12** ②
13 no use complaining
14 couldn't help laughing
15 He is afraid of losing his power.
16 to eat, eating

01
너는 식물을 기르는 데 관심이 있니?
전치사의 목적어로 동명사가 쓰이므로 빈칸에는 growing이 알맞다.

02
내일 할머니께 전화 드리는 것을 기억해. 내일이 생신이셔.
「remember+to-v」는 '(앞으로) ~할 것을 기억하다'라는 의미이다.

03
그는 저녁을 먹고 숙제를 하기 시작했다.
begin은 동명사와 to부정사를 모두 목적어로 취할 수 있다.

04
나의 남동생은 모형 비행기를 만드는 것을 ________.
① 원했다 ② 즐겼다 ③ 바랐다 ④ 계획했다 ⑤ 포기했다

enjoy와 give up은 동명사를 목적어로 취하므로 빈칸에 알맞다.

05

A: 액션 영화를 보는 게 어때?
B: 그거 좋은데! 나는 액션 영화를 정말 좋아해.

전치사의 목적어는 동명사의 형태가 되어야 하므로 빈칸에는 watching이 알맞다.

06

나는 지난달에 돈을 너무 많이 쓴 것을 후회한다.

「regret+v-ing」는 '(과거에) ~했던 것을 후회하다'라는 의미이다.

07

'~하기를 기대하다'는 「look forward to v-ing」로 표현한다.

08

동사가 문장의 주어로 쓰이려면 동명사나 to부정사가 되어야 하므로 Eating 또는 To eat의 형태가 알맞다. 이때 동명사 또는 to부정사 주어는 단수 취급한다.

09

• 우리 엄마는 커피를 먹는 것을 그만두셨다.
• 나는 이 노래 경연 대회에서 우승하기를 원한다.
• 집에 돌아오자마자, 그녀는 자신의 방으로 달려갔다.

quit은 동명사를 목적어로 취하고 want는 to부정사를 목적어로 취한다. 「on v-ing」는 '~하자마자'라는 뜻이다.

Words return 돌아오다

10

보기 해변에 누워있는 것을 상상해보라.
① 날고 있는 새들을 보아라.
② 그는 기타를 치고 있다.
③ 그의 직업은 영어를 가르치는 것이다.
④ 그들은 그 아이들을 돕고 있다.
⑤ 나는 새 운동화 한 켤레를 샀다.

보기와 ③, ⑤는 동명사이고, ①, ②, ④는 현재분사이다.

11

① Mike는 그의 집을 팔려고 계획하고 있다.
② 그녀는 욕실을 청소하는 것을 계속했다.
③ 나는 그녀를 처음 봤던 것을 절대 잊지 못할 것이다.
④ 이제 작별인사를 해야 할 때라고 말하게 되어 유감이다.
⑤ 당신의 편지에 제가 답하지 못한 것에 대해 용서해 주세요.

⑤ 동명사의 부정은 동명사 바로 앞에 not을 쓴다. (answering not → not answering)

12

① 나는 너를 집에 데려다 줄 것을 약속한다.
② Jessica는 혼자 먹는 것을 꺼리지 않는다.
③ Jennifer는 학교에서 나를 만나는 것을 피했다.
④ 나는 그 수프를 한번 먹어 보았는데, 맛있지 않았다.
⑤ 저에게 두 번째 기회를 주시는 것을 고려해 주세요.

mind는 동명사를 목적어로 취한다. (to eat → eating)

13

'~해도 소용없다'는 「It is no use v-ing」로 표현한다.

14

'~하지 않을 수 없다'는 「cannot help v-ing」로 표현한다.

15

전치사의 목적어는 동명사의 형태가 되어야 하므로 of 뒤에는 losing이 나와야 한다.

Words be afraid of ~을 두려워하다 power 힘, 권력

16

올해 초에, 나는 살을 빼기로 결심했다. 그래서 나는 매일 아침 조깅하는 것을 시작했다. 나는 또한 패스트푸드를 <u>먹기 위해 (→ 먹는 것을)</u> 멈췄다.

'~하던 것을 멈추다'를 뜻하는 「stop+v-ing」로 바꿔 써야 한다.

Words at the beginning of ~의 초반에 lose weight 살을 빼다

Lesson 06 | 분사

Point 047 현재분사

본문 90쪽

STEP 1

1 그는 불타고 있는 집에서 뛰쳐나왔다.
2 오리 몇 마리가 연못에서 수영하고 있었다.
3 너는 그 방에서 담배피고 있는 남자를 보았니?
4 엄마는 점심으로 계란 샌드위치를 만들고 있다.
5 12시에 파리로 떠나는 열차가 있다.

STEP 2

1 dancing 2 barking
3 shining 4 digging

STEP 3 ④

• 그것은 흥미로운 경기였다.
• 나는 산 정상에서 떠오르는 해를 보았다.

TIP 그녀는 음악을 듣고 있다.

STEP 3

• Eric은 침대에서 자고 있다.
• 그녀는 자고 있는 아기를 살포시 내려놓았다.

첫 번째 빈칸에는 be동사와 함께 쓰여 진행형을 만드는 현재분사 sleeping이, 두 번째 빈칸에는 진행의 의미를 갖는 현재분사 sleeping이 들어간다.

Point 048 과거분사

본문 91쪽

STEP 1

1 그녀는 떨어진 나뭇잎들을 쓸어냈다.
2 비행기는 공항에 방금 도착했다.
3 이 레스토랑에서 그 메뉴는 정기적으로 변경된다.
4 그녀는 새롭게 칠해진 자신의 집을 우리에게 보여 주었다.
5 모든 문과 창문은 굳게 잠겨 있었다.

STEP 2

1 shocked 2 found 3 invited
4 injured 5 named

STEP 3 ③

• 차고에는 부서진 자전거 한 대가 있었다.
• 이 삶은 달걀을 먹어도 되나요?

STEP 3

나는 쓰레기통에서 찢어진 편지를 보았다.

빈칸에는 '~된'의 수동의 의미의 과거분사가 알맞다.

Point 049 분사의 쓰임 (명사 수식)

본문 92쪽

STEP 1

1 designed 2 beeping 3 dancing
4 lost 5 invited

STEP 2

1 Do you know that lady talking to Ms. Wilson?
2 My dad bought my mom a bag made in Italy.
3 The picture hanging on the wall was taken ten years ago.
4 The boy bitten by a snake is in the hospital now.
5 Have you read any books written by Tolstoy?

STEP 3 ⑤

• 경찰은 도난당한 지갑을 찾았다.
• 파란색 모자를 쓰고 있는 소년은 내 남동생이다.

STEP 1

1 그녀는 내게 Valentino에 의해 디자인된 드레스를 하나 주었다.
2 나는 자명종 시계가 울리는 소리를 들었다.
3 퍼레이드에서 춤추고 있는 저 키 큰 소녀는 내 여동생이다.
4 나는 침대 밑에서 잃어버린 반지를 발견했다.
5 파티에 초대된 대부분의 사람들은 나타나지 않았다.

STEP 2

보기 저 새들을 봐. 그들은 둥지를 짓고 있다. → 둥지를 짓고 있는 저 새들을 봐.

1 너는 저 부인을 아니? 그녀는 Wilson 씨와 이야기 중이다.
→ 너는 Wilson 씨와 이야기 중인 저 부인을 아니?
2 나의 아빠는 엄마에게 가방을 하나 사주셨다. 그것은 이탈리아에서 만들어졌다.
→ 나의 아빠는 이탈리아에서 만들어진 가방 하나를 엄마에게 사주셨다.
3 그 사진은 10년 전에 찍힌 것이다. 그것은 벽에 걸려 있다.
→ 벽에 걸려 있는 그 사진은 10년 전에 찍힌 것이다.
4 그 소년은 지금 병원에 있다. 그는 뱀에 물렸다.

→ 뱀에 물린 그 소년은 지금 병원에 있다.
5 너는 책을 읽은 적이 있니? 그 책은 Tolstoy에 의해서 쓰였다.
→ 너는 Tolstoy에 의해 쓰인 책을 읽은 적이 있니?

STEP 3
수식어구를 동반하는 현재분사(covered with papers)는 명사(the table)를 뒤에서 수식한다.

Point 050 분사의 쓰임 (보어 역할)

본문 93쪽

STEP 1
1 listening 2 untouched 3 walking
4 solved 5 disappointed

STEP 2
1 He had his car repaired
2 His younger brother came crying loudly
3 The station remained unused
4 I noticed her attitude changed
5 I keep you waiting

STEP 3 ③

• 그는 TV를 보며 앉아 있었다.
• 그 배우는 팬들에게 둘러싸여 서 있었다.
• 그녀는 그를 너무 오랫동안 기다리게 했다.
• Jack은 자신의 방이 청소되어 있는 것을 발견했다.

STEP 1
1 Alice는 음악을 들으면서 누워 있었다.
2 그녀는 음식을 건드리지 않은 상태로 두었다.
3 Peter는 그녀가 계단을 걸어 내려가는 것을 보았다.
4 나는 그 문제가 즉시 해결되기를 원했다.
5 그는 그 소식에 약간 실망한 것처럼 보였다.

STEP 3
우리는 전구가 교체되도록 해야 한다.
목적어와 목적격 보어의 관계가 수동이므로 목적격 보어는 과거분사를 써야 한다.

Point 051 감정을 나타내는 분사

본문 94쪽

STEP 1
1 tired 2 confusing 3 touched
4 amazing 5 disappointed

STEP 2
1 interested 2 shocking 3 bored
4 annoying 5 exhausted

STEP 3 ②

• 그 소식은 놀라웠다.
• 우리는 그 소식에 놀랐다.

STEP 1
1 그들은 긴 여정 후에 피곤함을 느꼈다.
2 그 설명은 혼란스러웠다.
3 감동을 받은 관중들은 큰 박수갈채를 보냈다.
4 그 여행은 나에게 매우 놀라운 경험이었다.
5 나의 부모님은 내 성적에 실망하셨다.

STEP 2
1 Mike는 운동에 관심이 있다.
2 그 시합의 결과는 매우 충격적이었다.
3 나는 비행 중에 너무 지루했다.
4 John의 시끄러운 음악은 그의 이웃들에게 짜증스럽다.
5 그는 수 마일을 걸은 후 기진맥진해졌다.

STEP 3
• 그 축구 경기는 매우 흥미진진했다.
• 당신은 당신의 직업에 만족하십니까?
첫 번째 빈칸에는 주어가 '흥분한' 감정을 일으키는 것이므로 현재분사를, 두 번째 빈칸은 주어가 '만족하는' 감정을 느끼는 것이므로 과거분사를 써야한다.

Point 052 분사구문 만드는 법

본문 95쪽

STEP 1
1 Starting 2 Listening 3 Being
4 Getting 5 Not knowing

STEP 2
1 Entering the room 2 Turning to the right
3 Having many friends 4 Being late

STEP 3 ②

• 약을 먹은 후에, 그는 졸렸다.

STEP 1
1 지금 출발하면, 너는 너무 많이 뒤처지지 않을 것이다.

2 음악을 들으면서, 그는 숙제를 했다.
3 화가 나서, 그는 그 소년들에게 소리 지르기 시작했다.
4 스트레스를 너무 많이 받아서, 그는 직업을 바꾸기로 결심했다.
5 어떻게 할지 몰라서, 나는 그녀에게 조언을 구했다.

STEP 2
1 그가 방에 들어갔을 때, 그는 아이가 자고 있는 것을 발견했다.
2 오른쪽으로 돌면, 너는 은행을 발견할 것이다.
3 많은 친구가 있었지만, 그녀는 외로웠다.
4 우리는 늦어서, 기차를 놓쳤다.

STEP 3
우리가 해변에 도착했을 때, 우리는 해가 뜨는 것을 보았다.
접속사(When)와 공통된 주어(we)를 생략하고, 동사 arrived를 현재분사인 arriving으로 바꾸면 분사구문을 만들 수 있다.

Point 053 분사구문의 의미 (때)

본문 96쪽

STEP 1
1 ⓒ 2 ⓐ 3 ⓑ 4 ⓔ 5 ⓓ

STEP 2
1 When I heard the doorbell
2 After he got home
3 While he watched the movie
4 When you cross the road
5 After he finished his homework

STEP 3 ③

• 봉투를 열었을 때, 그는 콘서트 표 두 장을 발견했다.

STEP 1
1 손을 씻은 후, 그녀는 요리하기 시작했다.
2 피아노를 들려다가, 그는 허리를 다쳤다.
3 잠옷으로 갈아입은 후, 그는 잠자리에 들었다.
4 서랍을 정리하다가, 그녀는 오래된 사진 한 장을 발견했다.
5 구명조끼를 입은 후, 나는 수영장에 뛰어들었다.

STEP 2
1 초인종 소리를 들었을 때 나는 현관으로 급히 갔다.
2 집에 도착하고 나서, 그는 샤워를 했다.
3 그는 영화를 보는 도중에 잠이 들었다.
4 길을 건널 때는 양쪽을 살펴야 한다.
5 숙제를 다 한 후 그는 밖으로 놀러 나갔다.

STEP 3
자전거를 탈 때, 그는 항상 헬멧을 쓴다.
문맥상 '~할 때'를 의미하므로 When he ride a bike로 바꿔 쓸 수 있다.

Point 054 분사구문의 의미 (이유)

본문 97쪽

STEP 1
1 ⓒ 2 ⓓ 3 ⓔ 4 ⓐ 5 ⓑ

STEP 2
1 Being angry with her
2 Walking very quickly
3 Having an exam the next day
4 Feeling comfortable with us
5 Being the top basketball player

STEP 3 ④

• 몸무게를 줄이길 원해서 나는 요즘 덜 먹고 있다.

STEP 1
1 지난달에 일을 그만두어서, 나는 새로운 일을 찾고 있다.
2 자세한 지도가 있어서, 우리는 길을 찾을 수 있었다.
3 그는 엄격한 채식주의자라서, 고기를 절대 먹지 않는다.
4 새 사업을 시작해서, 그는 매우 바빴다.
5 일을 위해 프랑스어가 필요해서, 그녀는 그것을 매우 열심히 공부하고 있다.

STEP 2
1 그는 그녀에게 화가 나서, 한마디도 하지 않았다.
2 매우 빨리 걸어가서 나는 마지막 기차를 탈 수 있었다.
3 다음 날 시험이 있어서 나는 도서관에서 하루를 보냈다.
4 우리와 함께 있는 것이 편안해서, 그녀는 여기에 더 오래 머물고 싶어 했다.
5 최고의 농구선수여서, 그는 여자아이들에게 인기가 있었다.

STEP 3
① 너무 피곤해서 그녀는 휴식을 취했다.
② 학교 근처에 살아서 나는 점심을 먹으러 집에 간다.
③ 동물을 사랑해서, 그녀는 수의사가 되기를 원한다.
④ 감자 껍질을 벗긴 후 그는 그것들을 오븐에서 요리했다.
⑤ 자신의 건강에 대해 주의하므로 그는 좀처럼 아프지 않다.
④는 '때'를 의미하고, 나머지는 '이유'를 의미한다.

Point 055 분사구문의 의미 (조건, 양보)

본문 98쪽

STEP 1

1 그녀는 매우 아팠지만, 회의에 참석했다.
2 그는 많이 먹지만, 쉽게 살이 찌지 않는다.
3 그의 제안을 거절하면, 너는 후회할 것이다.
4 신문을 읽을 때, 그는 돋보기안경을 필요로 한다.
5 그녀는 친절한 사람이기 때문에 모두에게 사랑받는다.

STEP 2

1 Trying their best 2 Finishing your homework
3 Traveling to France 4 Having so much money

STEP 3 ⑤

• 창문을 열면, 너는 신선한 공기를 마실 수 있을 것이다.
• 그녀의 집에 가까이 살지만, 우리는 그녀를 거의 보지 못한다.

STEP 3

나이가 아주 많지만, 그는 자신에게 도전하는 것을 절대 멈추지 않는다.

문맥상 '~일지라도'의 뜻을 나타내는 양보의 접속사 though가 빈칸에 알맞다.

Point 056 분사구문의 의미 (동시동작, 연속동작)

본문 99쪽

STEP 1

1 책상에 앉은 다음, 그는 숙제를 하기 시작했다.
2 행복하게 미소를 지으면서, 그녀는 생일 선물을 열어보았다.
3 팝콘을 먹으면서, 그 소년들은 액션 영화를 보았다.
4 기적을 바라면서, 그 의사는 수술을 계속했다.
5 우리는 저녁을 먹고 나서, 후식으로 아이스크림을 즐겼다.

STEP 2

1 Waving her hands 2 barking at me
3 Knocking on the door 4 rubbing her eyes

STEP 3 ②

• 모자를 쓰면서 그는 작별인사를 했다.
• 우리는 주차를 하고 표 판매기를 찾았다.

TIP 샤워를 하면서 그는 노래를 불렀다.

STEP 3

보기 나에게 윙크하면서, 그녀는 내게 쪽지를 건넸다.
① 가난했지만, 그 커플은 매우 행복했다.
② 라디오를 들으면서, 그녀는 저녁을 준비했다.
③ 우리는 공항에 운전해서 가서, 비행기를 탔다.
④ 그는 아침에 떠나서, 정오에 집에 돌아왔다.
⑤ 카페인이 들어있어서, 커피는 당신을 깨어있게 할 수 있다.

보기 와 ②는 동시동작을 나타내는 반면, ①은 양보를, ③, ④는 연속동작을, ⑤는 이유를 나타내는 분사구문이다.

01회 내신 적중 실전 문제

본문 100쪽

01 ④ 02 ③, ⑤ 03 ④ 04 ⑤ 05 ③
06 ⑤ 07 ④ 08 ②, ③ 09 ① 10 ②
11 ④ 12 ① 13 ⓐ interested ⓑ boring
14 This is the sand castle built by the kids.
15 Traveling in Europe 16 Not feeling well

01

A: 꽃을 들고 있는 저 소년은 누구니?
B: 그는 내 사촌 Jeremy야.

꽃을 '들고 있는' 이라는 능동의 의미로 the boy를 수식하는 현재분사 holding이 와야 한다.

Words cousin 사촌 hold (손에) 들다, 갖고 있다

02

부사절로 쓰면 As I had no money이고 분사구문으로 바꿔 쓰면 접속사 As와 주어 I를 생략하고, 동사 had를 현재분사인 having으로 바꿔 써서 Having no money이다.

03

그는 기자들이 너무 많은 질문을 했을 때 약간 짜증이 났다.

주어인 He가 '짜증이 난' 감정을 느끼는 것이므로 과거분사 annoyed를 쓴다.

Words reporter 기자 annoy 짜증나게 하다

04

그녀는 거울이 깨진 것을 발견했다.

목적어인 거울이 '깨져 진' 것이므로 목적격 보어는 수동의 의미를 가진 과거분사 broken을 쓴다.

Words mirror 거울

05

Brian은 택시를 기다리며 서 있었다.

주어와 주격 보어의 관계가 능동이므로 빈칸에는 현재분사가 알맞다.

06

• 초록색 드레스를 입고 있는 여자는 아름다웠다.
• 엄마는 벽에 그림을 걸고 있다.

첫 번째 빈칸은 능동의 의미로 앞의 명사인 the woman을 수식하는 현재분사가 알맞다. 두 번째 빈칸은 be동사 뒤에서 진행형을 만드는 현재분사가 필요하다.

07

• 버스 정류장에서 발견된 우산은 John의 것이다.
• 너는 전화기가 울리는 소리를 들었니?

첫 번째 빈칸은 앞의 명사 the umbrella를 수식하는 분사로, 우산은 '발견된' 것이므로 수동의 의미의 과거분사 found를 쓴다. 두 번째 빈칸은 동사 hear의 목적격 보어 자리로 목적어인 the phone이 '울리는' 것이므로 능동, 진행의 의미의 현재분사 ringing을 쓴다.

Words belong to ~의 소유이다, ~에 속하다
ring (종 등이) 울리다(-rang-rung)

08

① 그의 행동은 실망스럽다.
② 그녀는 자신의 작품에 만족했다.
③ 그 액션 영화는 정말 흥미진진했다.
④ 그는 사고를 봤을 때, 충격을 받았다.
⑤ 그들은 아빠로부터 우울한 소식을 들었다.

② 그녀가 '만족시키는' 것이 아니라 '만족한' 감정을 느끼는 것이므로 과거분사 satisfied로 고쳐야 한다. ③ 액션 영화가 '흥미진진한' 감정을 일으키는 것이므로 현재분사 exciting을 써야 한다.

Words behavior 행동 depressing 우울한

09

그녀에게 아무런 메시지를 받지 못해서, 나는 그냥 거기에서 기다렸다.

분사구문의 부정을 나타낼 때는 분사 앞에 not을 쓴다.

10

보기 신발을 벗은 후, 그녀는 집으로 걸어 들어갔다.
① 얇은 옷을 입어서, 그녀는 추웠다.
② 쪽지를 쓴 후, Jason는 그것을 나에게 건넸다.
③ 남은 할 일이 없어서, 그는 집으로 갔다.
④ 우리의 웹사이트를 방문하면, 당신은 할인을 받을 수 있다.
⑤ 폭탄이 폭발해서, 10명이 사망했다.

보기 와 ②는 문맥상 '~한 후에(after)'를 뜻하는 때를 나타내는 분사구문이다. ①, ③은 이유, ④는 조건, ⑤는 연속동작을 나타내는 분사구문이다.

Words note 쪽지 bomb 폭탄 explode 폭발하다

11

보기 산꼭대기에 올라가면, 너는 항구를 볼 수 있다.
① 크게 울면서, 그녀는 방을 나갔다.
② 배가 고파서, 나는 간식을 좀 먹었다.
③ 그 버스는 7시에 출발하고 10시에 도착한다.
④ 그와 함께 일하면, 너는 그가 신뢰할 만한 사람이라는 것을 알게 될 것이다.
⑤ 버스를 기다리면서, 내 여동생과 나는 수다를 떨었다.

보기 와 ④는 조건을 나타내는 반면, ①은 동시동작, ②는 이유, ③은 연속동작, ⑤는 때를 나타내는 분사구문이다.

Words reliable 신뢰할 만한, 믿을 만한 chat 수다를 떨다

12

① 비가 와서, 우리는 소풍을 취소했다.
② 그녀는 가방을 열고, 책을 한 권 꺼냈다.
③ 고속도로를 운전할 때는, 너는 조심해야 한다.
④ 진실을 알게 되었을 때, 그는 웃지 않을 수 없었다.
⑤ 벽에 기대서, 그는 책을 읽고 있었다.

①에서 분사구문의 주어는 it으로 주절의 주어 we와 다르기 때문에 주어 it을 생략하여 분사구문으로 만들 수 없다.

Words take out 꺼내다 highway 고속도로
lean against ~에 기대다

13

• Sam은 영화를 만드는 데 관심이 있다.
• 역사는 Sam에게 지루한 과목이다.

첫 번째 빈칸은 주어가 '흥미로워하는' 감정을 느끼는 것이므로 과거분사 interested를, 두 번째 빈칸은 수식을 받는 명사인 subject가 '지루한' 감정을 일으키는 것이므로 현재분사 boring을 쓴다.

Words subject 과목

14

수식어를 동반하여 길어진 분사구(built by the kids)는 명사(the sand castle)를 뒤에서 수식한다.

Words sand castle 모래성

15

유럽에서 여행할 때, 나는 항상 유스호스텔에서 머문다.

접속사와 주어를 생략하고 동사를 현재분사로 쓴다.

16

A: Katie는 왜 빨리 자러 갔니?

B: 그녀는 몸이 안 좋았어.

대화의 상황을 부사절로 표현하면 Because Katie didn't feel well, she went to bed early.이다. 부사절의 접속사와 공통되는 주어를 생략하고 현재분사 feeling을 써서 분사구문을 만든다. 부정을 나타내는 not은 분사 앞에 쓴다.

02회 내신 적중 실전 문제

본문 102쪽

01 ④ 02 ① 03 ③ 04 ⑤ 05 ③ 06 ④
07 ⑤ 08 ④ 09 ⑤ 10 ① 11 ⑤ 12 ①
13 Coming 14 confused 15 amused, amusing
16 Having poor eyesight, he could not see clearly.

01

보기 배가 고파서, 나는 냉장고에서 뭔가 먹을 것을 찾았다.

이유를 나타내는 부사절인 Because[As, Since] I was hungry를 분사구문으로 바꾼 것이다. 접속사와 공통되는 주어 I를 생략하고 동사 was의 원형 상태인 be에 -ing를 붙여서 being으로 만든다.

02

그는 보통 그의 방에 있는 모든 창문을 하루 종일 닫아 놓는다.

빈칸은 keep의 목적격 보어 자리로 목적어와 목적격 보어의 관계를 살펴야 한다. 창문은 '닫히는' 것이므로 수동의 의미의 과거분사 shut이 와야 한다.

Words shut 닫다(-shut-shut)

03

- 나는 Lisa가 그녀의 상황에 대해 불평하는 것을 들었다.
- 소녀들은 그들의 학교 점심에 대해 불평하고 있었다.

첫 번째 빈칸은 동사 hear의 목적격 보어 자리로 목적어인 Lisa가 '불평하는' 것이므로 능동의 의미의 현재분사가 알맞다. 두 번째 빈칸에는 be동사 뒤에서 진행형을 만드는 현재분사가 필요하다.

04

- Henry는 피자의 마지막 조각을 먹었다.
- Maria는 그녀의 방에서 바이올린을 연습하고 있었다.
- 그녀는 울고 있는 작은 소녀에게 쿠키를 주었다.

(A) have[has]와 결합하여 완료형을 만드는 과거분사가 알맞다.
(B) be동사와 결합하여 진행형을 만드는 현재분사가 알맞다.
(C) '울고 있는'의 뜻으로 little girl을 수식하는 현재분사가 알맞다.

05

- 그 종이에는 아무것도 쓰여 있는 것이 없었다.
- Tom은 하늘을 날고 있는 새를 그렸다.

첫 번째 빈칸에는 '쓰여 있는'의 수동의 의미가 되어야 하므로 과거분사 written이 알맞다. 두 번째 빈칸은 '날고 있는'의 능동의 의미가 되어야 하므로 현재분사 flying이 알맞다.

Words fly 날다(-flew-flown)

06

그 아이들은 흥미로운 동물 쇼에 갔다. 그 흥분한 아이들은 깡충깡충 뛰었다.

첫 번째 빈칸은 쇼가 '흥분시키는' 것이므로 능동의 현재분사가, 두 번째 빈칸은 아이들이 '흥분하게 된' 것이므로 수동의 과거분사가 알맞다.

07

분사구문이나 시간을 나타내는 부사절(When+주어+동사)로 쓸 수 있다.

08

① Angela는 잡지를 읽으며 앉아 있었다.
② 나는 그 소년이 길을 건너는 것을 보았다.
③ 겁에 질린 아이들은 도와달라고 소리를 질렀다.
④ 내 충고를 따르지 않으면, 너는 곤경에 빠질 것이다.
⑤ 테이블에서 커피를 마시고 있는 여자는 나의 이모이다.

④ 분사구문의 부정을 나타낼 때는 분사 바로 앞에 not을 쓴다.

Words terrified 무서워하는, 겁이 난
get into trouble 곤경에 빠지다

09

다음 날 중요한 시험이 있지만, 그녀는 파티에 가고 싶어 했다.

분사구문은 맥락을 통해 생략된 접속사를 추측해야 한다. 중요한 시험이 있지만 파티에 가고 싶어 했다는 흐름이 자연스러우므로 양보를 나타내는 접속사 Although가 알맞다.

10

오른쪽을 보면, 너는 궁전을 볼 수 있다.

문맥상 조건을 나타내는 접속사 if가 알맞다.

11

보기 키가 매우 커서, 그는 농구 선수가 되었다.

① 저녁을 준비하면서, 그녀는 손가락을 베었다.

② 복도에서 기다리다가, Cathy는 그들이 이야기하는 것을 들었다.

③ 연세가 많이 드셨음에도 불구하고, 나의 할아버지는 여전히 운전을 하실 수 있다.

④ 높게 점프를 하다가, 그녀는 발목을 삐었다.

⑤ 변명을 하기 싫어서, 그는 더 이상 말하지 않았다.

보기 와 ⑤는 이유를 나타내는 반면, ①, ②, ④는 '~하는 동안'의 의미로 때를, ③은 양보를 나타내는 분사구문이다.

Words hall 복도 twist (발목 · 손목 등을) 삐다 ankle 발목 make excuses 변명하다

12

보기 전화 통화를 하면서, 그는 길을 걸었다.

① 휘파람으로 노래를 부르면서, 그는 설거지를 했다.

② 착한 소년이라서, 그는 항상 그의 엄마를 돕는다.

③ 돌부리에 걸려 넘어졌어도, 그는 경주를 포기하지 않았다.

④ 좋은 성적을 받고 싶어서, 그는 열심히 공부하기로 결심했다.

⑤ 아이스크림을 너무 많이 먹으면, 너는 배가 아플 것이다.

보기 와 ①은 동시동작을 나타내는 반면, ②, ④는 이유, ③은 양보, ⑤는 조건을 나타내는 분사구문이다.

Words fall over ~에 걸려 넘어지다 stomachache 복통

13

시간을 나타내는 부사절인 When dad came back home을 분사구문으로 바꿔야 한다. 접속사 When과 공통되는 주어 dad를 생략하고 동사는 현재분사의 형태인 coming을 쓴다.

14

주어가 감정의 대상이 되어 '~한 감정을 느끼는'의 의미일 때는 과거분사로 나타낸다.

15

나는 Jack의 농담을 좋아한다. 그의 재미있는 농담은 나를 항상 웃게 한다.

명사가 감정의 원인이 되어 '~한 감정을 일으키는'의 의미일 때는 현재분사로 나타낸다.

16

그는 시력이 나빴다. 그래서 그는 분명하게 볼 수 없었다.

Because he had poor eyesight, he could not see clearly.의 문장을 분사구문을 이용한 문장으로 바꿔 쓴다. 접속사 Because와 주어 he를 생략하고 현재분사 having을 써서 분사구문으로 나타낸다.

Words clearly 분명하게

Lesson 07 수동태

Point 057 수동태의 개념과 기본 형태

본문 106쪽

STEP 1
1 is loved 2 is cleaned 3 checks
4 are posted 5 carries

STEP 2
1 The movie of the month is played in the Grand Hall.
2 This palace is visited by many tourists.
3 A lot of money is spent on education.
4 The flowers are watered twice a week.

STEP 3 ④

• 엄마는 특별한 수프를 만드신다.
• 특별한 수프가 엄마에 의해 만들어진다.

STEP 1
1 그녀의 동화책은 많은 아이들에게 사랑받는다.
2 교실은 매일 청소된다.
3 그 정비공은 엘리베이터를 정기적으로 점검한다.
4 그의 사진과 동영상은 그의 조수에 의해 게시된다.
5 어미 캥거루는 새끼를 자신의 주머니 안에 넣고 다닌다.

STEP 3
자전거가 아빠에 의해 '수리되는' 것이므로 빈칸에는 수동을 나타내는 「be동사+과거분사」의 형태가 알맞다.

Point 058 수동태를 만드는 방법

본문 107쪽

STEP 1
1 resembles 2 was taken 3 disappeared
4 me 5 looks

STEP 2
1 is fed by Tony
2 was written by a famous poet
3 were packed by Diane
4 is trusted by us

STEP 3 ⑤

• 우리는 그 규칙을 지킨다.
• 그 규칙은 우리에 의해 지켜진다.

STEP 1
1 그 소녀는 그녀의 엄마를 닮았다.
2 그녀의 사진은 그녀의 허락 없이 찍혔다.
3 그 마술사는 갑자기 사라졌다.
4 저녁 밥상은 나에 의해서 차려진다.
5 당신의 가방은 무거워 보인다.

STEP 2
1 Tony가 그 개에게 먹이를 준다.
2 한 유명한 시인이 이 시를 썼다.
3 Diane는 가방을 쌌다.
4 우리는 우리의 새 지도자를 신뢰한다.

STEP 3
① 그가 공을 던졌다.
② 그 소녀들은 노래를 불렀다.
③ 그들이 그 집들을 지었다.
④ 그녀는 파티를 즐겼다.
⑤ 그녀는 여배우가 되었다.
⑤ become은 상태를 나타내는 동사로 수동태로 바꿀 수 없다.

Point 059 수동태의 시제 (과거시제)

본문 108쪽

STEP 1
1 were destroyed 2 were made
3 was delivered 4 was invented
5 was planted

STEP 2
1 was bitten by 2 were discovered by
3 was stopped by 4 was founded by
5 was opened

STEP 3 ③

• 그 고양이는 차에 치였다. (← 차가 고양이를 쳤다.)
• 그 쿠키들은 자원봉사자들에 의해 구워졌다. (← 자원봉사자들은 그 쿠키들을 구웠다.)

STEP 1
1 그 마을의 건물들은 지진에 의해 파괴되었다.
2 그 초대장은 며칠 전에 만들어졌다.

3 소포는 지난 금요일에 고객에게 배달되었다.
4 전구는 에디슨에 의해 발명되었다.
5 그의 집 앞의 참나무는 2003년에 심어졌다.

STEP 3
많은 사람들이 그 여배우를 사랑했다.
= 그 여배우는 많은 사람들에게 사랑받았다.
능동태를 수동태로 바꾼 문장이다. 과거시제의 문장을 수동태로 바꾸고 있으며 주어가 3인칭 단수이므로 「was+과거분사」 형태로 쓴다.

Point 060 수동태의 시제 (미래시제)

본문 109쪽

STEP 1
1 will be repaired 2 will be built
3 will be decorated 4 will be completed
5 will be solved

STEP 2
1 The patients will be checked by a new doctor.
2 Many workers will be hired by the company this year.
3 The museum will be visited by millions of people.
4 A bakery will be opened by Mr. and Mrs. Brown next month.
5 The contract will be signed by the manager tonight.

STEP 3 ⑤

• 당신은 다음 주 금요일에 지불을 받을 것입니다.
• 오늘의 토론은 많은 사람들에 의해 시청될 것이다.

STEP 1
1 그의 차는 몇 시간 내에 수리될 것이다.
2 마을에 새로운 쇼핑센터가 내년에 지어질 것이다.
3 교실은 내일 학생들에 의해 장식될 것이다.
4 그 프로젝트는 다음 달 말까지 완료될 것이다.
5 그 문제는 일주일 내에 해결될 것이다.

STEP 2
1 새 의사가 환자들을 검사할 것이다.
2 그 회사는 올해 많은 직원들을 고용할 것이다.
3 수백만 명의 사람들이 박물관을 방문할 것이다.
4 Brown 부부는 다음 달에 빵집을 열 것이다.
5 매니저는 오늘 밤 그 계약서에 사인을 할 것이다.

STEP 3
가구는 내일 당신에게 배달될 것이다.
미래시제를 나타내는 부사 tomorrow로 보아 미래시제의 수동태가 쓰여야 한다. 미래시제 문장의 수동태는 「will be+과거분사(+by+행위자)」의 형태로 쓴다.

Point 061 수동태의 부정문과 의문문

본문 110쪽

STEP 1
1 wasn't broken 2 Was 3 taken
4 wasn't solved 5 replaced

STEP 2
1 Were, moved 2 is not included
3 Was, mopped by 4 was not delivered
5 Are, produced

STEP 3 ④

• 그 거리는 아직 청소되지 않았다.
• 이 보고서는 Annie에 의해 작성되었니?

STEP 1
1 그 창문은 Tom에 의해 깨지지 않았다.
2 그 노래는 Elvis가 불렀나요?
3 그 개는 수의사에게 데려가졌나요?
4 그 문제는 Janet에 의해 해결되지 않았다.
5 그 컴퓨터들은 새 것으로 교체되었나요?

STEP 3
A: 일본어가 인도네시아에서 사용되나요?
B: 아니오, 그것은 거기서 사용되지 않습니다.
수동태의 의문문은 「be동사+주어+과거분사(+by+행위자)~?」로, 수동태의 부정문은 「be동사+not+과거분사(+by+행위자)」로 쓰므로, 공통으로 들어갈 말로 알맞은 말은 과거분사(spoken)이다.

Point 062 조동사의 수동태

본문 111쪽

STEP 1
1 may be forgotten 2 must be protected
3 Should these plants be watered
4 can not be solved 5 will not be paid

STEP 2

1 must be removed　2 will be sent
3 Can, be seen　4 may not be believed

STEP 3 ⑤

• 많은 종류의 새들이 그 지역에서 관찰될 수 있다.
• 전시회에 있는 물품들은 절대로 만져서는 안 된다.
• 세미나실은 내일 청소될까요?

STEP 1

1 그 암호는 쉽게 잊혀질지도 모른다.
2 아이들은 위험으로부터 보호되어야 한다.
3 이 식물들은 매일 물을 주어야 하나요?
4 그 문제는 우리에 의해 해결될 수 없다.
5 그 청구서는 우리에 의해 지불되지 않을 것이다.

STEP 3

조동사가 쓰인 수동태의 부정문은 「조동사+not+be+과거분사」의 형태로 쓴다.

Point 063 4형식 문장의 수동태

본문 112쪽

STEP 1

1 for　2 to　3 was handed
4 to his parents　5 was taught

STEP 2

1 were given snacks and drinks (by them)
2 was passed to me by Tom
3 was cooked for the couple by the chef
4 will be sent to you (by us)
5 was offered a job by

STEP 3 ②

• 그들은 고객들에게 크리스마스 카드를 보냈다.
• 고객들은 (그들에 의해) 크리스마스 카드를 받았다.
• 크리스마스 카드는 (그들에 의해) 그들의 고객들에게 보내졌다.

STEP 1

1 소녀의 엄마는 소녀에게 예쁜 모자를 사주셨다.
2 선생님은 학생들에게 흥미로운 이야기를 해주셨다.
3 그가 죽은 후, 그의 유언장은 그의 아들에게 건네졌다.
4 그의 부모님들은 그의 성적표를 보았다.
5 그는 체스의 기본적인 규칙을 그의 아버지에게 배웠다.

STEP 2

1 그들은 참가자들에게 간식과 음료수를 제공했다.
2 Tom은 내게 쪽지를 건넸다.
3 요리사는 그 커플에게 특별한 요리를 만들어 주었다.
4 우리는 14일 이내에 당신에게 그 결과를 보내 드리겠습니다.
5 '뉴욕 타임즈'의 편집장이 그에게 일자리를 제의했다.

STEP 3

소년의 할아버지는 소년에게 특별한 책상을 만들어 주셨다.

4형식 문장의 수동태에서 직접목적어를 주어로 하는 경우, 간접목적어 앞에 전치사를 쓰는데, make는 전치사 for를 쓴다.

Point 064 5형식 문장의 수동태

본문 113쪽

STEP 1

1 was kept　2 to change　3 was elected
4 to leave　5 was taught

STEP 2

1 Dr. Martin was considered a great leader (by them).
2 I was asked to wipe the tables by the manager.
3 Visitors are not allowed to take pictures in the museum (by them).
4 The lawyer was made famous by the case.

STEP 3 ③

• 그의 부모님은 그를 Alexander라고 이름 지었다.
  → 그는 그의 부모님에 의해 Alexander라는 이름으로 불렸다.
• 의사는 그에게 규칙적으로 운동하라고 충고했다.
  → 그는 의사에게서 규칙적으로 운동을 하라는 충고를 받았다.

STEP 1

1 그 문은 낮에 열려 있었다.
2 Jason은 그의 계획을 바꾸라는 말을 들었다.
3 그는 급우들에 의해 대표로 뽑혔다.
4 그 남자는 그 나라를 떠나도록 강요받았다.
5 그녀는 다른 사람에게 친절하게 대하라고 배웠다.

STEP 2

1 그들은 Martin 박사를 위대한 지도자로 여겼다.
2 그 매니저는 나에게 식탁을 닦아 달라고 요청했다.

3 그들은 방문객들이 박물관에서 사진을 찍도록 허락하지 않는다.
4 그 소송 건은 그 변호사를 유명하게 만들었다.

STEP 3
선생님은 우리에게 우리의 생각을 표현하라고 격려하셨다.
5형식 문장의 수동태를 만들 때, 능동태의 목적어는 수동태의 주어로 쓰고 동사는 「be동사+과거분사」의 형태로 바꾼다. 능동태의 목적격 보어는 동사 뒤에 그대로 써준다.

Point 065 동사구의 수동태

본문 114쪽

STEP 1
1 run over
2 was taken care of
3 be dealt with
4 was not handed in
5 be put off

STEP 2
1 was looked after
2 was looked up to
3 will be paid for
4 was brought up
5 was laughed at

STEP 3 ④

• 트럭이 그 개를 쳤다. → 그 개는 트럭에 치였다.

STEP 1
1 그 사슴은 차에 치였다.
2 그 새는 Maria에 의해 돌봐졌다.
3 폭력은 엄격하게 다뤄져야 한다.
4 숙제는 제때에 제출되지 않았다.
5 그 축구 경기는 나쁜 날씨로 인해 연기될까?

STEP 3
① 재판은 다른 날로 미뤄졌다.
② 그는 그의 아이들에게 존경을 받았다.
③ 그는 왕실에서 자라났다.
④ Joseph은 그의 형들에게 무시당했다.
⑤ 그 불만사항은 매니저에 의해 처리되었다.
④ 'look down on(~을 무시하다)'이 하나의 동사구이므로 수동태로 바꿀 때 함께 묶어서 써야 한다. (was looked down by → was looked down on by)

Point 066 by 이외의 전치사를 사용하는 수동태

본문 115쪽

STEP 1
1 with 2 in 3 at 4 for 5 of

STEP 2
1 was covered with
2 will be known to
3 is scared of
4 Are, satisfied with
5 am tired of

STEP 3 ④

STEP 1
1 그 방은 연기로 가득했다.
2 어떤 사람들은 스포츠에 관심이 없다.
3 Ann은 그 소식을 듣고 놀랐다.
4 California는 아름다운 경치로 유명하다.
5 그녀의 분홍색 드레스는 실크로 만들어진 것이다.

STEP 3
• 벨기에는 초콜릿으로 유명하다.
• 내 인생은 모험으로 가득하다.
be known for: ~로 유명하다 / be full of: ~로 가득 차다

01회 내신 적중 실전 문제

본문 116쪽

01 ④ 02 ⑤ 03 ② 04 ⑤ 05 ⑤ 06 ④
07 ①, ④ 08 ⑤ 09 ④ 10 ⑤ 11 ② 12 ③
13 (1) were told the good news by Jason
(2) was told to us by Jason
14 Was the letter delivered by Mr. Brown?
15 The door wasn't opened by me.
16 (1) can be recycled (2) will not be broken
(3) should be handed in

01
• 그 액션 영화는 많은 소녀들에 의해 시청되었다.
수동태는 「be동사+과거분사」의 형태이다. see(보다)의 과거분사는 seen이다.

02
그의 이름은 영원히 기억될 것이다.
미래시제 문장의 수동태는 「will be+과거분사」의 형태이다.

03

• 엄마는 머핀을 구웠다.

• 그 학교는 1988년에 지어졌다.

첫 번째 문장은 주어가 동작을 하는 주체이므로 능동태 문장이 와야 한다. 따라서 빈칸에는 동사의 과거형인 baked가 알맞다. 두 번째 문장은 주어가 동작을 받는 대상이므로 수동태 문장이 와야 한다. 따라서 빈칸에는 「be동사+과거분사」의 형태가 알맞다.

Words bake 굽다

04

① 그 편지는 Dave에 의해 쓰였다.
② 그 나무는 농부에 의해서 베어졌다.
③ 당신의 가방은 벨보이에 의해 운반될 것이다.
④ 그 건물들은 폭탄에 의해서 파괴되었다.
⑤ 그 그림은 어제 누군가에 의해 도난당했다.

행위자가 불분명할 때, 「by+행위자」를 생략할 수 있다.

05

과거시제 문장의 수동태는 「was/were+과거분사(+by+행위자)」로 쓴다.

Words ride 타다(-rode-ridden)

06

수동태의 의문문은 「be동사+주어+과거분사(+by+행위자)~?」로 쓴다.

Words grow 재배하다(-grew-grown)

07

A: 멕시코에서 무슨 일이 일어났니?
B: 강한 지진이 일어나서 많은 사람들이 죽었어[죽임을 당했어].

die는 자동사로 '죽다'의 의미이므로 수동태로 쓸 수 없고, kill은 타동사로 '죽이다'의 의미이므로 수동태로 표현해야 한다.

Words earthquake 지진

08

• 탁자는 먼지로 덮여 있었다.

• 나는 내 삶에 만족한다.

be covered with: ~로 덮여 있다 / be satisfied with: ~에 만족하다

Words dust 먼지

09

많은 학생들이 그 선생님을 존경했다.

동사구 look up to는 한 단어처럼 묶어서 수동태로 바꾼다. 따라서 동사구 looked up to는 was looked up to로 바꿔 써야 한다.

10

① 언니는 내게 점심을 요리해 주었다.
② 아빠는 내게 인형의 집을 만들어 주었다.
③ 나는 그에게 내 사진 앨범을 보여 주었다.
④ 그녀는 내게 신용카드를 건넸다.
⑤ 우리는 그에게 또 다른 기회를 주지 않았다.

② give의 직접목적어를 주어로 한 수동태 문장은 간접목적어(him) 앞에 전치사 to를 써야 한다.

11

① 초대장은 내게 보내졌다.
② 그의 아버지는 그에게 차를 사주셨다.
③ 그 시는 박 선생님에 의해 학생들에게 읽혀졌다.
④ 나는 크리스마스에 가족들로부터 선물을 받았다.
⑤ Mike는 어떤 일을 하기 전에 두 번 생각하라고 배웠다.

② buy의 간접목적어는 수동태의 주어가 될 수 없다. 따라서 The car was bought for him by his dad.로 써야 한다.

Words invitation 초대장

12

① 그 아기는 Amy라고 이름이 지어졌다.
② 그 채소들은 신선하게 보관된다.
③ 나는 컴퓨터를 사용하도록 허락받았다.
④ 그는 회원들에 의해 회장으로 선출되었다.
⑤ 그녀는 다른 나라로 도피하라고 경고를 받았다.

③ 5형식 문장에서 능동태의 목적격 보어로 쓰인 to부정사는 동사 뒤에 그대로 쓴다. (use → to use)

Words allow 허락하다 president 회장 warn 경고하다 escape 달아나다, 탈출하다

13

Jason은 우리에게 좋은 소식을 말해 주었다.

(1) 간접목적어를 주어로 하는 경우 직접목적어는 동사 뒤에 바로 온다. (2) tell의 직접목적어를 주어로 한 수동태 문장은 간접목적어 앞에 전치사 to를 쓴다.

14

Brown 씨가 그 편지를 배달했니?

능동태 문장의 목적어인 the letter가 수동태 문장의 주어가 된다. 수동태의 의문문은 「be동사+주어+과거분사(+by+행위자)~?」의 형태이다.

15

나는 그 문을 열지 않았다.

능동태 문장의 목적어인 the door가 수동태 문장의 주어가 된다. 수동태의 부정문은 「be동사+not+과거분사(+by+행위자)」의 형태이다. 시제가 과거이고 부정문이므로, wasn't opened를 쓴다.

16

조동사의 수동태는 「조동사+be+과거분사」의 형태로 쓴다. 조동사가 있는 수동태 문장의 부정문은 조동사 뒤에 not을 쓴다.

Words recycle 재활용하다 hand in (과제 등을) 제출하다

02회 내신 적중 실전 문제

본문 118쪽

01 ④	02 ③	03 ④	04 ②	05 ②	06 ③
07 ④	08 ⑤	09 ①, ④	10 ②	11 ⑤	12 ①

13 be kept warm by
14 I was persuaded to take part in the contest by my parents.
15 was not invited
16 must not be told

01

지구의 날은 '기념되는' 것이므로 수동태(be동사+과거분사)로 표현한다.

Words celebrate 기념하다

02

대부분의 인도 사람들은 소고기를 먹지 않는다.

수동태의 부정문은 「be동사+not+과거분사(+by+행위자)」의 형태로 쓴다. 주어가 3인칭 단수이고, 능동태 문장의 시제가 현재이므로 be동사는 is로 쓴다.

03

그가 너를 따라갔니?

능동태의 목적어 you가 수동태의 주어가 된다. 수동태의 의문문은 「be동사+주어+과거분사(+by+행위자)~?」의 형태로 쓴다.

Words follow 따라가다

04

그들은 내게 나만의 사업을 시작해 보라고 조언했다.

능동태의 목적어 me를 수동태의 주어 I로 쓰고, 동사는 「be동사+과거분사」의 형태로 바꾼다. 능동태의 목적격 보어인 to부정사는 동사 뒤에 그대로 쓴다.

Words business 사업

05

• 축구공은 그 아이들을 위해 구입되었다.
• 그 카메라는 나의 오빠가 내게 빌려준 것이다.

buy의 직접목적어를 주어로 하는 수동태 문장에서 기존의 간접목적어 앞에 전치사 for가 와야 한다. lend의 직접목적어를 주어로 하는 수동태 문장에서 기존의 간접목적어 앞에 전치사 to가 와야 한다.

Words lend 빌려 주다

06

이 프로젝트는 모레까지 완성될 수 있다/완성될지도 모른다/완성되어야 한다.

be done이 있으므로 빈칸에는 can, may, must, should와 같은 조동사를 써야 한다. has는 조동사가 아니다.

Words the day after tomorrow 모레

07

① 에펠탑은 1889년에 건축되었다.
② 그 방은 엄마에 의해 청소되었니?
③ Peter는 그의 개에게 집을 만들어 주었다.
④ 그 보물들은 선장에 의해 발견되었다.
⑤ 그 벤치는 학생들에 의해 노란색으로 칠해졌다.

① built → was built
② Did the room cleaned → Was the room cleaned
③ was made → made ⑤ painted → was painted

Words captain 선장

08

• 그 책상은 나무로 만들어진 것이다.
• 그 병은 쿠키로 채워져 있었다.
• Kevin은 똑같은 것을 먹는 것에 싫증이 났다.

(A) be made of: ~로 만들어지다 (B) be filled with: ~로 가득 차다 (C) be tired of: ~에 싫증이 나다

09

Fred는 Lilly에게 그 꽃을 주었다.

① give의 간접목적어를 주어로 하는 경우 직접목적어는 동사 뒤에 바로 온다. ④ give의 직접목적어를 주어로 한 수동태 문장은 간접목적어 앞에 전치사 to를 쓴다.

10

① 그는 죽은 채로 발견되었다.
② 그 일은 어제 일어났다.
③ 비는 곧 그칠 것으로 예상되었다.
④ 새 스니커즈 운동화가 그를 위해 구입되었다.
⑤ 그 돈은 그의 삼촌에 의해서 그에게 전해졌다.

② happen은 자동사이므로 수동태로 쓰이지 않는다.

11

① 그 여행은 미뤄져야 한다.
② 그녀는 약간의 휴식을 취하도록 권고 받았다.
③ 나는 벌금을 내라고 그 판사에게 명령받았다.
④ 그 소년은 그의 친구들에 의해 천재라고 불려진다.
⑤ 할머니는 엄마에 의해서 돌봐졌다.

⑤ 동사구 take care of는 수동태로 바꿀 때 한 단어처럼 묶어서 쓴다. 이때 전치사를 빠뜨리지 않아야 한다. (was taken care by → was taken care of by)

Words pay a fine 벌금을 내다 judge 판사 genius 천재

12

① Larry는 높은 곳을 무서워한다.
② 너는 마술에 관심이 있니?
③ 모든 사람은 희망으로 가득 차 있는 것처럼 보였다.
④ 두리안은 그것의 강한 냄새로 유명하다.
⑤ 그의 학급 친구들은 그의 성적에 놀랐다.

① be scared of는 '~을 두려워하다'라는 뜻이다. for를 of로 고쳐야 한다.

Words heights 높은 곳[위치] durian 두리안(열대 과일) grade 성적

13

능동태 문장은 The blanket will keep you warm.으로 미래시제의 5형식 문장이다. 미래시제의 수동태는 「will be+과거분사(+by+행위자)」의 형태로 쓴다. 능동태의 목적격 보어로 쓰인 warm은 동사 뒤에 그대로 쓴다.

Words blanket 담요

14

내 부모님들은 그 대회에 참가하라고 나를 설득했다.

능동태의 목적어 me를 수동태의 주어 I로 쓰고, 동사는 수동태로 was persuaded로 바꾼다. 능동태의 목적격 보어인 to부정사는 수동태의 동사 뒤에 그대로 쓴다. 능동태의 주어인 my parents는 수동태의 문장 맨 뒤에 by my parents로 써준다.

Words persuade 설득하다 take part in ~에 참가하다 contest 대회, 시합

15

A: 너는 그 파티 초대장을 받았니?
B: 아니, 나는 초대받지 못했어.

빈칸 앞에 No로 보아 '초대받지 못하였다'라는 말이 빈칸에 알맞다. 수동태의 부정문은 「be동사+not+과거분사」로 쓴다. be동사는 주어가 I이고 시제가 과거이므로 was를 쓴다.

16

A: 이 이야기는 다른 사람에게 알려져서는 안 돼.
B: 알겠어. 나만 알고 있을게.

대화의 흐름상 '이야기가 되어서는 안 된다'라는 말이 알맞다. 조동사가 있는 수동태의 부정문은 「조동사+not+be+과거분사」로 쓴다.

Words keep~to oneself ~을 비밀로 간직하다

Lesson 08 | 대명사

Point 067 부정대명사 one

본문 122쪽

STEP 1
1 one 2 it 3 one 4 It 5 ones

STEP 2
1 one 2 it 3 one 4 ones 5 it

STEP 3 ②

- A: 이 근처에 은행이 있나요?
  B: 네, 모퉁이 근처에 하나 있습니다.
- 저는 이 바지가 마음에 들어요. 더 큰 것도 있나요?
- 우리 아버지는 오래된 차를 팔고 새 것을 구입하셨다.

TIP 나는 네 새 셔츠가 마음에 들어. 어디에서 그것을 샀니?

STEP 1
1 나는 자가 필요해. 하나 가지고 있니?
2 이 차는 너무 뜨겁다. 나는 그것을 마실 수 없다.
3 버스가 만원이다. 다음 것을 기다리자.
4 나는 영화를 한 편 보았다. 그것은 지루했다.
5 나의 신발은 너무 작아서 나의 어머니는 새 신발을 사주셨다.

STEP 2
1 이 수건이 더러워요. 저에게 깨끗한 것을 주세요.
2 나는 내 열쇠를 찾을 수가 없다. 너는 그것을 봤니?
3 이 컴퓨터가 작동을 하지 않아요. 저것을 사용해도 될까요?
4 나는 그녀의 귀걸이가 마음에 든다. 나는 같은 것을 가지기를 원한다.
5 내가 펜 하나를 빌릴 수 있을까요? 내가 그것을 내일까지 돌려줄게요.

STEP 3
A: 샌드위치를 드시겠습니까?
B: 아니오, 괜찮습니다. 이미 하나 먹었어요.
앞서 나온 명사와 같은 종류의 사물을 나타내는 대명사는 one이다. 이때 one은 앞서 언급한 sandwich를 의미한다.

Point 068 부정대명사 another

본문 123쪽

STEP 1
1 another
2 another
3 another
4 others
5 another

STEP 2
1 have another glass of juice
2 we watched another movie
3 another way to solve this math problem
4 Show me another
5 moved to another company

STEP 3 ⑤

- 이 우산은 고장이 났어요. 또 다른 것을 주세요.
- 커피를 한 잔 더 드시겠습니까?

STEP 1
1 말하는 것과 행동하는 것은 다른 것이다.
2 만일 네가 이 계획이 마음에 들지 않는다면 나는 또 다른 것이 있다.
3 이 펜을 또 다른 것으로 교환해주실 수 있나요?
4 뒤에서 남들을 흉보지 마라.
5 음악이 끝났지만 음악가는 또 다른 음악을 연주하기 시작했다.

STEP 3
① 왼쪽에 또 다른 문이 있다.
② 나의 아버지께서는 또 다른 나라에 살기를 원하신다.
③ 나는 종이를 다 써버렸다. 또 다른 종이를 줘.
④ 그 전시회 이후에, 그 예술가는 또 다른 전시회를 개최할 예정이다.
⑤ 너는 가방 속에 잡지가 많구나. 내가 하나 읽어도 되니?
⑤는 앞에 나온 명사와 같은 종류의 사람이나 사물을 의미하는 one이 들어가야 한다. 이때 one은 a magazine을 의미한다.

Point 069 부정대명사 all, both

본문 124쪽

STEP 1
1 1 All 2 were 3 are 4 Both 5 All

STEP 2
1 All agreed on the new plan.
2 I watched both of the movies.

3 He read all the books in his room.
4 Both of us know your secret.
5 All the water in the well was polluted.

STEP 3 ②

• 모든 사람들이 그 소식에 흥분했다.
• 사람들 모두가 행복해 보인다.
• 둘 다 내 것이다.
• 그녀의 아들 둘 다 의사이다.

STEP 1
1 걱정 마. 모든 것이 괜찮을 거야.
2 모든 유명한 영화배우들이 그 시상식에 있었다.
3 두 자리 모두 비어있다.
4 나에게는 언니가 둘이 있다. 둘 다 승무원이다.
5 그 건물의 모든 사람들이 구출되었다.

STEP 3
① 나는 부모님 두 분 다 사랑한다.
② 내 돈이 모두 도난당했다.
③ 모든 무용수들이 무대 위로 올라갔다.
④ 이 책 두 권 다 베스트셀러이다.
⑤ 나의 반의 모든 학생들은 미술 수업을 좋아한다.

「all+(of)+명사」로 쓰인 경우 뒤에 나오는 명사의 수에 동사를 일치시킨다. money는 셀 수 없는 단수 명사이므로 동사 were가 아닌 was를 써야 한다.

Point 070 부정대명사 each, every

본문 125쪽

STEP 1
1 Every 2 has 3 members 4 Each 5 has

STEP 2
1 Every rule has an exception.
2 Each person has his own job.
3 The train leaves every ten minutes.
4 Each of the possible answers is shown below the questions.

STEP 3 ①

• 장난감들이 각각 모양이 다르다.
• 가족 구성원 각자가 일정이 다르다.
• 모든 국가는 고유의 전통 문화를 가지고 있다.

TIP 월드컵은 4년마다 개최된다.

STEP 1
1 모든 개는 자기 날을 갖는다.(쥐구멍에도 볕들 날 있다.)
2 각각의 학생은 자신의 컴퓨터가 있다.
3 그 그룹 멤버들 각자는 음악적 재능이 뛰어나다.
4 너희들 각자는 최선을 다해야 한다.
5 각각의 꽃들은 고유의 향기를 가지고 있다.

STEP 3
① 모든 버스는 승객들로 가득 차 있었다.
② 그들 각자는 성적이 향상되었다.
③ 각각의 언어는 고유의 문법을 가지고 있다.
④ 아이들 각자는 모자를 쓰고 있다.
⑤ 그녀의 가족은 5년마다 해외여행을 간다.

「every+단수 명사」는 단수 취급하므로 단수 동사를 써야 한다. (were → was)

Point 071 부정대명사 some, any

본문 126쪽

STEP 1
1 some 2 any 3 some 4 any 5 Some

STEP 2
1 Any time after 2 o'clock is fine.
2 I prepared some pasta.
3 Do you need any information about the contest?
4 Why don't you do some exercise?
5 I don't have any plans for the vacation.

STEP 3 ⑤

• 몇몇은 사무실에서 아직도 일을 하고 있다.
• 병 속에 약간의 물이 있다.
• 그것은 당신과 전혀 상관이 없다.
• 질문이 있으시다면, 물어보세요.

STEP 1
1 방 안에 몇 명의 사람들이 있다.
2 나는 네 도움이 전혀 필요하지 않다.
3 케이크를 좀 더 드실래요?
4 부산행 기차가 있나요?
5 음식이 약간 남아 있다.

STEP 3
① 간식을 좀 먹을래?

② 나는 점심으로 김밥을 조금 먹었다.
③ 나는 너와 이야기 나눌 시간이 좀 있다.
④ 내 휴대전화에는 약간의 음악 파일이 있다.
⑤ 나는 그 카메라를 살 돈이 조금도 없다.

나머지는 '약간,' '조금'의 뜻을 가진 some이 들어가야 하는 반면 ⑤에는 any가 들어가 「not ~ any …」의 형태로 '조금의 …도 ~아닌'의 뜻을 가진다.

Point 072 one ~ the other… / some ~ others…

본문 127쪽

STEP 1
1 others 2 the others 3 the other
4 One 5 another

STEP 2
1 Some, others 2 One, the other
3 Some, the others

STEP 3 ④

- 그녀의 두 아들 중 한 명은 변호사이고, 다른 한 명은 의사이다.
- 어떤 사람들은 축구를 했고, 다른 사람들은 구경했다.

STEP 1
1 전쟁에서 어떤 사람들은 죽고, 다른 사람들은 부상을 입었다.
2 내 동아리 구성원들 중에, 어떤 아이들은 캠프에 참여하고, 나머지 아이들은 참여하지 않는다.
3 나에게는 두 명의 이모가 있다. 한 분은 캐나다에 살고, 다른 한 분은 뉴질랜드에 산다.
4 나는 방과 후 수업을 두 개 듣는다. 하나는 춤이고, 다른 하나는 배드민턴이다.
5 그녀는 악기를 세 개 연주할 수 있다. 하나는 피아노이고, 다른 하나는 첼로이고, 나머지는 기타이다.

STEP 3
나는 펜 네 자루를 샀다. 하나는 빨간색이고, 다른 하나는 파란색이고, 나머지는 검은색이다.

셋 이상일 경우 하나는 one, 다른 하나는 another, 나머지는 the other(s)로 지칭한다.

Point 073 each other / one another

본문 128쪽

STEP 1
1 one another 2 each other 3 each other
4 one another 5 each other

STEP 2
1 differ from each other
2 communicate with one another
3 fight with one another
4 met one another
5 looked at each other

STEP 3 ③

- 두 팀이 서로 마주보고 있다.
- 우리는 서로에게 공손해야 한다.

STEP 1
1 나의 반 친구들 모두는 서로에게 우호적이다.
2 우리 둘 다 서로를 도울 필요가 있다.
3 두 대의 차가 서로 충돌했다.
4 사람들은 서로 연락을 하기 위해 이메일을 이용한다.
5 그 커플은 서로 어떻게 만났니?

STEP 3
- 두 사람이 걸어가다 서로 부딪혔다.
- 아이들 각자는 자신의 선물에 만족했다.

each other는 '서로'의 뜻이고, each는 「each of+복수명사」의 형태로 쓰여 단수 동사를 취하므로 빈칸에 공통으로 알맞은 말은 each이다.

Point 074 재귀대명사의 재귀 용법

본문 129쪽

STEP 1
1 yourself[yourselves] 2 ourselves 3 myself
4 me 5 herself

STEP 2
1 blame yourself 2 He cut himself
3 introduced herself 4 killed himself
5 talk to himself

STEP 3 ⑤

- 미나는 샌드위치를 만들어 먹었다.
- Jason은 너무 어려서 스스로를 돌볼 수 없다.

STEP 1
1 너[너희] 스스로를 잘 돌보아라.

2 우리는 잠시 동안 제정신이 아니었다.
3 나는 너에게 화가 난 것이 아니다. 나 자신에게 화가 난다.
4 면접관은 나에게 장래 계획에 대해 물어봤다.
5 유나는 이기적이다. 그녀는 항상 남보다 자신이 우선이다.

STEP 3
① 그 예술가들은 스스로를 낭만파라고 불렀다.
② 하늘은 스스로 돕는 자를 돕는다.
③ 구름이 하늘에 온통 퍼졌다.
④ 그 당원들은 자기들끼리 말다툼을 했다.
⑤ 그들은 길을 잃었지만, 그들을 도와 줄 사람이 아무도 없었다.
나머지는 재귀대명사 themselves가 들어가는 반면 ⑤는 목적격 대명사인 them이 들어가야 한다.

Point 075 재귀대명사의 강조 용법

본문 130쪽

STEP 1
1 myself, 내가 직접 그 건물을 디자인하고 지었다.
2 himself, 나는 대통령과 직접 악수를 했다.
3 himself, 나는 그가 직접 그 문제를 처리할 수 있다고 생각한다.
4 ourselves, 우리가 직접 교실을 청소하자.
5 herself, 나의 어머니는 직접 목도리를 짜셨다.

STEP 2
1 new here myself
2 me the secret recipe itself
3 finish the project yourself
4 speak to the store manager himself
5 I didn't like the musical itself

STEP 3 ①

• 선생님이 직접 나에게 말씀하셨다.
• 나는 바로 그 보고서를 썼다.
• 더러운 거지가 바로 왕 자신이었다.

STEP 3
① 그는 자신이 천재라고 생각한다.
② 네가 그 시를 직접 썼니?
③ 한 버스 운전사가 바로 그 사고를 일으켰다.
④ 우리가 직접 그 문제를 처리할 것이다.
⑤ 특별 손님은 바로 그 유명 배우였다.
나머지는 생략해도 문장의 성립에 지장을 주지 않는 재귀대명사의 강조 용법인 반면, ①은 재귀대명사가 동사의 목적어로 쓰인 재귀 용법이다.

Point 076 재귀대명사의 관용적 용법

본문 131쪽

STEP 1
1 by 2 yourself 3 ourselves 4 for 5 herself

STEP 2
1 for[by] herself 2 by himself 3 beside herself
4 Between ourselves 5 in itself

STEP 3 ①

STEP 1
1 민호는 혼자서 점심을 먹고 있다.
2 제가 케이크를 좀 만들었어요. 마음껏 드세요.
3 우리는 파티에서 즐거운 시간을 보냈다.
4 나는 스스로 숙제를 끝냈다.
5 수진이는 공손하다. 그녀는 항상 바르게 행동한다.

STEP 3
• 코트를 벗고 편안히 계세요.
• 원하시는 것을 마음껏 드세요.
make oneself at home은 '편안히 있다'의 뜻이고 help oneself는 '(~을) 마음대로 먹다'의 뜻이다. .

01회 내신 적중 실전 문제

본문 132쪽

01 ① 02 ④ 03 ② 04 ② 05 ① 06 ④
07 ② 08 ④ 09 ④ 10 ⑤ 11 ⑤ 12 ②
13 All of us have a duty to protect the environment.
14 enjoyed ourselves
15 Both daughters are teachers.
16 One is a vet, and the other is a banker.

01
• 나는 휴대전화를 잃어버렸다. 하나 사야 한다.
• 나에게는 두 명의 자매가 있다. 한 명은 키가 크고, 다른 한 명은 키가 작다.
첫 번째 빈칸에는 앞에 언급된 것과 같은 종류의 것을 나타내므로 one이 알맞다. 두 번째 빈칸에는 두 사람[사물]을 차례로 가리킬 때 쓰는 표현인 「one ~ the other …(하나는 ~, 다른 하나는 …)」의 one이 쓰여야 한다. 따라서 one이 빈칸에 공통으로 들어가야 한다.

02

보기 우리가 이 문제를 직접 해결하자.

① 나는 수영하는 법을 스스로 배웠다.
② 너는 스스로를 믿어야 한다.
③ 그는 "나는 할 수 있어."라고 혼잣말을 했다.
④ 나는 직접 크리스마스 트리를 장식했다.
⑤ 너는 영어로 자기소개를 할 수 있니?

보기 와 같이 생략 가능한 강조 용법으로 쓰인 것은 ④이다.

03

① 나는 돈이 하나도 없다.
② 우리 좀 쉬는 게 어떠니?
③ 만약 어떤 문제가 있다면, 내가 너에게 알려줄게.
④ 오늘 밤 쇼의 표가 남은 것이 있나요?
⑤ 소라는 구경만 하고, 어떤 옷도 사지 않았다.

나머지는 부정문, 의문문, 조건문에 쓰여 '어떤,' '약간'의 뜻을 가지는 any가 들어가며, ②에는 권유나 요청의 의미를 나타내는 의문문에 쓰이는 some이 들어간다.

Words look around 구경하다

04

'각각의'라는 뜻은 each를 사용해서 표현하며 뒤에 단수 명사와 단수 동사가 이어진다.

Words flag 기, 깃발

05

'모두'의 뜻으로 복수 명사 앞에 쓰여 복수 취급을 하는 것은 all이다.

06

'옷을 입다'는 뜻이 되려면 dress oneself가 되어야 하므로 her가 아닌 herself가 옳다.

07

검은색 운동화는 내 것이 아니다. 하얀 것이 내 것이다.

앞에 언급된 것과 같은 종류의 것을 나타내므로 one이 쓰여야 하는데 앞에 언급된 것이 복수 명사이므로 ones가 알맞다.

08

어떤 학생들은 영어를 좋아하고, 다른 학생들은 수학을 좋아한다.

'어떤 것[사람]들은 ~, 다른 어떤 것[사람]들은 …'의 뜻을 가진 표현은 「some ~ others …」 이다.

09

A: 빨간 것과 파란 것 중 어떤 펜을 사시겠습니까?
B: 둘 다 사겠습니다.

빨간색 펜과 파란색 펜 둘 중 어느 것을 살 건지를 묻고 있는 질문이므로, '둘 다'를 의미하는 both로 대답하는 것이 알맞다.

10

A: 이 파란색 스웨터가 저와 잘 어울리는 것 같지 않아요.
B: 걱정 마세요. 이 스웨터는 다른 색으로도 있어요.

'또 다른 하나(의)' 뜻으로 같은 종류의 또 다른 것을 가리키는 말은 another이다.

Words go well with ~와 잘 어울리다

11

① 두 소녀 모두 나의 여자 조카들이다.
② 모든 순간이 소중하다.
③ 모든 팬들은 그 가수를 보고서 행복했다.
④ 각 학생은 교복을 입고 있다.
⑤ 내 형제들 각자는 자신의 방이 있다.

each는 「each of+복수 명사」의 형태로 뒤에 복수 명사가 오더라도 단수 취급한다. 따라서 have를 has로 고쳐야 한다.

Words niece 여자 조카 precious 귀중한, 소중한

12

Mike는 혼자 자신의 공부 계획을 세운다.

on one's own은 문맥에 따라 혼자서(by oneself)와 스스로(for oneself)의 뜻을 둘 다 갖는다. 해당 문장은 두 가지 해석 다 가능하다.

Words on one's own 혼자서, 혼자 힘으로

13

우리들 모두는 환경을 보호할 의무가 있다.

「all (of)+명사」는 '모든 ~,' '~ 모두'의 뜻으로 명사의 수에 동사를 일치시킨다. 주어가 all of us로 복수이므로 동사는 has가 아닌 have가 맞다.

Words duty 의무 protect 보호하다 environment 환경

14

enjoy oneself는 '좋은[즐거운] 시간을 보내다'라는 뜻을 가진 재귀대명사의 관용적 표현이다.

15

A: 그들의 딸들은 직업이 무엇인가?

B: 두 딸 모두 선생님이다.

both는 '둘 다(의)'의 뜻으로 대명사와 형용사로 모두 쓰인다.

16

A: 그들의 아들들은 직업이 무엇인가?

B: 한 명은 수의사이고, 다른 한 명은 은행원이다.

두 사물[사람]을 차례로 가리키는 표현은 「one ~ the other …(하나는 ~, 다른 하나는 …)」이다.

02회 내신 적중 실전 문제

본문 134쪽

01 ①	02 ②	03 ①	04 ④	05 ④	06 ②
07 ③	08 ⑤	09 ④	10 ④	11 ⑤	12 ③

13 Every audience is enjoying the concert.
14 Both of my parents are dentists.
15 Modern people communicate with one another by e-mail.
16 Some students like listening to music, and the others like reading books.

01

• 모든 학생들이 안경을 쓰고 있다.
• 모든 돈은 금고에 있다.

'all(모든)' 뒤에 복수 명사가 오면 복수 취급하고, 단수 명사가 오면 단수 취급한다.

Words safe 금고

02

both는 '둘 다(의)'의 뜻으로 뒤에 복수 명사와 복수 동사가 이어진다.

03

① 내가 직접 그 그림을 그렸다.
② 그녀는 난로에 데었다.
③ 소크라테스는 "너 자신을 알라."라고 말했다.
④ 그 배우는 어제 자살했다.
⑤ 너는 스스로를 돌볼 만큼 충분히 나이 들었다.

나머지는 재귀대명사가 동사나 전치사의 목적어로 쓰인 재귀 용법인 반면 ①은 생략 가능한 강조 용법이다.

Words stove 난로 look after 돌보다

04

① 모든 개인은 유일무이하다.
② 끝이 좋으면 다 좋다.
③ 각 소녀가 배낭을 메고 있다.
④ 모든 사람은 법 앞에서 평등하다.
⑤ 우리들 각자는 그 일의 한 부분을 담당하고 있다.

나머지는 주어가 단수인 경우로 be동사 is가 알맞은 반면 ④는 주어가 「all+복수 명사」로 복수이므로 be동사 are가 알맞다.

Words unique 유일무이한, 독특한 equal 동등한
in charge of ~을 담당하는

05

A: 케이크 좀 더 드세요.

B: 아니오, 괜찮습니다. 저는 배가 불러요.

help oneself는 '마음대로 먹다'는 뜻을 가진 재귀대명사의 관용적 표현이다.

06

나는 어제 연필을 샀는데 그것을 잃어버렸다. 하나 사야한다.

첫 번째 빈칸에는 앞서 언급된 동일한 사물을 가리키는 it이 알맞고, 두 번째 빈칸에는 앞서 언급된 것과 같은 종류의 사물을 가리키는 one이 알맞다.

07

한국은 대통령을 5년마다 선출한다.

「every+숫자+기간」은 '~마다'의 뜻이다.

08

나는 아이스크림을 먹을 거야. 너도 좀 먹을래?

권유나 요청의 의미를 나타내는 의문문에 쓰여 '약간'의 뜻을 가지는 대명사는 some이다.

09

• 이 티셔츠는 나에게 좀 끼네요. 다른 것을 보여 줄 수 있나요?
• 가족의 모든 구성원들은 서로가 너무 다르다.

앞서 언급한 것과 같은 종류의 또 다른 것을 가리키는 대명사는 another이고, '서로'의 뜻을 가진 대명사는 one another이다. 따라서 공통으로 알맞은 말은 another이다.

10

① 냉장고에 과일이 약간 있다.
② 내 양 손 모두 추위에 얼었다.
③ 나는 빨간 장미를 사지 않았다. 노란 것을 샀다.
④ 내 두 삼촌들 중 한 명은 직업이 있고, 다른 한 명은 없다.
⑤ 나는 숟가락을 떨어뜨렸어요. 또 다른 것을 갖다 줄 수 있나요?

두 사물이나 사람을 차례로 가리키는 표현은 「one ~ the other …(하나는 ~, 다른 하나는 …)」이다.

Words frozen (꽁꽁) 언 drop 떨어뜨리다

11

① 그녀는 아름다움 그 자체이다.
② 기자는 나를 직접 인터뷰했다.
③ 우리가 직접 사과나무를 심었다.
④ 너는 직접 그 여배우를 본 적이 있니?
⑤ 나의 부모님께서는 아파트를 장만하셨다.

⑤의 재귀대명사는 buy의 간접목적어로 쓰였으므로 생략할 수 없다.

Words plant 심다 portrait 초상화

12

케이크 한 조각 더 먹을 수 있을까요?

앞서 언급한 것과 같은 종류의 또 다른 것을 가리키는 대명사는 another이다.

13

모든 관객들이 콘서트를 즐기고 있다.

똑같이 '모든'의 뜻이지만 all은 뒤에 복수 명사가 와서 복수 취급을 하는 반면 every는 뒤에 단수 명사가 오고 단수 취급한다.

14

우리 아버지는 치과 의사이다. 우리 엄마도 치과 의사이다.
→ 우리 부모님은 두 분 다 치과 의사이다.

both는 '둘 다(의),' '양쪽(의)'의 뜻으로 항상 복수 취급한다.

15

one another는 '서로'의 뜻으로 셋 이상의 사람 사이에 쓴다.

16

나의 반에는 30명의 학생들이 있다.

정해진 수의 사람이나 사물을 대조할 때는 「some ~ the others …」를 쓴다.

Lesson 09 | 비교 구문

Point 077 as ~ as 구문

본문 138쪽

STEP 1
1 as 2 so 3 much 4 yours 5 possible

STEP 2
1 as thoughtful as 2 as fast as
3 not as[so] heavy as 4 as clearly as

STEP 3 ④

• Kelly는 나만큼 한국말을 잘 한다.
• Jane은 그만큼 어리지 않다.

TIP 가능한 빨리 제게 전화주세요.

STEP 1

1 이 여행 가방은 저것만큼 가볍다.
2 오늘 서울은 대구만큼 덥지 않다.
3 Ben은 Ted만큼 많이 먹는다.
4 내 방은 네 방만큼 크다.
5 그것을 가능한 빨리 해주세요.

STEP 3

'~만큼 …한[하게]'의 뜻을 가진 원급[동등] 비교는 「as+형용사/부사의 원급+as ~」의 형태를 취한다.

Point 078 비교급, 최상급 만드는 법 (규칙 변화)

본문 139쪽

STEP 1
1 hotter, hottest 2 cheaper, cheapest
3 nicer, nicest 4 prettier, prettiest
5 more amazing, most amazing
6 more difficult, most difficult

STEP 2
1 fastest 2 more popular
3 thinnest 4 dirtier

STEP 3 ③

STEP 3

① 민호는 나보다 더 똑똑하다.

② 내 고양이는 내 강아지보다 더 뚱뚱하다.
③ 코끼리는 하마보다 더 무겁다.
④ 내 남동생은 나보다 더 열심히 공부한다.
⑤ 그 파이는 내가 기대했던 것보다 더 맛있었다.

「자음+-y」로 끝나는 단어는 비교급, 최상급을 만들 때 y를 i로 고치고 -er/-est를 붙인다. (heavyer → heavier)

Point 079 비교급, 최상급 만드는 법 (불규칙 변화)

본문 140쪽

STEP 1
1 best 2 worse 3 oldest 4 more 5 less

STEP 2
1 better 2 farther 3 less 4 worst

STEP 3 ②

STEP 1
1 나의 강아지는 나의 가장 좋은 친구이다.
2 그 방의 상태는 내가 들은 것보다 더 나빴다.
3 침대는 내가 가진 가장 오래된 가구이다.
4 아버지는 어머니보다 돈을 더 많이 버신다.
5 만약 네가 몸무게를 줄이길 원하면 이전보다 더 적은 밀가루를 먹도록 하라.

STEP 3
나는 내가 예상했던 것보다 더 늦게 숙제를 끝냈다.

late의 비교급은 두 개다. '시간이 늦은'의 뜻일 때는 later이고, '순서가 늦은'의 뜻일 때는 latter이다. 해석상 전자에 해당되므로 later가 알맞다.

Point 080 비교급+than

본문 141쪽

STEP 1
1 than 2 much 3 very 4 as 5 happier

STEP 2
1 He was a lot taller than I expected.
2 My brother went to bed later than I did.
3 Taking the subway is faster than driving.
4 Gold is still more valuable than silver.
5 Credit cards are more convenient than cash.

STEP 3 ③

• 내 여동생은 나보다 더 조심스럽다.
= 나는 내 여동생만큼 조심스럽지 않다.
• 나의 아버지는 어머니보다 훨씬 더 나이가 많다.

STEP 1
1 네 가방은 내 것보다 더 무겁다.
2 Jake는 평소보다 훨씬 더 일찍 학교에 왔다.
3 유나는 춤을 아주 잘 춘다.
4 세진은 진호만큼 활동적이지 않다.
5 나는 전보다 지금이 훨씬 더 행복하다.

STEP 3
어제도 추웠지만 오늘은 훨씬 더 춥다.

비교급 앞에 쓰여서 '훨씬'이라는 의미로 비교급을 강조하는 것에는 much, still, even, far, a lot 등이 있다. very는 비교급을 강조하는 데 쓸 수 없다.

Point 081 비교 구문을 이용한 표현 I

본문 142쪽

STEP 1
1 old 2 heavier 3 as 4 as 5 five times

STEP 2
1 He walked twice as fast as usual.
2 This exam was ten times more difficult than the previous one.
3 We finished the work twice as quickly as we expected.
4 Sumin's score is three times higher than Jisu's.

STEP 3 ④

• 나는 내 상사보다 세 배 더 열심히 일한다.

STEP 1
1 우리 엄마는 나보다 나이가 두 배 더 많으시다.
2 이 아령은 저 아령보다 네 배 더 무겁다.
3 수미의 스마트폰은 내 것보다 세 배 더 비싸다.
4 보름달은 반달보다 두 배 더 밝다.
5 이 건물은 저 건물보다 다섯 배 더 높다.

STEP 3

'~의 몇 배로 …한[하게]'는 「배수사+as+원급+as」와 「배수사+비교급+than」이 있는데, twice는 원급을 이용한 표현만 가능하다.

Point 082 비교 구문을 이용한 표현 Ⅱ

본문 143쪽

STEP 1
1 네가 책을 많이 읽을수록, 너는 더 현명해질 것이다.
2 더 열심히 노력할수록, 너는 더 성공할 것이다.
3 우리가 더 높이 올라갈수록, 공기가 더 희박해졌다.
4 네가 더 일찍 주문할수록, 네 음식은 더 빨리 도착할 것이다.
5 날씨가 추워질수록, 더 많은 사람들이 감기에 걸린다.

STEP 2
1 the healthier you will be
2 The more money you make
3 the more scared the children felt
4 the deeper he got into the mud
5 The longer I listened to the music

STEP 3 ④

• 그녀는 나이가 들수록 더 아름다워졌다.

TIP 네가 많이 먹을수록, 너는 더 체중이 늘 것이다.

STEP 3
그녀를 더 많이 알게 될수록, 너는 더 많이 그녀를 좋아할 것이다.
「the+비교급, the+비교급」은 '~하면 할수록 더 …한[하게]'의 뜻을 가진 표현이다.

Point 083 비교 구문을 이용한 표현 Ⅲ

본문 144쪽

STEP 1
1 모든 것이 점점 더 나아질 것이다.
2 점점 더 많은 아이들이 스마트폰을 이용하고 있다.
3 강은 점점 더 빠르게 흘렀다.
4 나무들이 점점 더 초록빛이 되어가고 있다.
5 그 새들은 점점 더 낮게 날았다.

STEP 2
1 The sky is getting darker and darker.
2 Suji is getting slimmer and slimmer.
3 Her health condition became worse and worse.
4 The price got higher and higher.
5 The workers were growing thirstier and thirstier.

STEP 3 ⑤

• 점점 더 많은 사람들이 혼자 살고 있다.

STEP 3
'점점 더 ~한[하게]'의 뜻을 가진 표현은 「비교급+and+비교급」이다.

Point 084 the+최상급

본문 145쪽

STEP 1
1 the 2 cheapest 3 worst 4 best 5 of

STEP 2
1 the most crowded city
2 the hottest month
3 the fastest
4 the happiest birthday
5 the highest mountain

STEP 3 ④

• 나는 우리 가족 중에서 가장 키가 작다.

TIP • 그 배우는 한국에서 가장 인기가 있다.
• 민수는 내 친구들 중에서 가장 재미있다.

STEP 1
1 재민이는 우리 반에서 키가 가장 큰 학생이다.
2 이것이 이 식당에서 가장 싼 음식이다.
3 나는 내 생애 최악의 실수를 했다.
4 그것은 그 영화에서 최고의 장면이었다.
5 유진은 학생들 중에서 가장 똑똑하다.

STEP 3
① 그것은 그 책에서 가장 웃긴 이야기였다.
② 우리 가족은 나에게 가장 소중하다.
③ 그녀는 자신의 마을에서 가장 유명한 스타이다.
④ 벤치는 소파만큼 편안하지 않다.
⑤ 기린은 동물들 중 목이 가장 길다.
나머지는 최상급으로 빈칸에 the가 들어가야 하지만, ④는 「not+as[so]+원급+as」 표현으로 빈칸에 as나 so가 들어가야 한다.

Point 085 최상급을 이용한 표현

본문 146쪽

STEP 1
1 best 2 most 3 greatest
4 students 5 heard

STEP 2
1 the most beautiful country that I have ever visited
2 one of the coldest countries in the world
3 one of the worst experiences I've ever had
4 one of the most famous movie directors in Korea

STEP 3 ⑤

• 세종대왕은 한국 역사상 가장 위대한 왕들 중 한 명이었다.
• 그것은 지금까지 내가 본 최악의 영화였다.

STEP 1
1 이곳은 도시에서 가장 훌륭한 식당들 중 하나이다.
2 그 반지는 내가 지금까지 산 것들 중 가장 비싼 물건이다.
3 베토벤은 세상에서 가장 위대한 음악가들 중 한 명이다.
4 유빈은 그의 학급에서 가장 똑똑한 학생들 중 한 명이다.
5 그의 농담은 내가 지금까지 들어 본 가장 웃긴 농담이었다.

STEP 3
이 스카프는 내가 가진 가장 좋은 물건들 중 하나이다.
「one of the+최상급」 뒤에는 복수 명사가 이어져야 한다.

Point 086 원급, 비교급을 이용한 최상급 표현

본문 147쪽

STEP 1
1 No 2 than 3 other 4 books 5 flower

STEP 2
1 No other sport is as exciting as baseball.
2 This is more expensive than any other bag in the shop.
3 No other mountain is higher than Mt. Everest.
4 She is more attractive than all the other actresses in Korea.

STEP 3 ③

STEP 1
1 우리 학교의 어떤 소년도 세훈이만큼 힘이 세지 않다.
2 한국의 어떤 코미디언도 그보다 더 웃기지 않다.
3 과학은 다른 어떤 과목보다 더 어렵다.
4 이것은 다른 모든 책들보다 더 재미있다.
5 장미는 다른 어떤 꽃보다 더 아름답다.

STEP 3
① 어떤 디저트도 치즈 케이크만큼 맛있지 않다.
② 치즈 케이크는 가장 맛있는 디저트이다.
③ 어떤 디저트도 치즈 케이크보다 덜 맛있지 않다.
④ 치즈 케이크는 다른 어떤 디저트보다 더 맛이 있다.
⑤ 치즈 케이크는 다른 모든 디저트들보다 더 맛이 있다.
나머지는 디저트 중 치즈 케이크가 가장 맛있다는 의미인 반면 ③은 치즈 케이크가 디저트 중 가장 맛이 없다는 뜻이다.

01회 내신 적중 실전 문제

본문 148쪽

01 ②	02 ③	03 ②	04 ④	05 ①	06 ⑤
07 ②	08 ②	09 ①	10 ④	11 ③	12 ②

13 Jisu's bag is twice as expensive as mine.
14 Bears are one of the most dangerous animals in the world.
15 Yubin is taller than Minho.
16 Namsu is the heaviest of[among] them.

01
① Judy는 Kate보다 나이가 더 많다.
② 그녀의 머리카락은 나만큼 길다.
③ 강이 점점 더 말라가고 있다.
④ 더 많이 먹을수록, 너는 더 뚱뚱해질 것이다.
⑤ 그 경기는 내가 지금까지 본 가장 흥미진진한 경기였다.
비교 대상이 그녀의 머리카락과 나의 머리카락이므로 me가 아닌 my hair나 mine이 되어야 한다.
Words dry 마른 fat 뚱뚱한, 살찐

02
보기 한국의 어떤 가수도 그만큼 인기가 있지 않다.
① 그는 한국에서 가장 인기 있는 가수이다.
② 한국의 어떤 가수도 그보다 더 인기가 있지 않다.
③ 그는 한국의 다른 가수들만큼 인기가 있지 않다.
④ 그는 한국의 다른 어떤 가수보다 인기가 있다.
⑤ 그는 한국의 모든 다른 가수들보다 더 인기가 있다.

③을 제외한 나머지는 '그가 한국에서 가장 인기 있는 가수이다.'라는 최상급의 의미를 가진다. ③은 그가 다른 가수들에 비해 인기가 없다는 뜻이다.

03

'~하면 할수록 더 …한[하게]'는 「the+비교급, the+비교급」으로 표현한다.

Words stressed 스트레스를 받는[느끼는]

04

길에 어제보다 훨씬 더 많은 사람들이 있다.

비교급 앞에 쓰여 '훨씬'의 뜻으로 비교급을 강조하는 말에는 much, still, even, far, a lot 등이 있다. very는 원급의 형용사와 부사를 강조한다.

05

① 진호는 나보다 더 창의적이다.
② Kate는 이전보다 더 예뻐 보인다.
③ Susan은 그녀의 여동생보다 더 날씬하다.
④ 그 은행은 여기에서 우체국보다 더 가깝다.
⑤ 인터넷은 우리가 생각하는 것보다 더 위험할 수 있다.

creative와 같이 -ive로 끝나는 2음절 단어는 앞에 more나 most를 붙여서 비교급, 최상급을 만든다. (creativer → more creative)

Words creative 창의적인

06

'점점 더 ~한[하게]'는 「비교급+and+비교급」으로 표현한다.

Words heavy (비가) 거센

07

건강은 인생에서 가장 중요한 것이다.

최상급 앞에는 the가 온다.

08

Alex는 그의 학교의 다른 어떤 소년보다 더 게으르다.

「비교급+than+any other+단수 명사」는 '다른 어떤 ~보다도 더 …한'의 뜻을 가진 비교급을 이용한 최상급 표현이다.

Words lazy 게으른

09

그 놀이터는 체육관보다 두 배 더 크다.

「배수사+as+원급+as」는 '~의 몇 배로 …한[하게]'의 뜻을 가진 표현이다.

Words playground 놀이터 gym 체육관

10

그 죄수는 점점 더 말라갔다.

「비교급+and+비교급」은 '점점 더 ~한[하게]'의 뜻을 가진 표현이다. elder는 '(순서상) 손위의'의 뜻이므로 내용상 적합하지 않다.

Words prisoner 죄수, 재소자 thin 마른

11

① 나의 언니는 대학교에 다닌다.
② 전자가 후자보다 더 낫다.
③ 우리는 그 문제를 좀 더 논의할 필요가 있다.
④ 그녀의 상태는 비 때문에 더 나빠졌다.
⑤ 요즘에 나는 하루에 6시간도 채 안 잔다.

farther는 '(거리가) 더 먼'의 뜻이다. 내용상 '(정도가) 더 나아간'을 의미하는 further로 고쳐야 한다.

Words the former 전자 the latter 후자 discuss 논의하다, 토론하다

12

벌새는 지구상의 다른 어떤 새보다 더 작다.

「비교급+than+any other+단수 명사」는 '다른 어떤 ~보다도 더 …한'의 뜻을 가진 최상급 표현이다.

Words hummingbird 벌새

13

내 가방은 5천원이다. 지수의 가방은 만원이다.
→ 지수의 가방은 내 것보다 두 배 더 비싸다.

'~의 몇 배로 …한[하게]'의 뜻을 가진 배수사 표현에서 twice는 항상 「배수사+as+원급+as」로 쓴다.

14

'가장 ~한 것들 중 하나'의 뜻을 가진 표현은 「one of the+최상급+복수 명사」이다.

15

비교급으로 물었으므로 비교급을 이용해 답한다. 비교급 표현은 「형용사/부사의 비교급+than」으로 나타낸다.

Words height 키 weight 몸무게

16

최상급으로 물었으므로 최상급을 이용해 답한다. 최상급 표현은 「the+형용사/부사의 최상급(+in/of 비교 대상)」으로 나타낸다.

02회 내신 적중 실전 문제

본문 150쪽

01 ④ 02 ② 03 ① 04 ④ 05 ④ 06 ④
07 ⑤ 08 ⑤ 09 ① 10 ③ 11 ⑤ 12 ⑤
13 The more you exercise, the healthier you become.
14 slower than any other animal
15 Seoul is as warm as Jejudo.
16 Dokdo is colder than any other region in Korea.

01

• 수지는 내 친구들 중에서 가장 예쁜 소녀이다.
• 칠레는 세계에서 가장 긴 나라이다.

최상급 표현에서 of 뒤에는 비교 대상이 되는 명사가 오는데, 복수 명사나 복수의 의미를 가진 명사가 온다. in 뒤에는 장소나 범위를 나타내는 단수 명사가 온다.

02

보기 내 방은 그녀의 방만큼 크지 않다.
① 내 방은 그녀의 방보다 더 크다.
② 내 방은 그녀의 방보다 더 작다.
③ 그녀의 방은 내 방보다 더 작다.
④ 그녀의 방은 내 방만큼 크지 않다.
⑤ 그녀의 방은 내 방보다 더 크지 않다.

「A is not as[so] ~ as B」는 'A는 B만큼 ~하지 않다'는 뜻이다.

03

배구는 모든 스포츠 중에 가장 흥미로운 스포츠이다.
= 어떤 스포츠도 배구보다 더 흥미롭지 않다.

「No (other) ~ 비교급+than」은 '어떤 ~도 …보다 더 ~하지 않는'의 뜻을 가진 최상급 표현이다.

Words volleyball 배구

04

나는 이렇게 형편없는 영화는 본 적이 없다.
= 그것은 내가 지금껏 본 최악의 영화이다.

bad의 최상급은 worst이다.

05

'가장 ~한 것들 중 하나'의 뜻을 가진 표현은 「one of the+최상급+복수 명사」이다.

06

① 나는 스파게티보다 피자를 더 좋아한다.
= 나는 스파게티보다 피자를 선호한다.
② 나는 Jessy만큼 영어를 잘 할 수 없다.
= Jessy는 나보다 영어를 더 잘한다.
③ 이것은 내가 지금껏 읽은 가장 지루한 책이다.
= 어떤 책도 이 책만큼 지루하지 않다.
④ 이번 시험은 이전 시험만큼 어렵지 않았다.
= 이번 시험은 이전 시험보다 더 어려웠다.
⑤ 우리 학교의 누구도 유나보다 피아노를 더 잘 치지 못한다.
= 유나는 우리 학교에서 피아노를 가장 잘 친다.

「A is not as[so] ~ as B」는 「B is 비교급 than A」로 바꿀 수 있다.

07

Alex는 우리 반에서 가장 인기 있는 학생이다.

popular를 제외한 나머지 형용사는 최상급을 만들 때 뒤에 -est를 붙여야 한다.

08

그의 차는 내 차보다 세 배 더 비싸다.

'~의 몇 배로 …한[하게]'의 뜻을 가진 배수사 표현은 「배수사+as+원급+as」 또는 「배수사+비교급+than」이다. 전자를 이용한 표현이므로 원급인 expensive만 들어갈 수 있다.

09

이것은 저것보다 더 ____________ 하다.
① 쉬운 ② 유명한 ③ 지루한 ④ 유용한 ⑤ 흥미로운

비교급에서 more를 이용하는 경우는 3음절 이상이거나 2음절이면서 -ous, -ful, -ive, -ing로 끝나는 경우이다. easy의 비교급은 easier이다.

10

우리 가족의 누구도 Joe 삼촌만큼 ____________ 하지 않다.
① 부유한 ② 뚱뚱한 ③ 더 현명한 ④ 활동적인 ⑤ 지적인

「No (other) ~ as+원급+as」는 '어떤 ~도 …만큼 ~하지 않는'의 뜻을 가진 최상급 표현이다. 원급을 이용한 표

현이므로 비교급인 wiser는 들어갈 수 없다.

11

① Tom은 Ben보다 키가 더 크다.
② Judy는 Frank보다 나이가 더 많다.
③ 내 자는 네 것보다 더 길다.
④ 수학은 영어보다 더 어렵다.
⑤ 이 건물은 저것보다 훨씬 더 높다.

나머지는 비교급 표현에서 '~보다'의 뜻으로 쓰이는 than이 들어가는 반면 ⑤에는 '훨씬'이라는 뜻으로 비교급을 강조하는 much, still, even, far 등이 들어가야 한다.

Words ruler 자

12

'점점 더 ~한[하게]'의 뜻을 가진 표현은 「비교급+and+비교급」이다. 따라서 warmer and warmer가 되어야 한다.

13

너는 운동을 더 많이 함에 따라, 더 건강해진다.
→ 운동을 더 많이 하면 할수록, 너는 더 건강해진다.

「the+비교급, the+비교급」은 '~하면 할수록 더 …한[하게]'의 뜻을 가진 표현이다.

14

「비교급+than+any other+단수 명사」는 '다른 어떤 ~보다도 더 …한[하게]'의 뜻을 가진 최상급 표현이다.

Words snail 달팽이 on earth 지구상에서

15

서울과 제주도의 기온을 비교하라.

서울과 제주도의 기온을 비교하라고 했는데 두 지역의 기온이 같으므로 원급[동등] 비교 표현을 이용한다.

Words compare 비교하다

16

한국에서 어느 지역이 가장 추운가?

한국에서 어느 지역이 가장 춥냐고 물었으므로 최상급을 이용해 답한다. 조건에 맞는 최상급 표현은 「비교급+than+any other+단수 명사(다른 어떤 ~보다도 더 …한[하게])」이다.

Words region 지역, 지방

Lesson 10 | 관계사

Point 087 주격 관계대명사 who

본문 154쪽

STEP 1

1 그녀에게는 유명한 예술가인 아들이 있다.
2 사진작가는 사진을 찍는 사람이다.
3 너는 선글라스를 낀 여자가 보이니?
4 자전거를 타고 있는 여자아이는 내 여동생이다.
5 Jenny와 이야기하고 있는 남자아이는 누구니?

STEP 2

1 Ms. Park is the teacher who teaches us history.
2 The gentleman who is carrying a cane is my grandfather.
3 There are several students who are playing basketball in the gym.
4 John is the boy who broke the window.
5 The woman who lives next door is kind to the neighbors.

STEP 3 ②

• 이분이 그 사람이다. + 그는 내 결혼식에서 축가를 불러 줬다.
→ 이분이 내 결혼식에서 축가를 불러 줬던 사람이다.
• 나는 아주 예쁜 소녀를 만났다.

STEP 2

1 박 선생님은 선생님이다. 그녀는 우리에게 역사를 가르쳐 주신다.
→ 박 선생님은 우리에게 역사를 가르쳐 주시는 선생님이다.
2 그 신사는 우리 할아버지시다. 그는 지팡이를 짚고 있다.
→ 지팡이를 짚고 있는 신사는 우리 할아버지시다.
3 학생들이 몇 명 있다. 그들은 체육관에서 농구를 하고 있다.
→ 체육관에서 농구를 하고 있는 학생들이 몇 명 있다.
4 John이 그 소년이다. 그는 창문을 깼다.
→ John이 창문을 깬 그 소년이다.
5 그 여자는 이웃 사람들에게 친절하다. 그녀는 옆집에 산다.
→ 옆집에 사는 그 여자는 이웃 사람들에게 친절하다.

STEP 3

① 최후에 웃는 자가 진정 웃는 자이다.
② 그 뉴스는 누가 은행을 털었는지 말하지 않았다.
③ 일자리를 얻기를 원하는 사람들이 많다.
④ 캐나다에 사는 내 친척이 나에게 선물을 보내 주었다.

⑤ 문 옆에 서 있는 키가 큰 남자는 우리 삼촌이다.

②의 who는 '누구'라는 뜻을 가진 의문사인 반면, 나머지 문장에서는 모두 who가 주격 관계대명사로 쓰였다.

Point 088 소유격 관계대명사 whose

본문 155쪽

STEP 1

1 whose 2 was 3 who 4 whose 5 of which

STEP 2

1 of which the wall[the wall of which] is pink
2 a man whose voice is soft
3 whose owner is a popular singer
4 of which the aim[the aim of which] is to develop writing skills

STEP 3 ④

• 내게는 친구가 있다. + 그의[그녀의] 아버지는 유명한 배우이다.
→ 내게는 아버지가 유명한 배우인 친구가 있다.
• 지붕이 빨간색인 집이 많다.

STEP 1

1 기린은 목이 매우 긴 동물이다.
2 나는 제목이 재미있는 책을 읽었다.
3 내게 영어를 가르쳐 주었던 사람은 우리 누나이다.
4 민호는 포지션이 투수인 야구 선수이다.
5 우리 엄마는 가격이 매우 비싼 가방을 사셨다.

STEP 3

① 내게는 털이 흰 강아지가 있다.
② 너는 다리가 부러진 그 탁자를 사용할 수 없다.
③ (옛날에) 이름이 Midas인 왕이 살았다.
④ Susan은 아름다운 것으로 알려진 소녀이다.
⑤ Tom은 가장 좋아하는 운동이 축구인 나의 친구이다.

④의 빈칸에는 주격 관계대명사 who가 들어가야 하는 반면, 나머지 문장의 빈칸에는 모두 소유격 관계대명사 whose가 들어가야 한다.

Point 089 목적격 관계대명사 whom

본문 156쪽

STEP 1

1 The politician **V** many people support is giving a speech.
2 Sumin is the boy with **V** I went to the flea market yesterday.
3 Ryan has a girlfriend **V** he has dated for a long time.
4 My schoolmate **V** I fought with the other day apologized to me.
5 The baby to **V** my aunt gave birth is so cute.

STEP 2

1 who(m) we met in Hong Kong
2 who(m) I introduced to you last week
3 who(m) I worked with[with whom I worked]
4 whose sense of fashion is quite good

STEP 3 ⑤

• 어제 나는 그 남자아이를 우연히 마주쳤다. + 나는 그를 과학 캠프에서 만났다.
→ 어제 나는 과학 캠프에서 만났던 남자아이를 우연히 마주쳤다.
• 나는 함께 일하는 사람들을 존경한다.

STEP 1

1 많은 사람들이 지지하는 정치가가 연설을 하고 있다.
2 수민이는 어제 내가 벼룩시장에 같이 간 남자아이다.
3 Ryan에게는 오랫동안 데이트를 해 온 여자 친구가 있다.
4 일전에 나와 싸운 학교 친구가 내게 사과했다.
5 우리 이모가 낳으신 아기는 매우 귀엽다.

STEP 3

① 여기에 나와 친한 사람들 중 몇 명이 있다.
② 너는 프랑스어를 한국어로 번역할 수 있는 사람을 아니?
③ 나는 네가 전에 언급했던 사람을 만났다.
④ 우리는 믿을 수 있는 변호사를 찾고 있다.
⑤ 교장 선생님과 악수를 하고 있는 소년은 학생회장이다.

⑤ 목적격 관계대명사 who 앞에는 전치사가 올 수 없다. 따라서 who를 whom으로 고치거나 전치사 with를 관계대명사절 뒤로 옮겨야 한다.

Point 090 관계대명사 which

본문 157쪽

STEP 1

1 which 2 who 3 which
4 of which 5 which

STEP 2

1 which is in the box is mine
2 which you recommended to me was very nice
3 which many dangerous animals live
4 which I'm listening to is peaceful

STEP 3 ③

• 이것이 우리 아버지께서 뒤뜰에 만들어 주신 그네이다.
• 너는 네가 소속되어 있는 동호회가 마음에 드니?

STEP 1

1 이것은 베트남 전쟁에 관한 책이다.
2 내게는 컴퓨터 공학을 전공하고 있는 여동생이 있다.
3 내가 가장 좋아하는 작가가 쓴 그 베스트셀러는 다 팔렸다.
4 내게는 자랑스럽고 아름다운 조국이 있다.
5 우리는 그 기사가 다루었던 주제에 관해 이야기를 나누었다.

STEP 3

① 내가 처리할 수 없는 문제가 많이 있다.
② 우리 아버지께서 근무하시던 회사가 파산했다.
③ 우체국이 어느 쪽인지 아시나요?
④ 네가 나에게 빌려준 책은 매우 재미있었다.
⑤ 우리가 산 세탁기는 수리될 필요가 있다.

③의 which는 '어느'라는 뜻의 의문사로 쓰인 반면, 나머지 문장에서는 모두 which가 관계대명사로 쓰였다.

Point 091 관계대명사 that

본문 158쪽

STEP 1

1 which, that 2 who, that 3 which, that
4 who, that 5 whom

STEP 2

1 This is the garden that my grandmother takes care of.
2 He is the only witness to the car accident that happened last night.
3 I helped the old lady that lived upstairs with her baskets.
4 What do you think of the woman that you met yesterday?

STEP 3 ⑤

• 나는 우리 할아버지께서 기르신 감자를 먹었다.
• 나는 Johnson 씨가 이야기하고 있는 것에 대해 하나도 이해할 수 없다.

STEP 1

1 너는 Tim Burton이 만든 영화를 본 적 있니?
2 우리는 수학을 잘하는 사람이 필요하다.
3 Michael은 난방 설비가 없는 주택에서 산다.
4 내가 태우고 갔던 승객은 내게 더 조심히 운전하라고 말했다.
5 White 선생님은 내가 감사 카드를 써 드린 선생님이시다.

STEP 2

1 이곳은 정원이다. 우리 할머니께서는 그곳을 돌보신다.
→ 이곳은 우리 할머니께서 돌보시는 정원이다.
2 그는 교통사고의 유일한 목격자이다. 그 일은 어젯밤에 발생했다.
→ 그는 어젯밤에 발생했던 교통사고의 유일한 목격자이다.
3 나는 노부인이 바구니를 드는 것을 도와 드렸다. 그녀는 위층에 사신다.
→ 나는 위층에 사시는 노부인이 바구니를 드는 것을 도와 드렸다.
4 너는 그 여자에 대해 어떻게 생각하니? 너는 어제 그녀를 만났어.
→ 너는 네가 어제 만난 여자에 대해 어떻게 생각하니?

STEP 3

사람을 선행사로 하고 관계대명사절에서 전치사 to의 목적어로 쓰였으므로 ③, ④는 오답이다. who나 that 앞에 전치사를 쓸 수 없으므로 ①, ② 역시 오답이다.

Point 092 관계대명사 that vs. 접속사 that

본문 159쪽

STEP 1

1 관, 에펠탑은 많은 관광객들을 파리로 불러들이는 탑이다.
2 접, 너는 화성에 생명체가 있다고 믿니?
3 관, 그것은 내가 태어나기 전에 인기 있던 코미디 쇼였다.
4 관, 내가 점심으로 먹은 핫도그는 짰다.
5 접, 진실은 그 식당의 서비스가 형편없었다는 것이다.

STEP 2

1 A vet is a person that takes care of sick animals.
2 We couldn't believe that Amy got her driver's license.

3 It is true that smoking is bad for health.
4 It is the funniest story that I've ever heard.

STEP 3 ①

- 우리 팀이 경기에서 이긴 것은 놀라운 일이었다.
- 나는 그가 정직하다고 생각한다.
- 사실은 그녀가 수영을 할 수 없다는 것이다.

STEP 3

① 나는 그 증인이 진실을 말하고 있다고 생각하지 않는다.
② 너는 내가 탁자 위에 놓아둔 시계를 보았니?
③ 그것은 내가 길에서 산 것과 똑같은 스카프이다.
④ 내가 네게 만들어 준 스파게티가 어땠니?
⑤ 긴 곱슬머리를 한 소녀는 우리 언니이다.

①의 that은 접속사인 반면, 나머지 문장에서 that은 모두 관계대명사이다.

Point 093 관계대명사 what

본문 160쪽

STEP 1

1 what 2 that 3 what 4 which 5 what

STEP 2

1 what I am saying
2 what makes me happy
3 what Sumi is waiting for
4 What Ben enjoys most
5 what I am reading

STEP 3 ③

- 내가 지금 원하는 것은 물이다.
- 그 소포는 내가 기다리던 것이었다.

STEP 1

1 네가 한 일을 보자.
2 나는 네가 해 달라고 부탁하는 것이면 무엇이든 할 거야.
3 네가 오늘 배운 것을 반드시 복습해라.
4 여기 네가 물을 줘야 하는 식물이 있다.
5 내가 너에게 말한 것을 남들에게 말하지 마.

STEP 3

- 나에게는 가죽 밴드가 달린 시계가 없다.
- 나는 네가 속삭인 말을 못 들었다.

첫 번째 빈칸에는 주격 관계대명사 which가 알맞고, 두 번째 빈칸에는 선행사를 포함하는 관계대명사 what이 알맞다.

Point 094 관계대명사의 생략 I

본문 161쪽

STEP 1

1 that, 나는 그녀가 말해 준 게 하나도 기억나지 않는다.
2 which, 내가 너를 위해 구운 쿠키를 좀 먹어 봐.
3 who, 네가 어제 도와 드린 노인은 우리 할아버지시다.
4 which, 내가 산 청바지는 세탁할 필요가 있다.
5 whom, 유나는 모든 선생님이 칭찬하는 학생이다.

STEP 2

1 This is the sports car I want to rent.
2 The movie my father likes most is *Ben-Hur*.
3 How did you find the key I lost at school?
4 I want to complain about this bag I bought last week.
5 The American I admire most is Barack Obama.

STEP 3 ⑤

- 나는 언제든지 전화할 수 있는 친구가 필요하다.
- 너는 그 건축가가 지은 건물을 봤니?

STEP 3

① 이것은 내가 지난번에 너에게 빌려준 그 책이 아니다.
② 나는 우리가 함께 본 영화가 마음에 들지 않았다.
③ 더 주문하고 싶으신 게 있나요?
④ 그 죄수가 법정에서 말한 모든 것은 사실이었다.
⑤ 과학 캠프에 참가하고 싶어 하는 학생들이 많다.

①~④의 밑줄 친 부분은 목적격 관계대명사로 생략이 가능한 반면, ⑤의 밑줄 친 부분은 주격 관계대명사이므로 생략할 수 없다.

Point 095 관계대명사의 생략 II

본문 162쪽

STEP 1

1 I don't have a pen **V** I can write with.
2 He has a daughter **V** he is very proud of.
3 That is the dog **V** my little brother is scared of.
4 Emily finally found the memo **V** she was looking for.

5 Love is a common topic **V** most writers write about.

STEP 2
1 The bed I slept in at the hotel
2 the city the Colosseum is located in
3 to the party she was invited to
4 the girl he is going out with
5 a friend I have shared joys and sorrows with

STEP 3 ②

• 나는 John과 이야기를 나누고 있는 소녀를 알고 있다.
• 이곳은 내가 자란 집이다.
• 야구는 Tom이 잘하는 운동이다.

STEP 1
1 나에게는 쓸 펜이 없다.
2 그에게는 그가 매우 자랑스러워하는 딸이 한 명 있다.
3 저것이 내 남동생이 무서워하는 개이다.
4 Emily는 마침내 찾고 있던 메모를 발견했다.
5 사랑은 대부분의 작가들이 쓰는 흔한 주제이다.

STEP 3
① 축구 동아리는 내가 속해 있는 동아리이다.
② 우리 부모님은 내가 의지할 수 있는 사람들이다.
③ 체육은 Tyler가 가장 흥미 있어 하는 과목이다.
④ 사전은 내가 정보를 얻는 출처이다.
⑤ 우리 할머니는 나를 키워 주신 분이다.

② 목적격 관계대명사는 전치사가 앞에 올 경우 생략될 수 없다.

Point 096 관계대명사의 생략 Ⅲ

본문 163쪽

STEP 1
1 which is 2 that was 3 ×
4 who are 5 ×

STEP 2
1 the man who[that] is limping
2 a lot of students who[that] are reading books in the library
3 knowledge which[that] is useful in life at school
4 Anyone who[that] is interested in art
5 The clothes which[that] were dry-cleaned at the laundry

STEP 3 ⑤

• 나는 나와 나이가 비슷한 남자와 결혼하고 싶다.
• 1990년대에 작곡된 그 노래는 내가 가장 좋아하는 노래이다.

STEP 1
1 자신감은 실패로부터 회복하는 데 있어 중요한 요인이다.
2 여기에 주차되어 있던 차는 경찰에 의해 견인되었다.
3 그 회사는 법을 전공한 사람들을 찾고 있다.
4 너는 무대 위에서 노래하고 있는 여자아이들을 아니?
5 우리는 케이크의 주재료가 되는 것들을 샀다.

STEP 3
• 담배를 피우고 있는 노인은 우리 할아버지시다.
• 난로 위에서 끓고 있는 물은 라면을 끓이기 위한 것이다.

두 문장 모두 맨 앞의 명사구와 분사구 사이에 「주격 관계대명사+be동사」가 생략돼 있다. 사람(the old man)이나 사물(the water)이 선행사일 때 관계대명사 that을 사용한다.

Point 097 관계부사 when

본문 164쪽

STEP 1
1 4월 5일은 우리가 나무를 심는 날이다.
2 5월은 휴일이 많이 있는 달이다.
3 2015년은 내 조카가 태어난 해였다.
4 지금은 우리가 그의 무사 귀환을 위해 기도해야 할 시간이다.
5 많은 사람들이 9.11 공격이 발생했던 날을 여전히 기억한다.

STEP 2
1 March is the month when the new school year begins in Korea.
2 Yesterday was the day when my father came back from a business trip.
3 Seven o'clock is the time when I leave home for work.
4 Spring is the season when lots of flowers blossom.

STEP 3 ②

• 나는 그날을 결코 잊지 못할 것이다. + 그날에[그때] 나는 너

를 처음 만났다.
→ 나는 너를 처음 만난 날을 결코 잊지 못할 것이다.

STEP 2

1 3월은 달이다. 한국에서는 새 학년이 3월에 시작된다.
→ 3월은 한국에서 새 학년이 시작되는 달이다.
2 어제는 날이었다. 우리 아버지께서는 어제 출장에서 돌아오셨다.
→ 어제는 우리 아버지께서 출장에서 돌아오신 날이었다.
3 7시는 시간이다. 나는 7시에 집을 나와 직장에 간다.
→ 7시는 내가 집을 나와 직장에 가는 시간이다.
4 봄은 계절이다. 봄에는 많은 꽃이 피어난다.
→ 봄은 많은 꽃이 피어나는 계절이다.

STEP 3

• 너는 한국 축구팀이 4강에 진출했던 날을 기억하니?
• 회의가 시작될 시간을 내게 알려 줘.

선행사가 시간, 때를 나타낼 때 사용되는 관계부사 when은 선행사에 따라 「in/at/on+which」로 바꿔 쓸 수 있다. day는 전치사 on과 어울린다.

Point 098 관계부사 where

본문 165쪽

STEP 1
1 where 2 where 3 in 4 who 5 which

STEP 2
1 the place where my family ate out yesterday
2 of the town in which the Earl of Sandwich lived
3 the country where we can find natural beauty
4 the city in which Monet was born

STEP 3 ②

• 이곳이 그 공원이다. + 나는 그 공원에서[거기에서] 강아지를 잃어버렸다.
→ 이곳이 내가 강아지를 잃어버렸던 공원이다.

STEP 1

1 뉴욕은 자유의 여신상이 있는 도시이다.
2 양로원은 어르신들이 쉴 수 있는 장소이다.
3 운동장은 사람들이 운동을 할 수 있는 장소이다.
4 비행기 안에는 부유한 사업가처럼 보이는 남자가 있었다.
5 경복궁은 조선 왕조 때 왕들이 살았던 궁이다.

STEP 3

① 나는 우리 아버지가 사셨던 마을에 갔다.
② 지금은 많은 관광객들이 제주도를 방문하는 계절이다.
③ 루브르는 유명한 그림인 '모나리자'가 걸려 있는 박물관이다.
④ 그들은 공기가 깨끗한 나라로 이사할 예정이다.
⑤ 이곳은 우리 부모님께서 결혼하신 예식장이다.

②의 빈칸에는 관계부사 when이 들어가야 하는 반면, 나머지 빈칸에는 모두 관계부사 where가 들어가야 한다.

Point 099 관계부사 why

본문 166쪽

STEP 1
1 why[for which] 2 why[for which] 3 which
4 which 5 which

STEP 2
1 I'm sure there is a reason why he didn't come here.
2 Is there some reason for which she is avoiding me?
3 One reason why I like this restaurant is its reasonable prices.
4 There's a reason for which the movie was a big hit.

STEP 3 ①

• 내게 이유를 말해 줘. + 너는 그 이유로 늦었어.
→ 네가 늦은 이유를 내게 말해 줘.

STEP 1

1 나는 그가 나에게 화가 난 이유를 전혀 생각해 낼 수가 없다.
2 내가 그것에 대해 말할 수 없는 어떤 이유가 있다.
3 그들은 곧 발표될 결과를 기다리고 있다.
4 그녀는 내가 이해할 수 없는 이유로 일을 그만두었다.
5 그들이 헤어진 이유는 간단하다.

STEP 3

• 그녀가 교회에 다니는 이유는 평화를 찾기 위해서이다.
• John은 마침내 나를 떠났던 이유를 말해 줬다.

두 문장 모두 빈칸 앞에 the reason이 있고 빈칸 뒤에 절이 이어지고 있다. 이 경우 관계부사 why를 넣어 선행사와 절을 연결해 주며, why 대신 「for+which」를 쓰기도 한다.

Point 100 관계부사 how

본문 167쪽

STEP 1

1 how 2 in which 3 how 4 in which 5 way

STEP 2

1 the way (in which) he acted
2 The way (in which) people communicate
3 how you made the robot
4 how she handles things
5 how I can put the baby to sleep

STEP 3 ⑤

• 우리들은 방법에 관해 배웠다. + 이집트인들은 그 방법으로 미라를 만들었다.
→ 우리들은 이집트인들이 미라를 만들었던 방법에 관해 배웠다.

STEP 1

1 너는 그 기계가 작동되는 방식을 아니?
2 Sam은 Laura에게 젓가락을 사용하는 방법을 알려 주었다.
3 네가 컴퓨터를 고친 방법을 나에게 알려 줘.
4 나는 네가 옷을 입은 방식이 마음에 들어.
5 그는 모두에게 친절하다. 그것이 그가 사람들을 대하는 방식이다.

STEP 3

① 너는 지금 이대로가 딱 좋다.
② 그것이 내가 단어를 암기하는 방법이다.
③ 사람을 겉을 보고 판단하지 마라.
④ 나는 그녀가 나를 향해 미소 짓는 모습이 좋다.
⑤ Daniel이 프랑스어를 하는 방식은 재미있다.

⑤ 선행사 the way와 관계부사 how는 같이 쓸 수 없고, 둘 중 하나만 써야 한다.

01회 내신 적중 실전 문제

본문 168쪽

01 ② 02 ② 03 ① 04 ⑤ 05 ① 06 ③
07 ③ 08 ④ 09 ③ 10 ① 11 ② 12 ②
13 A firefighter is a person who[that] puts out fires.
14 that
15 February 18 is the day when Mira was born.
16 John's Pizza is the place where Mira's birthday party will be held.

01

① 내가 기르고 있는 애완동물은 앵무새이다.
② 나는 어떤 것을 입어야 할지 결정할 수가 없다.
③ 내가 네게 사 준 향수가 마음에 드니?
④ 탁자 위에 있는 소금을 내게 건네줄 수 있니?
⑤ 낙타는 등에 혹이 있는 동물이다.

②의 which는 '어떤'의 뜻을 가진 의문사로 쓰인 반면, 나머지는 모두 which가 관계대명사로 쓰였다.

Words raise 기르다 parrot 앵무새 perfume 향수 pass 건네주다 camel 낙타 hump 혹 back 등

02

① 창문이 깨진 차는 우리 아빠의 것이다.
② 나에게는 별명이 많은 남동생이 있다.
③ 너는 제목이 'The Giver'인 소설을 읽어 봤니?
④ 머리카락이 금발인 여자는 나의 새로운 영어 선생님이다.
⑤ 이름이 잘 알려진 세계적인 영화배우가 한국에 왔다.

②의 빈칸에는 주격 관계대명사 who나 that이 들어가야 하는 반면, 나머지는 모두 빈칸에 소유격 관계대명사 whose가 들어가야 한다.

Words nickname 별명 novel 소설 title 제목 blond 금발인 international 세계적인 well-known 잘 알려진

03

① 미술은 내가 못하는 과목이다.
② 이것이 내가 서점에서 산 책이다.
③ 내가 함께 여행을 갔던 소년은 케냐 출신이다.
④ 자동차 아래에서 잠을 자고 있는 고양이를 봐라.
⑤ 축구를 하고 있는 아이들이 몇 명 있다.

목적격 관계대명사 바로 앞에 전치사가 있을 경우 관계대명사를 생략할 수 없다

Words subject 과목 bookstore 서점

04

• Jake는 네가 신뢰할 수 있는 사람이 아니다.
• Tom의 옆에 앉아 있는 소녀의 이름은 뭐니?

사람을 선행사로 하는 목적격 관계대명사 중에 바로 앞에 전치사가 올 수 있는 것은 whom밖에 없다.

Words trust 신뢰하다

05

• 너는 이유를 설명할 수 있니? 너는 그 이유로 숙제를 제출하지 않았어.
→ 너는 숙제를 제출하지 않은 이유를 설명할 수 있니?

이유를 뜻하는 선행사 reason을 수식하는 관계부사는 why이다.

Words explain 설명하다 hand in ~를 제출하다

06

그녀는 모국어가 한국어가 아닌 학생들에게 한국어를 가르쳐 왔다.

③ 문장의 의미상 주격 · 목적격 관계대명사 that을 소유격 관계대명사 whose로 고쳐야 한다.

Words native language 모국어

07

그들은 주차 금지 구역에 주차한 사람을 찾고 있다.

관계대명사 who가 쓰였으므로 선행사는 사람을 뜻하는 말이어야 한다.

Words park 주차하다 no parking zone 주차 금지 구역
vehicle 차량, 탈것

08

내가 적은 전화번호는 틀렸다.

빈칸에는 사물을 선행사로 하는 목적격 관계대명사인 which나 that이 들어가야 한다.

09

A: 저녁으로 뭘 먹고 싶니?
B: 내가 저녁으로 먹고 싶은 것은 초밥이야.

'~하는 것'이라는 뜻으로 선행사를 포함하는 관계대명사는 what이다.

Words sushi 초밥

10

A: 개미가 먹이를 나르는 모습[방식]을 본 적이 있니?
B: 응. 그것들은 먹이를 옮기려고 함께 일하더라.

'~한 방식[방법]'이라는 뜻을 표현할 때 쓰는 관계부사는 how이다.

Words carry 나르다, 옮기다

11

보기 Vincent van Gogh는 여전히 많은 사람들에게 사랑받는 예술가이다.
① 어떤 사람들은 UFO가 있다고 믿는다.
② 나는 그 해변에서 보았던 저녁노을을 잊을 수가 없다.
③ 너는 이 선생님이 다른 학교로 옮기신 것을 알았니?
④ 현대 사회에 그러한 일이 일어난다니 충격적이다.
⑤ 제 소망은 독자들에게 가치 있는 무언가를 전달하는 것입니다.

보기 와 ②의 that은 관계대명사로 쓰인 반면, 나머지 문장 모두 that이 접속사로 쓰였다.

Words UFO(Unidentified Flying Object) 미확인 비행 물체
sunset 저녁노을, 일몰 shocking 충격적인
modern 현대의 convey 전달하다 value 가치

12

① 나는 독일어를 할 수 있는 여자아이를 안다.
② Luke는 면으로 만든 바지를 입고 있다.
③ 기차를 기다리고 있는 사람들이 많다.
④ 악어는 큰 입을 가진 동물이다.
⑤ 이곳은 내가 어린 시절부터 익히 알고 지내 온 지역이다.

① 선행사가 사람이므로, which를 who[that]로 고쳐야 한다.
③ 「주격 관계대명사+be동사」는 한꺼번에 생략해야 하므로, waiting 앞의 are도 생략하거나 are 앞에 who[that]를 넣어 주어야 한다.
④ 관계대명사가 뒤에 이어지는 절에서 주어 역할을 하므로, of which를 which[that]로 고쳐야 한다.
⑤ 전치사 바로 뒤에 오는 목적격 관계대명사는 생략할 수 없으므로, with 뒤에 which를 넣어 주어야 한다.

Words German 독일어 cotton 면 crocodile 악어 area 지역
be familiar with ~를 익히 알다 childhood 어린 시절

13

보기
A: 비행기 조종사는 누구인가요?
B: 비행기 조종사는 비행기를 조종하는 사람입니다.

A: 소방관은 누구인가요?
B: 소방관은 불을 끄는 사람입니다.

who[that]는 선행사가 사람이고 관계대명사절 안에서 주어 역할을 할 때 쓰는 주격 관계대명사이다.

Words put out (불을) 끄다

14

• 내가 인터뷰했던 그 교수는 뇌에 관한 연구로 알려져 있다.
• 그들이 묵었던 호텔은 4성급이었다.

선행사가 사람이거나 사물이고 관계대명사절 안에서 동사나 전치사의 목적어 역할을 할 때 목적격 관계대명사 that을 쓴다.

Words professor 교수 interview 인터뷰를 하다 work 연구 brain 뇌 four-star 4성급의

[15~16]

너를 나의 생일 파티에 초대할게.
언제: 내 생일 (2월 18일)
어디서: John's Pizza

미라로부터

15

시간, 때를 나타내는 선행사를 수식하는 관계부사는 when이다.

16

장소를 나타내는 선행사를 수식하는 관계부사는 where이다.

02회 내신 적중 실전 문제

본문 170쪽

01 ⑤	02 ②	03 ①	04 ④	05 ③	06 ①
07 ⑤	08 ①	09 ④	10 ④	11 ④	12 ⑤

13 The concert that I bought a ticket for was canceled.
14 I want to know how King Sejong invented Hangeul.
15 Susan took off the sunglasses she was wearing.
16 I bought a pen made in Japan.

01

보기 나에게는 뉴질랜드에 사는 사촌이 있다.
① 그녀는 누구를 기다리고 있니?
② 너는 저 키 큰 남자가 누구인지 아니?
③ 나는 누가 네 우산을 가져갔는지 말해 줄 수 있어.
④ 너는 누가 한국 최고의 춤꾼이라고 생각하니?
⑤ 나는 초등학교에서 나를 가르쳐 주셨던 선생님을 방문했다.

보기와 같이 who가 주격 관계대명사로 쓰인 문장은 ⑤이고, 나머지 문장 모두 who가 '누구'의 뜻을 가진 의문사로 쓰였다.

Words cousin 사촌

02

① 나는 엄마가 나에게 만들어 주시는 것을 언제나 좋아한다.
② 생각나는 어떤 것이든 내게 말해 줘.
③ 우리 선생님은 내가 알아야 할 것을 가르쳐 주신다.
④ 내가 생일 선물로 원하는 것은 새 카메라이다.
⑤ 네가 이미 가진 것에 만족하려고 노력해라.

② 앞에 선행사 anything이 있으므로 관계대명사 what 대신 that이 와야 한다. 선행사가 anything일 경우 주로 which 대신 that을 사용한다.

Words come to mind 생각이 떠오르다 content 만족하는

03

① 네가 도움이 필요할 때는 나에게 전화해도 돼.
② 가을은 하늘이 푸르른 계절이다.
③ 지금은 딸기가 가장 맛있는 때이다.
④ 나는 아직도 고등학교를 졸업한 날을 기억한다.
⑤ 12월은 우리가 사랑하는 사람들과 선물을 나눠 갖는 달이다.

①의 when은 '~할 때'의 뜻을 가진 접속사인 반면, 나머지 문장 모두 when이 관계부사로 쓰였다.

Words strawberry 딸기 graduate from ~를 졸업하다 share 나누어 갖다

04

① 내가 자란 마을은 아주 작다.
② 프랑스는 지나가 자신의 약혼자를 만난 나라이다.
③ 우리가 아이스크림을 먹었던 카페는 오후 11시에 문을 닫는다.
④ 이것은 우리 아버지께서 십 년 전에 지으신 집이다.
⑤ 많은 회사가 위치한 그 건물은 현대적으로 보인다.

④의 빈칸 뒤에 이어지는 절에서 동사 built의 목적어가 빠져 있는 것으로 보아, 빈칸에는 목적격 관계대명사 which[that]이 와야 한다.

Words village 마을 fiancé 약혼자 firm 회사

05

Jack은 믿기 어려운 이야기를 나에게 들려 준 사람이다.

③ 관계대명사가 전치사의 목적어 역할을 할 때 전치사가 관계대명사 앞에 올 수 있는데, 이 경우 who 대신 whom을 써야 한다.

Words unbelievable 믿기 어려운

06

나는 회의가 지연된 이유를 모른다.

이유를 나타내는 선행사 the reason 뒤에 오는 for which를 관계부사 why로 바꿔 쓸 수 있다.

Words delay 지연시키다

07

표지가 빨간색인 그 책은 잘 팔린다.

빈칸 앞의 명사와 빈칸 뒤의 절을 연결해 주는 말이 필요하다. 이때 빈칸에 소유격 관계대명사 whose가 오는 것이 의미상 적절하다.

08

너는 오늘 배운 것을 이해하니?

'~하는 것'이라는 뜻으로 선행사를 포함하는 관계대명사는 what이다.

09

• 나는 실화를 바탕으로 한 영화를 좋아한다.
• 그 소문은 할리우드 스타가 그 작은 마을을 방문했다는 것이다.

첫 번째 빈칸에는 주격 관계대명사 which나 that이 들어갈 수 있고, 두 번째 빈칸에는 명사절을 이끄는 접속사 that이 들어가야 한다.

Words be based on ~를 바탕으로 하다 rumor 소문

10

• 잠수함은 물속을 들어갈 수 있는 배이다.
• 당신이 10킬로그램을 감량한 방법을 제게 알려 주세요.

사람이 아닌 선행사를 수식하는 주격 · 목적격 관계대명사는 which와 that이다. 그런데 that 앞에는 전치사를 쓸 수 없으므로, 빈칸에 공통으로 들어갈 말은 which이다.

Words submarine 잠수함

11

① 우리가 처음 만났던 장소에서 만나자.
② 낮 12시는 내가 학교에서 점심을 먹는 시간이다.
③ 바르셀로나는 Gaudi의 건축물이 존재하는 도시이다.
④ 아무도 그 죄수가 탈출한 방법을 모른다.
⑤ 추석은 우리가 송편을 먹는 날이다.

④ 방법을 나타내는 선행사 the way와 관계부사 how는 함께 쓸 수 없다.

Words noon 낮 12시 exist 존재하다 prisoner 죄수
escape 탈출하다

12

• 나는 마침내 필요로 했던 문서를 발견했다.
• 우리 엄마는 (앉아서) 쉴 수 있는 안락의자를 사오셨다.

동사나 전치사의 목적어로 쓰인 목적격 관계대명사는 생략할 수 있다. 두 문장 모두 선행사가 사물이므로 which[that]이 생략되었음을 알 수 있다.

Words document 문서 require 필요로 하다
armchair 안락의자 rest 쉬다, 휴식하다

13

목적격 관계대명사 that을 쓸 경우, that 앞에 전치사를 쓸 수 없음에 유의한다.

Words cancel 취소하다

14

선행사 the way와 관계부사 how는 둘 중 하나만 써야 함에 유의한다.

Words invent 발명하다

15

Susan은 선글라스를 쓰고 있었다. 그녀는 그것을 벗었다.
→ Susan은 쓰고 있던 선글라스를 벗었다.

동사의 목적어로 쓰인 목적격 관계대명사는 생략할 수 있다. 글자 수를 맞추기 위해서는 관계대명사 which[that]을 생략해야 한다.

16

나는 펜을 하나 샀다. 그것은 일본에서 만들어졌다.
→ 나는 일본에서 만들어진 펜을 하나 샀다.

분사구 앞에 오는 「주격 관계대명사+be동사」는 생략할 수 있다. 글자 수를 맞추기 위해서는 which[that] was를 생략해야 한다.

Lesson 11 | 가정법

Point 101 가정법 과거

본문 174쪽

STEP 1

1 were 2 had 3 would 4 knew 5 could

STEP 2

1 If she found the answer
2 If Tom were not sick[ill]
3 If people knew the truth
4 I could buy the camera
5 you would[could] understand this book

STEP 3 ⑤

TIP 만약 내가 부자라면 전 세계를 여행할 수 있을 텐데.
→ 나는 부자가 아니라서 전 세계를 여행할 수 없다.

STEP 1

1 만약 내가 새라면 너에게로 날아갈 텐데.
2 만약 그들에게 시간이 더 있다면 그들은 그 프로젝트를 끝낼 수 있을 텐데.
3 만약 그가 건강하다면 마라톤에 참가할 텐데.
4 만약 내가 그녀의 주소를 안다면 그녀를 방문할 텐데.
5 만약 그녀가 런던에 산다면 Big Ben을 볼 수 있을 텐데.

STEP 3

① 만약 날씨가 좋다면 우리는 산책을 할 텐데.
② 만약 네가 나를 도와준다면 나는 무엇이든 할 수 있을 텐데.
③ 만약 그녀가 열심히 공부한다면 시험을 통과할 수 있을 텐데.
④ 만약 그 가방이 조금 더 싸다면 나는 그것을 살 텐데.
⑤ 만약 그가 직장을 구한다면 그 집을 빌릴 돈을 충분히 벌 수 있을 텐데.

⑤ 가정법 과거 문장이므로 주절의 조동사 can을 과거형 could로 고쳐야 한다.

Point 102 가정법 과거완료

본문 175쪽

STEP 1

1 had hurried 2 have met 3 would
4 given 5 had

STEP 2

1 If I had not been busy
2 If you had heard the news
3 I would not have felt tired
4 you might have shed tears

STEP 3 ④

TIP 만약 네가 나에게 그 책을 빌려주지 않았다면 나는 숙제를 할 수 없었을 텐데.
→ 네가 나에게 그 책을 빌려줘서 나는 숙제를 할 수 있었다.

STEP 1

1 만약 그녀가 서둘렀다면 늦지 않았을 텐데.
2 만약 네가 파티에 왔다면 그를 만날 수 있었을 텐데.
3 만약 내가 아프지 않았다면 수학여행에 갔을 텐데.
4 만약 그가 나에게 충고를 해 주지 않았다면 나는 실패했을 텐데.
5 만약 John에게 차가 있었다면 그는 나를 태워줬을 텐데.

STEP 3

보기 나에게 전화기가 없어서 너에게 전화할 수 없었다.
① 만약 나에게 전화기가 있다면 너에게 전화할 수 있을 것이다.
② 만약 나에게 전화기가 있다면 너에게 전화할 수 있을 텐데.
③ 만약 나에게 전화기가 없다면 너에게 전화할 수 없을 텐데.
④ 만약 나에게 전화기가 있었다면 너에게 전화할 수 있었을 텐데.
⑤ 만약 나에게 전화기가 없었다면 너에게 전화할 수 없었을 텐데.

주어진 문장은 직설법 과거 문장이다. 이를 가정법 과거완료 문장(「If+주어+had p.p.~, 주어+조동사의 과거형+have p.p.…」)으로 바꿀 수 있다.

Point 103 I wish+가정법 과거

본문 176쪽

STEP 1

1 눈이 아주 많이 내린다면 좋을 텐데.
2 나에게 새처럼 날개가 있다면 좋을 텐데.
3 네가 여기에서 머무른다면 좋을 텐데.
4 그들이 서로 잘 지낸다면 좋을 텐데.
5 이것을 해결하는 쉬운 방법이 있다면 좋을 텐데.

STEP 2

1 were not too shy

2 could understand me
3 could run as fast as Usain Bolt
4 had magical powers
5 lived in the countryside

STEP 3 ③

TIP 내가 일본어를 할 수 있다면 좋을 텐데.
→ 내가 일본어를 할 수 없어서 아쉽다.

STEP 2

1 내가 수줍음을 너무 많이 타서 아쉽다.
→ 내가 수줍음을 너무 많이 타지 않는다면 좋을 텐데.
2 네가 나를 이해할 수 없어서 아쉽다.
→ 네가 나를 이해할 수 있다면 좋을 텐데.
3 내가 Usain Bolt만큼 빨리 달릴 수 없어서 아쉽다.
→ 내가 Usain Bolt만큼 빨리 달릴 수 있다면 좋을 텐데.
4 내가 마법의 힘을 갖고 있지 않아서 아쉽다.
→ 내가 마법의 힘을 갖고 있다면 좋을 텐데.
5 우리 할머니께서 시골에 살지 않으셔서 아쉽다.
→ 우리 할머니께서 시골에 사신다면 좋을 텐데.

STEP 3

내게는 이미 선글라스가 두 개 있다. 내가 갈색 선글라스도 한 개 갖고 있다면 좋을 텐데.

현재의 소망은 「I wish+(that)+주어+동사의 과거형~」의 형태로 나타낸다. 따라서 빈칸에는 have의 과거형인 had가 들어가야 한다.

Point 104 I wish+가정법 과거완료

본문 177쪽

STEP 1

1 had been　2 had got[gotten]
3 had not happened　4 had come

STEP 2

1 you had not said so
2 our plan had succeeded
3 the door had not been open
4 I had met you earlier

STEP 3 ④

TIP 내가 수영하는 법을 배웠다면 좋았을 텐데.
→ 내가 수영하는 법을 배우지 않아서 아쉽다.

STEP 3

보기 내가 그 일을 맡았다면 좋았을 텐데.
① 내가 그 일을 맡아서 기쁘다.
② 내가 그 일을 맡지 않아서 기쁘다.
③ 내가 그 일을 맡지 않을 것이라서 아쉽다.
④ 내가 그 일을 맡지 않아서 아쉽다.
⑤ 내가 그 일을 맡고 있지 않아서 아쉽다.

「I wish+가정법 과거완료」 문장은 직설법 현재 문장(「I'm sorry+(that)+주어+동사의 과거형~」)으로 바꿀 수 있다.

Point 105 as if+가정법 과거

본문 178쪽

STEP 1

1 나는 마치 꿈을 꾸고 있는 것 같은 기분이 든다.
2 그들은 마치 친한 친구인 것처럼 보인다.
3 Lucy는 마치 나를 환영하는 것처럼 미소 지었다.
4 그가 마치 누군가에게 고함을 지르고 있는 것처럼 들렸다.
5 네가 마치 우리 엄마인 것처럼 말하지 마.

STEP 2

1 He lives as if he were a millionaire.
2 I felt as if I were floating in the air.
3 Mark acted as if he didn't pay attention to anyone.
4 Mom treats me as if I were a baby.

STEP 3 ②

• 그는 마치 다른 세상에서 온 것처럼 보인다.
• 그는 마치 다른 세상에서 온 것처럼 보였다.

TIP 그녀는 마치 동물을 좋아하는 것처럼 행동한다.
→ 사실, 그녀는 동물을 좋아하지 않는다.

STEP 3

그는 마치 우리 삼촌을 아는 것처럼 말한다. 사실, 그는 그를 (우리 삼촌을) 모른다.

주절과 같은 시점에서 실제와 다른 상황을 나타낼 때, 「as if+주어+동사의 과거형~」으로 문장을 표현한다.

Point 106 as if+가정법 과거완료

본문 179쪽

STEP 1

1 그는 마치 아무 일도 일어나지 않았던 것처럼 행동했다.

2 너는 마치 아침 식사를 하지 않았던 것처럼 먹는구나.
3 Robin은 마치 화가 난 것처럼 황급히 방을 떠났다.
4 Jack은 마치 자신이 뉴욕을 방문해 본 것처럼 말했다.
5 Carol은 마치 아무 것도 모르는 것처럼 멍해 보인다.

STEP 2
1 as if you hadn't slept
2 as if he had been
3 as if she had been
4 as if they had fought

STEP 3 ⑤

• 그 신사는 마치 젊었을 때 가난했던 것처럼 말한다.
• 그 신사는 마치 젊었을 때 가난했던 것처럼 말했다.

TIP 마치 네가 어젯밤에 공부를 열심히 한 것처럼 들린다.
→ 사실, 너는 어젯밤에 공부를 열심히 하지 않았다.

STEP 3
사실, Paul은 일본에 있지 않았다.
→ Paul은 마치 자신이 일본에 있었던 것처럼 말한다.
실제 과거와 다른 상황을 나타낼 때 「as if+주어+had p.p.~」로 문장을 표현한다.

01회 내신 적중 실전 문제

본문 180쪽

01 ③ 02 ① 03 ③ 04 ① 05 ⑤ 06 ④
07 ③ 08 ② 09 ⑤ 10 ④ 11 ② 12 ③
13 I wish I had told you sooner.
14 You are talking as if you believed[trusted] him.
15 If I had been careful, I would not have fallen down in front of my friends.
16 I wish I could go back to yesterday.

01
나는 돈이 없어서 너에게 돈을 빌려줄 수 없다.
③ 만약 나에게 돈이 있다면 너에게 빌려줄 수 있을 텐데.
주어진 문장은 직설법 현재 문장이다. 이를 가정법 과거 문장(「If+주어+동사의 과거형~, 주어+조동사의 과거형+동사원형…」)으로 바꿀 수 있다.
Words lend 빌려주다

02
① 내가 그때 Michael에게 사과했다면 좋았을 텐데.
② 우리가 오래된 가구를 모두 처리할 수 있다면 좋을 텐데.
③ 만약 네가 내 입장에 처한다면 너도 똑같이 할 거야.
④ 만약 비가 오지 않았다면 우리는 축구를 할 수 있었을 텐데.
⑤ 그녀는 그 사고를 직접 봤던 것처럼 내게 그것에 관해 말해 주었다.
① 부사 then으로 보아 과거의 일에 대한 아쉬움이나 후회를 나타내는 문장이므로, 「I wish+가정법 과거완료」로 나타내야 한다. (have → had)
Words apologize 사과하다 get rid of ~을 처리하다, 없애다 furniture 가구 be in one's shoes ~의 입장에 처하다

03
• 만약 지금이 겨울이라면 나는 스키를 타러 갈 텐데.
• 그녀는 마치 미국인인 것처럼 영어를 한다.
첫 번째 문장은 가정법 과거 문장이고 두 번째 문장은 「as if+가정법 과거」 문장이다.

04
'~하면[이라면] 좋을 텐데'라는 의미를 가진 문장은 「I wish+가정법 과거」로 표현한다.

05
A: 나 어제 매장에서 진공청소기 샀어. 그거 꽤 비싸더라.
B: 만약 네가 그것을 온라인에서 샀다면 할인을 받을 수 있었을 텐데.
과거의 사실을 반대로 가정하는 문장은 가정법 과거완료(「If+주어+had p.p.~, 주어+조동사의 과거형+have p.p.…」)로 나타낸다.
Words vacuum cleaner 진공청소기 quite 꽤, 상당히 discount 할인

06
'마치 ~였던[했던] 것처럼'이라는 뜻의 문장은 「as if+주어+had p.p.~」의 형태로 표현한다.

07
만약 네가 굉장한 부자라면 무엇을 할 거니?
주절의 동사 형태가 「조동사의 과거형+동사원형」이고 그 뒤에 if절이 이어지는 것으로 보아 가정법 과거 문장이다. 따라서 빈칸에는 동사의 과거형이 들어가야 한다.

08

그는 마치 자기가 내 상사인 것처럼 행동한다. 실제로, 그는 그렇지 않다.

'마치 ~인 것처럼'이라는 뜻의 문장은 「as if+주어+동사의 과거형」으로 표현한다.

Words boss (직장의) 상사

09

Jake는 도둑을 보았을 때 마치 심장이 멎는 것 같은 기분을 느꼈다. 만약 그가 용감했다면 그 도둑을 잡을 수 있었을 것이다.

⑤ 과거의 사실을 반대로 가정하는 문장은 가정법 과거완료로 나타낸다. (could catch → could have caught)

Words thief 도둑 brave 용감한

10

그 운동선수는 마치 발목을 삔 것처럼 달리기를 멈췄다.
= 사실, 그는 발목을 삐지 않았다.
① 그는 발목을 삤다
② 그는 달리고 싶지 않았다
③ 그는 더 빨리 달리고 싶었다
⑤ 그는 전에 발목을 삔 적이 있다

주어진 문장은 「as if+가정법 과거완료」를 사용하여 실제 과거와 다른 상황을 나타내므로, 실제로 그는 발목을 삐지 않았음을 알 수 있다.

Words athlete 운동선수 sprain 삐다, 접질리다 ankle 발목

11

A: 내게 그 록 밴드의 콘서트 티켓이 있다면 좋을 텐데. 티켓이 전부 팔렸더라.
B: 그러게 말이야. 그거 정말 보고 싶은데.

실현 가능성이 희박한 현재의 소망을 나타내는 문장은 「I wish+(that)+주어+동사의 과거형~」으로 표현한다.

Words sell out 다 팔리다, 매진되다

12

① 나는 그녀가 그립다. 그녀가 여기에 있다면 좋을 텐데.
② 민지는 마치 모델인 것처럼 걷는다.
③ 만약 네가 거기에 있었다면 즐거운 시간을 보냈을 텐데.
④ 만약 우리 아버지께서 한가하시다면 나와 시간을 보내실 수 있을 텐데.
⑤ 만약 그 영화가 무섭지 않다면 너와 함께 그것을 볼 텐데.

③은 가정법 과거완료 문장이므로 빈칸에 had been이 들어가야 한다. 나머지 문장은 모두 가정법 과거 문장이므로 빈칸에 were가 들어가야 한다.

Words miss 그리워하다 enjoy oneself 즐거운 시간을 보내다 spend (시간을) 보내다 scary 무서운

13

내가 네게 진작 말해 주지 않아서 아쉽다.
→ 내가 네게 진작 말해 주었다면 좋았을 텐데.

과거에 이루어지지 못했던 일에 대한 아쉬움이나 후회를 나타낼 때 「I wish+(that)+주어+had p.p.~」를 사용한다.

14

'마치 ~인[하는] 것처럼'이라는 뜻의 문장은 「as if+주어+동사의 과거형~」으로 표현한다.

[15~16]

어제는 내 생애 최악의 날이었다. 나는 친구들 앞에서 넘어졌다. 나는 조심성이 없었다. 그러고 나서는 안경을 부러뜨렸다. 이렇게 바보 같을 수가! 어제로 다시 되돌아갈 수 있다면 좋을 텐데.

Words fall down 넘어지다 careful 조심성 있는 idiot 바보

15

만약 내가 조심했다면 친구들 앞에서 넘어지지 않았을 텐데.

과거의 사실을 반대로 가정하는 문장은 가정법 과거완료로 나타낸다.

16

'~하면[이라면] 좋을 텐데'라는 의미를 가진 문장은 「I wish+(that)+주어+동사의 과거형~」으로 표현한다.

02회 내신 적중 실전 문제

본문 182쪽

01 ④ 02 ③ 03 ③ 04 ② 05 ⑤ 06 ②
07 ③ 08 ⑤ 09 ⑤ 10 ⑤ 11 ④ 12 ③
13 had 14 as if you had been right all the time
15 If I were you, I would ask him to stop shaking his leg.
16 look as if you were a fire fighter

01

• 만약 내가 슈퍼맨이라면 위험에 처한 사람들을 구할 텐데.
• 만약 내가 그 충고를 받아들였다면 성공했을 텐데.

첫 번째 문장은 가정법 과거 문장이므로 빈칸에 were가 알맞다. 두 번째 문장은 가정법 과거완료 문장이므로 빈칸

에 would have가 알맞다.

Words rescue (위험에서) 구하다 in danger 위험에 처한 advice 충고 succeed 성공하다

02

보기 나에게 강아지가 있다면 좋을 텐데.

① 나에게 강아지가 있어서 기쁘다.
② 나에게 강아지가 있어서 기뻤다.
③ 나에게 강아지가 없어서 아쉽다.
④ 나에게 강아지가 없어서 아쉽다.
⑤ 나에게 강아지가 없어서 아쉬웠다.

「I wish+가정법 과거」는 「I'm sorry (that)+주어+동사의 현재형~」으로 바꿔 쓸 수 있다.

03

그녀는 마치 자기가 영화배우인 것처럼 행동한다. 사실, 그녀는 평범한 소녀일 뿐이다.

③ 주절과 같은 시점에서 실제와 다른 상황을 나타낼 때는 「as if+주어+동사의 과거형~」으로 표현한다. (is → were)

Words behave 행동하다 normal 평범한, 정상적인

04

① 만약 그녀가 친절하다면 인기가 있을 텐데.
② 만약 나에게 그 책이 있다면 너에게 그것을 빌려줄 수 있을 텐데.
③ 만약 내가 네 이메일을 봤다면 네게 전화했을 텐데.
④ 만약 네가 그곳에 있었다면 그 공연을 즐겼을 텐데.
⑤ 만약 카메라가 더 저렴했다면 나는 그것을 살 수 있었을 텐데.

① 가정법 과거 문장이므로 will을 would로 고쳐야 한다.
③ 가정법 과거완료 문장이므로 saw를 had seen으로 고쳐야 한다.
④ 가정법 과거완료 문장이므로 will enjoy를 would have enjoyed로 고쳐야 한다.
⑤ 가정법 과거완료 문장이므로 buy를 have bought로 고쳐야 한다.

Words popular 인기 있는 cheap 저렴한

05

① 나에게는 언니가 없다. 한 명 있다면 좋을 텐데.
② 그 영화는 오직 성인들을 위한 것이다. 만약 내가 나이가 더 많다면 그 영화를 볼 수 있을 텐데.
③ 그는 마치 자신이 나의 선생님인 것처럼 행동한다. 사실, 그는 나의 학급 친구이다.
④ 내가 어제 요가 수업에 참석하지 못해서 아쉽다. 수업에 갔다면 좋았을 텐데.
⑤ 만약 내가 통학 버스를 놓치지 않았다면 학교에 쉽게 갈 수 있었을 텐데. 나는 학교에 걸어서 가야 했다.

⑤ 두 문장을 내용상 자연스럽게 연결하기 위해서는 첫 번째 문장을 가정법 과거완료로 고쳐야 한다.

Words adult 성인 classmate 학급 친구 attend 참석하다 with ease 편하게 on foot 도보로

06

보기 그는 마치 그녀에게 관심이 없는 척했다.

① 사실, 그는 그녀에게 관심이 있다.
② 사실, 그는 그녀에게 관심이 있었다.
③ 사실, 그는 그녀에게 관심이 없다.
④ 사실, 그는 그녀에게 관심이 없었다.
⑤ 사실, 그는 그녀에게 관심이 있다.

「as if+가정법 과거」는 주절의 시제와 같은 시점에서 실제와 다른 상황을 나타낼 때 쓴다. 따라서 보기 문장은 그가 그녀에게 관심이 있었다는 속뜻을 가진다.

Words pretend ~인 척하다 be interested in ~에 관심이 있다

07

나는 요즘 너무 바쁘다. 한가하다면 좋을 텐데.

실현 불가능하거나 실현 가능성이 희박한 현재의 소망을 나타내는 문장은 「I wish+(that)+주어+동사의 과거형~」으로 표현한다.

Words these days 요즘

08

만약 날씨가 좋았다면 나는 등산을 갔을 텐데.

과거의 사실을 반대로 가정하는 문장은 가정법 과거완료(「If+주어+had p.p.~, 주어+조동사의 과거형+have p.p.…」)로 나타낸다.

09

지호가 대표로 뽑히지 않아서 아쉽다.
= 지호가 대표로 뽑혔다면 좋았을 텐데.

과거에 이루어지지 못했던 일에 대한 아쉬움이나 후회를 나타낼 때 「I wish+(that)+주어+had p.p.~」를 사용한다.

10

우리 아버지는 출장을 가셔서 나의 졸업식에 오실 수 없었다.
= 만약 우리 아버지가 출장을 가지 않으셨다면, 나의 졸업식에 오실 수 있었을 텐데.

과거의 사실을 반대로 가정할 때는 가정법 과거완료(「If+주어+had p.p.~, 주어+조동사의 과거형+have p.p.…」)로 나타낸다.

Words business trip 출장 graduation 졸업식, 졸업

11

A: 만약 너는 복권에 당첨된다면 무엇을 할 거니?

B: 나는 그 돈을 자선단체에 기부할 거야.

A는 가정법 과거를 통해 실현 가능성이 희박한 일을 가정하고 있다. 따라서 주절의 동사를 「조동사의 과거형+동사원형」으로 써야 한다.

Words win a lottery 복권에 당첨되다 donate 기부하다 charity 자선단체

12

A: 너는 왜 숙제를 제때에 제출하지 않았니?

B: 실은 밤늦게 숙제를 시작했거든. 그것을 더 일찍 시작했다면 좋았을 텐데.

① 내가 그것을 더 일찍 시작한다면 좋을 텐데.

② 내가 그것을 더 일찍 시작해서 기쁘다.

④ 내가 그것을 더 일찍 시작하지 않아서 아쉽다.

⑤ 네가 그것을 더 일찍 시작하지 않아서 아쉽다.

내용상 「I wish+가정법 과거완료」를 사용해서 과거에 이루어지지 못했던 일에 대한 아쉬움이나 후회를 나타내는 것이 적절하다.

Words hand in ~를 제출하다 on time 제때에

13

'~하면[이라면] 좋을 텐데'라는 의미를 가진 문장은 「I wish+(that)+주어+동사의 과거형~」으로 나타낸다.

Words facility 시설

14

너는 마치 네가 항상 옳았던 것처럼 말한다. 사실, 너는 항상 옳지는 않았다.

주절의 시제보다 앞선 시점에서 실제와 다른 상황을 나타내는 문장은 「as if+주어+had p.p.~」로 나타낸다.

15

A: 우리 반 친구가 항상 다리를 떨어서, 나는 그것이 신경 쓰여.

B: 그에게 다리 떠는 것을 멈춰 달라고 부탁하는 게 어떠니?

→ 만약 내가 너라면 그에게 다리 떠는 것을 멈춰 달라고 부탁할 거야.

조건으로 제시된 절(If I were you)은 실현 불가능한 일을 가정하는 내용이므로, 주절도 가정법 과거로 표현해야 함에 유의한다.

Words shake 떨다, 흔들다 bother 신경 쓰이게 하다

16

A: 엄마, 저 좀 보세요. 저 소방관처럼 변장했어요.

B: 와! 너는 마치 소방관처럼 보이는구나.

주절의 시제와 같은 시점에서 실제와 다른 상황을 나타내므로, 「as if+주어+동사의 과거형~」의 형태로 문장을 표현해야 한다.

Words dress up 변장하다 fire fighter 소방관

Lesson 12 | 접속사

Point 107 등위접속사 and, but

본문 186쪽

STEP 1

1 and 2 but 3 and 4 and 5 but

STEP 2

1 and closes at 6
2 but he didn't give up
3 but a vet
4 and took some medicine

STEP 3 ④

- 나는 셔츠와 바지 한 벌을 샀다.
- 음식이 비싸지만, 맛있었다.

TIP (1) 버터 바른 빵은 내가 가장 좋아하는 아침식사이다.
(2) 나는 아픈 게 아니라 피곤하다.

STEP 1

1 나는 춥고 배고프다.
2 John은 어제 아팠지만 학교에 왔다.
3 너는 이 책을 통해서 읽기와 쓰기 능력을 개발할 수 있다.
4 그는 그 상자를 들어서 조심스럽게 내려놓았다.
5 시험이 쉽지는 않았지만, 나는 겨우 통과했다.

STEP 3

① 시행착오는 위대한 스승이다
② 나는 매우 아팠지만 병원에 가지 않았다.
③ 관중들은 동시에 웃다가 울다가 했다.
④ 그녀는 여가 시간에 피아노 치는 것과 사진 찍는 것을 좋아한다.
⑤ 나는 운동은 잘 못하지만 악기 연주는 잘한다.

등위접속사 and가 연결하는 두 단어는 형태와 품사가 같아야 한다. 따라서 ④는 take가 아니라 taking이 맞다.

Point 108 등위접속사 or, so

본문 187쪽

STEP 1

1 or 2 so 3 or 4 or 5 so

STEP 2

1 or in the closet
2 so I didn't see his face
3 so it was canceled
4 or the daily newspaper
5 or are they dead

STEP 3 ③

- 차와 커피 중에 어느 것을 선호하니?
- 그는 정직하지 않다, 그래서 나는 그를 믿지 않는다.

STEP 1

1 너는 머물거나 지금 떠날 수 있다.
2 그는 열쇠를 잃어버려서, 방에 들어갈 수 없었다.
3 축구, 야구 또는 농구 중에 어떤 것을 더 좋아하니?
4 너희 아버지는 라디오 방송국과 소방서 중 어느 곳에서 일하시니?
5 나는 머리가 너무 아파서, 병원에 갔었다.

STEP 3

① 이 이야기는 사실이니 아니면 허구이니?
② 너는 그에게 지금 또는 나중에 전화하면 된다.
③ 내가 화분을 깨서 엄마가 화가 나셨다.
④ 너는 피자와 스파게티 중 어떤 게 더 좋으니?
⑤ 너는 오직 액체로 된 것들만 먹거나 마실 수 있다.

③은 인과관계를 나타내므로 so가 들어가야 하고, 나머지는 모두 or가 들어가야 자연스럽다.

Point 109 시간 접속사 when, as, while

본문 188쪽

STEP 1

1 나는 감기에 걸리면, 목이 아프다.
2 시간이 지남에 따라, 날이 어두워졌다.
3 그는 샤워를 하는 동안, 노래를 불렀다.
4 내가 태어났을 때, 나의 아버지는 해외에 계셨다.
5 네가 음식을 먹는 동안에는 말하지 않도록 해라.

STEP 2

1 when it snows
2 while the baby is sleeping
3 As I turned on the computer
4 When he jogged

STEP 3 ①

• 종이 울리면 쓰는 것을 멈춰라.
• 우리가 도시에서 멀어짐에 따라, 길은 더 좁아졌다.
• 내가 떠나 있는 동안 내 개를 돌봐주세요.

STEP 3

• 내가 거기에 도착했을 때, 경기가 시작되었다.
• 나는 운전을 하면서, 라디오를 듣는다.
• 나이가 듦에 따라, 그의 병이 악화되었다.

'~할 때', '~하면서', '~함에 따라'의 뜻을 모두 가진 접속사는 ① As이다.

Point 110 시간 접속사 before, after, until[till]

본문 189쪽

STEP 1

1 우리는 점심을 먹은 후에 산책을 했다.
2 나는 시험을 보기 전에, 크게 심호흡을 했다.
3 나는 엄마가 돌아오실 때까지 잠자리에 들지 않을 것이다.
4 그들은 시합이 끝난 후에 악수를 했다.
5 사람들은 지하철이 멈출 때까지 승강장에서 기다렸다.

STEP 2

1 after 2 until[till] 3 before
4 before 5 After

STEP 3 ②

• 나는 나가기 전에 불을 껐다.
• 내가 집을 떠난 후에 비가 오기 시작했다.
• 나는 엄마가 내 방에 들어 오실 때까지 일어나지 않았다.

STEP 3

① 종이 울리기 전에, 나는 시험을 끝냈다.
② 콘서트가 끝난 후에 너에게 전화하겠다.
③ 비가 내리기 시작하기 전에 우리는 집에 도착해야 한다.
④ 그는 결정을 내릴 때까지 너에게 아무 말도 하지 않을 것이다.
⑤ 지수는 최신 휴대전화를 살 수 있을 때까지 용돈을 모았다.

시간의 부사절에서는 미래의 일이라도 현재시제를 써야 하므로 ②는 after the concert is over가 맞다.

Point 111 이유 접속사 because, as, since

본문 190쪽

STEP 1

1 나는 늦게 일어났기 때문에 학교에 지각했다.
2 그녀는 몸이 안 좋았기 때문에, 학교를 조퇴했다.
3 그는 겨우 5살이기 때문에, 롤러코스터를 탈 수 없다.
4 너는 이곳이 처음이기 때문에, 내가 너를 안내해주겠다.
5 Susan은 선물을 많이 받았기 때문에 매우 행복했다.

STEP 2

1 because I was taking a shower
2 As Lisa is thoughtful
3 Since it is cold outside
4 because he had to take care of
5 Because he was tired

STEP 3 ③

• 나는 늦었기 때문에 택시를 탔다.
• 그는 배가 매우 고팠으므로, 점심을 많이 먹었다.
• 물이 없어서, 나는 샤워를 할 수 없었다.

STEP 3

① 그녀는 이기적이기 때문에 인기가 없다.
② 시간이 충분하지 않았기 때문에 우리는 서둘렀다.
③ 비행기는 폭우 때문에 이륙할 수 없었다.
④ 할머니께서 편찮으셨기 때문에 나는 할머니를 뵈러 갔다.
⑤ 한국 축구 팀이 경기에 이겼기 때문에 사람들은 흥분했다.

나머지는 뒤에 절이 이어지므로 이유를 나타내는 접속사 because, as, since가 들어가야 하는 반면, ③은 뒤에 명사구인 the heavy rain이 이어지므로 because of가 와야 한다.

Point 112 결과 접속사 so ~ that

본문 191쪽

STEP 1

1 so 2 to 3 that 4 enough 5 so

STEP 2

1 so, that 2 enough to
3 so, that 4 enough to
5 so, that

STEP 3 ①

• 그녀는 영어 회화를 매우 열심히 연습해서 경시대회에서 잘 할 수 있었다.
= 그녀는 경시대회에서 잘 할 정도로 영어 회화를 매우 열심히

연습했다.

TIP 케이크가 너무 맛있어서 모두들 좋아 했다.

STEP 1

1 날씨가 너무 좋아서 우리는 소풍을 갔다.
2 그녀는 많은 사람들의 마음을 끌 정도로 충분히 아름다웠다.
3 그 퍼즐은 너무 어려워서 아무도 풀 수 없었다.
4 나는 물을 세 잔이나 마실 정도로 충분히 목이 말랐다.
5 나는 너무 배가 고파서 식탁 위에 음식을 모두 먹었다.

STEP 3

보기 그는 그 상자를 옮길 만큼 충분히 강하다.
① 그는 너무 강해서 그 상자를 옮길 수 있다.

「형용사+enough to부정사」는 「so+형용사+that ~」으로 바꿔 쓸 수 있다.

Point 113 조건 접속사 if, unless

본문 192쪽

STEP 1

1 If 2 If 3 if 4 Unless 5 unless

STEP 2

1 If you have some money
2 Unless you keep the promise
3 unless it rains
4 if he joins our team
5 Unless you help me

STEP 3 ②

• 만일 네가 비밀을 지켜준다면, 나는 너에게 모든 것을 말해 줄 것이다.
• 만일 늦지 않았다면, 나는 그 팀에 합류하고 싶다.

STEP 1

1 네가 숙제를 끝내면, 외출해도 좋다.
2 너는 서두르지 않으면, 버스를 놓칠 것이다.
3 누구든 규칙적으로 운동을 한다면, 살을 뺄 수 있다.
4 내가 너무 바쁘지 않다면, 네가 일을 끝내는 것을 도와주겠다.
5 너에게 만일 지도가 없다면, 그 장소를 찾는 것은 어렵다.

STEP 3

① 추우면, 이 차를 마셔라.
② 네가 피곤하지 않다면, 영화를 보러 가자.
③ 너는 그녀를 만나면, 내가 왜 그녀를 좋아하는지 알게 될 것이다.
④ 네가 만일 그녀의 주소를 안다면, 나에게 알려 줘라.
⑤ 너는 지금 출발한다면, 첫 기차를 탈 수 있다.

②에는 내용상 Unless(만일 ~하지 않는다면)가 들어가야 하고 나머지는 If(만일 ~한다면)가 들어가야 한다.

Point 114 양보 접속사 though[although]

본문 193쪽

STEP 1

1 교통이 혼잡했음에도 불구하고, 우리는 제 시간에 도착했다.
2 많은 비가 오는 데도 불구하고 아이들은 산책을 나갔다.
3 나의 가족은 비록 부유하지는 않지만, 우리는 행복하다.
4 그가 나에게 거짓말을 했음에도 불구하고, 나는 그를 용서할 수 있다.
5 그 여배우는 비록 그리 상냥하지는 않지만 매력적이다.

STEP 2

1 Although he is short
2 Though the sun is shining
3 Although our team lost the game
4 Though it was true
5 Although my grandmother is old

STEP 3 ①

• 나는 배가 불렀음에도 불구하고, 그 디저트를 먹었다.

STEP 3

① 그것이 사실일지라도, 나는 그것을 믿지 않았다.
② 날씨가 더웠음에도 불구하고 그는 겨울옷을 입었다.
③ 나는 보통 아침을 거름에도 불구하고 건강하다.
④ 그녀는 노래를 잘 못 부름에도 불구하고 가수가 되고 싶어 한다.
⑤ 비록 그 식당은 인기가 있지만, 그곳의 음식은 훌륭하지 않다.

①의 Despite는 '~에도 불구하고'라는 뜻의 전치사이므로 뒤에 절이 오지 못한다. Despite 대신 Although 또는 Though가 와야 한다.

Point 115 both A and B / not only A but also B

본문 194쪽

STEP 1

1 Both 2 but 3 only 4 and 5 Not

STEP 2

1 both the guitar and (the) piano

2 not only China but also Vietnam (Vietnam as well as China)
3 not only handsome but also tall (tall as well as handsome)
4 Not only Linda but also her younger[little] brother (Her younger[little] brother as well as Linda)
5 Both Matt and John

STEP 3 ⑤

• Eric과 Ben은 둘 다 프로 농구 선수들이다.
• 그 사고로 운전자뿐만 아니라 승객들도 다쳤다.

STEP 1

1 민수와 그의 형은 둘 다 영어 선생님이다.
2 한국인들 뿐만 아니라 일본인들도 노인들을 공경한다.
3 그 수프는 뜨거울 뿐만 아니라 쓰기까지 했다.
4 그 책은 재미있고 교육적이다.
5 나 뿐만 아니라 너도 회의에 참석해야 한다.

STEP 3

① 축구와 야구 둘 다 인기가 있는 스포츠이다.
② 김 선생님은 친절하실 뿐만 아니라 지적이시다.
③ 우리는 그 소식에 슬픔과 분노 둘 다를 느꼈다.
④ 그녀의 엄마 뿐만 아니라 그녀도 땅콩 알레르기가 있다.
⑤ 나 뿐만 아니라 나의 형도 그 선수의 광팬이다.

「Not only A but also B」가 주어일 때는 B에 동사의 수를 일치시켜야 한다. 따라서 ⑤는 are가 아닌 is가 알맞다.

Point 116 either A or B / neither A nor B

본문 195쪽

STEP 1

1 Either 2 neither 3 either 4 nor 5 or

STEP 2

1 neither tall nor short
2 either pizza or spaghetti
3 neither read nor write
4 Neither Lisa nor I am
5 Either you or Minji is

STEP 3 ④

• Susan과 나 둘 중 하나가 아기를 돌봐야 한다.
• Tom도 그의 팀 구성원도 모두 결과에 만족하지 못했다.

STEP 1

1 너와 나 둘 중 하나가 틀렸다.
2 헬렌 켈러는 볼 수도 들을 수도 없었다.
3 너는 여기서 이탈리아 음식이나 인도 음식을 먹을 수 있다.
4 민호와 창민이 둘 다 축구팀에 선발되지 않았다.
5 그는 천재이거나 바보이다.

STEP 3

• 나와 너 둘 중 하나에게 책임이 있다.
• 나와 너 둘 다 그 문제에 대해 책임이 없다.

「either A or B」와 「neither A nor B」 두 표현 모두 B에 동사의 수를 일치시켜야 한다. B의 위치에 두 문장 모두 you가 있으므로 are가 들어가는 것이 알맞다.

Point 117 명사절을 이끄는 that

본문 196쪽

STEP 1

1 피는 물보다 진하다는 것은 사실이다. (주어)
2 나는 내가 재미있는 것을 알고 있다. (목적어)
3 문제는 우리에게 충분한 시간이 없다는 것이다. (보어)
4 네가 캠프에 올 수 없다니 유감이다. (진주어)
5 핵심 포인트는 우리가 그 문제를 통제할 수 있다는 것이다. (보어)

STEP 2

1 that money is most important
2 that we can't find the way out
3 That she is only 9 years old
4 that you are leaving for the United States

STEP 3 ③

• 그가 선거에서 패했다는 것은 충격이었다.
• 나는 그녀가 패션 감각이 있다고 생각한다.
• 사실은 그가 거짓말쟁이라는 것이다.
• 그가 똑똑하다는 것은 사실이 아니다.

STEP 3

① 나는 내가 어떤 것도 잘못했다고 생각하지 않는다.
② 네가 나에게 거짓말을 했다는 것이 실망스럽다.
③ 그녀가 외동딸이라는 것은 믿기 어렵다.
④ 중요한 것은 우리가 함께여서 행복하다는 것이다.
⑤ 그 음악가가 죽었다는 소식은 충격적이었다.

③에서 'She is the only child.'라는 문장 전체가 주어로 쓰였으므로 접속사 that이 앞에 있어야 한다.

Point 118 명사절을 이끄는 if, whether
본문 197쪽

STEP 1
1 whether 2 Whether 3 if 4 if 5 whether

STEP 2
1 if it is not in style
2 if she will come back soon
3 Whether it will rain or not
4 if he will move to another city

STEP 3 ①

- Mike가 나를 사랑하는지 아닌지 알고 싶다.
- 우리가 늦는지 아닌지 상관없다.
- 우리가 기금을 조성할 수 있는지 아닌지가 정말 중요하다.
- 그가 집에 있는지 아닌지 궁금하다.
- 문제는 그것이 여전히 존재하는지 아닌지이다.

STEP 1
1 너는 그녀가 아픈지 아닌지 알고 있니?
2 네가 그것이 마음에 드는지 안 드는지는 중요하지 않다.
3 나는 그곳에 갈지 말지 결정할 수가 없다.
4 우리가 이기든 지든 중요하지 않다.
5 문제는 우리가 호텔에 머물 수 있는지 없는지이다.

STEP 3
- 그녀가 병에서 회복할지 안할지 아무도 모른다.
- 네가 도와주지 않으면 나는 숙제를 끝낼 수 없다.

'~인지 아닌지'와 '~이라면'의 뜻을 모두 가진 접속사는 ① if이다.

Point 119 명령문+and / 명령문+or
본문 198쪽

STEP 1
1 or 2 or 3 and 4 and 5 and

STEP 2
1 or 2 or 3 and 4 or

STEP 3 ②

- 서로 도와라, 그러면 너희는 시간을 절약할 것이다.
- 마감일을 지켜라, 그렇지 않으면 너는 점수가 깎일 것이다.

STEP 1
1 재킷을 입어라, 그렇지 않으면 너는 감기에 걸릴 것이다.
2 엄마께 전화를 드려라, 그렇지 않으면 그녀는 너를 걱정하실 것이다.
3 약을 좀 먹어라, 그러면 너는 훨씬 나을 것이다.
4 우산을 가져가라, 그러면 너는 젖지 않을 것이다.
5 규칙적으로 운동을 해라, 그러면 너는 건강을 유지할 것이다.

STEP 3
① 일찍 잠자리에 들어라, 그렇지 않으면 너는 피곤할 것이다.
② 열심히 공부해라, 그러면 너는 좋은 성적을 받을 것이다.
③ 최선을 다해라, 그렇지 않으면 너는 목표를 이룰 수 없을 것이다.
④ 너무 많이 먹지 마라, 그렇지 않으면 너는 배가 아플 것이다.
⑤ 영어를 더 연습해라, 그렇지 않으면 너는 영어를 잘 말할 수 없을 것이다.

②에는 '…해라, 그러면 ~할 것이다'의 뜻인 「명령문, and ~」가 들어가는 것이 알맞고, 나머지는 모두 '…해라, 그렇지 않으면 ~할 것이다'의 뜻인 「명령문, or ~」가 들어간다.

01회 내신 적중 실전 문제
본문 199쪽

01 ① 02 ① 03 ② 04 ⑤ 05 ② 06 ⑤
07 ② 08 ③ 09 ③ 10 ① 11 ③ 12 ⑤
13 Unless you clean your room, your mom will scold you.
14 Do you know whether it will rain or not tomorrow?
15 go swimming after she meets Kevin
16 have lunch before she goes to the library

01
- 나는 너무 졸립고 피곤하다.
- 그녀는 영어와 프랑스어 둘 다 할 수 있다.

순조롭게 연결되는 내용을 대등하게 이어주는 접속사는 and이고, 「both A and B」는 'A와 B 둘 다'의 뜻을 가진다. 따라서 공통으로 알맞은 말은 ① and이다.

02
① 그의 형은 키가 아주 큰 반면 그는 키가 작다.

② 내가 잠을 자는 동안, 눈이 아주 많이 내렸다.
③ 내가 외출해 있는 동안 누군가 집에 침입했다.
④ 나는 설거지를 하는 동안, 컵을 깼다.
⑤ 너는 운전하는 동안 휴대전화를 사용하면 안 된다.

①은 '~인 반면에'의 뜻이고, 나머지는 모두 '~하는 동안'의 뜻이다.

Words heavily 심하게, 아주 많이

03

① 내 방은 크진 않지만, 아늑하다.
② 그 영화는 매우 길지만 매우 재미있었다.
③ 나는 어제 Susan과 Kathy 둘 다 만났다.
④ 너는 홍콩에 가봤니, 아니면 대만에 가봤니?
⑤ 시간이 충분하지 않아서 나는 도움을 요청했다.

등위접속사 and, but, or, so는 형태와 품사가 같은 단어와 구, 절을 연결한다. 따라서 ②의 but 뒤에 long과 품사가 같은 형용사 interesting이 와야 한다.

Words cozy 아늑한 ask for help 도움을 요청하다

04

① 추워지고 있어서, 우리는 집에 가야한다
② 그녀는 아팠기 때문에, 회사에 가지 못했다.
③ 그녀는 새로운 일자리를 구했기 때문에 댈러스로 이사를 갔다.
④ 비가 오기 때문에, 우리는 집에 있어야 한다.
⑤ 교통이 혼잡했기 때문에 우리는 늦었다.

Because of 뒤에는 절이 올 수 없으므로 ⑤에는 Because가 와야 한다.

05

그 신사는 너무 친절해서 나에게 길을 안내해주었다.
= 그 신사는 나에게 길을 안내해 줄만큼 충분히 친절했다.

「so+형용사/부사+that …」는 '너무 ~해서 …하다'의 뜻으로 「형용사/부사+enough+to부정사」로 바꿔 쓸 수 있다. 따라서 첫 번째 문장에는 so가, 두 번째 문장에는 enough가 들어가는 것이 알맞다.

06

'~임에도 불구하고'의 양보의 뜻을 가진 접속사는 ⑤ Although이다.

Words give up 포기하다

07

만일 피곤하다면, 좀 쉬어라.

'만일 ~한다면'의 조건의 뜻을 가진 접속사는 ② If이다.

08

나는 그 소식을 듣고 슬프지도 기쁘지도 않았다.

「neither A nor B」는 'A도 B도 아닌'의 뜻을 가진다. 따라서 ③ nor가 들어가야 한다.

09

사람들은 건강이 가장 중요하다고 말한다.

'~라는 것'의 의미를 가지고 명사절을 이끄는 접속사는 ③ that이다.

10

그만 떠들어라, 그렇지 않으면 너의 선생님께서 너에게 화를 내실 것이다.

명령문 뒤에서 '그렇지 않으면'의 의미를 갖는 접속사는 ① or이다.

11

① 우리는 우리가 곤경에 빠진 것을 알고 있었다.
② 너는 그가 선거에서 이겼다는 것을 들었니?
③ 그 때 나는 집에서 TV를 보고 있었다.
④ 그녀에게 쌍둥이 자매가 있다는 것은 흥미롭다.
⑤ 문제는 아무도 돈을 갖고 있지 않다는 것이었다.

나머지는 명사절을 이끄는 접속사로 쓰인 반면 ③의 that은 지시 형용사로 쓰였다.

Words in trouble 곤경에 빠져서 election 선거 twin 쌍둥이

12

나는 샤워를 했다. 그러고 나서, 나는 쿠키를 먹었다.
= 나는 샤워를 한 후에 쿠키를 먹었다.

'~한 후에'의 뜻을 가진 접속사는 ⑤ After이다.

13

만약 네가 방 청소를 하지 않으면, 너의 엄마가 너를 꾸짖으실 것이다.

If ~ not(만일 ~하지 않다면)은 unless로 바꿔 쓸 수 있다. unless로 바꿀 경우 not은 없어진다.

Words scold 꾸짖다, 혼내다

14

명사절을 이끌며 '~인지 아닌지'의 뜻을 가진 접속사는 whether와 if이다. 총 10단어로 쓰라고 했으므로 whether를 쓰고 or not을 붙인다.

15

지수는 수요일에 무엇을 할 것인가?

수요일에 먼저 할 일을 after가 이끄는 부사절에 쓰고, 나머지 일을 주절에 쓴다. 이 때 부사절의 시제는 현재 시제로 써야 한다.

16

지수는 금요일에 무엇을 할 것인가?

금요일에 나중에 할 일을 before가 이끄는 부사절에 쓰고, 나머지 일을 주절에 쓴다. 이때 부사절의 시제는 현재시제로 써야 한다.

02회 내신 적중 실전 문제

본문 201쪽

01 ③	02 ③	03 ⑤	04 ①	05 ①	06 ②
07 ⑤	08 ④	09 ③	10 ⑤	11 ①	12 ④

13 My father likes neither hiking nor fishing.
14 Hurry up, or you will miss the bus.
15 While Emily is short, Amy is tall.
16 Both Emily and Amy are outgoing and friendly [friendly and outgoing].

01

보기 나는 그 일을 맡을지 말지 결정할 수 없다.

① 네가 필요하다면 내 공책을 빌려주겠다.
② 질문이 있으면 나에게 연락해라.
③ 나는 그녀가 아직도 이 근처에 사는지 모른다.
④ 내가 시간이 있다면, 나는 친구들과 어울릴 것이다.
⑤ 너는 숙제를 끝내지 않으면 외출할 수 없다.

보기 와 같이 '~인지 아닌지'의 뜻을 가진 것은 ③이다.

02

① 자명종을 맞춰라, 그렇지 않으면 너는 늦게 일어날 것이다.
② 식물들에 정기적으로 물을 줘라, 그렇지 않으면 식물들이 죽을 것이다.
③ 밤 늦게 먹는 것을 멈춰라, 그러면 너는 살이 빠질 것이다.
④ 청소를 해라, 그렇지 않으면 너의 부모님께서 화를 내실 것이다.
⑤ 장갑을 껴라, 그렇지 않으면 너의 손이 얼 것이다.

③은 and가 들어가야 자연스럽고, 나머지는 or가 들어가야 자연스럽다.

Words mess 엉망인 상태(상황) freeze 얼다

03

① 지구가 둥근 것은 사실이다.
② 그녀가 음악을 좋아한다는 것을 모든 사람이 안다.
③ 많은 사람들이 그 남자가 성실하다고 말한다.
④ 사실은 누구도 그 자리를 원하지 않는다는 것이다.
⑤ 나무 옆에 서 있는 저 남자를 봐라.

⑤는 지시 형용사이고, 나머지는 명사절을 이끄는 접속사 that이다.

Words round 둥근 position 자리, 지위 diligent 성실한

04

① 수미와 나 둘 다 열쇠를 가지고 있지 않다.
② Amy뿐만 아니라 Eric도 요리를 좋아한다.
③ 너와 나 둘 중 하나는 여기에 남아야 한다.
④ 너와 너의 친구 모두 환영이다.
⑤ 주호 뿐만 아니라 그의 형도 결석했다.

「neither A nor B」가 주어로 쓰인 경우 B에 동사의 수를 일치시켜야 한다. 따라서 ①에는 has가 아닌 have를 써야 한다.

Words absent 결석한

05

• 날씨가 따뜻했으므로 나는 재킷을 벗었다.
• 차가 너무 뜨거워서 마실 수 없었다.

'그러므로'의 뜻을 가진 접속사는 so이고, 「so+형용사/부사+that …」은 '너무 ~해서 …하다'의 의미를 가진다. 따라서 빈칸에 공통으로 들어갈 말로 알맞은 것은 ① so이다.

06

그 야구 선수가 오직 한 손으로 공을 잡고 던지는 것은 놀라웠다.

that절이 문장에서 주어 역할을 할 경우 그 자리에 가주어 it을 쓰고 that절은 문장의 뒤로 보낸다. 따라서 surprising 뒤에 that절이 와야 한다.

Words catch 잡다 throw 던지다

07

그는 문이 열릴 때까지 계속 기다렸다.

'~할 때까지'의 뜻을 가진 접속사는 ⑤ until이다.

08

너는 이 책을 읽지 않으면, 이것에 관한 보고서를 쓸 수 없다.

'만일 ~하지 않는다면'의 뜻을 가진 접속사는 ④ Unless 이다.

09

헬멧을 써라, 그러면 너는 안전할 것이다.

명령문 뒤에 쓰여 '그러면 ~할 것이다'의 의미를 갖는 접속사는 ③ and이다.

10

방이 시끄러웠음에도 불구하고 아기는 곤히 잤다.

'~임에도 불구하고'의 뜻을 가진 접속사는 ⑤ although 이다.

11

① 그는 일할 때, 클래식 음악을 듣는다.
② 나는 돈이 없기 때문에, 쇼핑을 하러 갈 수 없다.
③ 버스가 이미 떠났기 때문에, 우리는 기다려야 한다.
④ 너는 14살 미만이므로, 그 영화를 볼 수 없다.
⑤ 나의 음악 선생님은 친절하시기 때문에, 학생들은 그녀를 좋아한다.

①은 '~할 때'의 뜻이고 나머지는 '~ 때문에'의 뜻이다.

12

A: 오늘 오후에 내가 케이크를 만드는 동안 여동생을 돌봐줄 수 있니?
B: 물론이죠, 학교가 끝난 후에 집으로 올게요.

'~하는 동안'의 뜻을 가진 접속사는 while이고, '~한 후에'의 뜻을 가진 접속사는 after이다.

13

아버지는 등산을 좋아하지 않으신다. 아버지는 낚시를 좋아하지 않으신다.
→ 아버지는 등산과 낚시 둘 다 안 좋아하신다.

'A도 B도 둘 다 아닌'은 「neither A nor B」로 쓴다.

14

「명령문+and ~」는 '…해라, 그러면 ~할 것이다'의 뜻을 가진다.

15

Emily는 키가 작은 반면, Amy는 키가 크다.

while은 '~인 반면에'의 뜻으로 서로 상반되는 내용을 연결한다.

16

Emily와 Amy는 둘 다 외향적이고 친절하다[친절하고 외향적이다].

both A and B는 'A와 B 둘 다'의 뜻을 가지고, 주어로 쓰인 경우 복수 취급한다.

Words outgoing 외향적인 friendly 친절한

마무리 10분 테스트

Lesson 01 문장의 형태

01 angry
02 to stay
03 taken
04 sleeping
05 bought a beautiful dress for her
06 asked an important question of them
07 cooked dinner for his friends that evening
08 lend your dictionary to me
09 to leave
10 talk[talking]
11 smile
12 watch
13 like an apology
14 of her sister
15 kept calm
16 allowed her to go
17 leave your sister alone
18 help me pack my suitcase
19 find your ring for you
20 got her son to clean up the kitchen
21 send a fax to
22 noticed him looking
23 made a huge cake for
24 have them move
25 expected me to do my best

Lesson 02 동사의 시제

01 has
02 is sleeping
03 was preparing
04 broke out
05 is
06 was driving
07 reads
08 called
09 speak
10 has used, for
11 has never traveled
12 haven't seen, since
13 have you known
14 Maggie wrote the report last night.
15 He hasn't been at work for a week.
16 I have used this cell phone for two years.
17 I haven't seen him since last year.
18 have lived in Suwon for three years
19 has lost his favorite toy car
20 have had this medal since 2002
21 has gone to London
22 has just come back
23 hasn't bought the flowers yet
24 have already read the novel
25 Have you ever eaten

Lesson 03 조동사

01 fix
02 couldn't
03 must not
04 had to
05 could not believe
06 Can[May, Could] I see
07 would, play
08 would not break
09 may not come
10 must be
11 cannot be
12 may need
13 must know
14 going → go
15 not to park → not park
16 staying → stay
17 eating → eat
18 You don't have to wash your hair every day.
19 She was able to solve the puzzle.
20 He does read a lot of books.
21 She used to drink coffee every morning.
22 He had to walk home.
23 You had better not touch the button
24 We didn't have to worry about him.
25 Would you like to try this on?

Lesson 04 to부정사

01 to travel with
02 to go
03 for her
04 something exciting

05 whom to help
06 as to
07 so clever that
08 is not easy to learn
09 good that she couldn't miss
10 easy to make
11 planned to travel
12 kind of you to carry
13 fun for him to play
14 fun nothing → nothing fun
15 to only → only to
16 for you → of you
17 enough smart → smart enough
18 is too salty to eat
19 need a yard to play in
20 would be upset to see the mess
21 to find himself alone
22 It was foolish of me to believe the story. [I was foolish to believe the story.]
23 He must be honest to tell me the truth.
24 They practiced very hard, only to lose the game.
25 She was happy to get so much support from her fans.

Lesson 05 동명사

01 Listening
02 going
03 not eating
04 is
05 answering
06 to refuse
07 making[to make]
08 spending
09 to write
10 opening
11 talking
12 telling
13 to lock
14 to run
15 hearing
16 to inform
17 reading
18 look forward to watching
19 cannot help loving you
20 feel like playing the guitar
21 kept on reading the newspaper
22 was busy taking orders
23 is no use worrying
24 has trouble reading
25 is worth keeping

Lesson 06 분사

01 disappointed
02 boring
03 confusing
04 thrown
05 singing
06 exciting
07 embarrassed
08 surprised
09 beating
10 the frightening noise
11 discussed in class
12 freshly baked
13 some children playing
14 stood surrounded by the players
15 we had to keep the windows closed
16 They felt the building shaking
17 The man waiting outside is
18 Graduating from college
19 Getting the lead in the school play
20 Going out without a jacket
21 rushing to answer it
22 Though he is a foreigner
23 Because we booked the tickets in advance
24 If you take a taxi
25 When she looked in her bag

Lesson 07 수동태

01 solved
02 are used
03 disappeared
04 be seen
05 was found
06 is spent
07 was not written
08 Was, damaged
09 should be carried
10 must not be taken
11 was told to me
12 was bought for me
13 to leave
14 to Bob
15 to the children
16 will be cooked
17 should not be trusted
18 was advised to lose weight
19 was brought up by her grandma
20 The ship was named Titanic
21 must be taken care of by
22 is interested in
23 were surprised at
24 is filled with
25 was covered with

Lesson 08 대명사

01 any
02 has
03 one
04 another
05 any money
06 Both of them
07 Each student
08 All, is
09 Tom is listening to music under the tree by himself.
10 I made the robot dog for[by] myself.
11 After his wife died, he was beside himself with grief.
12 I enjoyed myself in Hong Kong.
13 have → has
14 any → some
15 was → were
16 me → myself
17 was → were
18 Is there any fruit in the refrigerator?
19 Ms. Wilson knows every student in her school.
20 Both of us walk to school.
21 One of the two books is mine, but the other is not.
22 others like scary movies
23 I need to buy a new one
24 You might hurt yourself
25 It opened of itself

Lesson 09 비교 구문

01 early
02 easier
03 much[still, even, far, a lot]
04 cities
05 boy
06 as, as
07 twice as
08 The more
09 any other
10 I am as tall as Mina. 또는 Mina is as tall as I am[me].
11 Dongsu is heavier than I am[me].
12 No other food is as delicious as chicken.
13 Cheetahs are faster than all the other animals in the world.
14 famouser → more famous
15 colder → coldest
16 old and old → older and older
17 game → games
18 Susan is not so pretty as Clara.
19 Wolves are still faster than dogs.
20 Geneva is one of the finest cities in the world.
21 The more you sleep, the more tired you feel.
22 longer and longer
23 the angrier I became
24 four times as heavy as yours
25 one of the most difficult languages in the world

Lesson 10 관계사

01 whose
02 whom
03 what
04 which
05 whose color
06 in which
07 month when
08 What, is
09 I am riding the bicycle which[that] I borrowed from John.
10 Yujin can read the books which[that] are written in Chinese.
11 This is the hospital where[at which] my little sister works as a nurse.
12 The news reported the way (in which) the people on the ship were rescued. [The news reported how the people on the ship were rescued.]
13 that → what
14 when → where[in which/at which]
15 where → when[in which]
16 which → why[for which]
17 I will wear the dress my mom made for me.
18 I will show you how you can operate the machine.
19 Computer technology is the study I am interested in.
20 The picture taken by my father is hanging on the wall.
21 who wants to come
22 What I want to do this weekend
23 whose service was great
24 where Mozart lived
25 which was planted by my grandfather

Lesson 11 가정법

01 could
02 would
03 had been
04 were
05 had eaten[had]
06 as if, were
07 were, would
08 had had[got], would have
09 as if, had lived
10 I wish I had an older brother.
11 I wish you had come to the audition.
12 I could have picked you up if I had had a car.
13 If I knew his address, I could write a letter to him.
14 studied → had studied
15 am → were
16 are → were
17 never met → had never met
18 If I were free, I would go on a trip.
19 I wish I had had some money at that time.
20 Mina sounded as if she had been to London.
21 If he had not been sick, he would have come to the meeting.
22 you could see the fireworks with me
23 as if they were shocked at the news
24 I had gone to bed early last night
25 I could have entered the room

Lesson 12 접속사

01 sunny
02 but
03 and
04 are
05 until
06 but
07 As
08 either
09 Although[Though]
10 I didn't study hard, so I failed the test.
11 She can neither ski nor skate.
12 Both I and my mom love roses.
13 The book was so boring that I couldn't finish it.
14 whether → that
15 that → so
16 have → has
17 or → and
18 He is neither tall nor handsome.
19 Buy some milk before you come home.
20 Since the meeting room was empty, I turned off the lights. [I turned off the lights since the meeting room was empty.]
21 The soup was not only cold but also salty.
22 so I opened the door
23 while she was cutting the onions
24 unless my mom agrees [if my mom doesn't agree]
25 and you will achieve the goal

중학 영문법
MANUAL 119 ②